Praise for

RAW DEAL

"This is a deeply informed and eye-opening call for change."

—*Publishers Weekly*

"If you think you understand the meat industry, please think again. Chloe Sorvino provides a fascinating, gripping, and ultimately indispensable portrait of the powerful companies at the heart of our food system. This story is as shocking as it is revelatory, showing how the meat industry manipulates our political system, drives climate change, and hikes prices for American meals. This book is required reading for anyone who eats."

—Christopher Leonard,
New York Times bestselling author of
The Meat Racket and *Kochland*

"*Raw Deal* is Chloe Sorvino's deeply reported, firsthand account of how business imperatives drive the meat industry to mistreat workers, pollute the environment, fix prices, bribe, and manipulate the political process, all in the name of shareholder profits. She argues convincingly for holding this industry accountable and requiring it and other corporations to engage in social as well as fiduciary responsibility. *Raw Deal* is a must-read for anyone who cares about where our food comes from."

—Marion Nestle,
author of *What to Eat* and
professor emerita of nutrition, food studies,
and public health, New York University

"*Raw Deal* is poised to become the next definitive authority on the current state of the broken food system in America and our desperate fight to curb climate change. Insightful as it is harrowing, what can often seem like an impossible hornet's nest to untangle is illuminated. *Raw Deal* will shake you into sharp presence while shining light on a road toward a decentralized, community-centered food system."

—Camilla Marcus,
chef of Westbourne and cofounder
of the Independent Restaurant Coalition

"Some meat-packers will hate this book, but it will force everybody to think. The big-is-fragile problem also applies to other industries such as electronic chips and baby formula."

—Temple Grandin,
author of *Animals in Translation*

"Readers will gnash their teeth at Sorvino's vivid accounts of rapacious billionaires and the half-dozen mega-corporations that dominate the industry, pollute waterways, and exhaust farmland under the very gentle hand of government regulators . . . Convincing, often enraging, and no more optimistic than the facts call for."

—*Kirkus Reviews*

"A journalist who has spent nearly a decade covering food and agriculture for *Forbes*, Sorvino lays bare the inner workings of the meat industry with clear-eyed practicality—from the scale of the environmental cost of meat to the depths of corporate greed and consolidation of power."

—*Modern Farmer*

"Packed with a wide range of expert input, *Raw Deal* provides a firsthand look into a typically opaque industry and makes the case that changing our meat industry is both possible and necessary."

—*Civil Eats*

"*Raw Deal* is a meticulously researched account of what's wrong with today's meat industry and how we might overhaul it . . . What sets the book apart from many others in this genre is Sorvino's excellent deep dive into how the world's largest meat companies and retailers have been deploying illegal and irresponsible practices—including bribery, corruption, and collusion—to grab, hold on to and expand power and profits at the expense of people and the planet."

—GreenBiz

"Sorvino's captivating discoveries convey the vulnerabilities of a powerful part of the food system and the effects of this broken industry."

—Food Tank

"*Raw Deal* is a shocking and page-turning read that exposes the many ills that plague meat corporations in the US, including price-fixing, elite power grabs, and a systemic lack of transparency."

—*Green Queen*

RAW DEAL

HIDDEN CORRUPTION, CORPORATE GREED, AND THE FIGHT FOR THE FUTURE OF MEAT

CHLOE SORVINO

SIMON ACUMEN

NEW YORK   LONDON   TORONTO   SYDNEY   NEW DELHI

SIMON
ACUMEN

An Imprint of Simon & Schuster, LLC
1230 Avenue of the Americas
New York, NY 10020

First Simon Acumen trade paperback edition November 2024

SIMON ACUMEN and colophon is a trademark of Simon & Schuster, LLC

Simon & Schuster: Celebrating 100 Years of Publishing in 2024

For information about special discounts for bulk purchases,
please contact Simon & Schuster Special Sales at 1-866-506-1949
or business@simonandschuster.com.

The Simon & Schuster Speakers Bureau can bring authors to your live event.
For more information or to book an event, contact the Simon & Schuster Speakers
Bureau at 1-866-248-3049 or visit our website at www.simonspeakers.com.

Interior design by Kyoko Watanabe

Manufactured in the United States of America

1   3   5   7   9   10   8   6   4   2

Library of Congress Cataloging-in-Publication Data has been applied for.

ISBN 978-1-9821-7204-6
ISBN 978-1-9821-7205-3 (pbk)
ISBN 978-1-9821-7206-0 (ebook)

To the future generations who will not have the luxury
of deciding whether change is worth it.

And to My Dream Team, for your unconditional love.
Mom, for staying up with me.
Nick, for waking me up with coffee.
Emery, for keeping me fed.

CONTENTS

SECTION IV:
Maximizing What We've Got

RAW DEAL

Introduction:
A Pandemic Catalyst

In April 2020, as America's slaughterhouses transformed into hotbeds of COVID-19 outbreak, many livestock farmers had to accept their worst nightmare: killing off their own herds. In quick succession, fourteen plants from Sioux Falls, South Dakota, to Perry, Iowa, had closed. Exposed workers were calling in sick, and others stopped showing up. Without enough workers on the line, the plants couldn't run as many shifts, and the backups started to ricochet throughout the supply chain. Slaughterhouses curtailed how many animals they could accept. With more time to put on weight, some of the hogs and cattle became too fat to fit through slaughterhouse machinery. An industry that had shaved the slaughter and processing of livestock down to a fraction of a second came to a halt.

At the Smithfield facility in Milan, Missouri, a longtime pork slicer decided enough was enough. She had suffered UTIs in the past while working eleven-hour shifts with only two fifteen-minute bathroom breaks and a thirty-minute lunch break allowed a day. She was concerned by what could happen if Smithfield ignored its workers' health amid COVID-19. As a Jane Doe, she pushed the meat industry to high alert with an anonymous lawsuit, which was later dismissed.[*] Line workers in that plant continued to butcher shoulder to shoulder, cutting up to 1,100 hogs an hour. The conveyor belts moved so fast that workers trimming meat didn't have enough time to cover their mouths to cough. The lawsuit aimed to close the plant until workers could exist there with social distancing measures in place, insisting not

---

[*] The court ordered Smithfield to comply with CDC guidance in April, ahead of a hearing held in May. The lawsuit was ultimately dismissed, as lawyers for Smithfield argued to let OSHA handle violations and otherwise defer to state and county health officials.

just on masks and plexiglass dividers but a full six feet of spacing between each worker, based on the Centers for Disease Control and Prevention's guidelines. These changes would mean the amount of meat leaving the door would need to be slashed.

That lawsuit seems to have been enough to scare billionaire Tyson chairman John Tyson. The patriarch of America's largest meat supplier took out an ad in the Sunday *New York Times* just three days after the complaint was filed. The "food supply chain is breaking," he proclaimed. Tyson's motives behind the ad were far more complicated. He was pushing workers who were risking their lives to keep showing up on the line, while attempting to rally public support around meat processing. Tyson stoked fears, among both consumers and the government, that American grocery stores would soon face lasting shortages.

There was a veiled threat contained within the ad for anyone willing to look a little deeper. The ad was published within seven months of the 2020 presidential election. Americans, historically, haven't kept politicians in office when they're unhappy about meat. Yet the food supply chain was already broken, and Tyson helped break it. Did Tyson deserve to rally support through fearmongering after years of squeezing out producers and allegedly limiting employee compensation in an attempt to deliver record-breaking profits to shareholders?

An executive order signed by President Donald Trump employed the Defense Production Act to compel meat-packers to reopen and attempt to absolve them of worker safety liability. The order was based on a proposal drafted by Tyson's legal department. According to a congressional report released in May 2022, as Tyson and Smithfield worked to secure Trump's support, executives including the CEOs "engaged in constant communications" with Trump appointees at USDA and the White House, and the "eventual order adopted the themes and statutory directive laid out in Tyson's draft."* All fourteen plants had shifts back within a few days.

But backups continued.

Workers kept getting sick from the novel virus. The tragedy even inspired managers at a Tyson plant in Waterloo, Iowa, to create an office bet-

---

* Julie Anna Potts, CEO of meat processor trade group NAMI, said the report "uses 20/20 hindsight and cherry picks data." Tyson said it has prioritized its workers' safety. Smithfield declined to comment.

ting pool on how many workers would die. An independent investigation, spearheaded by former attorney general Eric Holder, concluded in December 2020 and led to the firing of seven plant managers.

There still was hardly a comprehensive shortage, despite what John Tyson seems to have wanted Americans to believe. The most popular cuts were harder in some places to secure. But meat production had been rising for years, and customers inside restaurants and grocery stores seeing temporary shortages were really experiencing the effects of several confounding factors: pandemic-related logistics woes, a decrease in the supply of meat from unnaturally high levels, and historic highs of meat leaving the United States as exports. Prices for fresh meat rose 11 percent. There was a lack of actual demand for frozen meat even though the supply remained high in freezers.

Highly centralized meat production was what was breaking. In quick succession: Kroger and Costco announced they would limit meat purchases, followed by Texas-based H-E-B, and then Wendy's, known for using only fresh beef, stopped making hamburgers at some locations. When I got the 9 p.m. text from my cousin in DC, asking if she should buy another chest freezer and stock up on meat, I realized panic was setting in across mom blogs and beyond.

Big and Fragile

In April, as potential shortages loomed, Temple Grandin called me from her home near Colorado's ranchlands. Temple's tone was gruffer than usual. The iconic slaughterhouse consultant had spent more than a half century pushing the biggest players in the meat industry—from McDonald's to Cargill to Tyson—to adopt more humane livestock practices as they charted global expansion. Grocery stores hadn't come this close to running out of burgers and bacon in decades.

My questions for Temple spilled out as I paced around my couch. The supply chain shocks were creating large amounts of waste. What was happening to the thousands of hogs not making it to the slaughterhouse? Why was the Department of Agriculture still reporting frozen beef and pork inventory nationwide at an all-time high? And why was meat still being exported while forty million people were unemployed and food bank lines lasted hours? Did Temple think industrial meat's supply chains were broken beyond repair?

Badly managed is bad, Grandin decided, her deep and guttural voice punctuating each *b*. Big is not bad, she explained; it is fragile. Temple then told me the story of when she first realized this. During a storm in 2013, she was driving back to her Fort Collins, Colorado, home and the interstate was flooded. After finding the backroads also impassable, she continued to drive. She made it out near the town of Greeley, the agribusiness hub where JBS's American division is headquartered. There, she found a massive feedlot where the cattle were all dry but the flooding was starting to hit the edges of the yard. A dry bridge came into view, just a foot out of water, and she drove over it to get home.

The bridge was submerged an hour later. JBS, the world's largest meat supplier, had the infrastructure, but after that bridge flooded, the entire feedlot was at risk. The floods ended up lasting for a week, killing at least eight people.

"When big breaks," Grandin told me, "you've got a real mess."

It would have been harder for a disaster to strike if the cattle were spread apart, not just clustered in confinement at this one feedlot. Grandin's tale remains a stark example of how the megaplants built in the past decade transformed the industry and have pushed it to the brink of centralization and efficiency. Since Grandin started her career designing cattle systems in the 1970s, she has become one of the few in the meat industry who have witnessed the entire arc of decades of consolidation—how the plants moved to the countryside, chasing after supersized feedlots that promised to make the industry more efficient, while the small ones left in cities got swallowed up or went bankrupt.

In the past fifty years, the number of US meatpacking plants has been cut in half. The cost of compliance for small, independent processors has eaten into already slim profits. Just 835 federally inspected slaughterhouses remain.

Those plants had to get bigger to survive. About 60 percent of all beef and pork processing in 2015 came from the top thirteen plants in each industry. Smithfield's Sioux Falls plant, where Jane Doe worked, is responsible for roughly 5 percent of the country's pork supply, and slaughters at a rate of nineteen thousand hogs per day, across three shifts. This consolidation has created fragility, easily threatened by a crisis.

Economics of Waste

Decades of centralization have damaged commodity markets and pushed industrial meat production to a breaking point. Waste abounds, according to Mary Hendrickson, associate professor of rural sociology at the University of Missouri. If all the world's food waste was a country, it would be the third-ranked world emitter of greenhouse gases. But that's just scratching the surface. The mass euthanasia of livestock during 2020 was an egregious example of what can happen in a worst-case scenario. By May, the pork industry was backed up—so much that 170,000 hogs a day that were ready to head to the slaughterhouse had nowhere to go. Some ten million hogs were at risk of the same fate before the end of the year, the National Pork Producers Council warned.

Taking a conservative estimate, if around 300,000 hogs were killed by their farmers during the pandemic spring of 2020, and those pigs were an average of 275 pounds, that would yield 29,000 tons of pork that went to waste. Those pigs ate millions of bushels of corn and soy.

"This is a breathtaking waste of resources," Hendrickson told me. "If it were really about efficient production and all of these kinds of things, rather than accumulating power or workers' power or farmers' power, we would not see that wastefulness."

Fewer, bigger plants can lead to more waste. One plant shutting down can cut down competition in a market that producers sell livestock to, especially if a market doesn't have enough competition, like in 2019 when a Tyson plant in Kansas caught fire and nearly shut down a market. If closures hit several plants at once—like in 2020 during the early pandemic and in 2021 when a cyberattack shut down all nine of JBS's American plants—the supply chain could crumble.

When It's Raining Gold, Get a Bucket

As slaughterhouse backups played out in the United States, the seeming supply shortage forced prices up double digits. Meanwhile, meat-packers were cresting in profits as prices hit fresh highs. At JBS, for example, strong beef and pork sales at higher prices due to the plant shutdowns had 2020 second-quarter net profits come in at twice as high as the average analyst's estimate—$630 million, compared to the projected $300 million. While 2020 was an anomalous year, to be sure, outsize profits for top meat-packers was the trend across the board: JBS's year-end results outed more than $4 billion in operating profit at a margin of 9.8 percent, while Tyson pulled in more than $5 billion, or an 11.6 percent profit margin (compared to 5.2 percent in 2014). Those profits are a result of price increases, thanks to swinging commodities, corporate consolidation, and accumulation of power in some uncompetitive markets.

Profits also come from export markets. Through the pandemic, top meat-packers exported more meat than ever before. Tyson's shipments abroad rose 43 percent to more than 640,000 tons compared to JBS USA, which exported nearly 770,000 tons, an increase of 19 percent since 2019. Smithfield saw exports grow 25 percent to over 750,000 tons, according to global data provider Panjiva, owned by S&P.

"They're on fire. Best my exports have ever been. On fire," a meat billionaire bragged to me in early 2021.

He added: "If it's raining gold outside, we're walking around with buckets."

At what cost? At least 298 COVID-19 slaughterhouse deaths, according to the Food and Environment Reporting Network and the tireless work of journalist Leah Douglas, with more than fifty-nine thousand exposed, exponentially spreading the virus to their families, communities, and beyond.

What did the meat-packers get in return? A light tap on the wrist from the Occupational Safety and Health Administration, or OSHA, that meat-packers like JBS and Smithfield have fought paying. The fines, levied in September 2020, ended up hitting just those two firms and totaling less than $30,000. Compare that to the $17 million fine Blue Bell ice cream got for its 2015 listeria outbreak that caused three deaths, or a salmonella outbreak from the Peanut Corporation of America that caused nine deaths and hundreds of illnesses, and sent the CEO to jail for twenty-eight years.

Security Threat

In the past decade, foreign billionaires have acquired huge swaths of the country's meat supply. In pork, Smithfield, owned by Hong Kong–based WH Group, controls 26 percent and JBS controls 19 percent. That's 45 percent of US pork foreign-owned. Brazilian outfits JBS and Marfrig then command a third of the US beef industry. JBS also has 17 percent of the chicken industry, while German-owned EW Group controls about 50 percent of the US market for broiler chicken genetics, which means American farmers pay them for fresh birds after every harvest. In another decade, how much more could be gobbled up, and what demands will arise?

Rural communities are harmed while American waterways, soils, and air get polluted for the benefit of international slaughterhouse billionaires, who now have all the power and little incentive to reshape operations. Yet the crisis from climate change will continue to exacerbate global tensions, and foreign-owned corporations have already been handed the chance to dictate what we eat. That's how an industry responsible for a large amount of the nation's protein consumption has become a national security risk.

The meat industry—driven by the quest for more profits, buoyed by subsidies, tax breaks, insurance coverage, lax regulatory enforcement, and federal food purchases—has become a threat to itself. Major federal investigations and hundreds of lawsuits related to price-fixing may be only the start of an overdue reckoning for the meat industry. More than two dozen American meat processors are implicated in the industry's latest conspiracy, including Tyson and JBS. The Brazilian meat-packer became the world's largest meat-packer and a domineering force in American markets. This exponential growth came from an acquisition spree fueled by a Brazilian bribery scheme led by the parent company. Yet grocers keep placing orders, and customers buy up the meat.

A Breaking Point Coming a Mile Away

COVID-19 threw this fragile system into crisis, but it is far from an isolated incident. A large mess awaits all eaters, meat lovers or otherwise. There are countless threats, from topsoil degradation to industrial meat factory-borne disease. It's time to course-correct for decades of mistakes before climate change makes it too late. According to a 2021 report from the United Nations, the global food system (from feed production to transportation to packaging) produces more than a third of all greenhouse gas emissions annually. In the United States, agriculture is one of the largest contributors to greenhouse gases, accounting for 10 percent of annual emissions. If global warming from meat isn't limited, there will be no chance at stymieing catastrophic environmental change.

Major changes to how we produce food—and specifically meat, since it commands outsize resources—are necessary. The latest United Nations Intergovernmental Panel on Climate Change report, put together with input from more than seven hundred contributing scientists from sixty-six countries around the world, is a reality check. Limiting global warming to the crucial target of 1.5° to 2°C will be completely out of reach without a massive pivot. Even if all fossil fuels were eliminated quickly, the meat industry would still need to overhaul its operations.

The meat industry has one of the strongest concentrations of power in the nation. It exerts influence on a wide variety of crucial policy areas, from economics and trade to employment and immigration to federal nutrition policy and school lunches. Lobbyists for the meat industry and its North American Meat Institute have secured regulations that have benefited the ultra-consolidated while squeezing out smaller independents. NAMI spent more than $325,000 on lobbying in 2020, its single largest yearly total in two decades. Meatpackers counter that the meat business is one of the nation's most heavily regulated industries. Some regulations have eroded public trust in the meat supply. Ag gag laws, the first of which passed in Kansas in 1990, have restricted public access to what actually goes on inside plants. A Kansas appeals court ruled one such law unconstitutional on First Amendment grounds in August 2021, and the Supreme Court declined to review the case in 2022, upholding the decision.

Environmental degradation is at the center of much of the lobbying. According to a 2021 study published by New York University researchers, the largest meat producers in America have collectively blocked climate legislation that could limit their annual output, while six of the largest meat trade groups—NAMI, the National Cattlemen's Beef Association, the National Pork Producers Council, the National Chicken Council, the International Dairy Foods Association, and the American Farm Bureau Federation and related state groups—have spent at least $200 million since 2000 on lobbying for climate-related issues including cap-and-trade, the Clean Air Act, and greenhouse gas regulations.

These systems of production have harmed the long-term health of the communities, often Black, Latinx, or Indigenous, who live near a part of the meat supply chain. Hidden impacts threaten personal health, in addition to the broader health-care system. Institutions like the Rockefeller Foundation say the health system must address the relationship between food and nutrition differently. After the foundation released a landmark report on how America's industrialized production systems shunt $2 trillion annually in health and environmental costs to consumers and taxpayers, I spoke with Devon Klatell, managing director of the organization's food initiative, who said hospitals need to center food and nutrition during treatment. But the main takeaway, Klatell said, lies with who bears these externalized costs: "Even though we didn't put a single dollar number on inequity, across every issue area we looked at, communities of color bear disproportionate costs. Having the hard conversation about who bears the cost and who is in a position to help lessen or minimize or mitigate that cost is an important part."

The Cost of Cheap Meat

In a world where industrial meat passes the costs down the line, someone along the way pays the price. There are dozens of factors to consider when designing a system where good meat exists. Good meat is not just meat that is made in a way that does not directly worsen climate change, although that is a crucial element. It must be good for all the other parts of the system too: the animals, the workers, the producers, food waste, land use, biodiversity, the nutrition and health of the community around production.

I'm not going so far as to say everyone must be a vegan. Bill Gates, in his 2021 book *How to Avoid a Climate Disaster: The Solutions We Have and the Breakthroughs We Need*, suggests that everyone in wealthy nations should eat only synthetic meat. *Far less* meat should be consumed overall, and meat from cramped factories that pollute must come to an end. But the leading alternatives, meat and meatless, are still double the price of industrial meat, and meat from livestock that graze and rotate on pasture has a critical role to play in our future, if it can become more accessible.

That's not to say that voting with your dollars is a panacea. The concept betrays its underlying goals. Consumers have been trained to believe spending power can signal changing preferences and thereby shifts in demand. In reality, billionaires' whims are far more influential when it comes to deciding what food people can buy. The government's power to rein in corporate greed is probably strongest of all, yet the most rarely used. There is some power in sourcing food with a strict ethical code, especially if it's supporting alternative systems with fewer brokers and middlemen. The problem is figuring out which purveyors are worth the time.

That's harder today than ever before, because the lines between what's ethical to support and what's not have blurred, almost beyond the point of recognition: there's now Amazon-owned Whole Foods, venture-backed subscription services, and frothy IPOs turned popular household brands. How do you make sure not only that your vote gets placed but that the message you want it to convey is heard clearly? Small suppliers will feel that dollar exponentially more than massive operations selling to distributors and megaretailers.

At the heart of this book are the tensions between centralized systems—built for globalization, big capital spending, billionaire profits, and exports—and regional ones, rooted in community. For too long, these supply chains have been erected independently of one another. There's no time to completely rebuild from scratch. But we might create a patchwork of systems that prioritize communities and strengthen access to more nutritious, sustainably produced foods.

The pandemic showed many Americans for the first time that the meat industry is failing, but the details have been obscured. It's essential to understand how we got here and how we might choose better for ourselves and the future. It is only through collaboration between a network of farmers, processors, manufacturers, retail and food services (like restaurants, cafeterias, and hospitals), and consumers that we can combat the devastating impact of industrialized meat—on climate change, human rights, hunger, health—and avoid a tragic future in which only a few powerful players control the entire industry, where more price hikes, human health threats, commodification, and inhumane working conditions abound.

The Future of Meat

A growing number of eaters have decided to stop right here and go vegan. Others are experimenting as so-called flexitarians or reducetarians—opting to go meatless with mushrooms, beans, tofu, or often with an array of venture-backed brands. Yet another group is limiting their meat consumption to only the most ethical meat, like bison or certain operations with livestock raised on pastures under rotational management. Some of these alternative challengers show promise, but most are not set up to effectively make a dent in overall industrial meat consumption. A certain level of scale is needed to avoid a fate like the past decade of locavorism, which has barely affected the total annual volume.

Ignoring meat is not the answer to the future of sustainable food. Meat production has been a staple of the American economy, culture, and diet for generations, but industrial agriculture that values profits over people and the environment is careening toward a food-insecure future. Food wealth needs to be available to everyone, and people—farmers, workers, packers, and eaters—need to be at the center of the problem-solving.

The pitfalls of a food system dictated by big money and consolidation are not novel. Meat's consolidation problem is decades old. After five decades of mass consolidation, a tight grip on the markets exists. In beef, the top four packers control more than 80 percent of the industry, while the top firms in poultry have more than half and pork's largest producers dominate 70 percent.

As I've become *Forbes'* go-to reporter for agribusiness valuations, I've dug deeper into the challengers making a dent in industrialized and consolidated agriculture's grip on America's food system. On a hen farm in Paris, Texas, I interviewed Matt O'Hayer, the founder of pasture-raised egg brand Vital Farms, about how he proved consumers were willing to pay a premium for ethical treatment of animals and farmers. I became the first journalist to try the Impossible Whopper and have examined the burgeoning plant-based foods industry with a critical eye to its reliance on environmentally destructive commodity row crops, flavor science, and engineered ingredients.

When the pandemic hit, it tested the emerging alternative protein industry and its full cases of fakes by Beyond, Impossible, and their bevy of competitors, mostly from traditional meat-packers like Tyson, JBS, Smithfield, and Hormel. I began to wonder if the plant-based bubble was bursting before it ever really got going. But then fears over meat supply shortages ahead of barbecue season led to a new round of panic buying into May 2020, and more shoppers reached for the vegan alternatives.

Plant-based foods sales at grocery stores, according to NielsenIQ, hit $900 million in retail sales in 2020. These alternatives started considerably outpacing total food sales during the pandemic, with refrigerated alternatives like Beyond and Impossible surging 240 percent during the spring peak of meat panic buying. The bump outpaced animal meat sales, which started to decline.

If all you see with this is shifting consumer demand, take a step back. Plant-based still amounts to less than 1 percent of total US meat sales. In 2021 sales stagnated. The movement is threatened by the same problem that the past decade's push to localize the food system has experienced. Local food systems can be just as fraught. I asked Temple Grandin back in April 2020 what she thought could be a solution. Her answer was simple: "This pandemic is going to be a wake-up call. I expect many to become a lot more interested in more distributed, local supply chains."

The gigantic rise in large-scale industrial meat production, however, has been solidified over the past decade, even as the farm-to-table movement has been fueled by the popularity of Michael Pollan's *The Omnivore's Dilemma* and grown into a ubiquitous feature of strip malls and other suburban landscapes. The supply chains erected to provide an alternative to cheap meat and industrial produce have grown to new heights while continuing to fail their farmers. For all the excitement, local food is still just 1.5 percent of total agricultural output, or the roughly $400 billion in agricultural commodities like corn, soy, wheat, and produce that US producers sell annually. That's partly because it's harder than ever to run a small-scale operation successfully. As a result, few are left. While farmers' markets are heralded as an easy way to directly support a farmer, they institutionalize and normalize the unprofitability of small-scale farming because of hidden costs like transportation and packaging. At the same time, alternative models like community-supported farm shares more evenly distribute the added expenses but have been overshadowed—perhaps because they are competing for algorithmic placement and ad rates on Instagram with venture-backed brands raising millions just to acquire customers online—and have failed to grow as widely.

So what *is* good to eat? Food that actively works to build stronger and healthier communities, with workers who are treated justly and have a seat at the table. What's grown isn't just okay for the environment. It's produced sustainably, with minimal inputs, and preferably in a way that replenishes soils and encourages biodiversity, without leaving behind waste and water pollution. This definition should exist at all ends of the supply chain, from ranch to slaughterhouse to distributor to retailer.

Almost no meat in America is produced this way today. But there are several businesses, old and new, trying. Those succeeding have figured out a way to leverage assets for scale—giving them a chance at competing with industrialized prices and markets. Almost all the meat that is good to eat is sold for at-home use, which limits access to those who can spare convenience or pay a price for it. The meat is also rarely accessible at mainstream supermarkets. It needs to be sought out—which takes an obsessive ready to invest time in digging through the jargon and greenwashing. That's not okay. Cut out problematic production and repurpose as much of the assets as possible. There's not enough time or money to start completely from scratch.

SECTION I

—

THE INDUSTRIAL GRIP

CHAPTER 1

How Goliath Got So Big

Americans have no idea where their meat comes from. And while that's hurting us, it's also making others rich. These aren't old fortunes discussed in history books alongside the Rockefellers. Most of the wealth and power now concentrated within the meat industry has been carved out within the past five decades.

The Great Depression brought the Tyson family to the meat industry. A fifth-generation farmer, twenty-six-year-old John W. Tyson moved his wife and one-year-old son, Don, to Springdale, Arkansas, in 1931 with half a load of hay and a nickel in his pocket. Tyson wound up selling chickens to customers in Kansas City and St. Louis. In 1936, he packed up a truck and went to Chicago. The Tysons moved into raising chickens during World War II, when demand started soaring because poultry, a rarity in a lot of American diets up until then, was not rationed like pork and beef. Strong sales enticed the Tysons to expand. Their first plant opened in 1958—$15,000 over budget. By 1963, the firm was a publicly traded company.

Going public meant the Tyson family could take some risk off the table and bring in more shareholders, whose capital would help fuel an acquisition boom. The biggest shareholders continued to be the Tyson family, who control the majority of voting power, thanks to a dual-class stock structure that has insulated their shares. But Tyson's stock was on a roller-coaster ride at the whim of the market, alternating between record highs and lows. Then Tyson landed on a profitable win when it introduced Rock Cornish game hens. Soon access to cheap capital was fueling mergers of neighboring competitors. Regional processors including Arkansas neighbor Prospect

Farms and others throughout the South and Midwest like Omaha's Ocomo Foods got rolled up quickly under the leadership of John's son, Don, who had dropped out of college to start at the family company.

Don took over after his father and stepmother died in a car-train crash in 1967. He left his mark, creating a standard-issue Tyson uniform of khaki coveralls embroidered with the employee's name. An affable gambler who cultivated a cadre of presidents and politicians, his corporate strategy left a mark on the entire industry: "grow or die."

Grain Domination

The silent giant is agribusiness powerhouse Cargill, founded by William W. Cargill, one of five sons born to a Scottish sea captain, who set up a small grain trader in the frontier outpost of Conover, Iowa, in 1865. When Cargill died in 1909, the husband of Cargill's daughter who grew up across the street, took over operations. The new patriarch's name: John Hugh MacMillan. The Cargill and MacMillan families ran the company from there.

Cargill focused on grain until 1950. Thereafter the company dumped decades of profits into dozens of other commodities-based businesses, like cattle feedlot Caprock Industries in 1974 and beef processor MBPXL Corporation in 1979. Cargill transformed itself into an agribusiness conglomerate. The business swelled to more than $10 billion in annual revenue. Grain became a mere third of the business. Cargill became a top soybean producer, a top manufacturer of feed for livestock, America's second-largest beef packer, a poultry processor, a corn marketer, and seller of a myriad of products based on Cargill's network of commodified inputs—soybeans, flour, wheat, tapioca and sunflowers, chicken, turkey, and eggs. Other ventures included commodities futures trading, life insurance, barge construction, chemical processing, salt mining, and production of sugar and cotton.

Hog Wild

Tyson's and Cargill's aggressive acquisitions sparked the meatpacking industry to consolidate, but these two large firms were hardly the only ones. The Luter family founded hog processor Smithfield in 1936 in the ham-famous town of Smithfield, Virginia. It started when a father and son saw no future for themselves at the pork plant where they worked, Gwaltney of Smithfield. They raised $10,000 from local investors and decided to open up their own plant across the street instead.

Operations took off with third-generation CEO Joseph Luter III, who ran the company as CEO from the day after he graduated college at Wake Forest. Until 1966, a "genuine" Smithfield ham had to be fed only peanuts and aged for six months. But as Smithfield gobbled up more of its neighbors and made deals to source hogs from the Midwest, they shifted to corn-fed hogs. Meanwhile, Luter pressed his slaughterhouses to keep pumping out bacon, hams, and deli-style cuts.

In 1969, a DC-based firm acquired Smithfield for $20 million. Luter stayed on but was fired six months later. Luter returned in 1975 after creditors begged him. The firm was slaughtering 890,000 hogs annually and careening toward bankruptcy. Luter, who was developing a ski resort in Virginia, eyed the challenge as a way to buy back the family firm. Smithfield was losing $1 million a year with mounting debt. But once Luter came back, Smithfield quickly returned to making money. Luter then started acquiring more competitors, including Milwaukee's Patrick Cudahy and Baltimore's Schluderberg-Kurdle.

Ahead of the Curve

Packers back then only cut carcasses into massive sections, usually each animal just cut into quarters. Breaking the meat down further rested with butchers and their customers. But IBP, or Iowa Beef Processors, started cutting beef into smaller cuts easier for retailers to handle, vacuum-sealing it and calling it boxed beef.

Accounts flocked to IBP, and IBP secured a strong foothold ahead of competition. The invention also eliminated fat, bones, and trimmings from shipments, and gave meat-packers another avenue for moneymaking by reselling these parts to other industries, like pet food. The invention created a ripple effect in the beef industry: revamp the plant to cut and package boxed beef, too, or close up shop.

Merger Mania

A string of conflating factors has underwritten a major shift in American diets. The introduction of chicken as a mainstream source of protein gave rise to an entirely new market dominated by a fresh group of emerging processors. Then, in the 1970s, the USDA subsidized agribusiness. The government has funded price supports, crop insurance, disaster payments, tax credits, and depreciation allowances. The preferential treatment helped bigger industrial players root out smaller ones, which couldn't handle the competition amid their own rising costs.

The Reagan administration, relaxing antitrust regulations, then ushered in an open season for mergers and acquisitions. Among the rapid-fire mergers that followed, consider a survey of deals from 1981. Smithfield's Luter bought his father and grandfather's former employer, Gwaltney of Smithfield across the street, for $34 million. Occidental Petroleum then acquired IBP. Hubris joined the party: Perdue Farms, the first to brand commodity chicken popularized through television ads featuring CEO Frank Perdue, opened its first chicken restaurant that year.

The pressure to create cheaper meat and more of it became all-consuming, and the agriculture department's policy of "get big or get out" started revealing its own limitations. The farm crisis of the 1980s hit when the Federal Reserve imposed austere measures to try to bring down high interest rates, and farmland values fell drastically. Between 1970 and the peak in 1982, the value of farmland per acre across America soared 355 percent. But from 1982 to 1987, values crashed 34 percent. In Midwestern states like Iowa, the impacts were severe: acre prices reached a record increase of 431 percent before dropping 62 percent by 1987. But American agriculture has coalesced around a system where farms often lose money, and land ownership helps to offset taxes. The rapid changes, at a time when many farmers had taken out way too much debt, created an unexpected crash. Income dropped and exports halted. Farmers defaulted on their loans in droves: In 1970 there was $52 billion in US farm debt, compared to $162 billion in 1979. The banks that doled out these loans failed—sixty-two banks that primarily gave agricultural loans shuttered in 1985. That accounted for more than half of all US bank failures that year. Yet Wall Street chugged along.

Bankers turned to new prospects and welcomed the public listings of more meat processors. Smithfield stock quintupled in 1985. Pilgrim's Pride, then a forty-year-old chicken processor in Pittsburg, Texas, went public in 1986, followed by Mississippi-based Sanderson Farms, another family-founded-and-run company, the next year. Then 49 percent of IBP started trading when owner Occidental Petroleum wanted to partially cash out. Cargill, by then America's largest privately held company, with more than $30 billion in annual revenue, remained a crucial link at several junctures in the meat supply, controlled by three branches of family heirs.

This era is also when Joe Grendys, a Chicago billionaire, joined the chicken company Koch Foods after the original owner Fred Koch (pronounced "cook") offered Grendys in 1984 a chance to earn 50 percent equity in the business. It was a one-room processing plant where Grendys, Koch, and several other employees took the bones out of chicken and butchered it down for customers. Grendys bought out his mentor in 1992. Grendys' own acquisition spree started from there. In 1995, he bought Aspen Foods in Chicago's Fulton Market area. Under Grendys, Koch processed chicken much more than before. Grendys brought Koch into chicken nugget production and other popular formats, pushing Koch to grow into a top poultry processor.

Accounts with fast-growing fast-food chains like KFC and McDonald's boosted the industry. None more than Tyson. As its stock grew, Tyson soared to new heights, as Christopher Leonard's *The Meat Racket* lays out, and inched out in front of the hungry pack. In the five years leading up to 1989, Tyson doubled in size. That year it acquired Holly Farms for $1.5 billion, its largest acquisition at that point. Of Tyson's forty-seven plants, the vast majority were acquired. Tyson had built just two.

Consolidation created a profit multiplier for meat-packers, which has continued to bankroll the top operations into the present day. Firms used to tiny net margins were eventually amassing more cash than ever before. Some of that money helped meat-packers expand internationally, but most went toward dividends, stock buybacks, more acquisitions, and managerial compensation, all while low-paid plant workers continued to face one of the most dangerous jobs in America.

That cash in the bank has fueled bidding wars. Tyson and Smithfield fought over IBP in 2000, raising bids against each other for more than three months before a flurry of competing offers came in rapid fire over the New

Year holiday. Tyson won by January 2—even though Smithfield had offered a higher price overall. IBP agreed to $3.2 billion in cash and stock.

The megadeal put Tyson closer to the center of American dinner plates.

Tyson won another crucial bidding war in 2014, this time against Brazilian outfit JBS. Tyson ended up paying $8.55 billion, including debt, for Jimmy Dean breakfast sausage maker Hillshire Farms. Tyson might have not wanted to deal with JBS having another pipeline to prime customers. Tyson spent a 71 percent premium to Hillshire's share price before it became an acquisition target.

JBS's American acquisition spree started in 2007. Majority owned and run by the Batista family from central Brazil, JBS got into its Hillshire bidding war after invading Tyson's backyard and spending close to $2 billion rolling up other competitors. Tyson likely didn't bid to avoid antitrust scrutiny.[*] Unrestrained, JBS found many American meat-packers cheap. The Batistas' first US deal was for Greeley, Colorado–based Swift, once the gem of the beef industry. JBS paid $225 million in cash and assumed $1.2 billion of debt to acquire twelve US and Australian plants responsible for twenty-three thousand cattle slaughtered per day.

This book will explore what these acquisitions really entailed and how a billionaire-owned foreign entity acquired iconic American brands and crucial infrastructure, fueled in part by a mass bribery scheme in Brazil led by top JBS shareholders—who, at one point, even attempted to buy Brazil's 2014 elections.[†‡]

These deals became a major force driving the meat industry to consoli-

---

[*] To measure market competitiveness, the Department of Justice often considers the Herfindahl-Hirschman Index, or HHI, which is a simple equation that calculates market concentration by tallying up the market shares of firms in an industry. DOJ considers 15% to 25% to be a moderately concentrated marketplace, and more than 25% control to be a highly concentrated marketplace. Top meat companies often control a large share of their markets. In beef, Tyson has 24% market share, while Cargill has 22% and JBS has 21%. In pork, Smithfield controls 24%, while JBS has 21% and Tyson has 16%. In chicken, JBS-backed Pilgrim's Pride has 23%, while Tyson has 21%.

[†] JBS used funds and loans from Brazilian state bank BNDES to acquire Swift, Pilgrim's Pride, and Smithfield Beef.

[‡] J&F Investimentos is a private investment holding company based in São Paulo, Brazil, which is the ultimate parent company of JBS. J&F owns 48.25% of JBS shares as its controlling group. J&F is wholly owned by the brothers Wesley and Joesley Batista, according to a Securities and Exchange Commission cease and desist order.

date under the Batista family's banner.* After losing out on IBP, Smithfield decided to focus only on pork, and instead of off-loading its large beef division to competitor Tyson, Smithfield sold it to JBS in 2008 for $565 million. The same week, JBS announced it would also acquire National Beef, founded in 1992. But both beef deals at once triggered regulators' concerns. While the Smithfield beef deal stuck, National Beef got cut. JBS moved into poultry in 2009 instead, after Pilgrim's Pride went bankrupt and JBS purchased majority ownership for $800 million.

---

* A J&F Investimentos spokesperson said, "All acquisitions made by J&F-controlled companies were made with legally-raised funds in accordance with all regulatory and legal requirements" and that J&F is implementing "one of the most extensive" compliance programs in the world. J&F legal counsel Francisco de Assis e Silva said the details described in the Batistas' and J&F collaboration agreements refer to electoral donations and that in Brazil companies were allowed to donate to politicians until 2015: "The fact is that Brazil faced a period in which any private-public relation and all political activities were considered illegal."

CHAPTER 2

Consolidation of Power

Sheldon Lavin was thirty-eight years old in 1970 when German immigrant Otto Kolschowsky and his sons approached Lavin for help. They ran Des Plaines, Illinois–based Otto & Sons. The business was proudly the first fresh hamburger meat supplier to McDonald's after sealing the deal with a Ray Kroc handshake in 1955. Since then, Kroc's suppliers list had grown to some 150 fresh burger manufacturers nationwide and Kroc wanted to cut down. Kroc, the legendary McDonald's franchise mastermind, decided just five suppliers could cryogenically flash-freeze burgers on an industrial scale, and he was offering Otto & Sons one of the slots. But the Kolschowsky family needed to figure out if they could finance a plant as big as McDonald's would need. The Chicago-based banker might have been able to help the Kolschowsky family with their predicament.

Lavin, the heavyset financial consultant, had spent years as an independent operator, bushy eyebrows furrowed while crunching the numbers. Lavin agreed to help and got the Kolschowskys their money. As the story goes, the loan officer was apparently so impressed that he suggested Lavin should have ownership in the processing plant. Lavin walked away from that at the time, but he did stay on as a key strategist, charting potential growth and keeping an eye on the money—and over the years remained active in the business at McDonald's urging. Executives at the chain apparently went as far as suggesting Lavin should make a full-time commitment to OSI, no doubt worried that Lavin could sell his consulting services to a competitor. When a business's only customer like McDonald's makes a friendly suggestion like that, the owner tends to listen. When the elder

Kolschowsky stepped down a few years later, Lavin held a third of the company's ownership and later the CEO post.

It's the start of how Lavin became a modern meat baron. For the past fifty years, Lavin has invested in crucial choke points across the meat industry while inking deals with some of the emerging alternatives trying to take it over.

Lavin's OSI Group is one of the world's largest contract manufacturers, with a network of sixty-five plants in eighteen countries. OSI remains a major supplier to McDonald's. Lavin earned the Golden Arches' trust, and a huge portion of their business, as he traveled the globe to open up international markets as the unofficial chief meat supplier, often scouting out local markets ahead of any formal expansion. OSI took off in the 1980s when Lavin gained control of the business after buying out one son and eventually the other.

"I decided there was no reason for me to stay if I didn't build OSI into something big," Lavin told the Meat Hall of Fame, into which he was inducted in 2013. "I might as well have gone back to finance. I wouldn't have stayed if I couldn't have grown it."

Lavin eventually diversified OSI's customer list with many of McDonald's fast-food competitors, like KFC and Pizza Hut. The roster has also included Chipotle, Whole Foods, Kraft Heinz's Oscar Mayer, Impossible Foods, and many others—annual revenues top $6 billion.

There's also a hand in the slaughter business. OSI owns a chicken processor called Amick Farms. For years, OSI also held a board seat as a large shareholder of Brazil's second-largest meatpacking company, Marfrig, which owns America's fourth-largest beef packer, National.

Lavin has surely made other investments I haven't been able to track. One that came up for his son Steven is MeaTech 3D, an Israeli start-up that became the first in the emerging industry of lab-grown meat to trade publicly in the United States. It transferred its listing to Nasdaq in 2021. Lavin served as the chairman of the start-up until 2022 and remains one of the largest individual shareholders. It hopes to manufacture the pricey equipment needed to produce lab-grown meat for a range of locations and business customers, from industrialized plants to maybe one day grocery stores.

Lavin is among the richest meat processors in America, according to

Forbes. His net worth is $3 billion. Cargill's dozen or so heirs are richer, with a combined fortune topping $40 billion, but none are involved in the day-to-day business.

The meat industry has created substantial wealth for those who have hoarded it. There's third-generation Tyson patriarch John H. Tyson at $3.1 billion, Chicago's chicken titan Joe Grendys with a fortune estimated at $3.3 billion, and Omaha beef packer Henry Davis with $2.3 billion. The Batista brothers Joesley and Wesley from Brazil-based JBS count $4.4 billion each, while Wan Long, who acquired Smithfield through his Chinese conglomerate WH Group, has $1.3 billion. Several billionaires have diversified their wealth by investing in slaughterhouses, feed milling operations, or other junctures in the meat supply chain, including Minneapolis *Star Tribune* owner Glen Taylor, estimated at $2.4 billion, and Ted Turner, the cable mogul turned bison rancher, worth $2.3 billion.

Meet the most extreme examples of consolidation of power within the meat industry. These billionaires and their companies underpin the meat supply chain. They invest in start-up challengers while maintaining strategic ties to competitors by acquiring firms that they want to off-load. Ultimately, these companies have the potential to transform either into well-funded proving grounds for change or untouchable holdouts that could prevent the entire system from crucial progress.

Efficiency, Feedlots, and Megaplants

Subsidized and industrialized corn and soy reduced the cost of production and helped animals get bigger quickly. But it also created the need for a new kind of intermediary—defined by the Environmental Protection Agency in 1976 as a concentrated animal feeding operation, or CAFO. Inserting feedlots between the farmer and the slaughterhouse created a new sector where the animals would spend their last few months getting much bigger, often squeezed close together with a bunch of other animals. Feedlots opened up in small towns dotting Iowa, Nebraska, and Colorado to bring the animals closer to where the corn was grown. Meatpacking megaplants were erected to maximize economies of scale that, in turn, forced other smaller plants to close because they couldn't compete on price or volume. Weaker operations were acquired in an acquisition frenzy that ratcheted up in the 1980s.

Wall Street's merger mania gutted the meat industry while simultaneously forcing meat-packers to supersize their plants. In 1976, the beef industry counted 145 midsize plants, which killed fifty thousand cattle a year, or about 22 million collectively. Just five plants at the time could slaughter more than half a million cattle a year. Their production made up less than 15 percent of all commercial beef. But the aftermath of mass consolidation and centralization on America's meat supply is stark. By 1998, midsize plants fell to thirty-eight overall, responsible for about 27 million cattle a year. A stunning fourteen plants had started slaughtering one million cattle or more, which that year accounted for more than two-thirds of total beef slaughter. The pork industry experienced a similarly grim story: in 1976, just twelve hog processing plants had the capacity to kill more than one million a year. Those large plants made up less than 30 percent of total hog slaughter. Yet, by 1998, megaplants like that had more than doubled, to thirty, and were responsible for more than 90 percent of commercial production.

Over the years, as economists have dug into the long-term data, they have realized that while the consolidation and centralization drove efficiency and eventually led to the takeover of the industry, the corporations were the most profitable *long term* because they could drive away competition *while* outlasting drought, market fluctuations, and thinning margins, which led dozens of other operators to close.

That's according to the University of Missouri's John Ikerd, a retired agriculture economics professor, who saw firsthand, from purchasing records farmers sent in by mail, how integrating hog production, slaughter, and distribution drove even the most efficient independent hog producers out of business in the 1990s. As the pork industry's corporatization began fully, prices for hogs dropped to a low while the average production costs were more than quadruple the market price. The least efficient producers went bankrupt or closed. The last survivors became corporate contract producers. Eventually many of the best couldn't last either. Once agribusiness conglomerates got control, those corporations pushed into most related areas, from genetics to the finished packages of grocery store bacon.

"The packers lowered wholesale pork prices enough to allow the pork from hogs under their control to clear the market, but only enough to leave prices seriously depressed in markets where independent producers were forced to sell. Any corporate losses on their owned or contract hogs were largely offset by wider margins of profit for hogs purchased from independent producers. Independent producers were not only forced to sell at large losses, some couldn't find markets at any price," Ikerd wrote.

"The least efficient independent producers are the first to be forced out of business by more efficient corporate producers," added Ikerd. "Once the corporations gain control of a significant share of the total market, they can begin to manipulate market prices available to remaining independent producers."

During times of excess, Ikerd explains, the corporations "depress and hold market prices" for independents, creating an unprofitable and unsustainable situation. Soon enough, the least efficient of the survivors are out of business.

That has driven, in the past five decades, the number of meatpacking plants to drastically recede. The top four firms in each meat sector control most of the processing capacity and dominate the rest of their industries. In beef, Tyson, JBS, Cargill, and National control more than 80 percent.* In pork, Smithfield, JBS, Tyson, and Hormel have more than 70 percent and, in chicken, Tyson, JBS-owned Pilgrim's Pride, Sanderson Farms, and Perdue control more than 50 percent.†

American meat output then increased more than twofold. Initially, consumers got steadier and cheaper meat prices, largely due to major declines in feed costs from government subsidies. Those cost savings have leveled out. Yet the combination of corn and large, centralized plants remains crucial to JBS's strategy, according to JBS North America CEO Andrés Nogueira. In Brazil, few cattle touch corn. They only eat grass (which helps to explain why, as the industry has become bloated, the Amazon rain forest has been clear-cut away).

"We operate plants of all sizes. We know the reality of all sizes of plants,"

---

* Some estimates for beef industry concentration have the top four firms' share at more than 85 percent.

† In beef, Tyson commands more than 24 percent of the market, while JBS counts about 21 percent, Cargill has 22 percent, and National Beef has 14 percent. The top pork producers start with Smithfield, which has a market share of more than 24 percent, while JBS has more than 21 percent, Tyson has more than 16 percent, and Hormel has 8 percent. JBS-backed Pilgrim's Pride controls 23 percent of the chicken industry, while Tyson has 21 percent, Sanderson 9 percent, Perdue 7 percent, and Koch 6 percent.

Nogueira explained. "We know how much better the quality and the impact that these plants we have in the US can operate. In Brazil, most cattle are grass-fed, not grain. They need to have smaller plants. Otherwise, you need to move the cattle a distance that would be bad for animal welfare. Because you can have grain-fed, you can have more concentration, and so you can have bigger plants. We know the reality of bigger and smaller. I can assure you that bigger is much better for farmers, for cost for sure, and impact.

"When you have a plant that can process six thousand cattle per day or twenty thousand hogs a day, that makes the plant very efficient," Nogueira said. "That's why when you go to retail in the US and buy pounds of beef or a pound of pork or a pound of chicken, it will be on average 30 percent to 40 percent cheaper than what you would buy in Europe. Or 50 percent to 60 percent from Japan or Korea. So, why? Because the size of the plant is part of the efficiency."

From the onset of merger mania through 2010, the number of US beef-packing plants declined by about 80 percent. But it wasn't just a crunch among slaughterhouses. The number of cattle feedlots had also declined by 32 percent since 1980. That period saw over thirty-six thousand feedlots exit the industry. Between 2003 and 2005, some six thousand feedlots went out of business alone. Nearly all that have survived have a capacity of more than a thousand cattle per day.

But the survivors are now rolling in it. In recent years, beef packers have captured a record amount of the industry's profits, and they'd like to keep it that way. Rabobank's animal protein analyst estimated operating income for packers from 2002 to 2014 was at a loss of at least $10 per head on average, compared to over $100 operating income per head in 2015.

Tyson has never before relied on beef to be its most profitable division, a title that chicken has held, but in the past five years beef has become a huge driver for the business. These yields have risen as the dividend that Tyson pays out quarterly to its shareholders has grown consistently during that time, yielding more than forty cents per share each quarter of 2020 and into 2021. That's a more than 2 percent yield, which is up by a factor of eight from paying just five cents a share in 2013. JBS, meanwhile, has an annual dividend of just under twenty cents per share. Its dividend yield, or the ratio that measures the payout compared to the overall stock price, is 8 percent. There are also stock buybacks, which is when a company repurchases some of its shares using cash generated from the business, investor capital, or debt to pay it off. After a buyback, the share price often rises. JBS spent more than $350 million on share buybacks in 2020, and another $700 million in 2021. Tyson had enough cash to repurchase more than $350 million in shares at the end of 2021.

Taking a Bite out of Rising Demand for Meat

There's an uneasy connection between supply and demand and a stable democracy. Usually where there's growing demand, there's pressure to meet it, but this kind of talk conveniently ignores a complicated history where meat shortages have been linked to all sorts of upheaval around the world. In Italy in 1976, masked gunmen kidnapped purveyors and threatened to kill them if meat prices didn't drop in working-class Roman neighborhoods. In the past decade in Venezuela, years of food shortages have caused riots and have contributed to millions fleeing. Two decades after the state's takeover of most food plants, meat production has contracted by two-thirds. Most Venezuelans who remain in the country can't afford to buy meat, if they're lucky enough to find it outside the black market. In the United States, out-of-reach meat prices have contributed to protests, worker strikes, and even the 1946 toppling of the Democratic party's sixteen-year control of Congress.

That's stuck with me as I've unwrapped the allegations of price manipulation against the country's largest meat-packers. Puffed up from a period of unprecedented moneymaking, all they have to do is keep making more and more meat—and mouths across the world will be ready to chow down.

Take what Tyson's then freshly appointed CEO, Tom Hayes, told me over deviled eggs and pumpkin soup at Bobby Flay's midtown Manhattan lunch haunt Bar Americain in 2017: "Worldwide protein consumption continues to grow on a global basis. When you have developing countries and they start to become wealthier, the first thing they do is spend more money on protein"—every meatpacking CEO's favorite talking point. Not the true cost of meat, the human toll, or the environmental impact.

Protein consumption in the United States was "fertile ground," added Hayes, who joined Tyson after it beat JBS to acquire Hayes' employer, Hillshire Brands, in 2014. "Half the population in the US wants more protein.

People are trying to actively increase their protein consumption," Hayes said.

He had just reported stellar annual earnings to Wall Street, including news of $2.9 billion in profit, a record. Voice recorder on the white table-cloth at the table with Tyson's top brass, I carefully ate bites of salad and tried not to let my mind drift too much to the odd combination of velvety pumpkin and mayonnaise-whipped yolks. I asked Hayes to clarify Tyson's growth strategy—would it be contingent on future mergers and acquisitions, like the massive Hillshire deal just completed? "Let's just pick what we want to do—protein, sustainable protein, brands, growth—and drive that. That's enough to keep us busy for a long time.

"A lot of food companies aren't growing today," he added, "and we want to continue to grow and deliver the financial results, deliver on account-abilities, but then also make the company sustainable." For each quarterly earnings report, we get further from a sustainable model.

It will be harder to keep delivering on growth as climate change continues to test systems of production. Sustainability has historically been a low priority. Processors have made little attempt to accept and change their role in supporting better systems fundamentally—like shifting away from synthetic fertilizer degraded cropland for feed or contracting cattle that eat not at feedlots but while grazing on forage through a system of managed rotations. Industrial meat-packers, meanwhile, continue to control massive amounts of power and profits, to the detriment of producers and consumers.

Meat-packers are not likely to give up future gains willingly. In 2018, the United Nations published potential scenarios, and its business-as-usual model has meat consumption increasing 50 percent, to 450 million tons annually, in the next three decades. It is almost entirely driven by a 23 percent production increase in China as well as a quadrupling of meat consumption in sub-Saharan Africa. A sustainability-minded model expects people living in high-income countries to decrease their meat consumption per capita—from 796 calories per day in 2012 to 738 per day by 2030 and 700 per day by 2050. It pegs 2050 global production levels at 380 million tons annually and 2030 levels closer to 350 million tons.

"So the future is bright, right?" JBS USA CEO André Nogueira told me over the phone at the end of 2020. "Protein consumption is growing on a global basis. We are a supplier with the globe in mind. We will continue to grow. The demand is very strong."

He followed up with an example.

"Last week we exported from the US one thousand containers of protein. That's one thousand containers, forty feet. Just JBS. Just one week," he boasted. "Where is this going? Everywhere, because we are very competitive. But there's no question, Asia is growing consumption at a very fast pace. China is a part of that, but it's not only Chinese."

This strategy is by design. China and Brazil are expected to lead the surge in meat consumption, but the projections are still based on imperfect trends, according to researchers from a University of Oxford project that analyzes decades of United Nations statistics, called Our World in Data. "One of the strongest determinants of how much meat people eat is how rich they are. This is at least true when we make cross-country comparisons," the researchers write, adding that "the direction and rate of change across countries has been highly variable. Growth in per capita meat consumption has been most marked in countries who have underwent [sic] a strong economic transition—per capita consumption in China has grown approximately 15-fold since 1961; rates in Brazil have nearly quadrupled. The major exception to this pattern has been India: dominant lactovegetarian preferences mean per capita meat consumption in 2013 was almost exactly the same as in 1961 at less than 4 kilograms per person." That is a lot of people and individual preferences—and it is not fair for entire industries to plan years in advance for increased consumption while ignoring generations of traditions. Assuming all countries will follow the trend of rising intake, especially for cultures known for millennia for adopting vegetarian diets, bets a lot on major variables.

Meat consumption per capita in the United States, meanwhile, has been stagnating. Americans' appetite for beef has dropped by around half since the late 1970s, while poultry consumption has doubled. US per capita beef consumption is down from its peak, but it's still four times higher than the world average. In a single year, the average American consumes around 275 pounds of all meat, compared to 170 pounds for the average European. It's a heck of a lot of demand to balance out. As HSBC's global food industry analyst Alessia Apostolatos puts it, "The demand side of the equation is driving the discourse."

CHAPTER 3

Monopsony Just Doesn't Have the Same Ring to It

After years of feeling squeezed and cut out of their livelihoods, independent cattlemen decided that they had had enough. A class-action suit called out Tyson as a market manipulator and demanded retribution. The case got to trial in 2004, and it promised to be the cattle trial of the century.

Henry Lee Pickett, a cattleman with a farm thirty-five miles south of Montgomery, Alabama, led the lawsuit, which was alleging violations of the Packers and Stockyards Act that had become one of the most widespread examples of manipulating the cash markets in beef history. Over thirty-five days in federal court in Alabama, Pickett alleged Tyson and its subsidiary IBP used contracts with cattlemen to deflate the price of cattle on the cash market. IBP, which Tyson acquired in 2001 after outbidding Smithfield, had benefited from lower prices overall. During the jury trial, it was estimated that Tyson depressed the prices paid for cattle between 1996 and 2004 by at least 4 percent on every animal, or at least $32 missed. That represented a value of more than $2 billion over the nine-year period.

For violating the Packers and Stockyards Act, the jury awarded the class-action group $1.28 billion. As many as thirty thousand cattlemen who made a cash market deal in that time were estimated to have a claim to a piece of that. But the victory was short-lived. Tyson, which had fought the lawsuit for years, asked the presiding judge to ignore the jury's decision. The Reagan-appointed judge decided the burden of proof for damages hadn't been met. Pickett and the cattlemen appealed to the federal appellate level, which affirmed the trial court's dismissal. Eventually the case made it to the

Supreme Court in 2006. But the justices declined to hear the appeal, in favor of Tyson, and the producers walked away empty-handed.

The case doesn't sit well with Colorado-born rancher Mike Callicrate, who would have qualified for part of the payout. Three years before the Pickett trial, in 2001, Callicrate traveled to San Antonio for the National Cattlemen's Beef Association convention and had a run-in. John Tyson, the son of Don Tyson and at the time the presiding CEO of Tyson, was there to give a speech about his company's acquisition of IBP and what it would mean for the beef industry. Callicrate spied Tyson going to the bathroom a few minutes before the keynote was set to start, and hung around outside the door to the men's room to introduce himself. After what Callicrate recalls as a weird post-bathroom handshake, Callicrate explained that he would be testifying as part of the class-action suit. Tyson didn't seem to be familiar with the case, so Callicrate laid out the stakes on the line: "Well, you know, Mr. Tyson, if we win this lawsuit, it could cost IBP more than its entire market capitalization."

As the story goes, then Tyson told Callicrate bluntly: "You're suing the wrong people here. You should sue Walmart. They dictate the price to us, and we have no choice but to pay you less."*

"Well, the reason you can pay us less is because you have the market power to do so," the rancher recalls saying. Callicrate, who also owns a meat market in Colorado Springs, still sniffs at the memory.

"He didn't win his argument," Callicrate recalled to me. "Tyson was absolutely right, but he had the power to pay less."

Chickenshit Lawsuits

There are few industries more consolidated than meatpacking, and even fewer where that environment has existed as long and with as much market power unchecked by regulators. In the years since that bathroom run-in, allegations of price-fixing have evolved that rival the scope of Tyson's Pickett class action. Scores of lawsuits allege that more than a dozen of America's top meat producers have conspired to keep supplies tight and customer prices high.

---

* A representative for Tyson Foods denies that John Tyson said this.

Many of the lawsuits have named a defendant called Agri Stats, a tool selling reports with confidential data on the meat industry. The firm is a data aggregator founded at a kitchen table in Fort Wayne, Indiana, in 1985, but controversy has overshadowed the business for nearly two decades. It's hard to imagine a legal system that doesn't call out Agri Stats at the very least as "facilitating collusion, if not fomenting it," according to antitrust lawyer Peter Carstensen.

Carstensen says that Agri Stats has helped the meat industry become more profitable at the expense of producers, workers, and consumers. Agri Stats created a platform for sharing confidential data and broke down each meat industry into key metrics on a spreadsheet. According to the class-action complaints, Agri Stats receives and shares financial information like monthly operating profit per live pound, sales per live pound, and cost per live pound, as well as facility-level information on production, breed of chicks, average weight at slaughter, flock inventory levels, feed and housing expenses, processing line speeds, birds per man-hour, and labor hours per pound. Agri Stats has been able to maintain its benchmarking business using anonymized data to obscure which plant the numbers come from and who the ultimate owner is. According to sources I spoke to, the data is easy enough to decode.*

Agri Stats, which did not return requests for comment, gave each chicken complex its own number. A coding system denoted which region the chicken complex was in and stated each plant surveyed in the region. The number never changed. Agri Stats even worked to prevent cheating, or what might happen if a firm tried to make a short-term gain with the knowledge that competitors were working in tandem to hold back supplies to drop prices.

Agri Stats created a blueprint for any business looking to aid meat market manipulation, according to the complaints. It does so by exploiting how hard it is for American regulators to enforce antitrust laws. Agri Stats turned over more than 385,000 pages of documents between 2010 and 2012 when the Department of Justice investigated the business. Federal investigators closed the case without recommending changes to the business or bringing forth any charges.

---

* However, a Justice Department investigation found this was sufficiently anonymized.

Yet sharing proprietary information that limits competition between food industry suppliers and favors a small few should be prohibited, according to the Packers and Stockyards Act of 1921, which aims to "assure fair competition and fair trade practices to safeguard farmers and ranchers . . . to protect consumers . . . and to protect members of the livestock, meat, and poultry industries from unfair, deceptive, unjustly discriminatory and monopolistic practices." Carstensen, who describes Agri Stats as leading "intentional" and "conscious" facilitation, is putting together a proposal to amend the Packers and Stockyards Act to prevent meat processors from sharing highly competitive data, which could starve companies like Agri Stats in the future.

By 2018, when a legal complaint alleged that Agri Stats had the best financial performance in its thirty-three years with $7 million in profits, the chicken industry's relationship with Agri Stats had become the target of lawsuits. Parties to the class-action lawsuit came from all ends of the food industry, from customer purchasers to retailers like Walmart and distributors like Sysco. Those parties eventually created a class action against twenty-five chicken processors. The class action includes Chick-Fil-A, Target, White Castle, Aldi, Wawa, Kraft Heinz, Conagra, and Nestlé. More than one hundred private lawsuits, from customers who have opted out of the class action, will play out in the courts for years.

A blockbuster federal settlement came next. In October 2020, JBS-backed Pilgrim's Pride, the second largest in the poultry industry, announced it would settle with the federal government. In February 2021, Pilgrim's Pride pleaded guilty for its participation in a conspiracy to suppress and eliminate competition and agreed to pay $107 million. The government estimated that between 2012 and 2017 at least $361 million in Pilgrim's chicken sales were impacted by Pilgrim's Pride's involvement. That's more than $1 for every American.

Tyson has also been settling private allegations of price-fixing with customers while denying wrongdoing. In January 2021, Tyson agreed to set aside about $220 million to dole out to groups of buyers suing Tyson and other processors. Tyson maintains that Agri Stats is a legitimate benchmarking service and that the claims have no merit. DOJ investigators have not charged Tyson or other meat processors, aside from Pilgrim's Pride, with any crimes. DOJ investigators have also not charged Agri Stats. Tyson agreed to work with federal prosecutors after internally investigating and finding a small subset of rigging related to broiler chicken bids among a small group of customers, unrelated to Agri Stats. Tyson claims the employee responsible was low-level and did not have pricing authority.

McDonald's still joined the class action against the top chicken processors and Agri Stats later on in 2021. So far, six poultry processors have settled with some class-action customers for a total of $169 million, all while denying wrongdoing.* Tyson's bill tops $80 million, while Pilgrim's Pride agreed to pay $75 million and OSI-owned Amick Farms settled for $3.95 million.

Collusion on a Mass Scale

This kind of activity is not unique to chicken. Several retailers, including Winn-Dixie, restaurant chains like LongHorn Steakhouse, and other meat-buying customers have also filed class-action claims against meat-packers that used Agri Stats for pork. JBS paid $57 million in three public settlements related to allegations of pork price-fixing, and as part of the agreements denied wrongdoing. Smithfield is the only other major pork producer to have settled claims, while also denying wrongdoing. Smithfield has agreed to pay $83 million. Other processors face settlements or possible trials.† Tyson is among them, and has stopped using Agri Stats for pork. Tyson claims Agri Stats pork data hasn't been as useful as the poultry data, which Tyson still pays for.

These lawsuits, which name Agri Stats as a defendant alongside the slaughterhouse customers, claim that once meat-packers got comfortable with Agri Stats data, Agri Stats expanded its offerings. The data provider started with the chicken industry but expanded its services to pork. Agri Stats even allegedly supplied some data to the beef industry starting in 2015, through a price-forecasting subscription service it owned called Express Markets, according to a class-action lawsuit filed in 2019. Agri Stats has denied the allegations that the supply of data it receives constitutes collusion.

---

* Law firms representing defendants have made at least $56 million so far.

† Defendants in the pork processor class action are Agri Stats, Hormel Foods, Smithfield Foods, Clemens Food, Hatfield Quality Meats, Triumph Foods, Seaboard Foods, JBS USA Food Company, and Tyson Foods.

As of May 2022, the main antitrust class action for the beef industry, filed in 2020, remains ongoing.* JBS became the first to settle with one customer group in the case, again denying wrongdoing. JBS agreed to pay $52.5 million in February 2022. JBS says it "entered into an agreement to partially settle the In re Beef Antitrust Litigation to avoid excessive litigation costs." JBS says the settlement, which is subject to court approval, "has nothing to do with antitrust claims from cattle ranchers, and the company will vigorously defend its interests against these allegations."

Ranching advocates have for a long time claimed that a tepid cash market and the rise of longer-term contracts with processors in the cattle industry have devastated prices paid to ranchers, while the meat processors are capturing more of the consumer dollar. The majority of beef produced gets sold to meat-packers through long-term contracts, but sales from the cash market help set the standard for prices on those contracts. That makes any manipulation of the cash market reverberate throughout the industry. Large meat-packers, on the other hand, say long-term contracts with producers lower risks and costs, and that they are committed to fair compensation for their farmers and ranchers.

According to the beef antitrust class-action complaint, that is what happened by 2015, when the prices of cattle going to slaughter and beef shipping to retailers stopped moving in tandem. Processors began charging their customers more money even as the price paid to producers dropped. The country's top meatpackers have testified that they cannot control market forces and deny that there has been collusion since 2015.

The complaint alleged that the reason for the odd blip in the commodity markets is that the top four meat-packers seem to have tried to cut out producers and bring down prices through a series of what, taken together, appears to be coordinated plant closures. Here's what happened: Cargill closed its Plainview, Texas, and Milwaukee, Wisconsin, plants (4,000 and 1,300 cattle slaughtered per day) in February 2013 and August 2014; National Beef shut its Brawley, California, plant (2,000 per day) in June 2014; JBS left its newly acquired Nampa, Idaho, plant closed; and Tyson closed its Denison, Iowa, plant (2,000 per day) in August 2015. The meat-packers

---

* Defendants in the beef antitrust class action are Tyson, JBS, Cargill, and National Beef Packing Company.

followed a simple rule, according to the complaint: if there are fewer plants processing animals, there are fewer businesses to purchase animals.

Tyson had already shut down its plant in Cherokee, Iowa, and, according to the *Des Moines Register*, Tyson refused to lease the plant to competition. The plant eventually sold in 2018 after Tyson amended its deed with a requirement that the next owner limit the number of cattle that could be slaughtered at the plant for the next decade. According to the deed, the new plant owners had to agree to confirm at least every three months the amount harvested was not violating its agreement with Tyson. "The aforesaid covenants, conditions and restrictions shall," the deed reads, "be enforceable by Tyson . . . to recover damages for such violations."*

In some markets, a packer rarely met competition for an open-market bid. One estimate alleges that cattle prices were artificially depressed by an average of 7.9 percent between 2015 and 2018. The top meat-packers pulled record-shattering profits out of the beef industry and played off these war chests as necessary to stay competitive amid the cycles of supply and demand. Why? They claim it is because they, too, deal with market pressures.

What's Monopsony Got to Do with It?

Walmart is America's largest meat seller, and the bigger Walmart gets, the more it wants to deal with suppliers that are bigger, too. Unlike monopoly, which describes producers, monopsony describes the buyers. In this case, that's retailers and other major operations that act as middlemen connecting producers with consumers. Like an oligopoly, which is when a seller's market is dominated by a handful of producers, there's also oligopsony, which is defined as a buying market that is controlled by a small few. The pressure comes into play on multiple levels: the meat-packers exert oligopsony pressure on producers, but select few large retailers also exert oligopsony pressure on the meat-packers.

Centralization and consolidation, from the meat-packers' perspective, are a chance to survive in a world that is squeezing them too, because Amazon and Walmart are behemoths that have unmatched scale and the power

---

* Tyson says it had to buy out the lease on the plant, which was supposed to last until 2020. The plant had been producing deli meat when Tyson closed it in 2014.

to dictate prices and terms. "You basically have Walmart dictating what they're going to pay, and every producer is hostage to the buyer because there's not that many buyers anymore on retail," Mark Lauritsen, the head of the meatpacking division for the nation's largest private-sector union, the United Food and Commercial Workers, told me.

"We have a monopsony problem along with a monopoly problem," Lauritsen continued. "If we solved the monopoly problem on beef and pork and chicken, if you think there was one there, and we broke up all these companies, and we don't fix the monopsony problem on the buyer side, all these small little meat-packers that we are now creating because we broke up the big meat-packers are going to get just stampeded like buffalo by companies like Walmart. We can't fix one problem without the other. Otherwise, consumers and workers and farmers are all going to get screwed up.

"We all grew up playing the game Monopoly. We all learned about the Rockefellers and the Carnegies. We get the concept. If you grab the average person on the street and say, 'What's monopsony?' they don't know about the concentration of buyer power, which can be just as bad," Lauritsen added. "I've been in the meat industry for thirty-five years. I've had a ton of barroom conversations. If you've got them in a barroom, they would all say, 'You're absolutely right.' There's a monopsony problem, but you'll never get one of them to say it. Because when you look at the amount of purchasing that Walmart has, there's not one of these employers that are going to speak up and say they're bad, because then Walmart just cuts them off. I've seen plants where Walmart puts them on a restricted list, where we have lost a hundred and fifty people to layoffs because, all of a sudden, half the business and the plant is gone because Walmart decided to restrict the business there, for whatever reason."

The union, which represents over 250,000 meatpacking workers at companies like JBS, Tyson, and Cargill, has a fundamental reason to want the meat-packers to be steady. But the point is fair. Some of the meatpacking industry consolidation through the 1990s and afterward was driven by Walmart becoming the nation's top grocer.

The Rise of the Superstore

Walmart entered the grocery industry in 1988 when its first supercenter opened in Washington, Missouri. Within a decade, twenty-five large regional grocery companies went out of business and Walmart had gobbled up 6 percent of the nation's grocery market. Walmart's share jumped to 23 percent by 2008, roughly the same share it has in 2021.

As America's largest grocer, Walmart has $200 billion in annual grocery sales, 3,500 American supercenters, and an overall market cap of more than $400 billion. Operations run smoothly across fifty-five distribution centers with 44 million square feet of warehouse space. Capturing more than 50 percent of grocery sales in forty-three metropolitan areas, as well as more than 70 percent across thirty-eight regions, means Walmart brings unparalleled dominance wherever it expands. Walmart's annual grocery revenue is more than double that of its next-biggest competitor, Kroger.

Retailers are taking an increasing portion of the dollar spent, which only tightens Walmart's grip. In 1990 each dollar spent by consumers on beef would have been distributed across the food supply chain as 59 cents for the rancher or farmer, just 8 cents for the packer, and 33 cents for the retailer. By 2009, the farmer's share had dropped to 42 cents and the packer's share rose slightly to 9 cents. But the retailer's share rose the most, to roughly half, or 49 cents of every dollar spent. In 2020, the producer earned 37 cents of every dollar spent on beef at retail, a drop of nearly 40 percent since 1990. Slaughterhouses retained 18 cents and retailers held on to 44 cents. A similar breakdown exists in pork and chicken. These numbers illustrate that while the retailer's share has swelled, so has the meat-packer's.

According to a report UFCW put out in 2010 called *Ending Walmart's Rural Stranglehold*, Walmart's scale gives it "unprecedented buying power over the packers to continue exerting strong downward pressure on prices paid to suppliers, preventing the meat-packers, workers and farmers from recovering their previous share of the consumer meat retail dollar." The report asserts: "It is clear that in order to right America's crippled agriculture economy caused by the oversized power that Walmart has over packers and farmers, appropriate government intervention is needed to curtail this company's excessive buyer power and to bring fairness back to the marketplace."

According to a National Grocers Association report on buyer power and economic discrimination from 2021, Walmart puts its muscle to work in new ways all the time. Take its requirement to provide at least 75 percent of deliveries on time and in full. The requirement increased to 85 percent and then 87 percent in 2019, only to get hiked up—to 98 percent—again as suppliers struggled with supply chain backups in 2020. If suppliers didn't meet Walmart's demands, the supplier got charged 3 percent of the cost of the goods sold. According to several grocery insiders, if Walmart's actions are not addressed, there may continue to be a destructive race to the bottom that could destroy communities that require access to healthy food.

"They are becoming bigger and bigger clients, and the negotiating power that food companies have with these retailers has fallen through. It's been hard for them to renegotiate," says Alessia Apostolatos, a global food industry analyst at HSBC.

Suppliers like Tyson and JBS generally renegotiate with Walmart and Amazon once a year. That's one of the main reasons why meat suppliers are so focused on trying to hedge their grain costs, meaning many meatpackers buy and trade commodities futures to shelter their businesses from risks like a sudden price surge.

Amazon is the biggest threat to Walmart's dominance. Aside from Walmart, no other single customer represented more than 10 percent of Tyson's sales. But Amazon may become a more powerful share. Walmart has centralized buying, and Amazon doesn't. Whole Foods is still the biggest part of Amazon's grocery business, estimated to have 2 percent market share of the US grocery industry. According to Marc Wulfraat, the founder of supply chain consultancy MWVPL, Walmart has 30 percent of the online grocery market compared to 27 percent for Amazon. JBS doesn't disclose its top customers, but HSBC estimates that JBS USA may have 5 to 7 percent coming from Walmart. (Pilgrim's Pride's top customer in Mexico is Walmart, for one.)

The actual amount of meat that sells on Amazon is unknown, and Wulfraat says it is a figure he's never seen in his fourteen years of systematically tracking Amazon's network of warehouses and distribution centers.

"All this data you're looking for is extremely secretive for everybody," Wulfraat shared. "Nobody wants their competitors to know what volume they are doing. The industry is very competitive. If Target finds out how much meat Walmart is selling, they may spend more time studying what Walmart is doing and try to figure out how to emulate Walmart and send spies into their stores. They're all spying on each other."

But academically and officially, it's hard to accurately test for whether monopsony market power is present, says C. Robert Taylor, a professor emeritus of agricultural economics and public policy at Auburn University. The data that shows costs isn't usually publicly available. Cost data is essential for testing for market power, and it generally *is* available in litigation. The problem is, the data and associated analyses are forever covered by court-ordered confidentiality, so useful studies may never see the light of day. But Taylor is one of the few people alive who had confidential access to the records for *Pickett v. Tyson*.

"When I first got into this, meat-packers had the upper hand in terms of market power, but during the past twenty to thirty years that has changed. The grocery chains have more power than the packers do now. It's a tiered power structure now with the Walmarts at the top and the packers below that and the farmers and ranchers at the very bottom," Taylor said. "Monopsony is a definite problem in agriculture, more so than oligopoly."

It's an uphill battle. Taylor recalls in 2011 arranging to meet with policy experts and economists at the Federal Trade Commission, which has antitrust authority over fertilizer markets. The main objective was for the FTC to investigate further because they could get nonpublic data. But after forty-five minutes of discussing the findings, an FTC bureaucrat cut the presentation off: "If we initiate such a study, we will get a call from the Hill telling us to back off or our funding will be cut. It has happened to us in the past."

Recalling it, Taylor added, "Refreshing honesty, but deeply troubling. The case was not prosecuted, even with considerable evidence of a global cartel."

Enforcing Antitrust

The beef industry's Big Four today are Tyson, JBS, Cargill, and National, owned by Brazil-based Marfrig. They have come under scrutiny for controlling more than 80 percent of the beef industry. That level of concentration of power isn't far off from a century ago when the federal government investigated the Big Five, then Swift & Co., Armour & Co., Wilson & Co., the Morris Packing Company, and the Cudahy Packing Company. In 1919 Senator John B. Kendrick of Wyoming noted history had repeated itself, but it just as easily could have been said about modern times as well: "This squall between the packers and the producers of this country ought to have blown over forty years ago, but we still have it on our hands."

Nothing was broken up then. At present, much of these sectors have been consolidated for three decades.

"The problem from an antitrust perspective is, it's very hard to unwind a consummated transaction," antitrust lawyer Seth Bloom, whose clients have included Amazon, told me. "The eggs have been scrambled. How do you unscramble the eggs if the damage has been done?"

Bloom was longtime general counsel for the Senate Judiciary's antitrust subcommittee, which held hearings that led to the Department of Justice blocking the acquisition of National by JBS in 2008, one of the rare modern instances of a beef merger being stopped.

Halting more mergers is the clearest way to prevent more consolidation, and the Department of Justice is scrutinizing the acquisition of third-largest poultry processor Sanderson Farms by a joint venture backed by historic grain traders Cargill and Continental Grain, which also owns poultry processor Wayne Farms. But Bloom thinks it remains a fool's errand to try to break up big meat-packers retroactively.

The Department of Justice is the agency that would enforce antitrust within the meat industry, as well as the Department of Agriculture, which has authority through the Packers and Stockyards Act. The FTC has power over retail and other agribusiness sectors like fertilizer. Antitrust lawyer Peter Carstensen thinks the eggs can still get unscrambled anytime, but he would prefer the market to solve these problems without needing regulators to step in. "The law is still clear," Carstensen said. These reverse decisions in the past have amounted to an "our bad" mistake. "There's no statute of limitations. I'm skeptical that anybody is willing to come forward and enforce that."

A coalition of food and retail associations, including the National Grocers Association, Organic Farmers Association, and American Beverage Licensees, would like to see the Robinson-Patman Act enforced. "Current enforcement efforts have failed to address these anticompetitive harms, and judges have inappropriately limited the scope of the law despite clear statutory language," a 2021 letter sent to Federal Trade Commission regulators reads. "Despite Congress' broad goals in 1936, the FTC has not brought a case under the Robinson-Patman Act in more than 20 years. Nor has the FTC brought an enforcement action against economic discrimination using the other antitrust laws."

Recommendations for reform come from nearly every corner of the industry, and from many outsiders. Ideas for meat pricing vary. Could all packer-to-packer communications and transactions be monitored and publicly reported? Should meat-packers be required to report their trades on the Chicago Mercantile Exchange like reporting requirements for insider trading in corporate stock?

A contentious idea is creating a producer's union, or a bargaining co-op, Carstensen tells me. An example of how this could be helpful occurred in Mississippi, when chicken growers for Sanderson Farms were offered a "one-sided" new contract, which proposed slashing their income by a third and created an impetus for those chicken growers to negotiate together as a unit. The surprise was announced just two days after Sanderson revealed it would be acquired by a joint venture backed by Cargill and Continental Grain. Carstensen's idea for a producer's union would go a step further, creating a standard contract for livestock producers that have decided to raise animals for a meat-packer like Tyson or Sanderson. That would give producers more bargaining power, if it works. None have been successful. But unions could lead to fairer contracts. "They have to be very careful," Carstensen told me. "You can get into some serious difficulty, because it sure looks like a cartel otherwise."

Buying groups that represent up to 35 percent of the total volume of a sector are a good place to start. The Department of Justice's Antitrust Division has stated that it will not object to a buying group's creation at that level. Carstensen analyzes how else this framework could succeed. In a 2010 paper in *William & Mary Business Law Review* titled "Buyer Cartels Versus Buying Groups: Legal Distinctions, Competitive Realities, and Antitrust Policy," Carstensen noted that buyer cartels are technically illegal but buying groups are subject to the "rule of reason" in antitrust law, which means that unlike price-fixing, which is automatically deemed illegal, there is a stringent four-part legal test that needs to be met to prove harm.

CHAPTER 4

The Human Cost of Eating Meat

Carmenlita started working for JBS USA in October 2011. The rocks were just starting to cool after a hot summer in Utah. She had decided to try out the beef plant job. Ahead of every shift, she traveled two and a half hours away from her home in Box Elder County, the rocky area northwest of Salt Lake where she had easy access to nature. But Carmenlita had a job.

The beef slaughterhouse in Hyrum, Utah, was more than seventy years old, formerly belonging to the historic Swift & Co. The plant smelled of ammonia. Fumes lingered in the air. Carmenlita made her way to her assignment in the fabrication department. There, she spent hours sealing large bags of beef and throwing them onto a conveyor belt.

According to a complaint Carmenlita filed in 2014, the repetitive motions created an elbow injury.* Then, the complaint alleged, a series of mishaps shuffled her around the plant over the next few years. Each move put her increasingly in harm's way. In April 2012, she slipped and hurt her elbow, back, and hip when water had overflowed from a janitor's closet into the hallway at the plant. Later that autumn, she reinjured her elbow after hitting the floor while attempting to save a falling thirty-two-pound chuck roll, a cut of beef that extends from the shoulder blade to the ribs and backbone.

These kinds of serious injuries are common in meatpacking jobs. Slaughtering and processing jobs for decades have ranked among the highest for occupational rates of injury, according to Human Rights Watch's

---

* According to the legal documents publicly available, it's unclear whether JBS accepted liability or admitted wrongdoing in this settlement.

analysis of Bureau of Labor Statistics data. The rate is far more than for the average manufacturing worker. In 2017, meatpacking workers were nearly twice as likely to get hurt and fifteen times as likely to contract a job-related illness as the average private-sector worker. Meatpacking is among the most dangerous jobs in America. According to the US Occupational Health and Safety Administration, meatpacking workers have a high risk of developing serious musculoskeletal disorders, in addition to hearing loss from high noise levels and injuries from slippery floors and dangerous machinery. Amputations, crushed fingers or hands, burns, and blindness are common. During 2021, at the same JBS beef plant in Greeley, Colorado, for example, a worker's left arm was amputated after his smock sleeve got caught in a sprocket on a conveyor belt. The next month, another worker died after falling into a vat containing toxic chemicals used to treat animal hides. OSHA found JBS to have failed its workers in both instances, and charged the meat giant $230,000.

Meatpacking workers and the plant-cleaning crews are also exposed daily to hazardous chemicals, like ammonia, used for refrigeration in plants, or disinfectants used to clean the meat like chlorine, hydrogen peroxide, and peracetic acid. Exposure might cause skin rashes, eye, nose, and throat irritation, burns to the skin and eyes from splashes, cough, or shortness of breath. Meatpacking workers also have an increased risk of lung cancer, as well as a host of other bacterial infections from handling the livestock and the meat. That includes a higher likelihood of contracting an antibiotic-resistant infection like methicillin-resistant Staphylococcus aureus, or MRSA.

Carmenlita, according to her complaint, had to push against resistant management to have an appropriate reassignment. The plant transferred her to scraping spinal cords in early 2013, but Carmenlita's situation allegedly got worse. She claims a sexually aggressive coworker started harassing her at the new station, making sexual comments and twice getting physical when he shoved half-ton beef carcasses into her. She claims management ignored her complaints of retaliatory harassment. But Carmenlita's injuries also weren't going away, and eventually her physician ordered that she not scrape spinal cords, pass big bags, or lift more than ten pounds. That's how Carmenlita made it to a post in the laundry room, where another coworker accused her of faking injuries. Once more she got transferred. This time it was to work with hides becoming leather in the plant's rendering department.

On March 1, 2013, Utah temperatures were mild. It was just above freezing, and the sun was shining. In the rendering department, Carmenlita alleged that she was assaulted by a coworker, who groped her, restrained her, and attempted to kiss her, according to her complaint. After she reported the incident to supervisors, they accused her of making it up. Then the interrogation was over. She returned to her post at the rendering department within a few feet from her alleged attacker.

A few days later, according to the complaint, she was assigned to work in a specific portion of the rendering department. Her new station was known as the gut bin.

Where her supervisor brought her was deeply disturbing, as described in detail in her legal complaint. She found "a filthy, vermin-infested room, an open trench through which flows a river of cow manure, and a raised metal platform suspended above a pit. The pit contained rotating saw blades grinding and mutilating portions of the slaughtered animals," according to her lawsuit later filed. Carmenlita was sent there to reach a long metal hook into the gut bin to pull out foreign objects. As an active member of a Native American tribe, she described in her lawsuit her dedication to "maintain balance and harmony with the Earth, to respect nature, and to live in harmony with man, animals, plants, and even insects" and practice her traditional religion. But the conditions of the gut bin conflicted so deeply with her beliefs that she had "an immediate psychological breakdown," according to her complaint.

When given the option to return to the gut bin or go home, she went home. She "could not cope with the horrors of the gut bin." The next day, when she reported to the gut bin and requested reassignment through her union representative, her bosses pointed to her complaints of discrimination and told her there was "no other place we want to put you." Within a few months, Carmenlita was fired. The notice came the day after she took time off to visit a doctor planning to perform surgery on her injuries. JBS declined to comment on the case. Her lawsuit was settled over the summer of 2014, eight months from the date of filing.*

---

* It is unclear from the publicly available settlement documents whether JBS accepted liability or admitted wrongdoing in this settlement.

Breeding Workplace Violence

In the meatpacking industry, which receives hundreds of discrimination and harassment complaints, Carmenlita's case is tragically common. In a lawsuit from 2015, a group of seventeen Black employees from a plant in Pilgrim's Pride's hometown of Mount Pleasant, Texas, filed a discrimination and harassment lawsuit over a culture where Black employees alleged to have been regularly subjected to hate speech and sexual violence. According to the complaint, the bathrooms were allegedly weaponized against Black workers with graffiti of hangings, Nazi pride symbols, hate speech, and racially charged phrases scrawled in Spanish.

Black employees who worked there had to raise their hand and be granted permission to use the bathroom, according to the legal complaint, while Hispanic and white workers did not. This was the case for one former worker in the lawsuit, who complained of having to raise her hand and being denied permission. Despite assurances that something would be done, nothing changed. Then she found out she was pregnant and asked to stop standing on the line for eight-hour shifts. She requested moving to a position where she could sit down. According to the complaint, "She inquired about moving to a more suitable position given her pregnancy or, in the alternative, any medical leave she would be eligible for. Both requests were denied without any discussion or consideration." Then she miscarried, and she was given disciplinary points for missing a week of work. A year later, she was fired for missing work while sick, according to the complaint.

Other testimony from that class-action lawsuit includes reports alleging near-daily sexual harassment, forced touching, threats of rape, and verbal attacks. The complaint included allegations of Hispanic employees routinely taking overtime work before Black employees, and Hispanic employees starting at a higher rate of pay and receiving raises sooner than Black employees. The lawsuit asserts:

> Rather than encourage and foster an inclusive and balanced workplace, a culture has been created wherein an almost exclusively Hispanic hierarchy encourages an environment that reminds Black workers of "their place" in the organization through exclusion, in-

timidation, segregation, steering, displacement and discouragement. Where possible, Black employees are steered away from certain departments within the plant and are kept together. At times, some Hispanic employees refuse to work with Black employees and are granted their wish when management quickly transfers the Black employee to work with other Black employees. Much like a plantation environment, a handful of Black employees are also placed in supervisory positions to "deal" with other Black employees that are segregated into certain areas of the plant. These Black supervisors serve as the buffer between Black line workers and upper management. Upon information and belief, if said Black supervisors did not "play along" with upper management's rules favoring the Hispanic workforce, they too would be disciplined. As a result, Black employees are subjected to unequal hiring practices, lower starting pay, assignment to less-desirable positions, segregation, delayed and unequal pay raises, disproportionate discipline, lack of advancement, unequal application of company policy and unlawful termination.

The lawsuit went to a mediator before a settlement was reached in 2016.*

In another case against Pilgrim's Pride, this time at a plant in Enterprise, Alabama, a manager was accused of raping a line worker. After luring Robyn to his office to get some paperwork, according to the complaint, he shut the door, closed the blinds, and allegedly told her that they were going to have sex in exchange for four hours of overtime. According to her lawsuit, she told him no, that she had kids at home, and even said she couldn't be fired for not having sex with him. He replied, according to the complaint, that it would not be the first time, nor the last. The Pilgrim's Pride manager then allegedly forced her into the bathroom and raped her. Two days later, she reported not the rape but other employees harassing her. On the same day, she was told that an "investigation" was completed and nothing had been found.

Then the retaliation started, according to her complaint. She claims

---

* It's unclear from the publicly available settlement documents whether Pilgrim's Pride accepted liability or admitted wrongdoing in this settlement.

to have reported at least two more instances of harassment. After a third assault over the course of a week, she alleged, she "began shaking uncontrollably" from suffering a nervous breakdown. She visited the emergency room and took a leave of absence the following week.

When she returned, she discovered that her abuser was fired for stealing chickens. She still continued to complain of the harassment, as well as retaliation she experienced at the plant, but, according to her lawsuit, "no remedial actions were taken to address the matter." She settled the case in 2013.*

The entire industry must do so much better on behalf of its workers. The meat production business can be harmful, and a lot of the harm is hidden from consumers.

Manipulating Workers Financially

Chicken industry executives even allegedly came together to hatch a plan. According to the class action lawsuit, originally filed in 2019, executives from some of the industry's top processors and two data firms colluded over wages and benefits offered, specifically to "depress the compensation paid to poultry workers" in violation of the Sherman Antitrust Act of 1890.

Each year between 2000 and 2019, several poultry processors surveyed compensation rates among competitors, and between 2001 and 2019 the poultry companies held private roundtable meetings to discuss the results and compare practices, according to a sworn declaration made public as part of a settlement of a class-action lawsuit. A "secret" steering committee of executives at different poultry companies created a survey, distributed by a third-party, "to compare the hourly wages, annual salaries, and employment benefits paid to dozens of categories of workers. The surveys featured both current and future compensation data, such as projected increases to salary pay ranges and the timing of those increases," according to the lawsuit's complaint. "And for many years, [processors] designed the survey in

---

* It is unclear from the publicly available settlement documents whether Pilgrim's Pride accepted liability or admitted wrongdoing in this settlement.

a format that made it easy for them to determine exactly how much each processor paid each worker at each of its plants."*†

The committee's roundtable meetings were often held at the Hilton Sandestin Golf Resort & Spa in Destin, Florida. According to the complaint, corporate envoys from more than a dozen companies were invited there to meet with their competitors—from the industry leader Tyson to billionaire-owned Koch Foods and publicly traded Pilgrim's Pride—at an unofficial meeting.‡ The backdrop of these meetings, usually held in May, created more opportunities to discuss compensation with competitors, according to the complaint, which notes that "senior executives gathered for 'dinners, drinks and other outings.'" In 2019, for example, the complaint quotes from an obtained email, which presented outing options for members of the survey group: "Let us know if you are still willing to join a group activity and vote for your favorite option." They chose from excursions including a five-hour party fishing trip, a tiki bar boat ride, or a dolphin boat cruise.

Before every annual meetup, according to the lawsuit, employees from each firm allegedly submitted highly detailed current compensation data to a third-party provider, Pottstown, Pennsylvania–based Webber, Meng, Sahl and Company, which is known as WMS.§ WMS is a small, three-person company that was paid a flat annual rate by each member of the group to survey the processors and distributed the data. WMS's survey, according to the complaint, asked critical competitive information, including average hourly wages, annual salaries for each processing line position, as well as the number of people employed in each position. WMS also got benefits data, including identifying which health insurance plans were offered, the price

---

* The president of WMS's sworn statement explains that poultry processors "reached agreements regarding what positions to cover in the Survey, which compensation data to seek in the Survey, how to structure the questions in the Survey, how to revise the Survey, how often to conduct the Survey, which participants to include in the Survey, and what information to display in the Survey Results Reports."

† The steering committee consisted of between three to five executives from different poultry processors. According to the third amended complaint, the five processors represented on the steering committee the most between 2000 and 2019 were Tyson, Perdue, Foster Farms, Fieldale, and Pilgrim's Pride.

‡ The lawsuit was filed against Agri Stats, Butterball, Cargill, Fieldale Farms, George's, Jennie-O Turkey Store, Keystone Foods, Koch Foods, Mountaire Farms, Peco Foods, Perdue Farms, Pilgrim's Pride Corporation, Sanderson Farms, Simmons Foods, Tyson Foods, Wayne Farms, Mar-Jac Poultry, Amick Farms, Allen Harim, OK Foods, Case Farms, Foster Farms, and Webber, Meng, Sahl and Company.

§ WMS did not return requests for comment.

of health insurance premiums, how much of that premium was paid by the employer, and the number of paid time-off allowances.*

WMS used a similar method to Agri Stats and randomly assigned a number to each attending firm at the meeting, according to a sworn declaration. Agri Stats, which is also a defendant in the class action, has also denied the lawsuit's allegations. WMS, according to the complaint, then circulated the results of the compensation survey to the attendees of the in-person meeting, with the names of the processors replaced by their randomly assigned number.†

WMS employees then, according to a sworn declaration, allegedly delivered a PowerPoint presentation that emphasized the average and median hourly rates and salaries for each poultry processing plant position, based on the survey data provided. WMS's presentation focused on year-to-year changes in the data reported.

According to the lawsuit, "though a letter code replaced each processor's name to purportedly anonymize the data, the report also included detailed demographics for each letter code. Throughout the year they supplemented the survey information with their regular Agri Stats data and meetings. (Agri Stats, which is also a defendant in the class action, has denied the lawsuit's allegations.)

Emails obtained over the course of settlements and the lawsuit discovery, according to settlement documents, show that "executives of poultry processors communicated directly about compensation practices by email, often seeking their competitors' input before making changes to their own wages or benefits."‡

---

* The survey provided the following metrics, according to the complaint, including base salary, the average bonus paid for the last twelve months, bonus eligibility, and the average bonus paid for the last twelve months for those actually receiving a bonus. The surveys, according to the complaint, provided detailed data about the value of contributions made to pension plans, the amount of life insurance coverage, the amount of insurance coverage for accidental death and dismemberment, the amount of coverage for long-term disability insurance, the amount and duration of short-term disability insurance, the provision of sick leave days, and the number of annual holidays. From 2000 through 2017, according to WMS, the survey included detailed data regarding future salary increases.

† Agri Stats did not return requests for comment.

‡ According to settlement documents for WMS, "For example, in one email, a Fieldale executive reminded the group to 'bring you[r] Data manual' to the meeting 'in case others have questions for you concerning your data.' In another email, a Tyson executive noted that future compensation data, including 'hourly production projected budgets,' were 'typically a discussion item during the roundtable sessions.' Mr. Meng believes that the Poultry

The group allegedly had strict rules to membership, too: the complaint says, "A poultry processor would be expelled from the Poultry Industry Survey Group if it failed to attend the annual in-person meeting two years in a row." In March 2016, for example, according to the complaint, a representative for Foster Farms emailed a warning to members that had not yet booked their lodging for the meeting: "Reminder that to remain a participant in the survey, attendance each year is not optional, but rather a requirement."

Poultry processors took steps "to conceal both the existence of, and their participation in," the surveys, according to the complaint. Each member of the group had to "agree and ensure that shared survey data or other information from discussions will be used and treated in a 'confidential' manner and definitely should not be shared with companies not participating in the survey. Failure to meet these requirements will result in immediate removal from the survey group."

The poultry industry systematically fixed wages and benefits, according to the suit. If these allegations are true, it creates new harm in an industry that is already a hazardous place to work. This would have hurt workers who are among America's most vulnerable—many of them immigrants, migrant workers, refugees, asylum seekers, the mass incarcerated, and participants in court-ordered substance-abuse programs. The scheme has impacted 250,000 chicken industry workers, holding them at "artificially depressed" wages as they work one of the already lowest-paying but most dangerous jobs in the country, according to the complaint.

Most poultry workers' annual incomes come in right at the federal poverty level, around $25,000 a year, according to a 2015 report by the nonprofit Oxfam America, which estimates the average poultry worker supporting two children qualifies for food stamps and the school lunch program. "Workers often turn to local charities and food banks to supplement their income," the report reads. "In many poultry towns, thrift stores and food banks dominate local storefronts."*

Industry Survey Group asked him 'to leave [the room] so that the attendees could engage in improper discussions about the Survey results and compensation practices without my halting or witnessing those discussions.' "

* As of May 2022, Tyson says its average pay is more than $18 an hour. With the value of medical insurances, vacation, and other benefits, Tyson claims its hourly workforce has an average total compensation valued at more than $50,000. Tyson CEO Donnie King testified in 2020 that Tyson has been making "significant investments" in its workforce.

That's the backdrop for the poultry industry's alleged subjugation of its workforce's pay as chicken processors experienced a period of record-setting industry profits. In July 2021, Pilgrim's Pride reached a $29 million settlement. Smaller processors have also settled, including George's for $5.8 million and Peco Foods for $3 million. WMS also settled and did not have any money to pay as part of its deal. These corporations did not deny wrongdoing as part of the settlement agreements. They did agree to cooperate against the dozen other defendants.*

The 400,000 documents that WMS turned over, as well as the testimony from its employees, became a turning point in the case. Sworn declaration totaling 109 pages from WMS president Jonathan Meng, taken in November 2021, was credited with "laying bare previously unknown facts," including that WMS was hired for an extra decade and that, to participate, companies had to submit information about poultry hatcheries and feed mills, not just processing plants.

"Unlike other clients with which I have worked, decisions regarding the content of each Poultry Industry Compensation Survey and each Survey Results Report, as well as the participants in each Survey, were made exclusively and collaboratively by a group of competing poultry processors," Meng's sworn statement reads.

According to the lawsuit's third amended complaint, which incorporated Meng's sworn declaration, Meng "repeatedly warned" the processors "that they were improperly exchanging compensation data in a manner that was inconsistent with federal antitrust law—but his warnings were regularly disregarded." In his sworn statement, Meng stated that the poultry processors "used WMS as an unwitting tool to conceal their misconduct." Meng often gave the group their annual presentation. He or the other WMS executive was eventually excused from the room so the corporate representatives could, according to settlement documents, "hold hours of entirely private roundtable discussions (often spanning two days) to discuss the Survey results and their future compensation plans." According to the com-

---

* The lawsuit was filed against Agri Stats, Butterball, Cargill, Fieldale Farms, George's, Jennie-O Turkey Store, Keystone Foods, Koch Foods, Mountaire Farms, Peco Foods, Perdue Farms, Pilgrim's Pride Corporation, Sanderson Farms, Simmons Foods, Tyson Foods, Wayne Farms, Mar-Jac Poultry, Amick Farms, Allen Harim, OK Foods, Case Farms, Foster Farms, and Webber, Meng, Sahl and Company.

plaint, "In March 2007, for example, Meng received an email from a human resources representative from Pilgrim's, which explained the situation: "While the meeting is scheduled for 1½ days, we ask that you be available through lunch on the first day to discuss the survey results. You will not need to attend the remainder of the meeting, as this time will be spent discussing future meetings and best practices between the poultry companies."

Meng alleges that, according to settlement documents and Meng's declaration, an executive from Fieldale repeatedly told Meng that, in the 1990s, executives from the poultry processors regularly met "to directly exchange and discuss compensation data with one another" without a third-party watching. Meng testified that he concluded WMS was only hired in 2000 to "create an appearance of compliance" while they "continued to exchange disaggregated and deanonymized compensation data and continued to discuss and harmonize their compensation practices." Meng stated that he was asked to leave the room "so that the attendees could engage in improper discussions about the Survey results and compensation practices without my halting or witnessing those discussions."

Meng, who has been president of WMS since 2000 and the primary administrator of the survey since 2004, also revealed that from at least 2001 to 2004 the compensation survey "included disaggregated, raw data on salaries, wages, and benefits that was sorted by processor" which allowed participants to "match each participating processor" to relevant data through a code. There were charts identifying starting salaries and future salary increases reported by each participating processor as well as the average hourly wages for each plant operated by each processor. The complaint describes "sham anonymization techniques" based on Meng's sworn declaration, which explained that "the inclusion of such detailed information about each letter code—which greatly facilitated deanonymization of the compensation data—in the Survey Results Reports distributed from 2001 through 2004 was a highly unusual practice. For that reason, WMS would have only done so at the explicit instruction of the Steering Committee."

According to WMS's settlement, in 2005, Meng halted that practice "because of antitrust concerns" and removed the disaggregated, raw data on salaries and hourly wages. Yet from 2013 to 2016 the steering committee again agreed to distribute "disaggregated, raw data that covered poultry processing workers—including production, maintenance, and refrigeration workers—and it was broken down by both plant and location." Meng testified that he "warned" the steering committee that disaggregated, raw wage data in a format that allows for members to easily deanonymize would violate federal antitrust law. In emails, Meng raised concerns but was overridden by the steering committee, and Meng, according to the complaint, "subsequently wrote each member of the Poultry Industry Survey Group to confirm their agreement with the inclusion of this disaggregated, raw data in the forthcoming Survey Results Reports. Each member of the Poultry Industry Survey Group expressly consented, and none made any objections or raised any concerns." The method prevailed for four annual surveys.

"While the names of the poultry processors that operated the plants was not disclosed in the disaggregated raw data, it is evident that Poultry Industry Survey Group members could ascertain which poultry processor operated which plant by analyzing the data," Meng's sworn testimony reads.

From 2013 to 2015, according to Meng's testimony, Tyson also sponsored a separate survey that detailed hourly plant maintenance and production worker salaries. Meng testified that it "provided even more disaggregated, raw, plant-level data than the Poultry Industry Compensation Survey." Meng said the Tyson-sponsored survey "facilitated the ability of members of the Poultry Industry Survey Group to identify the sources of plant-level compensation data in that survey." According to Meng's sworn declaration, Tyson scheduled a call with WMS to discuss this request in January 2013, which included multiple human resources executives from Tyson. During the call, Meng said he again warned Tyson the survey would not be compliant but was overridden. (Tyson denies the allegations of illegal collusion.)

After some top poultry processors were named in a class action alleging price-fixing conspiracy in September 2016, Meng testified that many in the survey group companies stopped participating. According to settlement documents, for example, on April 28, 2017, a representative of Pilgrim's Pride informed the rest of the group that Pilgrim's would not be attending that year's meeting: "Unfortunately, due to some current legal proceedings, we've been advised by counsel not to attend our comp meeting next week. Best of luck and apologies for any inconvenience this may cause," the email quoted in the complaint reads. In February 2018, a representative of Mountaire notified WMS that "Mountaire would not be able to participate in the Group due to instructions from its general counsel." In 2017, the survey changed due to the antitrust concerns: the companies, according to legal summary of Meng's testimony, "stopped reporting raw, disaggregated hourly wage data from each company's plants and, in 2018, removed all metrics regarding future salary increases." Then, starting in 2018, Meng was required to attend all of the roundtable sessions. According to part of the presentation WMS gave in 2019, included in the complaint, OK Foods, Mountaire, George's, Allen Harim, Keystone Foods, and Simmons had left the group.

"If you can coordinate with your competitors for inputs, whether it's labor or some other component, there's an incentive to do that. That undermines the ordinary functioning of the market," said antitrust lawyer Peter Carstensen. "Labor economics used to think that labor markets, especially for most skilled work, was highly competitive. Then, when they began to do more empirical work, what they found was that the markets are very local, very specialized, and therefore very much vulnerable to exploitation."

Agri Stats Meets the Bargaining Table

America's second-largest poultry processor, Pilgrim's Pride, filed for Chapter 11 bankruptcy in the Northern District of Texas in December 2008 and within a few months Brazil-based JBS swooped in to acquire a majority of shares. Pilgrim's problems sent shock waves throughout the poultry business. Pilgrim's, according to the complaint, strictly adhered to ranges deduced from Agri Stats data as well as the WMS-suggested industry average wage. That grip on Pilgrim's operations revealed itself when Pilgrim's renegotiated its collective bargaining agreement with the United Food and Commercial Workers International Union as part of its bankruptcy reorganization in 2009. According to the complaint, "During the course of those negotiations, Pilgrim's executives insisted that labor costs be within the Agri Stats average range in each of the company's domestic poultry processing plants."

"Notably, Pilgrim's . . . only disclosed 'average' industry-wide pay figures obtained from Agri Stats to the unions when engaging in collective bargaining negotiations—not disaggregated, company-specific or plant-specific Agri Stats wage data or any actual Agri Stats written reports," the complaint reads. "Because Agri Stats will only sell its reports to processors who also provide data for inclusion in those reports, unions and their members were not able to obtain the Agri Stats reports themselves."

The poultry industry is the least unionized of any kind of meat. About a third of all hourly poultry processing workers are in a union, and some 90 percent of them are organized with UFCW.

"Small operators can go in and basically shave labor costs down and abuse labor, and abuse farmers and ranchers, and then they turn around and take that half a cent that they save per pound of meat and cost the other operators, the bigger operators, business," UFCW's Mark Lauritsen told me. "That's what causes this cutthroat industry to thrive."

CHAPTER 5

The JBS Takeover of America's Meat

On the night of March 7, 2017, Joesley Batista was invited to Jaburu Palace, the official residence of Brazil's second-in-command, at 10:30 p.m. He was there to record and implicate the freshly installed president of Brazil.* The corruption scheme started with politicians fighting to stay in power in Brazil and ended with producers in America's Corn Belt answering to a new meat-packer. Batista, then forty-five years old, entered the modern, brutalist home from a discreet entrance. Inside, he found President Michel Temer, and awkward small talk began.†

The conversation, according to a plea agreement later signed, turned toward the Batistas' legal predicament. A key conspirator was about to be sentenced, and the two men were on edge.

Joesley tried to calm Temer down about his own potential risk of whistleblowing, conveniently while Joesley was secretly recording. Senators and politicians implicated in a sweeping anti-corruption probe in Brazil were signing plea bargains and implicating those higher up to get out of their own

---

* Joesley Batista turned over the recording to Brazilian prosecutors as he negotiated a cooperation agreement.

† The conversations and perspectives quoted directly and described in the following pages come from hours of research and analysis, spanning thousands of pages of legal documents, translated sworn testimony, video, and other recordings of the Batistas and their confidants. Interviews with me are denoted as such. Among the legal documents reviewed: J&F Investimentos' leniency agreement and the original cooperation agreements of Joesley and Wesley Batista from Brazil, as well as the Foreign Corrupt Practices Act plea agreement with the US Department of Justice and violations with the Securities Exchange Commission. J&F Investimentos maintains Joesley and Wesley Batista "have never been convicted of any crime, in any jurisdiction." They were charged in Brazil and were imprisoned for six months each, ending in 2018, and also agreed to violations of the Foreign Corrupt Practices Act with the Securities and Exchange Commission in 2020.

sentences. Former senator Eduardo Cunha, among the latest to be charged, needed to stay silent to keep Temer safe. But an arrangement had to be locked down, which is why Batista was invited. During the visit, Joesley told Temer that he was "taking care" of Eduardo Cunha and his fixer. Temer replied that it was "important" to keep bribes going to Cunha so he stayed happy.

"I want to hear you, President," Joesley said. "How is your situation with Eduardo Cunha?"

"Cunha decided to harass me . . . ," Temer responded.

"Let me tell you, within my reach, I did everything I could," Joesley said. "Zeroed it all out, so I'm on good terms with Cunha."

"That has to be maintained, okay?" Temer demanded.

"Every month," replied Joesley, who knew Cunha well after years of keeping him on his kickback payroll, just like Temer. Cunha and his fixer had helped the Batistas favorably reform meat export regulations—and Joesley paid handsomely for it, even once transferring ownership of an Agusta helicopter that Joesley had owned to Cunha's fixer.[*]

As Joesley left, Temer's political fate was sealed, and Joesley's cooperation with the government is alleged to have helped him and his brother negotiate their own plea agreements. That leverage helped them remain international businessmen with fortunes secure.

In May 2017, a few months after Batista's taped meetup with Temer, the recording got leaked.[†] The Batista brothers' plea bargain in connection with Brazil's sweeping anti-corruption probe, signed May 3, 2017, agreed to having committed unlawful conduct, a 100 million real fine, and truthful cooperation to spare them from jail time.[‡] The disclosure barely made US headlines. According to a Securities and Exchange Commission cease-and-desist order, the brothers' involvement was not disclosed to shareholders of Pilgrim's Pride in time for the annual shareholder meeting prior to the Batistas' reelection to the board. They resigned from the board of Pilgrim's after the plea agreements were made public. J&F Investimentos, which held the Batistas' more than 44 percent stake in JBS, reached its own leniency agreement and agreed to pay a landmark $3.2 billion fine (due over twenty-

---

[*] In March 2017, Cunha was sentenced to fifteen years in prison.

[†] Temer denied wrongdoing after the recordings were leaked and was never charged with a formal crime in Brazil.

[‡] All figures in this chapter are in Brazilian reals unless otherwise noted.

five years). In testimony, the Batistas and J&F Investimentos admitted to bribing Brazilian politicians for a total of more than $150 million to illicitly acquire loans and financing from the Brazilian Development Bank, BNDES, and several Brazilian pension funds—in addition to more than three dozen other incidents of bribery. As far as the public was concerned, it was business as usual at JBS. Key customers like McDonald's barely flinched. All the while, JBS became a major force of consolidation in the meat industry.

The Batistas' US buying spree started in 2007 and rolled up grocery store staples like Swift & Company and Smithfield Beef Group, while buying a majority of Pilgrim's Pride. JBS has become the biggest meat supplier in the world, dominating the United States with about 21 percent of the beef market, 21 percent of pork, and 23 percent of chicken.

Not all of those acquisitions were financed through the controversial Brazilian National Bank for Economic and Social Development, known as BNDES,[*] and its low-cost loans. JBS USA, the American subsidiary, has racked up more than $15 billion in debt to financial institutions from Barclays to Royal Bank of Canada. Major US institutions aren't just lenders; they're shareholders, too. The top two are Fidelity and BlackRock, which have increased their stakes since the Temer recording was leaked in May 2017. Both hold about 2 percent of total shares, worth more than $1 billion each.[†]

JBS has repeatedly attempted (and failed) to raise money on US public markets. The first attempt in 2010 never got off the ground. Then the company's scandals derailed another potential chance in 2017, according to sources I spoke to. A splashy public listing of its international assets remains in JBS's long-term potential plans. But a scandal could easily pull it back once again.

As Joesley Batista responded to an investigator during an interrogation with the Brazilian attorney general in May 2017, who asked if a US acquisition would have ever happened if it hadn't been for those kickback-hungry

---

[*] A J&F Investimentos spokesperson said, "BNDES' investment in JBS proved to be one of the most profitable for the bank. International auditors retained by BNDES to conduct an independent investigation found no improper relationship between J&F and BNDES. J&F companies fulfilled all legal and technical requirements to be eligible for an investment by BNDES."

[†] Figures as of May 31, 2022.

relationships: "Oh, no way. It wouldn't have happened. We wouldn't have made the deal."

The Origins of JBS

JBS stands for José Batista Sobrinho, the nearly ninety-year-old patriarch of the Batista family. At age twenty, in 1953, he got into butchery with his two brothers on their family farm in Anápolis, a rural region in central Brazil. Each day, he killed a few oxen and cut up the meat into quarters to sell to a local purveyor. He didn't know it at the time, but his business was actually well located for distribution. It would eventually be on the outskirts 125 miles to the east of where Brazil would move its capital and erect the city of Brasília. When he started supplying local restaurants with meat, business took off. He took advantage of a tax exemption for companies willing to invest in the new capital and in 1968 acquired his first slaughterhouse, outside Brasília. Another plant came two years later, increasing production to five hundred cattle a day. Wesley and Joesley were born into this environment. As Brazil's beef production rose between the 1960s and '70s, the family butchers could not slice meat off the bone fast enough. Meat was booming across Brazil, as was deforestation in the Amazon to make room for more cattle to graze and corn to grow.

These near-twin Batista brothers grew up buying and selling oxen while watching their father butcher while covered in specks of blood. Learning by doing was prioritized. At age seventeen, their elder brother José dropped out of high school to manage the family's slaughterhouses. Wesley and Joseley did the same when they hit that age, too. By their early thirties in 2005, Wesley and Joseley began leading their family operations. Their eldest brother, José, had just left the family firm for an ill-fated attempt at Brazilian politics, after spending twenty years running the company and building operations into one of the largest beef producers in Brazil. In the years leading up to his retirement, the company acquired twelve slaughterhouses and had grown its capacity to killing 5,800 cattle a day. Then, boom: a new crop of Batista brothers were the fresh faces leading this growing business, ready to industrialize it and take it global.

The Bribery-Paved Road to America

A chance to pitch well-connected investors on the Batistas' international dreams came in 2005.* According to translated videos of his testimony to prosecutors, Joesley had bribed his way into securing a meeting with Guido Mantega, who had become president of BNDES, Brazil's state development bank. Joesley claimed that Mantega, through an associate, had been on Joesley's payroll for months, both retained for a split monthly fee of R$50,000 in exchange for regular access to and preferential treatment from Mantega.† The payments had yet to amount to much of anything, according to Joesley, until Mantega's recent promotion. But Joesley was ready to move quickly when the opportunity came up, according to his own testimony. His family appreciated the R$100 million check BNDES first wrote the company in 2004 and wanted to lock up funds again.

Joesley arrived at BNDES headquarters—a tinted dark and looming tower with twenty-nine floors in Brazil's capital—and went up to the president of the board's office, where the entire board and all the bank's vice presidents were assembled to hear Joesley's presentation. BNDES had been operating since 1952, when it was first formed by the Brazilian government. But Joesley had a new idea for how to leverage BNDES money. His proposal hinged the success of JBS on the future of Brazil's entire economy. The pitch was simple: the previous administration had jump-started Brazil's global profile by easing policy so that Brazilian products got exported around the world cheaply. But few Brazilian companies still made goods in other countries. That next step was crucial if Brazil wanted to become a real contender with a top-ranking gross domestic product, Joesley argued. "That meeting was pretty remarkable, because a lot of the vice-presidents that were there couldn't believe it," Joesley later recalled in testimony to Brazilian prose-

---

* As a reminder, the sourcing in this section mainly comes from analysis of a trove of legal documents, which include the Brazilian leniency agreement of J&F Investimentos, the cooperation agreements of Joesley and Wesley Batista, the filings that explained what ultimately brought them to be arrested, as well as Joesley's interview with Brazilian prosecutors. I also reviewed DOJ and SEC documents related to the American side of the corruption investigation.

† Mantega has denied the allegations made by the Batistas and J&F; Mantega was temporarily arrested on corruption and bribery charges unrelated to the Batistas in 2016.

cutors. "We were all so used to multinational companies, buying Brazilian companies. Not Brazilian companies, becoming multinational companies."

Mantega thought the idea was strong and told Joesley that BNDES was interested. Joesley's relationship with Mantega, a pale Italian immigrant from Genoa with a graying, receding hairline, was formal then, but a deep personal connection was starting to develop.

"Right after leaving that meeting, I went back to my company," Joesley recalled. "We got right to work on prospecting companies that would be good candidates. That's when the journey to internationalize JBS started."

But the Batistas moved a lot faster than BNDES expected them to. A prime international acquisition was ready to become their test case. They purchased Argentina's largest beef producer and exporter, Swift Armour, for $200 million.

"When we made the deal with them, and bought the company, we went back to the BNDES and said, 'Look, that thing that you guys didn't believe in? It happened. We already bought the first company,'" Joesley recalled in testimony. BNDES ended up lending R$80 million toward the plan through a five-year loan, according to the plea agreement. Mantega delivered quickly: the first credit line was available in a few weeks; the second within a few days of submitting the request. For each loan or deal, Mantega and his fixer earned a 4 percent commission. "The deal was a bit rushed, because BNDES wasn't really prepared for it. BNDES didn't really believe in our plan, in our capabilities," Joesley added.

Joesley soon went back to BNDES to ask them to buy stock in the privately held company. Just as they came close to a deal that would have had BNDES put in $500 million for a 25 percent stake, the Batistas got a better offer from banks tantalizing them with a public offering instead, at practically double the value of the other deal, Joesley testified. The Batistas listed directly on the Brazilian stock exchange.

But the IPO disappointed. Just ten months into trading, the stock price was down nearly 40 percent from its original open. Soon after, Swift & Company's legendary beef-packing assets were overwhelmed with debt and looking for a buyer. Joesley wanted to pounce, he recalled: "We didn't have enough money to make the purchase. We went back to BNDES saying, 'Look, right now, there's an opportunity for you guys to come in and buy stock—because we can have an issuance of new shares.'"

Then BNDES changed leadership—Mantega became Brazil's minister of finance, and a new president was installed at BNDES. A week after the incoming chief took the job, an equity transaction with JBS was confirmed for $750 million. But then they hit a snag—the offer was dropped to $500 million. Meanwhile, in May 2007, the Batistas announced they would acquire Swift. Joesley testified that closing would be contingent on whether BNDES money came through. In the thick of it, Joesley claims, he turned to Mantega, who pushed it through. Mantega has denied the Batistas' allegations. BNDES ended up purchasing 12.94 percent of the stock of JBS for $580 million—and the Swift deal was able to close.

"That's when the operation took off," Joesley testified. "That only happened thanks to Guido's coordination of it. The minister made it happen, everything."

Coming to (North) America

A year after Michael Pollan's *The Omnivore's Dilemma* became a bestseller in 2007, the Batistas planted roots in the United States, at the Greeley, Colorado, headquarters of Swift. Then the worst-performing company in the American beef market, Swift had twelve plants in the United States and Australia that could slaughter twenty-three thousand cattle a day. JBS paid $225 million in cash and assumed $1.2 billion in debt. A Brazilian audit court later investigated JBS for its US acquisitions and found at least $362 million of BNDES funds went toward the Swift acquisition and other purchases at the time.

Joesley's older brother Wesley was dispatched to turn Swift around, and he moved his family to Greeley for the next four years. From his first moments in the old Swift plant, Wesley hopped on the line and got a little blood-spattered while making a show of how he liked to do it. For forty-five days before closing the deal, Wesley interviewed three hundred Swift workers. He worked with a translator, since he spoke no English, and many meatpacking workers come from a wide variety of immigrant or refugee backgrounds. Under Swift, the factories had been operating at 80 percent, but Wesley soon added a second shift and had the plants running more productively than before.

The buying spree didn't end there. Mizuho's John Baumgarten, who met Joesley Batista and some of his executives while at Goldman Sachs around

2008, has told me over the years how he was struck by Joesley's intensity after taking a meeting to help explain opportunities in the US food market: "They are really aggressive. Real dealmakers. Deal guys."

Joesley went back to BNDES around this time in 2008 to get more funds. At least four more companies looked ripe, and the Batistas wanted to buy all of them. BNDES ended up purchasing another 12.99 percent of JBS stock for $1 billion, in a joint operation with two Brazilian pension funds.

JBS then announced the acquisition of Smithfield Beef for $565 million in cash, which cemented its place as the world's largest beef supplier. It added about 1.5 billion pounds of fresh beef processing to JBS USA operations, in addition to the largest cattle feedlot operation in America, called Five Rivers—which alone could feed more than eight hundred thousand cattle at a time.*

The Batistas kept going and announced a third beef acquisition in 2008: America's fourth-largest beef processor at the time, National, based in Kansas City. The intended purchase price was $560 million. National had been struggling to keep up amid industry-wide consolidation but had a considerable $5 billion in revenue.

That's when Washington regulators stepped in and held a hearing through the Senate Judiciary's antitrust subcommittee in May 2008, led by Senator Herb Kohl, who also cofounded retailer Kohl's with his father and brother. The hearing is one of the few modern times when a beef packer's size and scope have been challenged so directly. Wesley Batista was brought in to testify in front of the group of senators.

Senator Kohl started off the hearing with a stirring introduction that put JBS's quick rise to market power into context: "By reducing the number of major buyers for ranchers' cattle from five down to three, and in some regions even two, this deal will give the remaining beef processors enormous buying power. With little choice to whom to sell their cattle, ranchers will increasingly be left in a 'take it or leave it' position. We should be equally concerned with effects on millions of beef consumers across the country in

---

* In 2008, according to a Debtwire shareholder report, "To finance the acquisition of Smithfield Beef and the attempted acquisition of National Beef, BNDESPar and SOE pension funds Petros and Funcef form Fundo de Investimento em Participações PROT, which acquires a 14.3% stake in JBS for BRL 1.4bn. JBS issues new shares to BNDESPar, raising BRL 335m and increasing BNDESPar's stake to 17%."

this era of rising food prices. Will only three major national sellers of beef be enough to ensure a competitive market for supermarkets, small grocery stores, and restaurants? Or will consumers need to go on a diet while the giant meatpacking firms grow ever fatter?"

Kohl questioned the connection with BNDES. Kohl asked, "Mr. Batista, is it true that the Brazilian Government has subsidized your acquisitions of National and Smithfield—or Swift?"

"No, Senator, to my knowledge, that is not the case," Batista replied. "JBS today is a public company. We have had investments from BNDES, a federal development bank, in Brazil. BNDES, a federal public company, has normal investments in JBS stock and has also extended JBS modest loans at competitive rates. JBS is a public company, and BNDES has some participation, but there was a public offer and there are a lot of JBS shares traded on the São Paulo stock exchange in Brazil. I believe that a lot of U.S. investors have JBS shares."

The response was sufficient for the time, but it didn't stop the DOJ and several states from officially filing an antitrust lawsuit after the hearing in October 2008. It alleged the deal would create a "fundamental restructuring of the U.S. beef-packing industry" and bid up prices for consumers. The lawsuit warns: "The acquisition would increase JBS's share of fed cattle packing capacity from close to 20% to approximately 35% and eliminate one of three large packers that compete with JBS. Post-merger, over 80% of the nation's fed cattle packing capacity would be controlled by a three-firm oligopoly—JBS, Tyson Foods, Inc. with approximately 25–30%, and Cargill, Inc. with approximately 20–25% share."

The complaint notes that this market dominance would make it more difficult for new companies to enter. Construction of a new plant would require over $250 million, and two years at least for the permits, designs, and build-out. "The transaction likely would substantially increase the incentive and ability of these major packers to engage in coordinated conduct in output and pricing decisions," according to the complaint. "As a result, grocers, food service companies and ultimately United States consumers likely will pay higher prices for USDA-graded beef, and cattle producers, ranchers and feedlots likely will receive lower prices for their fed cattle."

The lawsuit also notes that the acquisition would upend key cattle markets where ranchers have relied on cash sales for generations. "JBS's purchase of National would reduce the number of competitively significant actual or potential bidders for fed cattle from 4 to 3 in the High Plains, resulting in less aggressive competition and lower prices for feedlots and producers of fed cattle," the lawsuit reads. "JBS's purchase of National would eliminate actual and potential competition between JBS—via the Smithfield Beef Group plant it is acquiring—and National, leaving feedlots in the market with only one major buyer of fed cattle."

JBS backed off. National was nixed, but other JBS acquisitions Smithfield Beef and Five Rivers feedlot had already skated through. The brothers then decided to move into chicken instead. As Joesley recalled in Brazilian testimony, "An opportunity to buy chicken breasts emerged—really big ones." That's when the Batistas found Pilgrim's Pride in bankruptcy. JBS paid $800 million for a 64 percent interest in the publicly traded Texas chicken processor. Through that stake, JBS became the second-largest poultry producer in the world.

With an enterprise value of $2.8 billion, it was another major deal made possible by BNDES's funding. According to a press release from BNDES, which provided up to $2 billion in financing and restructuring, the deal was a milestone for JBS's aggressive strategy beyond Brazil. According to the DOJ indictment against the holding company J&F Investimentos, the bribe Joesley deposited into a US bank account held for Mantega was more than $55 million.

Pilgrim's was in bankruptcy, which gave the Batistas the power to decide how the operations would be restructured and how labor contracts would be renegotiated. In the case of Pilgrim's, JBS moved the offices to Greeley and cut 860 corporate and administrative positions. The debt load quickly fell from $2.1 billion to $1.3 billion by the end of 2010. By 2011, 70 percent of total JBS S.A. revenues came from the United States. Wesley Batista served as CEO of JBS and chairman of the board for Pilgrim's, while Joesley Batista served as CEO of the Batistas' holding company J&F and a member of Pilgrim's board.

Three Presidents and $150 Million of Kickbacks

In his filmed interview with Brazilian prosecutors, Joesley testified that his bribes made it to three presidents and even attempted to sway Brazil's 2014 presidential elections.

Joesley set up a separate account and paid Mantega the agreed-upon kickback whenever Mantega was owed money. Joesley claimed that Mantega explained the arrangement to Joesley cryptically: "One day, if I need it, I'll tell you."

Joesley says he only realized Mantega was really a front man, and who the ultimate beneficiaries were, in 2010 around the end of the presidency of Luiz Inácio Lula da Silva and the transition to his handpicked successor, Dilma Rousseff. That's when, after Joesley's next deal with Mantega, Joesley prepared to deposit Mantega's next kickback into the original account. But Mantega chided him.

"No, no, no," Mantega told Joesley, according to Joesley's testimony. "Now you have to open up a new account."

"Oh, why open a new account?" Joesley asked.

"No, no, no," Mantega continued. "This account is Lula's account. We have to open one for Dilma."

"Huh," Joesley caught himself musing, "Lula? Dilma? But do they know about this? Does Lula know about this? Does Dilma know?"

"They know," Mantega responded, according to Joesley's claims. "I tell them everything."*

Batista says he didn't press further at the time: "I didn't dig any deeper to find out if it was President Lula's, or if it was the Lula government's, or if it was the Dilma government's."

Joesley testified that Mantega called on him to dole the funds out in 2014. A recession and accusations that Dilma had overseen the misuse of state bank funds in the scandal of state-owned petroleum corporation Petrobras had Dilma's 2014 reelection campaign looking like a pipe dream. But Joesley's two offshore accounts had roughly $150 million combined— and that money may have started to look like the Workers' Party's last chance at staying in power. Suddenly, early during the summer of 2014, the demands to donate to thousands of politicians came in quick succession. Mantega called up Joesley, according to Joesley's interview with prosecutors, and laid it out: "Joesley, I need you to make these donations."

Joesley testified that he replied: "Let's do it."

Brazil's Workers' Party won the election and sustained thousands of pol-

---

* Lula and Dilma have denied the allegations.

iticians. Mostly the bribes were paid out by a loyal Batista family employee. But certain occasions called for Joesley's personal touch. The first instance, Joesley testified, brought him in October 2014 to São Paulo, where he met the former Brazilian president Lula, the founding face of Brazil's Workers' Party. Joesley recalled that he handed over cash and made clear that he was worried the demands for money would create unnecessary attention. But Lula didn't say a word and responded only with a blank stare. (Lula has denied these allegations.) Another instance brought Joesley directly to Dilma, just as she eked out her presidential election runoff victory with 51.6 percent of the vote.

Joesley's second run-in with a chief of Brazil became a shakedown. He claimed that it started with Joesley getting bombarded with demands for a R$30 million payment from a representative for Fernando Pimentel, another Workers' Party candidate and the governor-elect of the Brazilian state of Minas Gerais. (Pimentel has not responded to these claims.) But the kickback accounts were pretty much dry, and the request was coming from a distant associate with no authority to really ask.

Joesley testified that he ended up meeting Dilma at Planalto Palace, Brazil's modernist presidential workplace in Brasília, originally designed in 1958. Dilma, Joesley testified, was blunt. After confirming she had made the request, she asked Joesley to find Pimentel to plan to pay the bribe. But Joesley barely had enough.

"There's two accounts, and they're still asking me for R$30 million more," Joesley told Dilma, according to his testimony. "I did the math correctly. We've spent this much, and it's kind of running out. If we spend this R$30 million, it's finished."

Dilma, Joesley recalled in testimony, kept her reply brief: "No. It's important. We have to do it." Dilma has denied the allegations.

Joesley claimed he got Pimentel's instructions to meet up in Belo Horizonte at the Pampulha–Carlos Drummond de Andrade Airport, a teal and brown flat building. Inside the hangar, Joesley heard the plan: make the payment by acquiring a 3 percent interest in the company that runs the concessions of Mineirão Stadium, the large circular soccer stadium that was part of the network that hosted the 2014 World Cup in Pimentel's region. Pimentel arranged for the owner of a construction company to come by Joesley's office in São Paolo to make a trade. Pimentel has not responded to these claims. Joesley paid R$30 million and, in return, got 3 percent of the stadium contract. According to his testimony, Joesley exchanged the money, legally, through bank transfers and wrote up an official sales contract.*

Joesley then refocused on Dilma's vice president Michel Temer, who, according to Joesley, had independently been on Joesley's kickback payroll since 2010 and would soon become president himself.† Temer tested Joesley's loyalty at a time of critical political maneuvering. By 2016, Dilma faced an impeachment trial. Temer wanted to protect himself. According to Joesley's testimony, Temer called Joesley to his law offices in the upscale enclave of Jardins in São Paulo and asked for a kickback of R$300,000 to cover political marketing on the internet. Temer noted he was getting attacked over his connection to corruption scandals and Dilma, and then asked Joesley to arrange his help. Joesley asked the designated publicist to stop by his house to pick up the cash.

Temer was sworn in at the end of August 2016, just as the bribery schemes were unraveling. Joesley's house had been raided. He had already gone to the authorities to strike a deal. The Brazilian government's prosecutors were handing out plea deals to nearly anyone who could implicate others in the broader corruption investigation. The risk of getting caught up in someone else's plea negotiations was real, but it didn't stop Joesley from making new bribes. Another taped conversation from the time featured a politician allegedly discussing arrangements of who would pick up his payment of R$625,000 with Joesley, and says without any hint of irony, "It has to be someone we'd kill before he makes a plea bargain."

Joesley can be heard agreeing: "Yes, yes."

In June 2017 official bribery charges were filed against Temer, but the case never progressed due to a rule in Brazil that stipulates that a president can only stand trial after a two-thirds vote from a government body. Twice, there were never enough votes to move forward, and Temer was never convicted of any crimes. One of those votes, in October 2017, was over charges related to the Batista allegations. It failed, with 233 deputies voting to put Temer on trial, and 251 voting against.

---

* Dilma has denied wrongdoing and the allegations.
† Temer denied the allegations that he took bribes from Joesley and at the time of the leaked recording in 2017 refused to resign.

How the Batistas Got Jailed

JBS got close to $5 billion in equity and debt financing from BNDES. A large amount of that financing helped JBS acquire distressed American companies like Swift and Pilgrim's Pride. In exchange for funding one of the most aggressive corporate acquisition sprees in the food industry ever, Joesley created a series of shell companies and opened bank accounts for the shell companies at an investment bank in the United States. According to the Security and Exchange Commission cease-and-desist order, Joesley maintained accounts there for Mantega's use. Some of the meetings with Mantega took place in the United States. Another bribe was the transfer of a $1.5 million Manhattan apartment. Some kickbacks were cash transfers that Joesley dropped off himself. Others that Joesley detailed were paid through fake invoices as cattle purchased, or the transfer of ownership of an asset, like Joesley's Agusta helicopter.

Publicly traded Pilgrim's Pride, according to the Securities and Exchange Commission cease-and-desist order, became a slush fund for the Batistas, unbeknownst to management. The Batistas also indirectly received about $800 million in 2015 and 2016 in the form of dividend payments by Pilgrim's to JBS USA. As the SEC order described the funds from the bribery schemes:

> From 2009 to 2015, unbeknownst to Pilgrim's management, the Respondents carried out the bribery scheme and its funding using, at times, certain JBS operating accounts which contained funds that were commingled with funds obtained from Pilgrim's through intercompany transfers, special dividend payments, and other means. Pilgrim's books did not reflect this. The Respondents then paid bribes out of the operating accounts using various mechanisms including fake invoices, official election donations, and cash. In some instances, the Minister would direct the bribe payments to be made as official election donations.

BNDES spent more than $2 billion for about 21 percent ownership of JBS. In addition, BNDES and related pension funds gave an estimated $580 million toward the Swift acquisition and others at the time. A BNDES-led investment group of pension funds also helped JBS acquire Smithfield Beef and feedlot operation Five Rivers Cattle Feeding for $565 million in cash. BNDES later offered JBS up to $2 billion in collateralized debt so the 64 percent acquisition of Pilgrim's Pride could go through—for $800 million.

The Batistas' legal issues, meanwhile, didn't end with those original Brazilian plea agreements. Joesley failed to disclose other bribes to prosecutors. In fact, they came to light only after he accidentally sent audio recordings of incriminating conversations to the prosecutor's office. As soon as Brazilian officials figured it out, they started trying to rescind the Batistas' plea deals, which triggered allegations of obstructing justice. The prosecutors also had a case to overturn the deals for two other key reasons.

Wesley and Joesley Batista were arrested on charges of insider trading by Brazil's federal attorney general's office in September 2017. Before the plea bargain terms were disclosed to the public, Wesley sold shares of JBS at a high and repurchased them at the future low, according to legal documents from Brazil's attorney general's office. Wesley also acquired dollar futures contracts and dollar fixed-term contracts in the value of $2.815 billion. He made a profit in the financial markets of approximately R$100 million. The disclosures led to Brazil's worst financial market sell-off in at least a decade, a nearly 10 percent devaluation of the Brazilian real, and massive street demonstrations. Between May 12 and May 22, 2017, the JBS stock price was slashed in half.

What finally incarcerated the brothers was threefold: the additional bribes after signing the plea agreements, the manipulation of financial markets, and the advice they got from Brazil's then attorney general on how to negotiate their plea deals in Brazil and the United States. Prosecutors allege that it was yet another apparent attempt to secure preferential treatment. Their plea bargains originally promised no criminal cases would be brought against them: according to one of the accidental recordings sent to prosecutors, Joesley is heard saying, "We're the jewel in their crown. We're going to come out of this as everybody's friends, and we're not going to be arrested."

But these acts of disregard for authorities and their signed agreements sealed the Batista brothers' fate. Both ended up serving sentences of about six months, starting in September 2017 and lasting until February and March 2018. When they got out, they came back to the international meat empire they built in a decade.

Repercussions on the Soil Where the Assets Are

One of the most ambitious global acquisition sprees in Brazilian corporate history turned out to have been embroiled in a nationwide corruption investigation. Yet it was not publicly denounced by brands that benefit from the meat. Eventually the US Justice Department started looking into it, interviewing the Batistas in Brazil at the end of 2018. Several lawmakers requested investigations, including Senator Marco Rubio (R-FL) and Senator Bob Menendez (D-NJ), who sent the first of several joint letters in 2019 to ask the Treasury Department to investigate the US acquisitions, since the deals have "serious implications for the security, safety, and resiliency of our food system." But the most dogged in following up has been House Representative and Appropriations Chair Rosa DeLauro (D-CT), who has focused on the Department of Agriculture's role in regulating JBS.

"I called on Congress and I called on USDA to conduct an investigation into JBS to determine whether or not they should continue to receive government contracts, including trade aid," DeLauro told me in March 2021.

Despite her attempts, not much happened, and the Batistas stayed quiet. Joesley Batista staged his corporate comeback in the fog of the pandemic spring of 2020. His lawyers successfully appealed to a Brazilian judge to get him reinstated at J&F Investimentos, the Batista family's investment vehicle that holds the brothers' 44 percent ownership stake in JBS, and the Brazilian judge extended it to Wesley, too. In March 2020 they were allowed to join and participate in J&F board meetings, without voting rights. A few weeks after that, the courts again ruled in favor of the Batista brothers—they were allowed to rejoin the companies they control as part of management. All of a sudden, the Batistas were coming out of hiding and had little holding them back.

Within a few months, in October 2020, the US Department of Justice reached its settlements. J&F pled guilty to US foreign bribery charges and agreed to pay $128.25 million in criminal fines. The firm also agreed to an additional $27 million to the Securities and Exchange Commission. Wesley and Joesley also had to pay $550,000 each for their SEC violations. Part of the deal included cooperating in any ongoing and future investigations involving the firm and its employees. But the overall scope was narrow, mainly revolving around the shareholder entity J&F and the Batista brothers directly.

When the charges and settlement were jointly announced, DOJ claimed the damage was worth $256.5 million. But J&F got a break on half of it because of its record-setting $3.2 billion fine in Brazil.* That prosecution seems to join "The Chickenshit Club," James Comey's name for prosecutors who settled readily and only brought to trial cases they were sure they could win—as described in the book by journalist Jesse Eisinger titled that. It's a sweetheart break on paying the full thing. The Batistas have been appealing the remaining unpaid portions of their fine in Brazil, according to reports in Brazil's *O Globo* and others.

JBS's American businesses were then implicated in price-fixing schemes. Pilgrim's Pride pleaded guilty over price-fixing and agreed to pay the federal government approximately $107 million. Pilgrim's Pride, which JBS owns the majority of, also has paid out $75 million in class-action settlements related to rigging poultry prices. JBS has also settled with customers who alleged price-fixing for pork and beef. While denying wrongdoing, JBS made three pork-related settlements, amounting to $57 million, and also settled for $52.5 million with a group of customers who purchased JBS beef.†

"There's been price collusion," Sysco CEO Kevin Hourican told me in 2021 about his publicly traded food distributor's lawsuit against JBS for pork price-fixing which, at the time this book went to print, had yet to be resolved. "It's bad behavior and it needs to be addressed and the government's addressing it. We've been harmed and, frankly, select customers of ours have been harmed as well, so that will resolve itself in the courts and through some negotiation."

There continue to be questions about how the Batistas handled the fallout of their role in the bribery scheme, particularly in America. According to a lawsuit brought against them by a shareholder, the Batista brothers continued to serve as directors on the board of Pilgrim's while they were being indicted by—and cooperating with—Brazilian prosecutors. But a private shareholder claimed that they were not made aware of this fact, in a case that was dismissed on procedural grounds in 2015. The brothers were renominated to the board in March 2016 despite indictments dating to at least

---

* This fine figure is in US dollars; the original figure was R$10.3 billion. J&F agreed to pay a fine of R$8 billion and to contribute R$2.3 billion to social projects in Brazil.
† For more on beef, pork, and chicken class actions, refer to Chapter 3.

two months earlier, according to the lawsuit. The suit also alleged that the cooperation was also not disclosed in Pilgrim's subsequent annual report, in February 2017, just weeks before Joesley secretly recorded President Temer. The 2017 proxy statement, posted at the end of March, after the Temer tape was leaked, renominated Joesley and Wesley.

"Mr. Batista brings to the Board of Pilgrim's Pride significant senior leadership and industry experience. Mr. Batista has long been one of the most respected executives in Brazil's protein industry, and his reputation is now firmly established worldwide," the proxy advertised to shareholders about both brothers. "Mr. Batista grew up in the protein industry, and it is his strategic insight and entrepreneurial spirit that has facilitated the growth of JBS through numerous acquisitions, expanding its reach across the globe."

The US shareholder was filing that lawsuit at the same time as the brothers were negotiating a plea deal with Brazilian authorities. Both brothers accepted another stint on the board while handing over evidence of bribery to prosecutors. The lawsuit contends that this information would have been material and that even when the brothers did resign in May and June 2017, they did not disclose the reasons to shareholders.* In actuality, at the time of the proxy, the lawsuit asserts that Wesley was "one of the most disgraced and disrespected men in the nation of Brazil." Pilgrim's lacked a code of conduct until 2015, more than five years after being acquired, and as of 2018, according to the complaint, Pilgrim's was still in the process of rolling out an official anti-bribery compliance program. Although Joesley and Wesley Batista signed the code of conduct prohibiting bribery, neither received any anti-corruption or ethics training. According to the SEC order, Wesley Batista had failed to disclose his knowledge of any bribes paid during an internal audit.

The Batista brothers became billionaires and acquired dominance in the US meat market for JBS through a string of bribery-fueled acquisitions. But the American meat market was already vulnerable to manipulation. Too much consolidation limited the potential buyers for struggling meatpacking firms. All it took was JBS, on the quest to become the world's largest meat-packer.

---

* The case was dismissed, with the ability to refile the case, in 2018 while other related litigation played out.

CHAPTER 6

JBS Goes to Washington

Rapid consolidation has afforded JBS an outsize presence in American ranching and meat selling. Just as J&F and the Batistas got out of their foreign corruption charges with the US Department of Justice and Securities and Exchange Commission in the summer of 2020, a dozen lawmakers asked antitrust regulators to investigate JBS for creating another problem on US soil. JBS's acquisition of a lamb plant in Greeley was in question. JBS had sold the plant to a co-op of more than 145 families in 2015. But the lamb business struggled. Five years later, the co-op filed for bankruptcy. JBS purchased the plant through a bankruptcy auction in July 2020 with the hopes of turning it into a beef plant for making manufactured products like burgers. The group of concerned representatives, including six senators and six congressmen, warned that this decision could upend the American market for lamb. That one plant accounts for a fifth of the total US market. Policymakers feared JBS could destroy a huge portion of the American industry and then meet demand with its other lamb produced in Brazil, since JBS is America's largest lamb importer. Despite the concern, JBS reopened the plant in November 2020 after $13.5 million of investment as a beef plant making premium, retail-ready products. A JBS USA representative told me "the acquisition presented an exciting opportunity" to meet consumer demand as well as create new jobs in its headquarters' hometown.

JBS has exposed failures of government oversight. Many policymakers turned away as a billionaire-owned foreign entity acquired iconic US meat brands with funds obtained in part through foreign corruption and bribery. Industry workers, consumers, and farmers have suffered the impacts.

Top meat-packers like JBS can exert pressure on prices paid to producers, which has the potential of rippling through much of the industry. That's why independent livestock producers like Greg Gunthorp who have been at it for decades have been considering calling it quits. When Gunthorp overhauled practices in 1998 at his hog farm in LaGrange, Indiana, he was selling his pigs into the commodity market for less than his grandfather had done during the Great Depression. Business got better after transitioning to selling his pasture-raised hogs and chickens directly to restaurants. Gunthorp built an on-farm poultry slaughterhouse and attracted a customer base. Sales were strong for years. But then in early 2020 some of Gunthorp's largest poultry customers dropped him, including Indiana's own Patachou group of six restaurants helmed by the local food advocate and restaurateur Martha Hoover. He outlasted the year but didn't buy more chicks for 2021. "I tell people we're taking a break," he told me the week the painful announcement came out. "But I don't know that we have any intention whatsoever to go back."

Gunthorp had been slaughtering chickens on his farm for sixteen years but struggled to maintain margins amid a consolidated industry. Gunthorp was previously able to maintain his niche in the chicken market by doubling and tripling production—and by selling to high-end restaurants. But as independent restaurants struggled through the pandemic, so did Gunthorp. The fourth-generation farmer is furious over JBS's commandeering of American agribusiness. As an independent producer, he sits alongside JBS's representative on the USDA's meat inspection committee and says the conglomerate must be stopped.

"JBS does not deserve the right to be in the meat business in the United States of America, and I'm not afraid to say that. There's a lot [who] are," Gunthorp said. "JBS is the most egregious on price-fixing and bribery of politicians and inspectors.* That's the kind of activity which is the reason why we have a Meat and Poultry Act, which is as much about keeping criminal activity from the meat industry as it is to ensure we have a safe product. The secretary of agriculture has ultimate authority to say, 'Hey, you can't play in the meat industry.'"

The extent of the JBS problem is twofold, because JBS also imports meat, which impacts the US market and competition among US producers. The

---

* This quote references activity in the United States as well as Brazil.

American government has rules that stipulate how labels should note which country the meat comes from. They are called country-of-origin labeling requirements. But notably, the rules were repealed for beef and pork in 2015—passed through a legislative rider in the Appropriations Committee's year-end omnibus package. It opened up US beef markets to compete with some $3 billion of imports a year. The imported meat can still be labeled as "Product of USA"—as long as the beef is processed a bit more at a US plant. Gunthorp describes it as "the largest extraction of wealth in the meat business from farms."

"That benefited JBS more than it benefited anyone in the country," Gunthorp told me. "Largest importer. Largest beef player in the world. JBS made billions off that whole thing."

Importing Brazilian beef has been called into question as the safety of Brazilian beef has spent years reeling from major scandals. In March 2017, Operation Weak Flesh exposed Brazil's Ministry of Agriculture's negligence in exporting bad meat to the United States and other countries. Police raided JBS plants in Brazil along with several other plants and found widespread evidence of meat-packers bribing inspectors and politicians to export unsanitary and rotting meat with traces of salmonella.* Over the next three months, the agency inspected all imported meat from Brazil, and at the end of June announced the USDA was temporarily halting all imports. According to the USDA audit, the tainted meat had abscesses from hoof-and-mouth disease vaccination as well as visible blood clots and lymph nodes. A shocking 11 percent of all the beef had to be denied at the border. According to industry insiders, the major blow gave JBS another reason to table a potential American asset listing on the public markets. Though JBS denied it's related to Operation Weak Flesh.

Amid persistent calls to suspend tainted meat from Brazil for good, in June 2019 USDA veterinarians audited Brazilian slaughterhouses, including four owned by JBS, to determine whether it was safe to restart beef imports from Brazil. The audit found unsanitary conditions inside JBS plants in Brazil: from leaking pipes attracting flies to poor trash collection to more severe instances of failing to prevent brain tissue leakage among the carcasses.

---

* The investigation led to the arrest of a JBS employee but according to JBS "did not mention or raise any suspicions about the quality or the safety of JBS products."

But the ban was only partial. Imports from Brazil eventually restarted and have increased. After Brazil claimed hoof-and-mouth disease was eradicated among its herd in 2018, Brazilian beef imports increased more than 15 percent. Brazil is the fifth-largest beef importer to the United States, after Australia, Canada, New Zealand, and Mexico. Brazilian beef in the United States shot up another 35 percent in 2020, when imports topped 220 million pounds. But then mad cow disease was again detected in two Brazilian cattle in June 2021 and authorities failed to report it quickly.

Calls to ban all Brazilian beef have reemerged. Senator Jon Tester (D-MT) responded by introducing a bill in November 2021 to institute a ban on all Brazilian beef until the government could certify the meat complies with US regulations. That same month, Brazil exported a record amount of meat to the United States, overtaking the amount purchased by the usual top buyer, China, which had not yet reopened import markets after Brazil's mad cow incident.

Congress is still hearing calls to take the final step and make country-of-origin labeling mandatory for meat. Since 2020, the Federal Trade Commission has been addressing concerns that country-of-origin labels on meat are voluntary. In September 2021, a bipartisan coalition of lawmakers unveiled a bill to reinstate the labels for beef. "Product of USA" regulations are also expected to come up as an issue in the 2023 Farm Bill—which advocates are hopeful will set stricter standards, in addition to stronger incentives for supporting pasture-raised meat.

On the Government Gravy Train

On a balmy seventy-degree June day in the heart of America's Salad Bowl in 2019, I was standing backstage inside a massive tent set up on Main Street in Salinas, California. Just footsteps from the John Steinbeck museum, I had a recorder pushed in the face of then USDA secretary Sonny Perdue. As a magazine journalist, I rarely scrum, knocking elbows and jostling amid a horde for an interview, but the higher-ups at *Forbes* had secured the federal government's agriculture chief to be the final keynote for our fifth annual *Forbes* AgTech Summit, and as I pushed my recorder into the mess of nearly a dozen others, I decided to ask my nagging question.

A few months before the Salinas summit, *Forbes* magazine had added the Batista brothers to the billionaire ranks, thanks to their stake in the world's largest meat processor. Since then, it had come out that the Trump administration had purchased more than $60 million of pork products from JBS USA using funds meant to help US farmers hurt by the trade war with China. The headline in the *New York Daily News* read: "Trump administration showers Brazilian crooks with $62M bailout money meant for struggling U.S. farmers." A smaller check announced for Smithfield, a Virginia-based pork company owned by a Chinese billionaire's publicly traded conglomerate, had been canceled after public backlash.

I found myself backstage and face-to-face with Perdue, who a few hours before the *Forbes* summit had stopped over at Impossible Foods' headquarters in Silicon Valley. Perdue had waved his hand tepidly onstage when asked what he thought of the bleeding vegan burger, which was a clue for me as I sized up his demeanor going into the scrum. Backstage, Perdue had been answering questions about immigration and worker shortages from a gaggle of reporters around me, and then it was my turn.

"You were talking about the bailouts," I ventured.

"I don't like to use that word," responded Perdue.

I smiled. "Will you put protections in place so money doesn't go to JBS again?"

Perdue sighed. "Let me address the JBS issue. They bought Swift there in Greeley and they buy a lot of beef and hogs from US producers. Everything we are purchasing from them was produced by US producers. Now, we can't buy from every swine farmer there and that's not the way it's done. The beneficiary here was not JBS. It was the American hog farmer and that was our intention and, yes, we will do that again."

Perdue was true to his word. JBS got more trade war bailouts, along with other government funding. These federal procurement contracts continue to come under fire. To sell goods like meat to the federal government, a business must be law-abiding.

JBS's contracts have been in jeopardy before—not due to an investigation by USDA. Back in 2016, Department of Labor prosecutors called out JBS for discriminating against women, Black, Native American, and Latinx workers at plants in Hyrum, Utah, and Cactus, Texas. In 2018, JBS agreed to pay $4 million to settle the allegations while denying wrongdoing in each case.

Food contractors rarely go through procurement investigations. If regulators created a probe, Houston-based federal procurement contracts lawyer John Edwards says there would be an entire investigation and hearing process. But the impact is still limited: suspensions usually last a year, while debarment lasts three. The punishments are short-term because they are not intended to be punitive.

Agencies are disincentivized to go through the effort, says Edwards, unless it's really worth it. "It has serious effects on vendors and actually the agencies themselves," Edwards explains. The agencies still have to buy the products, in this case meat, and consolidation in the meat industry means there are few other options for supplying the government at the scale and price point they require. Adds Edwards, "It's a pretty involved process that they don't really jump into without very careful consideration."

The USDA shouldn't be supporting shady businesses with taxpayer dollars to supply public school kids with cheap meat, according to the chair of the House of Representatives Appropriations Committee.* Since arriving in America, JBS companies have earned nearly $900 million from federal contracts. That's including a $9 million contract signed on the day the Temer recording leaked in May 2017. More than $400 million in contracts through the USDA has been paid to JBS and Pilgrim's Pride for its meat in the last five years—over $150 million of which was purchased in 2019 alone. JBS gets millions more from other US government agencies.

Purple-haired Rep. Rosa DeLauro, who leads the House of Representatives' purse strings, has taken this fight from the Trump administration to the Biden administration. She has pointed to the fact that the federal government shelled out more than $70 million for JBS and Pilgrim's Pride meat in 2020, and JBS remains in good standing, despite years of calls for investigations.

"This is outrageous," DeLauro told me in March 2021. "You would be hard-pressed to find a more corrupt group of individuals. The brothers are criminals. The US, by law, should not be doing business with corrupt companies."

DeLauro has consistently argued that lawless behavior helped the Batistas take over the meat supply quickly and rely on a production system that is

---

* In response to DeLauro's allegations, a representative for JBS USA pointed to examples of how JBS has invested in being a good employer, from "competitive wages and benefits" to tuition aid to its net-zero emissions by 2040 commitment.

often dangerous for the environment, workers, farmers, local communities, and customers. DeLauro told me there was a clear and present danger to national security. Indeed, two months later, JBS's USA division was temporarily shut down by Russia-affiliated hackers, who were paid a ransom of $11 million in Bitcoin so plants could reopen.

"It is a question of national security when you have the level of violation, the corruption involved, and laws on the books which say we don't do business with these kinds of foreign corrupt practices," DeLauro said. "We are in violation of our own law."

"The consolidation leads to massive power over our government in terms of dictating agriculture policy and the market by dictating supply and price," DeLauro told me. "The more we shine a light on who they are and what they are about, we call into question our own government."

That's still easier said than done. JBS has locked up key hires, among the most notable being Al Almanza—the USDA's former food safety and inspections division chief who worked for the USDA for nearly forty years. Three days after Almanza retired at the end of July 2017, amid JBS's tainted beef scandal, he took up shop as JBS's global head of food safety and quality assurance. Right after Almanza, JBS appointed former Speaker of the House John Boehner and former SEC chairman Harvey Pitt to an independent advisory board. According to a press release, the advisory board was created "to support the company's executive leadership on matters related to corporate governance, government and regulatory affairs, commodity risk management and marketing." In April 2021 JBS then hired a former Federal Trade Commission antitrust regulator to fill its newly created position of chief legal officer. These appointments created JBS's own network of US-based government insiders and bureaucrats.

When I brought up the potential threat of the federal government rescinding its contracts to the head of JBS's American division, André Nogueira, during the phone interview in November 2020, said the company had already resolved the shareholder concerns. "The DOJ settlement is with a shareholder. We always said that. That was a shareholder issue," he said. "We would expect that would be settled the same way it was settled in Brazil. Pay the penalty and move on. It has nothing to do with JBS or the shareholder issues."

But others, like Representative DeLauro, do not think the situation is so simple. In April 2021 at a budget request committee hearing, DeLauro brought it up to USDA chief Tom Vilsack (who previously served in the same position under President Barack Obama during key years of JBS's rise).

"I've been an outspoken critic during the previous administration when what I view as the corrupt Brazilian meat-packer, JBS. They received more than $100 million as part of the department's so-called trade aid package. JBS is eligible and has received additional procurement contracts through the USDA's Agricultural Marketing Service. That concerns me because the Batista brothers, who own the parent company, have pled guilty to violating the Foreign Corrupt Practices Act," DeLauro stated. "The question is simple. Why are we using federal procurement process at USDA to subsidize a foreign corrupt owned meat-packer? And would you agree that this procurement process could be reformed, better utilized to support local farmers [and] regional food systems instead of this corporate monopoly?"

"Madam Chair, I agree with you," Vilsack started. "There's a number of different avenues in addition to procurement that we need to explore and need to look at within the department so that we have the strongest, most resilient food supply system, a system that's fair and equitable that treats people well and that rewards good behavior."

But in 2021, the US government spent $38 million on JBS or Pilgrim's Pride meat purchases. That includes a December 2021 payment to JBS for nearly $6.5 million of pork, earmarked through the Biden administration's economic recovery agenda, Build Back Better. "The lack of transparency with where and how taxpayer dollars are being used is real and it's very intentional," says Tim Gibbons from the advocacy group Missouri Rural Crisis Center. "They don't want us to know how our taxpayer dollars are being used to fuel corporate control like JBS's control over our markets."

A US Listing Washes Away JBS's Ill-Gotten Gains

Listing plans have been announced and pulled back many times over the past decade, but an American offering of assets on the public markets continues to be a goal. That's because JBS has always been a disappointment on the Brazilian stock exchange—as of the time of print, the stock trades at half the multiple of its global competitors, which are all smaller and less diversified.

JBS's international assets trading publicly on US markets is expected to ramp up competition in the already cutthroat meatpacking industry—and could even reignite another consolidation frenzy, according to industry experts. It could give these historically aggressive acquirers access to cheaper capital, and more of it. As HSBC managing director Carlos Laboy told me: "It's a problem for Tyson more than JBS. I don't know of any industry where the number two player leads the discourse on the industry."

Laboy and his colleague Alessia Apostolatos have questions: Where were the JBS executives who sit on Pilgrim Pride's board when their direct reports were engaged in price-fixing? What role will the Batistas have at JBS if it's traded on the NYSE? Before going public, HSBC's economic model applied a 1 percent discount for these governance concerns—equal to $2.7 billion.

"The most important element with the New York Stock Exchange listing is really greater disclosure on new corporate governance rules that will be put on this company," Laboy says. "What will the percentage ownership be of the Batistas? What is the level of independence that the board of directors and independent shareholders are going to have to be able to define the direction of this company? That to us is the most important thing for driving the valuation of JBS going forward. A US listing is really a onetime chance to reset the governance standards for the long term of this company and to infuse it with credibility."

In August 2021, one day after JBS proposed purchasing the remaining publicly traded shares in Pilgrim's Pride and privatizing the company, Senators Marco Rubio and Bob Menendez asked Federal Reserve chair Janet Yellen, the secretary of the Treasury, and the Committee on Foreign Investment in the United States to investigate any firm owned or controlled by Wesley and Joesley Batista, of which there are at least 250 in thirty countries. While the Batista brothers have been removed from the day-to-day at JBS, their shareholding entity J&F remains the single largest shareholder of JBS. The ultimate owners of J&F remain the Batista brothers, and JBS is still a family affair. Wesley's son, Wesley Mendonça Batista Filho, is the president of JBS Latin America, while family patriarch and founder José Batista Sobrinho remains the J&F representative on the JBS board. But a US listing, some analysts argue, could wash away the ill-gotten gains and major governance problems.[*]

"There's just a lot of uncertainty about what you're investing in," Brian

---

[*] A representative for JBS said a potential listing in the US is not linked with Operation Weak Flesh or the suspension of Brazilian beef in 2017.

Weddington, then vice president and senior credit officer at Moody's, told me in 2021. "They haven't addressed it head-on. It's a hard question to answer—that the Batista brothers are back in the business and in control."

Loss of trust is not an easy hurdle to get over. When I called up nutrition expert Marion Nestle to ask her what she thought, she retorted dryly: "Why would anybody trust them?

"Stockholders are interested in profits. They don't care whether it's food or a widget," Nestle continued. "From the standpoint of a stockholder, food is a widget. It has no other meaning besides something that can be bought and sold for a profit. Here you have products that people rely on for life and health that are being treated as if they're automobile parts."

The counterargument is that trading in the United States will put JBS's companies increasingly under the purview of US regulators. That is powerful when considering the ongoing threat of disease like African swine fever, which has decimated hog herds in China, and avian flu, which spread across America in 2022, reaching nearly forty million birds and even transmitting to a worker in Colorado.* Listing in the United States might provide stricter oversight over JBS operations and practices than if it were to relist in Asia. Wouldn't JBS becoming publicly traded ensure its shareholders have the authority to push for change? Sure, to a point.

That is only a fraction of the value that JBS would be gaining overall: the real benefit is the company's fiduciary duty to provide growth and value to its shareholders. There are many food advocates who think food companies should not be publicly traded for this very reason. Take an example from Nestle's 2020 book, *Let's Ask Marion*. In it she describes White House meetings spurred by Michelle Obama prioritizing childhood obesity and health where "food company representatives flatly drew the line at having to stop marketing to kids: 'We have a fiduciary duty to our stockholders,' they told us. From their standpoint, corporate profits had to come first; considerations of children's health were decidedly secondary." Having to answer to that purpose above all else is limiting, and while investing around "ESG," or environment, social, and governance, is trendy, that could shift. Demand for shareholder returns is what persists.

---

* The worker was a prison inmate who was placed on the poultry farm as part of a pre-release program.

CHAPTER 7

How Big Is Too Big?

I found myself in Omaha, Nebraska, inside my first beef slaughterhouse in June 2017, and it wasn't long before I was on my way to the kill floor. There was no time to anticipate it. I grabbed a hairnet and white smock in the hallway outside Greater Omaha Packing's slaughterhouse entrance. I walked through the doors and was immediately hit by the cold air, coupled with the faint smell of ammonia and iron.

Every day here in Omaha, 2,400 steer, only Angus or Hereford breeds mostly from surrounding Nebraska ranchlands, come to the slaughterhouse. Then a conveyor belt starts moving, and the steer gets closer to a stun gun. Usually there's only one shot, and suddenly the animal transitions into meat.

What happens after is perhaps more gruesome. Each is strung up by the legs. A machine strips the hide clean off—in a swift pull that takes only a few seconds. The meat then moves to the chillers for the next two days. I walk past thousands of carcasses hanging in rows and imagine punching them like the iconic scene from *Rocky*. They air out as USDA inspectors grade each by its marbling—select, choice, or prime.

From there, the meat winds through seven stainless-steel rooms on conveyor belts that stretch and turn as the meat is cut farther and farther down the line. It was lab-like, but I was still surprised that I could wear my own black boots inside without any rubber protection, and after I stepped through thin puddles of blood, errant fat trimmings, and soap mixing on the slippery ground, I decided to leave my ankle boots in the hotel room trash bin.

Toward the end of my tour, my guide was impressed, and offered me a special finale: "Usually people are puking by now," he told me, straight-faced, "but since you're not, we can go into the feces room, if you want."

With a steak house dinner planned a few hours later, I surprised myself as I nodded yes. We walked up a metal staircase and across what felt like a gangplank. From a walkway a few feet above, I watched intestines unravel as machines cleaned them out to be sold as tripe. There was a special hum to the machine that I'll never forget—when it got to the end of the intestine all stretched, there was a loud snap back before the machine quickly recoiled for the next one.

The Best Steak of My Life

A few hours after grinning my way through the room of guts, I met back up with Greater Omaha owner Henry Davis, a slight but fit then-sixty-six-year-old, and two of his top slaughterhouse managers. We sat down at a dimly lit, oak-paneled steak house in downtown Omaha called Spencer's, an establishment that lets Davis and his tobacco-chewing pals bring their own meat, fresh off the line.

I was energized from the day and even looking forward to the meal. I wondered if a fattier cut would appear, or if they'd give me a filet. The uncertainty added a level of suspense as I waited at the round wooden dining table. When asked earlier, I told them I'd eat whatever they normally bring out. Davis' beef has ended up at some of the country's top restaurants, from New York City's Minetta Tavern to the French Laundry in Yountville, California, so I was expecting it to be good. But I was still shocked when the tomahawks arrived, vacuum-sealed and featuring a bone the length of my forearm. The chef collected the meat and ducked back into the kitchen as soon as the handoff was complete.

As the steaks seared, to a cool-blue center for Davis and slightly more medium-rare for the rest of us, we discussed the luck of picking this date for my trip, after scheduling it a few months prior. It ended up being just one day after Davis' then-ninety-seven-year-old company shipped its first box of beef to China since 2003, mere hours after the USDA finalized a new trade deal that reopened the $2.5 billion market to American meat-packers. His plant was one of two slaughterhouses in the United States initially approved to ship to China, and his beef beat Tyson's. It was time to celebrate.

In fact, it was Davis' second night in a row at Spencer's. A large group of dignitaries from China were chewing on Davis' chops just twenty-four hours before, partly why my presence at the table was such a shock when our tomahawks came out. As the waiter set down each massive steak, plates searing hot, he came to me last. Confusion overtook him as he carefully looked at the plate in his hands and back at me and placed it in front of me. Then he asked, a little too concerned: "Little lady, are you going to be able to finish that?"

A few days before, when I had enough time to really process that I'd committed to touring a slaughterhouse in ninety-eight-degree heat and eating a steak house dinner afterward, I started to worry if I'd be a vegan by the time I was back in New York. But that moment cinched it for me.

"I plan on it," I responded. I should have winked.

Then I asked how big these steaks really were. Apparently, thirty-six ounces. I'd never had anything that looked like that tomahawk before. Whenever I'm reporting, I always accept whatever food my hosts offer me. I've smiled and popped digestive aides through extensive menu tastings over the years, from Arby's and Sonic to suppliers' selections of highly processed pizza cheeses. This time I was lucky to have a host in steaks, but I was still daunted.

None of my fretting mattered anyway. I tasted and devoured most of it within a few minutes. Polished it off easy. It was different from other corn-fed cuts I'd tried before, and I wondered out loud where the nuttier taste in the fat came from. Could it be a result of Greater Omaha's buyers selecting each steer individually from independent ranches instead of buying whole tracks from industrial-scale feedlots where subprime cattle can enter the mix?

Davis just smiled. He's worked every job at his family's slaughterhouse— from cattle buyer to line butcher—since summers during high school. He has lived the difference and fought to keep it going against the odds. A third-generation Nebraskan packer, Davis has been running the company since 1987, when revenues were $130 million and the company was shipping to a few states. After writing the company's software system and redesigning the slaughterhouse from scratch, Davis built Greater Omaha into a billion-dollar operation that exports to seventy countries and is now the fifth-largest beef packer in the industry overall. That adds up to more than 2 percent of total US production versus the more than 80 percent controlled by the top four producers: Tyson, JBS, Cargill, and National Beef.

I began to understand what that meant as I ate Davis' steak. I realized it would be difficult to expect *this* kind of quality from any other larger operation. It was already a feat that Davis had systematically manufactured this at scale. While Greater Omaha processes all three USDA grades of beef, it's known in the industry for its prime steaks, which has the highest amount of fat. About 10 percent of cattle earn that grade. The distinction used to be rarer: a decade ago, just 4 percent earned the grade, but cattle seem to be eating more corn-based feed to try to earn the top price.

In the face of industry-wide consolidation, Davis had grown his business tenfold while holding on to 100 percent equity and without taking on debt. I was impressed, or maybe I just had the meat sweats. None of my dinner mates ate their whole tomahawk, but they were amused watching me finish mine. I gnawed on the bone and even picked through the sides of mac and cheese, mashed potatoes, and creamed spinach piled on the table. I wish I were dainty. Toward the end of the meal, the metal clasp on my TJ Maxx wrap dress broke open. I caught it under the table before getting exposed and casually held it in place with one hand under my napkin until I put my jacket on to leave.

Omaha's Rise and Fall as the American Capital of Beef

The next day, Davis took me on a driving tour of beef industry history. Racing is an outlet for his slaughterhouse stress, and over the years Davis has built up a collection that includes a 1965 Lotus, a 1966 Alfa Romeo, and his trophy, a 1966 Ford GT40, the first American car to win Le Mans, raced by fearless driver Ken Miles before his fatal crash. But that day we drove the car he normally takes to work, a Mercedes-Benz S550 coupe. Accelerating onto L Street, we were just a few blocks from Omaha's historic ten-story Livestock Exchange Building, which decades before was surrounded by blocks and blocks of stockyards. Thousands of cattle a week would wait there to be sold and then killed. Because of the exchange, Davis' Greater Omaha Packing plant has operated in the neighborhood for a century.

"There used to be thirty-six packers here," Davis told me while driving around for a feature published in *Forbes*.

Pointing to a redbrick building on his right, he added, "That was one right over there."

The exchange became an out-of-use landmark, sometimes hosting weddings or catered events. Just four packers are left in Omaha, and, behind JBS, Davis' plant, still in view of the brown brick exchange building, is the largest remaining.

Davis is a testament to what has changed. Greater Omaha's history starts when its founder, Herman Cohen, Davis' grandfather, emigrated from Russia in 1905 at eleven years old—escaping pogroms and anti-Semitic discrimination. After serving in World War I, Cohen ended his tour with $100 in his pocket. In 1920 he moved to Omaha, keen on investing in beef. At the stockyards, Cohen picked a single steer a day, butchered it himself, and sold the beef, while a partner sold the hides. Their small operation on the exchange floor grew slowly to a few animals a week.

Davis' father, Pennie, joined the business in 1945, after marrying Cohen's youngest daughter, and soon became president as America doubled its beef consumption in the boom years following World War II. Families spent nearly one-fourth of their food budget on meat in 1950, according to the American Meat Institute. The company kept it simple, only cutting the meat down to hindquarters and forequarters sections. A distributor or butcher then purchased the meat and would break it down further so it was ready to cook at a restaurant or home.

Born in 1951, Davis' life spans the rise and decline of Omaha's beef market. When he was four years old, Omaha stole the country's top spot from Chicago as the largest beef-processing city. He grew up walking through the livestock auctions on the exchange floor and attended meetings with his father and other slaughterhouse owners. He worked in the processing plant through summer vacations in high school and college during the 1960s. Then he witnessed the industry collapse.

As the exchange became outdated, most of the big packinghouses left Omaha for feedlots in rural locations around the Midwest. The ones that remained in cities struggled to keep up—as the bigger rural slaughterhouses could bring costs down further while exerting local influence on ranchers. Within a few years, Omaha slaughterhouses shuttered, went bankrupt, or were acquired.

"Some of the plants in this town made the choice not to compete anymore. They wanted things to stay the way they were. You see that with other businesses all the time—they just want to make things the way they used to make them, and that does not work anymore. The market's not there anymore," Davis recalled. "When I was in my late teens and during college, I started to see that. What would happen is they were small family-owned businesses and whoever ran them, their family didn't care to participate in that business, and they would get shut out."

By the time Davis graduated from the University of Denver in 1973, Greater Omaha was among the last of a dying breed. "We were too small to have roles. Everybody did everything," Davis explained. At the time, Greater Omaha had forty employees and processed 232 steer a day. Davis watched early industry consolidation and decided to fight back, soon putting his degree in business and minor in computer science to work.

In 1980 he purchased his company's first computer—a Polymorphic (the brochure Davis pulls out of his filing cabinet boasts it can track receivables and project future sales)—for $5,870. The rest of the industry wasn't as far ahead, and there was little software on the market for a slaughterhouse producing "carcass beef." Recalls Davis: "We had a good business model back then, and I wasn't going to change my business to fit the software. The best thing for me to do was to either hire somebody to write the software, which at that time I didn't feel like we could afford, or write it myself."

As he started to write the code for the system that his company still runs on today, Davis focused first on building software that would make it easier to analyze data points, like how many pounds of meat were shipped and how many cattle had hit the target weight. For the first time, the company could predict the number of cattle purchased for the next week, how much each truckload cost the company to process, and how much they would make off the sale to a meat purveyor.

Davis took over the business when it slaughtered about 650 cattle a day. He soon made another major change, which saved the business. It had already been two decades since Iowa Beef Packers (known as IBP and later acquired by Tyson for $3.2 billion in 2001) drove the industry to keep up as the processor expanded rapidly with boxed beef. IBP started breaking down carcasses further into one kind of cut, like a loin or rib, and shipping them out in vacuum-sealed packages that were more manageable for a grocery store or restaurant distributor. Greater Omaha had yet to hop on the trend, but more cuts meant higher prices. Davis launched Greater Omaha's line in 1992. "Most of the industry followed along. Those that didn't are no longer in business," he said. In 1996, he expanded the plant just for its boxed-beef business, which nearly doubled production to 1,400 cattle a day.

The lines couldn't run fast enough. Meanwhile, across the industry, corn-finished cattle started growing quickly, pushed by the cheap economics of high-volume feedlots. Within three decades, the average weight of a steer nearly doubled—and it was becoming cumbersome to butcher the meat in such a tight space. "All of a sudden they didn't fit through the line," Davis recalls, and he decided in the 1990s to design a new Greater Omaha plant from scratch. He didn't hire an engineer because "we knew this better than anybody else." Instead, he and his executives spent a year identifying every issue on the floor and then designing the flow of the conveyor belts around those problems.

When the stainless-steel space in South Omaha opened in 2000, daily production rose 70 percent, to 2,400 cattle a day. Designed for ultimate flexibility, it became the first beef plant to incorporate a compartmentalized design that divides the process into seven areas with separate, computer-controlled air-handling systems. Those air conditioners force air that may contain contaminants away from the carcasses being processed, and the fans are why there's barely a whiff of smell in the plant itself. Davis also left as much space as possible unfilled, and when it first opened, he was struck by the idea that there was enough room to play soccer in the middle of the processing floor.

"We didn't know what was going in there. It hadn't even been invented yet, but we knew at some point in time, there's going to be a piece of equipment that we can use," he recalls. He also made sure the processing line—where workers stand side by side—was not attached to the outside wall, so that eventually building out would not stop production. That has led to four expansions of forty thousand square feet in the past seventeen years.

Davis' control of his plant stands out. While JBS has nine US plants and processes 200,000 cattle a week, Greater Omaha processes more than 14,000 a week, all under one roof. It even includes a sixty-five-thousand-square-foot robotic cold-storage warehouse that cost $40 million. There are no outside vendors or middlemen. And Davis says there are no plans to open another. He has toured two plants in recent years that were even designed after his, and he still didn't bite.

A fiercely independent survivor amid industry-wide consolidation,

Greater Omaha has become an attractive business. Davis says he fields inquiries nonstop from bigger companies that want to acquire his plant, financiers assessing private equity investments, or bankers looking for an IPO. The day after he started shipping to China, Davis received two calls. Davis has made a point of carefully charting his company's expansion. Despite being one of the oldest beef packers in the country, Greater Omaha has opted not to grow too big. It sells 700 million pounds of beef a year, a tiny slice of the 25 billion pounds processed in the United States annually.

He chooses not to sell to big retailers like Costco and Walmart. "The big chain stores?" Davis says, listing off grocers like Winn-Dixie and Raley's. "We don't have enough beef that if they run a sale, it would be too large of a percentage of our product."

While Greater Omaha is the biggest American beef seller to the European Union, Davis limits these exports, as well as any others, to under 20 percent of sales. "The big packers have to compete with us," he said.

Davis has set his sights on growing the business to around $1.5 billion, but he told me he worried about risking too much. "I'm very careful how I do that," Davis said. "We don't get overdependent on any market or any raw material or any customer."

But as Davis adds occasional product lines, there's a delicate balance between butchering further and making a higher margin on each cut while taking away business from one of their long-standing customers. For example, Greater Omaha has historically sold beef trimmings to butchers and distributors that would grind the meat further into burgers. That's how much of Greater Omaha's beef sent to New Jersey–based butcher-distributor Pat LaFrieda ends up as burgers for chains like Five Guys. But in 2016, Greater Omaha invested $12 million to grind its own beef with a production line making 100,000 pounds a day. "I'm not going to ever process all the subprimal cuts and whole-muscle cuts. I'm never going to do that all," Davis told me. "I would never take that away from my customers."

Could Greater Omaha's Size Be the Key for the Meat Industry?

Antitrust lawyer Peter Carstensen has suggested that plants would still get benefits of operational efficiencies if they commanded 3 to 5 percent of total beef industry production. If the country's packers reorganized based on that limit, each meat sector would have seven to ten total firms with three plants each. That norm would create a stronger environment for specialization and diversity of sourcing, Carstensen explains. Davis' Greater Omaha, at about 2.5 percent for one plant, is a similar proxy, which shows that the beef industry could be broken up in a way that still might not change efficiency or prices much.

I asked Davis what he thought about plant size, because I was toying with the idea of what the meat industry would look like if there weren't any plants bigger than Greater Omaha. Davis replied that he doesn't think it's possible for a beef plant to run effectively while processing fewer than two thousand cattle a day: "Because they are small, it's hard to make some of these investments. You have to be of a certain size to afford a half-a-million-dollar hot-water evisceration wash. You can afford it if you're doing two or three thousand a day, but if you're doing five hundred head a day or less, I don't know how they afford it, because that's only one item."

Many industry pioneers think an operation like Greater Omaha's is ideal not only for worker safety, due to how much can be reinvested in better machinery, but also for the animals and potential for waste. Legendary California grass-fed beef rancher Bill Niman says Greater Omaha understands that, which is why Niman has used Greater Omaha's slaughterhouse for years. Niman says he's concerned by the animal welfare standards at some of the smaller state-inspected or more regional slaughterhouses, and that bigger operations make better use of the whole animal because of their global distribution network. Certain cuts like tripe have more popularity abroad. Given those concerns, Niman has decided that it's just as smart for producers in a remote region to pool their resources to share transportation to a better, larger plant, like Greater Omaha, rather than wait for a spot at an overcommitted state plant. "These animals could be properly transported, professionally, to those kill plants," Niman explains, "who will, one day a week, process as a more custom matter."

More slaughterhouse capacity in the beef industry is needed. Some regional slaughterhouses have long wait lists to secure an open time slot. Industrial operations have contracts set years in advance, which makes adding capacity a long-term problem. Meat-packers have been hesitant to add more, because the shifting market dynamics would bring prices down and reduce potential profits.

Many industry experts have indicated that the best way to expand slaughter capacity in the beef industry is through technology that increases plant efficiency. An example would be automation that allows for a smaller workforce to take on a new Saturday shift. The other, harder way is through new construction of a small or medium-size plant that can differentiate itself.

Not the Only Way

But there are so many other ways to add capacity to slaughter operations—and sometimes they come with sovereignty. Food has always played a critical role in the Osage Nation. At feasts and celebrations, there's usually a brown paper bag under a guest's seat. Before leaving, the guests often fill up the bag with fruit and fry bread. It's a tradition that started in the earliest days of being forced onto a reservation in Oklahoma, when distant tribe members would travel for days to meet up.

Oklahoma is the heart of cattle country, producing some five million cattle across stolen lands. But a few years ago, the Osage Nation purchased a more than forty-thousand-acre ranch. They rematriated the land with a bison herd. It rekindled a journey for the Nation that became even more crucial as slaughterhouses backed up and wait lists grew throughout 2020, impacting Osage Nation cattlemen who ranch for a living. As supply shortages made getting some items in their area even more difficult, the Nation decided it would take its food supply out of the industrial system. With an $8 million check from the CARES Act, the Osage Nation built a small beef and bison slaughterhouse from scratch. As James Weigant, head of the Nation's COVID-19 task force, told me in early 2021 as the plant was opening: "As a Nation, we saw the pieces of the supply chain. But if we could just complete the chain, we could have our own supply chain insulated from exterior factors."

The facility can process fifteen to twenty livestock a day. The plant is a cornerstone of the Osage Nation's food sovereignty. It contributes greatly to the tribe's access to traditional and otherwise whole foods, as most of the surrounding area is a food apartheid—meaning there's little access to fresh fruits and vegetables.

The Osage Nation's plant is small, but it allows independence from industrial supply chains for the Nation's community. It is also a highly replicable concept, made from stainless steel and cement. Says Chris Roper, a consultant based in Oklahoma who has set up plants for several Indigenous groups, including the Osage Nation and the Quapaw Nation: "Small plants can be put up economically and can take care of communities. It's been proven, it can be done, and it needs to happen more often so we can take care of these smaller areas."

The Osage Nation's plant is nineteen thousand square feet. The inside is unlike most slaughterhouses—it's not just about what is killed within. It's also about what can be cooked from the sacrifice: when the plant opened in the beginning of 2021, it was equipped with a smoker to make jerky and sausages. The plant also gives the nation something else that's critical: the chance to control the full spectrum of ingredients and additives going into their food, and the ability to ban preservatives and other chemicals that it believes are unnatural (like chemical washes to clean meat and red dyes added to keep meat looking fresh longer).

It's far from the only path forward. There are few examples today of well-run and successful cooperatives, but they do exist. One that supplies Whole Foods is Country Natural Beef in Oregon. Co-ops tend to come with a stigma because most experiments have been utter disappointments, destroyed by competing interests, financial mismanagement, and disorganization. A recent example is the lamb plant in Greeley, Colorado, JBS's acquisition of which in 2020, with the intention of turning it into a beef plant, sparked antitrust concerns. It was really a repurchase: JBS sold it off to a cooperative years before. But the co-op producers couldn't turn the plant around during their time at the helm. C. Robert Taylor, formerly a professor at Auburn University, says the problem with the cooperative structure historically comes from open membership. But the same principles of multiple owners pooling resources can still come together, he explains. The trick is to incorporate the business as a limited liability company, or LLC, so that it provides more legal flexibility.

Another small-scale example, which animal rights advocate Temple Grandin has even endorsed, is mobile slaughterhouses fashioned out of trailers. Quick and cheap. The options get more expensive from there. Regional diversity is limited in meat production because the current industry is overwhelmingly set up so that plants are located close to corn-growing areas and feedlots for economic viability. But if feedlots dispersed, or, better, if there was less of a reliance on corn and feedlots, regional slaughter could flourish a bit easier. Getting there would be a major challenge—but not an impossible one.

One example is the operations of Missouri Prime Beef Packers. It's a joint venture between a cattle-breeding, feedlot, and processing company called NextGen Cattle and cattleman Stacy Davies. Davies' partners sold a tech start-up and reinvested their proceeds in feedlots. Their NextGen Cattle feeding operation is a key cattle supplier for all the labels Missouri Beef wants to market thanks to its two feedlots in Kansas. But their operation, and their partnership with Davies, a respected grass-fed rancher in his own right, is rare. Even though they repurposed an old pork plant, it still took luck, their deep pockets, several years, and $75 million invested in the project. A lot can go wrong when building infrastructure. But Next-Gen's operation pulled it off. The slaughterhouse opened in March 2021 and soon started killing five hundred cattle a day, including a fair amount of grass-fed.

"There are so many ranchers producing some wonderful animals without a plant to get those animals harvested. I see this plant as an opportunity to make a lot of dreams come true for a lot of people," Davies said. "It's big enough to have our costs low enough, but we can have the best packaging equipment. But it's also small enough to really allow some niche products to market and we can specialize."

Domestic customers crave grass-fed, especially as carnivore-friendly diets like paleo, keto, and Whole30 have been popularized. That demand has driven up the value of offal like liver, heart, and tongue—which is fascinating, considering it's in these bits—in addition to parts like the hide, bones, and blood, where slaughterhouses have historically made their profits. Big operations like Tyson or Cargill have these unit economics down to a science, and small farmers have a hard time winning. But operations like NextGen can use the same industry tricks to make a premium and build a market for grass-fed in the United States. Those who adhere to the paleo diet eat based on a model of humans' cavemen ancestors, who likely ate organ meat. Dedicated followers stipulate that meat must come from grass-fed animals, due to high amounts of vitamins, minerals, and fatty acids. These consumers understand that meat is less nutritious when sourced from animals that ate grain in confinement. NextGen's plant has top-of-the-line equipment to capture every piece of offal available, including tripe, tendons, feet, and bones from marrow to neck. "In the United States and worldwide, demand for those items, because of the health benefits, has increased the value of the heart, the liver, the kidneys, sweetbreads. Oxtail is one of the most valuable items in an animal now," says Davies. "The opportunity for the grass-fed program off all of this, there's a premium."

SECTION II

CHALLENGING THE INDUSTRIAL MEAT STATUS QUO

CHAPTER 8

How Climate Change Will
Upend Industrial Meat

The stench of a large hog producer hits before the operation comes into view. The hogs raised there exist in confinement—and their conditions can be brutal. Industrial hog farms can have hundreds or thousands of hogs, which are smarter than dogs or cats, stuck in one area. Breeding mothers are often locked in small metal cages and forced to lie down on one side because the cages are that tight. Sometimes they don't move onto the other side for months. The main objective is rapid reproducing. It creates a lot of hogs quickly and, by extension, a lot of manure. The growing herd's excess waste falls through slats in the floor and gets flushed into massive waste lagoons, where anaerobic bacteria work through the slurry. These lagoons—often the size of multiple football fields—spread fumes and adulterants that seep into the soil. Lagoons release significant amounts of ammonia, hydrogen sulfide, and other pollutants into the atmosphere, degrading local air quality while also contributing to global warming. Lagoons shed greenhouse gases, including methane, carbon dioxide, and nitrous oxide. The expansion of these lagoons in recent decades has driven an increase in greenhouse gas emissions from industrial hog production.

The toxic sludge has been known to kill people who fall in. In August 1992, a twenty-seven-year-old hog farm worker in Minnesota went into a manure lagoon to switch out a clogged pump and was poisoned by hydrogen sulfide. Then a forty-six-year-old co-owner of the multi-farm complex, which harvested ten thousand hogs annually, died during a rescue attempt. A similar story came up in Virginia in 2007 when four family members and a farmworker died, as well as in 2015 when two different father-son pairs, in Iowa and Wisconsin, died from noxious fumes while trying to perform maintenance.

Waste might fester in lagoons for years. Eventually the lagoons are drained out, only to be refilled. The polluted mixture left over is unloaded into rivers and streams, processed into biogas or aerosolized, and sprayed as manure on fields. Studies have shown that the spray is linked to asthma, upper-respiratory issues, low birth weight, anemia, high blood pressure elevation, and more among neighboring communities such as in counties like Duplin and Sampson in North Carolina, which tend to be predominantly Black, Latinx, and Indigenous. Many have noted that these impacts contribute to growing environmental injustice concerns. According to a 2018 study from Duke University scientists published in the *North Carolina Medical Journal*, death rates of all studied conditions—infant mortality, anemia, kidney disease, septicemia, and tuberculosis—were higher in communities located near large hog operations.

Industrial farms owned by or contracted for Smithfield, the largest hog producer in the United States, include some of the largest manure lagoons in America. Some of Smithfield's neighbors have suffered. In addition to headaches and nausea, some residents near Smithfield farms or contractors in North Carolina claim they have experienced elevated blood pressure and asthma symptoms. About five hundred mostly Black residents filed more than a dozen lawsuits in 2014 to collect damages and call out Smithfield as a private nuisance. The lawsuits allege they couldn't garden, host barbecues, or hang laundry outside. Juries in 2018 and 2019 awarded the neighbors about $550 million overall. Smithfield has denied all wrongdoing. After North Carolina passed a law that capped awards from punitive damages, the US District Court in Raleigh cut back the neighbors' award to $98 million.[*]

In 2019, Duplin County, North Carolina, resident Elsie Herring testified in front of the House Committee of Energy and Commerce that health risks and harm from a nearby manure lagoon have upended life on land that has been in her family for three generations, after her grandfather was born a slave on the property and later purchased it outright.

"The land where I live is precious to me and my family. We have lived

---

[*] The case was ultimately settled in 2020.

there since we were enslaved there," Herring, who died in 2021, told representatives in 2019. "I know that there's a better way to raise livestock and dispose of the waste than simply digging a hole in the ground and shooting it into the air. Those of us living near these facilities need the industry to adopt better waste controls. The industry cannot be allowed to continue to dump toxic material into our air and water."

The Southern Environmental Law Center sued the EPA over permits granted to Smithfield-owned hog operations on behalf of the Duplin County branch of the NAACP in 2021, and the EPA launched a formal investigation into allegations of environmental injustice in January 2022. Waste lagoons are the ugly side of the bacon industry, and a key example of how meat production can harm not just air but also water and soil. During crisis, those harms can multiply. When hurricanes hit hog-filled eastern North Carolina, where the hog industry creates about ten billion gallons of manure annually, lagoons flood and the waste spreads as far as the water. In 1999, Hurricane Floyd caused nearly fifty lagoons to leak, and the untreated waste created algae blooms and massive fish die-offs. The consequences were still felt more than a decade and a half later, in 2015, when a group of researchers representing Johns Hopkins and the University of North Carolina, Chapel Hill, tested for high concentrations of fecal bacteria upstream and downstream from industrial hog operations.

All this compounds with each storm. After Hurricane Florence in 2018, at least 59 lagoons impacted the surrounding environment, either from structural damage, discharges, or getting inundated with surface water from the hurricane. Lots of antibiotics stew in those lagoons, too, which means as the antibiotic-laced waste spreads, more water and soil become contaminated. Nearby rivers and streams have tested for high concentrations of E. coli or other antibiotic-resistant bacteria, while the soil sucks up all the chemicals, antibiotics, and other adulterants. Heavy metal buildup in soils hurts good bacteria in the soils while decreasing crop productivity.

As Elsie Herring testified to Congress: "We are on the front lines of climate change. The same lagoon and sprayfield system that endangers us on a daily basis becomes even more dangerous in the face of superstorms."

Big Meat's Threatened Resources

Until 2020, the meat industry largely avoided addressing its environmental impact. According to a 2020 report by the nearly $50 trillion investor network FAIRR, or Farm Animal Investment Risk and Return, only two—Tyson and Marfrig—in forty-three of the world's largest meat companies had undertaken and published results from a climate "scenario analysis." That's a paltry rate of just 5 percent of the meat industry's top companies, which is particularly small when considering, for comparison, that the oil, gas, mining, and utilities industries had done similar studies at a rate of 23 percent. Since then, many companies in the meat industry have publicly committed to change their ways by a certain point, years away in the future.

There are few ways for individual consumers to hold corporations accountable to their commitments while conglomerates are trying to blindly pilot-test their way into solutions. These goals still largely avoid lasting questions around environmental justice, biodiversity, and industrial crop production, which use synthetics that end up in waterways and lead to soil erosion. As climate change worsens, those impacts will worsen, and attempts at adapting will get even harder.

Outsize Emissions and Demands for Cleaner Air

Corporate commitments focus on cutting back on greenhouse gases. Globally, 14.5 percent of annual greenhouse gas emissions come from livestock production, and some 65 percent of that is due to industrially raised cattle. That trend holds up when looking at the United States. A 2019 study published in *Agricultural Systems* pegged the total footprint of beef production at 3.7 percent of total US emissions. Emissions from agriculture account for 10 percent of America's annual total, compared to transportation emitting 29 percent or 23 percent coming from burning fossil fuels like coal or natural gas for energy. While agriculture commands a fraction of the total, failing to reduce output from agriculture will prevent global goals from being met.

Air pollution from greenhouse gases comes from all ends of the meat supply chain: input manufacturing, feed production, and livestock production, to name a few. Fertilizer contributes roughly half of all US agricultural production emissions, and the bulk of the fertilizer used goes to row crops farmed for livestock feed. Nitrous oxide, a by-product of one of the most common fertilizers, is emitted as a potent greenhouse gas during manufacturing and application. Then there are the emissions from holding so many animals together in confinement, and the waste lagoons that emit superpotent greenhouse gases.

Packing livestock in while relying on cheap and low-grade feed has even increased the rate of emissions that come from livestock digestion—otherwise known as enteric fermentation, or burps—over the past three decades. Like waste lagoons, enteric fermentation creates a lot of methane, which traps more heat and heats the earth even faster. In 2021, the United Nations called curbing methane "the strongest lever we have to slow climate change over the next 25 years." But the Environmental Protection Agency has failed to stymie the growth of methane from confined livestock operations: since 1990, overall methane emissions in the United States have decreased, but methane from agricultural sources has jumped 16 percent as regulators have turned away from the problem. In April 2021, an alliance of twenty-five environmental and rural advocacy groups, representing more than 2.4 million members, petitioned the federal government to require concentrated hog production to receive a higher level of monitoring and increase regulations around methane.

The White House Office of Domestic Climate Policy released an action plan in November 2021 on how to cut methane emissions, which fell short of imposing limits on agriculture, even though agriculture is the single-largest contributor to methane. The plan focuses on rewards for reducing methane and incentives for transforming it into biogas, in which large balloons called digesters are installed around the lagoons to capture methane. The energy source is controversial. A petition with California's Air Resources Board has called into question the possibility that the industry could take advantage of the innovation as a carbon offset while encouraging more methane production, and asked that biogas be removed from any incentive-based credit program due to the civil rights concerns. Meanwhile, Smithfield's joint venture has poured about $500 million into producing biogas in North Carolina, Missouri, and Utah.

Researchers from Colorado State University found biogas production creates nearly four times more nitrogen than if the lagoon is open. Critics, meanwhile, suggest turning waste sludge from lagoons into biogas only

creates a potential market for an externality, meaning a side effect of industrial production, without addressing the fundamental reason the externality
exists in the first place. Expectations of shareholder returns drive incentives
that favor overproduction.

Focusing solely on greenhouse gas emissions to decrease the amount of
methane released into the atmosphere eclipses other fundamental problems
with industrial meat production, according to climate and environmental
justice advocates.

According to animal behaviorist and author Fred Provenza, who dis-
cusses how what animals eat really matters in his 2018 book *Nourishment*,
climate change is expected to make food even less nutritious. He writes, "As
atmospheric carbon dioxide increases, nitrogen (protein) concentrations
decline in a wide range of plant species. Lower levels of protein have been
observed in leaves, stems, roots, tubers, seeds, and grains and are correlated
with negative effects on human nutrition worldwide. Elevated CO_2 is also
associated with decreases in zinc and iron in grasses and legumes." In the
decades ahead, Provenza claims, farmers and food producers will have a
harder time accessing feed, and there are reasonable expectations that feed
prices will soar as harsher conditions, unpredictable storms, and degraded
land make farming harder. Water costs will add to expenses. Row crops like
corn or soy grown for feed need water to grow, as do the actual livestock.
But industrial production has polluted waterways for generations.

Industrial meat relies on each of these resources—rooted in healthy
water and soil—which won't be easily accessible in a changing climate.
Regulators and policymakers still have time to make crucial changes. So
far, attempts at reform have been too focused on air while largely ignoring
access to water and land.

Drought, Rancid Rivers, and Water Scarcity

Climate change compromises access to water, while runoff from agriculture
has already polluted too much of the nation's freshwater supply. There's
less snow expected in the West and aquifers drying out in the Great Plains.
Drought will be more common. Yet growing the crops for the animal feed
and then the actual livestock requires a lot of water, and livestock and crops
are expected to be thirstier if temperatures are hotter.

If a waterway is close to part of the meat production supply chain—from the farms that grow row crops turned into feed to the actual slaughterhouses—chances are it's either at risk or already tainted. Pollution from industrial runoff has hit dangerous heights across much of America's farmland. It doesn't matter if it's a tiny tributary or the Mississippi River, which collects water from the entire Midwest, or a tiny tributary: about 20 percent of nitrogen fertilizer is usually lost through surface runoff or leaching into groundwater. That pollution stimulates algae growth and creates low-oxygen dead zones that kill off aquatic life while transforming waterways into public health hazards. Some pollution remains close to areas of intense production. Other adulterants flow through the system, making their way down the Mississippi River and into the Gulf of Mexico, where the annual dead zone in 2021 was more than six thousand square miles—more than the size of the state of Connecticut.

The concentrated animal feedlot operations, or CAFOs, and the slaughterhouses where the livestock meet production lines create huge amounts of waste that need to be treated and deposited. Dirt, biological fluids, and blood flow from the killing floor into the sewer. Water is used to rinse carcasses, remove hair and feathers, and sanitize processing equipment. Slaughterhouses also use ammonia, nitrogen, and phosphorus, which end up in a plant's wastewater tanks alongside grease, fecal bacteria, and pathogens. High concentrations of these pollutants damage waterways, even often when they are processed by municipal wastewater treatment plants or a slaughterhouse's own program. Yet, thanks to lax regulations, citations are rare. The waste still gets dumped into a lot of public waterways.

Take JBS's pork plant in Beardstown, Illinois, which kills almost twenty thousand animals a day. A 2018 study ranking the country's top water polluters have named this 430,000-square-foot plant, surrounded by waste lagoons, as among the country's worst. On an average day in 2017, the plant was responsible for more than 1,800 pounds of nitrogen landing in a tributary that leads into the Illinois River. That's the equivalent amount handled by a sewage system for a small city with a population of nearly eighty thousand.*

---

* JBS says its Beardstown pork plant operates "well within its permitting requirements" and has invested in upgrades since acquiring the plant in 2015.

For years, environmental advocates have raised concerns over the country's largest meat suppliers' compliance with Clean Water Act regulations. In 2003 Tyson paid $7.5 million over Clean Water Act violation claims and in 2018 Tyson was sentenced in federal court to pay a $2 million criminal fine, and $500,000 of direct remedy harm "caused when it violated the Clean Water Act . . . that led to a major fish kill event." JBS, as another example, in 2011 agreed to pay $1.3 million to the federal government and state of Nebraska to settle alleged violations of the federal Clean Water Act at a beef plant in the state.*

The Environmental Protection Agency last updated its baseline slaughterhouse regulations in 2004. About two decades later, those limits on how to treat wastewater and how much can be dumped into waterways daily are woefully inadequate, according to environmental lawyers. In 2021 the agency said it would address concerns, but formal changes have not yet been made.† For example, flooding streams and lakes with waste that has close to three times the concentration of nitrogen found in raw household sewage remains legal. Environmental activist organizations have challenged the efficacy of the Clean Water Act in court. A patchwork of site-specific permits, approved on an individual basis, regulate plants. That creates a lot of leeway when it comes to permitting at the state level, deepening holes in the nation's safety net. The Clean Water Act, meanwhile, relies on states' further adopting standards. Studies have shown that local governments and policymakers in places like Iowa, the leading state contributing pollution to the dead zone in the Gulf, have largely ignored disastrous levels of water pollution for years.

Communities surrounding industrial meat production face serious health concerns due to groundwater contamination. In a 2020 study focusing on the impact of a CAFO in Iowa, of fifty-four thousand private wells tested, 40 percent were contaminated with coliform bacteria. Additionally, twelve thousand household wells tested positive for elevated levels of nitrates, at a level linked to an increased risk of cancer. These results highlight the fact that industrial production disproportionately affects predominantly Black, Indigenous, and Latinx communities. Additional treatment can be expen-

* Tyson says it is actively working to "limit our impact on the environment."
† The Supreme Court decided to take on a challenge to the Clean Water Act in 2022.

sive for local governments to take on, and the investments end up creating higher bills for taxpayers. Comprehensive cleanup and pollution mitigation plans are rare.

Accessing Healthy Land

Livestock requires a lot of resources to be turned into meat, whether it's grass-fed or corn-fed. That's why, in terms of human calories produced, industrial meat is highly inefficient. Just 3 percent of the feed consumed by beef cattle is converted into calories consumed by humans. Pork retains 9 percent, while chicken stands at 13 percent.

Government subsidies have propped up environmentally harmful farming practices like relying on synthetics and chemicals to boost production. Since 1995, the USDA has doled out more than $400 billion in subsidies, mainly to commodity row crop farmers and dairy producers, in the form of crop insurance, price supports, and conservation and disaster payments. Meat has been kept cheap through subsidies, especially subsidies that have impacted meat production's top expense: the grain used to pack weight onto livestock quickly. Subsidies supporting meat and dairy production in the United States are estimated at $38 billion annually. Yet there is no environmental or social benefits compliance requirement to receive subsidized money.

Subsidies have pushed monoculture into the mainstream. But monoculture sprayed into submission with harsh chemicals drives the cheap ingredients in livestock feed. Monoculture degrades soil, and, with biodiversity lacking, soils lose absorption and nutrients. Yet, a third of America's corn crop annually—about five million bushels—are the carbohydrate-laden calories that fatten up livestock. The protein in animal feed comes from soybeans. Livestock production is responsible for a whopping 70 percent of the annual US soy crop.

Industrial production of corn and soy strips American soils of nutrients, thanks to artificial fertilizers and other chemicals. Like meatpacking, the fertilizer industry is dominated by a handful of corporations, which the Department of Justice has been asked to investigate for antitrust concerns. The fertilizer industry's control of industrial crop farming is powerful. The vast majority of US farms rely on synthetics. Organic acres account for less than 1 percent of total US cropland. Few suppliers control the entire market.

Just two companies, Nutrien Limited and the Mosaic Company, supply the entirety of North America with potash, the commodity potassium-based fertilizer, while just four firms control more than 75 percent of production of all nitrogen-based fertilizer.

According to a landmark study on soil erosion published in 2017 in *Nature Communications*, biodiversity has receded across America's Great Plains to underwrite this catastrophic shift toward feed-fueled animal agriculture. We are losing precious biodiversity and degrading soil, which will only escalate the climate crisis. Human activity is the primary cause of accelerated soil erosion, which threatens "nutrient and carbon cycling, land productivity and in turn, worldwide socio-economic conditions."

"Impacts can be severe, not only through land degradation and fertility loss, but through a conspicuous number of off-site effects (e.g., sedimentation, siltation and eutrophication of waterways or enhanced flooding). The impact on climate through erosion-induced changes in soil carbon cycling also remains poorly quantified, as erosion can both increase or decrease CO_2 emissions through enhanced mineralization and sediment burial," the study reads. "Feeding Earth's growing population with increasing dietary preferences towards livestock products is undoubtedly enhancing the pressure on fertile soils thus exacerbating the erosion problem. Sustainable governance of soil has therefore become a topic of fundamental importance."

Soil degradation is a central threat to human health. Agriculture already commands too much land. But industrial agriculture is pushing forward and ignoring the consequences as America's soils are getting worse. Available farmland is decreasing. Between 2001 and 2016, more than eleven million acres of farmland were lost to other development. Moreover, the United States loses nearly one billion metric tons of soil every year through erosion. On top of that, decades of synthetics and other pollution have stressed soils across the country to their tipping point. Roughly a third of America's Corn Belt is degraded, according to a 2021 study.

Reframing How Much Production Is Really Needed

There's an impending food crisis. Corporations claim the industrial supply chain must produce more food, with fewer resources, by 2050. But that's true only if gross waste continues across the global supply chain. If a third of food wasn't wasted each year in the first place, ten billion people could already be sustained. The amount of food wasted each year is equivalent to more than double the number of people hungry around the world. Estimates suggest two billion people could be fed.

Yet meat is a large share of what ends up rotting in the trash. One study found that forty-one pounds of meat, poultry, and fish were wasted per capita in America in 2010. That is a lot of environmental resources to use for production of food that is not consumed.

Prioritizing Profits and Increasing Demand

The pressure to secure constant returns and growth has pushed meat-packers to expand unnecessarily and unsustainably. Take the case of the Chinese company WH Group, formerly Shuanghui Group, which has owned Virginia-based hog producer Smithfield since 2013. Its strategy to secure solid financial performance since then has hinged on increasing demand in China for American-style breakfast meats.

According to Wenxin Fan of the *Wall Street Journal* and analysts I've interviewed, WH Group's billionaire chairman, Wan Long, is attempting to underwrite a cultural shift in Chinese diets. His Hong Kong–headquartered meat conglomerate acquired the iconic American ham maker Smithfield in 2013 for $4.7 billion. With a valuation including debt of $7.1 billion, the deal was the largest acquisition of a US company by a Chinese business at the time, and Wan used the momentum to take his company public the next year on the Hong Kong stock exchange. But after rolling up the Smithfield deal with another, the acquisition of California's largest pork processor in 2017, Wan needed to make good on his big American investments with a hefty return to show for it.

That helped push Smithfield to export meat at record levels. A scourge of African swine fever then decimated China's domestic hog herd. Smithfield's total exports rose 44 percent in 2020, boosted by key months during some of the worst exposure rates of the pandemic, according to export-import data firm Panjiva.* For the first five months of 2020, Smithfield's monthly exports were at all-time highs—nearly 100,000 tons of pork each month,

---

* All exports sent through ports.

compared to 60,000 tons shipped each from JBS USA and Tyson. Smithfield exported more than 877,000 tons of meat in 2020. JBS shipped more than 760,000 tons, while Tyson shipped 640,000 tons. The rising exports exemplify a startling trend: export markets have helped meat-packers profit. US exports of meat remained consistently below 5 percent of total production from 1960 through the 1990s. But by 2017, more than 10 percent of total US beef production, 15 percent of poultry, and 20 percent of pork was exported—rather than sold through US markets, which would have lowered US meat prices.

The exports are even more controversial given the environmental ramifications. According to analysts I've spoken to, Wan's strategy of exporting popular American-style pork products appears to be completely out of sync with global environmental goals and consumer demand. Based on the United Nations' business-as-usual climate scenario, by 2050 China is expected to have the most meat consumption growth of any country. Yet WH Group appears to be building a market that does not yet exist.

Wan joined the original meat-processing firm, then a state-owned entity, in 1968 and over the next five decades turned it into the meat conglomerate known as WH Group. The success has rewarded him handsomely. He remains one of the largest individual shareholders, with 16 percent of stock. In 2019, his annual salary of $2 million was augmented with stock options worth $150 million.

But that payment and others have been called into question by Wan's eldest son, Wan Hongjian, who is the conglomerate's disgraced former heir apparent and previous board deputy chairman. In 2021, Wan Hongjian, then fifty-three, disagreed with his father over whether the business should sell more American-style breakfast pork to Chinese consumers. He thought WH Group overpaid for Smithfield and that WH Group must course-correct its strategy by importing less from the United States and selling cuts that Chinese meat eaters are already used to, like pork knuckles, braised pig cheeks, and glazed pork belly. As he told the *Wall Street Journal*, "There should be many views and ideas about Chinese and Western flavors."

The disagreement boiled over into a blowup between Wan Hongjian and his father in June 2021. During the incident, according to the *Wall Street Journal*, Wan Hongjian punched a door with his fist, hit his head against a glass closet, and then was pinned to the floor after being tackled by a bodyguard. WH Group dismissed Wan Hongjian soon after and replaced him with his younger brother, which prompted Wan Hongjian to cut deeper. In August 2021 he alleged Wan Long has used WH Group to profit personally while excessively trading on foreign exchange rate speculation and evading taxes. WH Group has denied the claims, yet the aftermath has tainted the legacy of the Smithfield acquisition. The mess also calls into question the multiple roles that a US meatpacking acquisition can play in the broader scheme of a billionaire's personal finances.

It remains to be seen whether the Chinese breakfast table will welcome bacon and American-style breakfast sausage as a staple. But a massive marketing budget by a billionaire may ultimately change the way the Chinese eat. As climate change intensifies, the question of rising demand and the pressure to meet it continues to echo. Is there enough actual demand to justify the depletion of resources from air, water, and soil to meet manufactured demand?

CHAPTER 9

The Threat of Antibiotic Resistance

Superbugs like E. coli, MRSA, and others resistant to antibiotics can colonize our bodies and lie dormant and undetected for years.

Some superbugs activate immediately or within days. Others may never. Some activate only decades later, often ignited by another opportunistic bit of inflammation. The superbug remains undetected until maybe Patient X is in the hospital with cancer or pneumonia, only to have a superbug she caught while working a meatpacking job decades before, all of a sudden, fire itself up. Then the infection runs rampant, and, without drugs to treat the infection, surprisingly quickly, Patient X may die.

Modern advances in molecular biology have allowed for an emerging field of study to retrace the evolution of antibiotic-resistant bacteria, and from those labs have emerged some of the strongest calls to reform meat production. Take the work of Lance Price, one of the leading experts on antibiotic resistance. He has been at the forefront of tracing the epidemiology of antibiotic-resistant strains from livestock production for two decades. His scientific work has been coupled with pushing policymakers to curb the use of unnecessary antibiotics in meat production because of the inequities he had witnessed. "Workers can get exposed, become colonized, and succumb to disease much later down the road," explained Price, an environmental and occupational health professor at George Washington University's public health school. "There are these ramifications, and the workers are on the front line."

Price does a lot of research in Denmark, because the country has pioneered antibiotic-free livestock raising at scale and the government tracks the data necessary to analyze how its workers are faring compared to the broader population. A study there Price worked on, published in 2015, found nearly 70 percent of all cases of resistant staph infection came from workers exposed to livestock as farmers or slaughterhouse workers. Danes with no livestock contact who still got sick from the strain of MRSA lived in areas with a lot of livestock production. It's hard to get access to enough data in the United States, or a funder to help with the costs of the study. Price has done one US-based study, shortly after he graduated with a doctorate from Johns Hopkins University in 2007. The study tracked chicken workers near the Delmarva Peninsula. Results showed those workers were thirty-two times more likely to be carrying a resistant strain of E. coli than their non-meatpacking working peers.

Price has seen antibiotic use persist. When he or his colleagues have tried to do more current research in the United States, they have hit roadblocks. "It's pretty disturbing, because every time my colleagues have tried to study workers and infections in the US, they get shut down," Price told me. "When you have big, powerful individual players who are not necessarily good stewards of antibiotics, they can drive a lot of resistance in the food supply."

The US meatpacking industry employs about five hundred thousand people, and then there are farmers, veterinarians, and many others with exposure from raising the livestock. It's unlikely even a fraction know the true extent of the risks of antibiotic resistance in their workplaces. Antibiotic use, and the drug resistance of diseases commonly treated with antibiotics, are on the rise. Antibiotic-resistant superbugs pose one of the biggest public health threats of our time. The next one could create a home inside an industrialized feedlot, according to the CDC as well as the United Nations, which have warned the silent threat of a superbug is lurking, and might even start the next pandemic.

The World's Greatest Public Health Threat

Antibiotic resistance will be responsible for as many as ten million deaths annually by 2050, according to United Nations estimates. As of May 2022, COVID-19's global death toll topped six million over two years. A study of deaths across 204 countries published in the *Lancet* in January 2022 suggests that antibiotic-resistant bacteria are already a leading cause of death globally. Annually in the United States, nearly three million people contract an antibiotic-resistant disease, according to the CDC, and at least thirty-five thousand die from superbugs that antibiotics can't cure. A 2018 study by the Washington University School of Medicine suggests that's a low estimate, and the death toll due to drug-resistant superbugs could be as high as 160,000 a year, which would make antibiotic resistance the fourth-leading cause of death in the United States. Compare that figure with the nation's ninth- and tenth-leading causes of death—flu and pneumonia—which each kill more than fifty thousand Americans a year.

A group of five Harvard researchers with a mix of public health, infectious disease, and pediatric medicine expertise, led by Derek MacFadden and Sarah McGough, first found in 2018 that an increase in temperature of 10°C was associated with increases in antibiotic resistance of common pathogens E. coli, *Klebsiella pneumoniae* (which can cause pneumonia, bloodstream infections, meningitis, and urinary tract infections), and *Staphylococcus aureus* (which can cause skin infections, pneumonia, heart valve infections, and bone infections). The study, published in *Nature Climate Change*, is based on clinical tests in forty-one states from 2013 to 2015 and suggests the projected figures for the burden of antibiotic resistance is significantly underestimated. A second study, led by McGough and four other researchers and published in November 2020, analyzed data from one of the world's most comprehensive antibiotic-resistance databases, with four million isolates from twenty-eight European countries between 2000 and 2016. It found evidence of long-term effects of temperature on antibiotic-resistance rate increases. "Antibiotic resistance poses one of the world's greatest public health threats today, with the potential to render many existing classes of antibiotics ineffective in the near future," reads the second study, "however, the impact of climate change on the distribution of antimicrobial resistance has been relatively ignored."

Antibiotics are routinely used by industrial meat producers to help animals gain weight quicker—which means more profit for a farmer—and overuse of antibiotics helps farmers cram more hogs in closer together. The alternatives to overuse are usually simple fixes like access to outdoor air, the ability to roam, or changing out water more frequently. But those practices come at the cost of more resources and effort, which most operations are unwilling to do for free.

Antibiotics help livestock reach slaughter weight faster, in part, because they suppress the growth of gut bacteria that compete for nutrients. When an animal ingests antibiotics, the hog may absorb more nutrients. Less feed is required for the animal to grow. Therefore, according to corporations' balance sheets, that antibiotic-fed animal is more efficient. From 1955 to 1995, the average weight of a chicken going to slaughter in America increased 50 percent, while the time it took to reach market weight declined 35 percent. Antibiotics became necessary to keep up in the meat business. A USDA economic report in 2014 found antibiotics increased hog output by about 2 percent and that ending the use of antibiotics for growth promotion would hurt output for nearly half of all hog producers that use the practice. The FDA began requiring a veterinarian to sign off on any antibiotic use in 2015, though conflicts of interest continued to arise as corporations employed their own veterinarians on-site.

Pilgrim's Pride, Perdue, and Tyson decided to start converting the majority of chicken production to antibiotic-free around 2015. The FDA's 2020 data on antibiotic sales for livestock shows poultry received 2 percent of the total antibiotics purchased, while cattle and hogs received the most antibiotics, at more than 40 percent each. Some of the most unchecked use is still happening within meat production. Lacing water and feed with antibiotics became the most common method for administering the drugs to animals when the goal was growth, and the preference remains: more than 60 percent of antibiotics in 2020 were added to feed, while 30 percent came from water.

Sometimes a farmer doesn't want to use antibiotics, but must. There are fair and humane reasons to administer antibiotics to animals. One uncomfortable truth about antibiotic-free meat production is, even if the trend is to eat antibiotic-free meat, livestock still get sick. When animals are sick, treating them with antibiotics is the right thing to do. But that creates potential waste, if Tyson is selling only no-antibiotics-ever chicken. In reality, that never happens, because Tyson diverts the sick chickens to a specific sick house where they will be fed antibiotics for treatment. Rather than discard those birds and create waste, birds that have been treated for illness with antibiotics end up being sold into the "precooked" market, which supplies school lunches and prisons. Because of the use of antibiotics as treatment for sick animals, a "no-antibiotics-ever" chicken may in fact come from a producer who does or has used antibiotics on certain birds for certain purposes, just not on the specific bird you have paid a premium for.

Customers pay an average of $1 more per pound for antibiotic-free meat. In practice, there are few ways to ensure the antibiotic-free meat being sold in stores was in fact raised without any exposure to any antibiotics at all. The USDA requires plants to submit their antibiotic-free labels for approval once a year, and then there's random testing on a tiny fraction of 1 percent of all of it. Otherwise, there's no validation process between the producer and the seller.

Whole Foods' supply chain is an example. In 2011, when the meat department set stricter animal welfare standards and started requiring third-party audits on some 3,500 farms every fifteen months, the chain lost 30 percent of its pork suppliers and 40 percent of its beef suppliers.

"That was a big shocker to me," recalls Theo Weening, Whole Foods' vice president of meat and poultry, during a call the week of 2020's pandemic Thanksgiving. As he boasted that organic turkeys are outpacing no-antibiotics-ever labels by 30 percent, I asked him about how the chain verifies the antibiotic-free claims on its labels, and he replied that every year it requires suppliers to resubmit their labels for approval. Mainly, he said, the chain relies on the animal welfare certification program, Global Animal Partnership, known as GAP, and the USDA's own extremely limited testing, but did not have its own internal process for verifying each label.

There is no rigorous testing done to verify antibiotic-free claims. The USDA's insufficient system has left major gaps in what's produced and what's advertised, without any procedure for validation. Yet corporations are collecting higher prices for products with an antibiotic-free tag.

The Murky State of Antibiotic Use in Meat

Overuse of antibiotics harms water, soil, and human health. Antibiotics end up in waterways that people swim in and otherwise contact. The antibiotic amoxicillin, for example, which is often given to people and animals, is released from bodies quickly. In humans, about 60 percent comes out in urine unchanged within about six hours. From the toilet, antibiotics might end up in a wastewater treatment plant, if the municipality is lucky enough to have one. The same holds true if a slaughterhouse has invested in its own. But treatment isn't perfect. Plants treat wastewater only to regulatory standards, which are minimal, without taking emerging science or new chemicals into consideration. The result: antibiotics often persist in reclaimed water. Consider further that livestock don't use toilets, and any contamination from livestock production while grazing on land isn't getting treated. Networks are doing wastewater analysis to map where resistant bacteria are most prevalent, but research is far from comprehensive.

Researchers at the University of Idaho found in December 2021 that when antibiotics seep into the ground, the soils store less carbon. The antibiotics stress soils more than they can handle. The study reads, "As soils encounter multiple stressors, ecosystem efficiency, stability and resilience may be diminished."

These threats will compound. Yet, despite the risks and growing trends of more consumers buying antibiotic-free meat, sales of antibiotics are still relatively high. The FDA's most recent report shows domestic sales and distribution of antibiotics for livestock decreased just 3 percent through 2020. Progress has stagnated, following two years in a row of sales increases. In 2019, sales of antibiotics for animals grew 3 percent, after growing 9 percent in 2018. Those insipid results come after the FDA prohibited the use of antibiotics for animal growth promotion in 2017, to quell more sales. The policy change created a moment of encouragement. Between 2015 and 2017, there was a 41 percent drop in sales, according to the Pew Charitable Trust. But the short-lived results have been sobering. Use on American farms is still down from peak sale years of 2015, a 38 percent drop, but those who watch this annual sales data closely are concerned. American livestock still ingest far more antibiotics than in Europe. The American industry, it seems, has given up on more progress.

It's not fully known why. The data on antibiotics used on livestock is far from perfect, but what we have available—mainly top-line sales that don't detail the reason the antibiotics were used—paint a problematic picture. Livestock operations could be reverting to bad practices or treating an increasing number of sick livestock due to animals' poor living conditions. The question is, will antibiotic use on farms remain at these quite high levels?

Livestock often receive the same kinds of antibiotics that treat serious human diseases. More than 60 percent of medically important antibiotics used in the United States go to livestock, compared to 35 percent in humans. Even though there are animal health companies like Elanco, a publicly traded spin-off of pharmaceuticals conglomerate Eli Lilly, most of the antibiotics used in livestock have not been developed specifically for them.

Overuse of antibiotics comes with a big cost: spending in the United States treating antibiotic-resistant infections alone is estimated at $5 billion annually. According to research, that figure, and the problem of antibiotic resistance, will only get worse as climate change does.

Up Close With FoodID

If you're purchasing antibiotic-free meat because you're worried about antibiotic resistance, chances are a fair amount of it has not been independently verified by the companies that sell it to consumers. Antibiotic researchers continue to come up with more evidence that a lot of antibiotic-free meat is not what it claims to be.

A technology start-up called FoodID has inserted itself into notoriously closed-off industrial slaughterhouses to find out how much of the meat has antibiotics. At these slaughterhouses, meat fresh off the line is swabbed and tested for more than ninety antibiotics and other adulterants. Within thirty minutes, tests from FoodID, akin to the technology used for a home pregnancy test, can detect it all, pull any contaminated meat aside for different labels, and keep up with the flow of the production line.

Until FoodID, the leading alternatives were tests sent out to independent labs that took days before results came back. The meat was long gone by then and en route to fast-food chains and grocery stores—leaving America's booming antibiotic-free business with a validation problem. But FoodID's tests do not hold up conveyor belts. That's the key—and why FoodID or validation checkpoints like it should maintain a station in any slaughterhouse in the future.

So far, FoodID has been otherwise unable to verify many "no-antibiotic" label claims.

A peer-reviewed study published in *Science* in April 2022, co-authored by public health professor Lance Price and FoodID CEO Kevin Lo, provides some empirical proof. Their study sampled 699 cattle from certified antibiotic-free operations which accounted for more than 38,000 cattle, or 12 percent of the total raised-without-antibiotics beef supply over the seven-month testing period. Findings show more than 40 percent of feedyards sampled had at least one case of cattle testing positive for antibiotics, while lots with at least one positive test represented approximately 15 percent of the cattle processed during the study period. "There's ample evidence that there are financial incentives to cheat," says Price. "The deck is stacked against honesty." The study found that 26 percent of cattle sampled from the Global Animal Partnership welfare certification program, which is used by Whole Foods and hundreds of other retailers and purchasers, had at least one positive test.* GAP executive director Anne Malleau told me the study prompted a "deep dive" into the program and its four hundred million animals certified every year. "It looks like there may have been a problem and we're doing something about it," Malleau said. Farms are already audited every fifteen months. While GAP never received the study's raw data, Malleau says the organization is now considering whether it could take on additional testing itself. But that may come down to price. As Malleau explains, "Everyone wants a lot of scrutiny, but what level of scrutiny are people willing to pay for?"

Price wants to see more testing from the USDA and more transparency, such as a public ledger that identifies suppliers selling meat certified as raised without antibiotics that actually tests positive. While this kind of testing is cheap and easy to reproduce, it's not free, and Price suggests the USDA could charge a fee to approve the antibiotic-free labels in the first place. That fund could also dole out payments to producers who have to treat their animals every now and again when sickness does happen.

"If you have to treat, it shouldn't be this financial conflict of interest. They shouldn't have to choose between good animal welfare and their own financial welfare," Price says.

As Bill Niman told me during the start-up's stealth phase: "Whether it's

---

* A Whole Foods spokesperson said "We have extensively reviewed the information made available to us and have no reason to believe that the cattle tested in this study ended up in products in our stores. We take compliance very seriously and never hesitate to act if a supplier has failed to meet our rigorous Quality Standards." The retail chain said every meat supplier at Whole Foods must pass an on-site visit by a third-party auditor who is given full access to facilities, record-keeping, and medical supplies. Whole Foods has worked with a third party, IEH Laboratories and Consulting, according to a spokesperson, "to test for the presence of antibiotics in beef and chicken products sold at Whole Foods Market and ensure that our suppliers are in compliance with our Quality Standards."

5 percent or 55 percent, it's a deceit and deception." The legendary rancher of grass-fed cattle in Northern California is approaching eighty years old. He sold his original Niman Ranch amid financial issues in 2006 and then sold his second, BN Ranch, to Blue Apron in 2017. He cashed out for more than many ranchers could dream of, but he couldn't stay away after he saw Stanford microbiologist and immunologist Dan Denney's research on repurposing simple lateral-flow tests, the kind of technology behind at-home pregnancy and rapid COVID-19 tests. Denney realized applying these quick tests to meat production could change the course of antibiotic resistance in America. Niman met Denney in 2014. They then joined forces with Facebook and Google veteran Kevin Lo, who took over day-to-day operations as CEO.

It is hard to trace whether what ends up being labeled as antibiotic-free is as it claims. The pressure of the markets has incentivized some producers to pass off livestock or chickens that were treated with antibiotics as antibiotic-free. But is the meat being sold with an antibiotic-free label on purpose? It depends. Lo explained to me: "They really run the gamut. On one end, there's malicious behavior. On the other end, innocent mistakes. But all of this comes back to the fact that nobody's watching and nobody's paying attention to it. We have a system right now where you sign a piece of paper with a checkmark, and you get the premium associated with selling that product." But government regulators and food industry insiders have ignored the gap when they could have stepped in.

The integrity of label claims, it seems, really doesn't exist. At least, not when the supplier is relying on audits like the USDA's, which can be helpful but are ultimately insufficient, according to Lo. Currently, the USDA may even allow for some companies to self-approve their own labels. "USDA-approved labels lack credibility," Lo said. It's easy enough to move some cattle or pigs that have been treated with antibiotics when the inspector arrives to audit. The lasting problem is that there's financial incentive to cheat. An inspector general's report that audited the USDA's label verification, published in June 2020, estimated that approximately 15 percent of labels the USDA is required to approve "may have one or more exceptions."

"Meat, poultry, and egg product labels may reflect inaccurate statements and claims made by establishments," the inspector general's audit reads.

Niman, Denney, and Lo got early funding from S2G Ventures, a fund fronted by the founder of OpenTable, Chuck Templeton. But from what I hear in investor circles, it's really backed and majority controlled by Lukas Walton, the grandson of Walmart's founder, a thirty-six-year-old who majored in environmentally sustainable business at Colorado College. Walton even had a personal tie to the transparency that FoodID wants to scale across the meat industry: Walton survived cancer as a kid, which his mom reportedly credits to transitioning to an all-organic diet. While nearly a quarter of the portfolio is invested in alternative protein, millions of dollars are still backing meat or start-ups that touch it. The fund pictures a future where animals roam on land and meat is still on plates. "We've got to get antibiotics out of our meat," Templeton told me. "Meat is not going away anytime soon."

With S2G's capital, FoodID has become the meat industry's first platform to comprehensively test for the presence of antibiotics and other chemical adulterants. It tests for seven drug families, including 95 percent of the most common antibiotics and other adulterants usually given to livestock through feed or water. The tests are quick, cheap, independently verifiable, and a potential game changer that has been used inside industrial slaughterhouses since 2020.

I spoke with Niman, who served on the Pew Commission on Superbugs and Industrial Farm Animal Production in 2014, many times as the company was getting off the ground. I brought up the concerning transmission of superbugs and asked him if he saw antibiotic resistance as a threat to long-term food security. As climate change intensifies, the superbugs rampant throughout the meat supply chain are expected to multiply. That's hard to fathom, considering meat production has already become a major driver of drug resistance, while many antibiotic-resistant bugs left on the meat have created dangerous recalls that doctors have been unable to fight with the common roster of food poisoning remedies. Yet overpopulated livestock production, enabled by the overuse of antibiotics, persists. All the while, the glut of antibiotics pollutes soils and waterways, further threatening the resources that farming and food production rely on.

"It's hard to deny that there's going to be unrest about food shortages," Niman replied solemnly. At that point during the interview, there was nothing else I could do but release the big gulp resting in the back of my throat. Food shortages, and who has access to what, are the unspoken threat behind the food system's many inefficiencies and inequalities.

That's why increasing transparency across the meat supply chain is a well-intentioned goal. This issue has increasingly been weighing on Niman, who has been struggling with how to communicate news about the data his start-up has from the slaughterhouses. "One thing I am really worried about—there are people that are doing the right thing and doing it right, because they believe it's the right thing to do, and they are religious about doing it correctly," he said. "I'm afraid that if we don't manage this carefully, we will create so much skepticism. I could see how people could say, 'I'm just going to buy the cheapest thing.' Why bother?"

That would be a mistake, he says, because companies need the consumer incentive. Yet so long as government subsidies artificially suppress the price of industrial meat, consumer incentive won't be enough.

At its heart, this is a product liability issue. But there's an implied safe harbor associated with relying on USDA label claims, which is a false pretense. As long as that safe harbor exists, the USDA has no incentive to actually test a comprehensive number of labels before they hit restaurants or grocery shelves, which charge more for antibiotic-free meat. As FoodID's CEO Kevin Lo told me, the USDA needs a framework that incorporates scientific testing as part of the label approval process. "Once you look, you bear responsibility for all sorts of claims, and that is an issue," says Lo. "Everybody in the supply chain makes money along the way. Ultimately, the incentives in the industry are such that people don't want to look."

Proliferation of antibiotics leads to antibiotic resistance, which in a hotter world due to climate change is a greater threat to human health. Consumers rely on antibiotic-free labels to shop more responsibly, but when up to 40 percent of those certifications may actually contain antibiotics, consumers are kept in the dark.

CHAPTER 10

Meat's Accessibility Gap

Too many families have a tough time securing enough healthy food. The cruel reality of the meat industry is that most pasture-raised meat is far too expensive or hard to find, so consumers relying on federal assistance must decide how to divvy up their limited funds to secure their own. That fact coexists with gross overconsumption: butcher counters at grocery stores overflowing with too much commercial meat alongside rows of refrigerated shelves lined with plastic packages of sausages, bacon, chicken breasts, and the like.

Even without the climate crisis, the meat industry is in deep trouble. Cheap meat is killing the most vulnerable. Yet meat is one of the most nutrient-dense foods commercially available, and, in crisis, access to meat can make a huge difference. Especially when survival is in question. But meat and other relief can also be weaponized against those who need it most.

When José Andrés and his team at World Central Kitchen fly to a destination around the world ready to cook as a form of relief, they meet hungry masses reeling from all forms of crisis. "It's day one in the middle of mayhem. If the only thing we have is cans of SPAM, I have no problem doing that," Andrés told me. "But this is day one. We are going to be there for many days, weeks, and months."

I caught up with Andrés after his 2021 trip to India, one of more than a dozen countries where he cooked during the extended pandemic. Andrés and volunteer chefs prepared rotis, dals, rices, paneers, and okra. Doctors and nurses in hospitals overrun from the pandemic got flatbreads, green pea rice, potato curry, and cucumber coriander salad. His team worked hard to source as much as possible from local markets and with farmers close by, checking their freezers and warehouses for extra food to buy. In Gaza in June 2021, World Central Kitchen purchased from local fishermen who were allowed to return to their boats following a cease-fire. During a busy hurricane season, though, the team may fly in food from Florida to islands in the Caribbean.

"As we can, we always rely on the private sector, which will always be better and more efficient than anybody else," Andrés said. "If the private sector is not up and running, we try to cover that ourselves because I don't want to be dependent on anybody." Government included.

Andrés, an immigrant from Spain, came to DC to work in restaurants in 1993. After watching the aftermath of Hurricane Katrina and wondering why there wasn't more of an effort to feed the displaced, Andrés decided to start his own relief work. Since the beginning, he has envisioned a global network of cooks "that in any collapse of our communities, we can come together and make sure that food and water will not be one of the issues."

The work will only get more difficult as climate change progresses, warns Andrés. Irreversible damage has already taken place and begun to reveal itself. World Central Kitchen has recently worked through one of the worst hurricane seasons to hit the Atlantic, floods in Germany, refugees at the US-Mexico border, wildfires in California, and an earthquake in Haiti, to name instances just from 2021. "We see that our job is not going to get any easier, but it's going to be heavier," Andrés said. "Climate change is a reality."

The work has put a spotlight on Andrés. A few weeks after our first interview, Andrés was granted a $100 million "Courage and Civility Award" from Jeff Bezos, a billionaire who, with his acquisition of Whole Foods, commands an increasingly large amount of influence in the food industry. A few weeks before the award was announced, Andrés scoffed at the lack of effectiveness of many deep-pocketed aid organizations: "Having money in the bank didn't allow many organizations to make the right decisions to bring relief to the people. What I need more is will. What we need the most is an intangible. If there is a will, there is a way."

A Crisis in the Richest Country in the World

The gap between those who have access to healthy food and the hungry in America is astonishing. In 2020, over sixty million Americans sought help from a food bank. At least forty million Americans lack consistent access to enough healthy food. Some thirteen million children live with pervasive hunger.

Many of those who rely on SNAP and charitable organizations work for meat suppliers. A 2014 survey found that among farmers whose sole income is raising chickens, 71 percent live below the poverty line. Processing jobs, especially at nonunionized chicken plants, are also notoriously low paying. Michael Foster, a then-eighteen-year employee of Georgia-based chicken processor Wayne Farms, was making $13 an hour when we spoke in May 2020. What he was making left him with barely enough to shell out for chicken himself. The then forty-year-old was fed up.

"Nobody is recognizing or appreciating us for what we're doing. My company could have afforded to at least give every worker they have a box of chicken," he told me. "I do not have chicken in my freezer."

Centuries of institutional racism are intrinsically linked to widespread hunger as well as the proliferation of diet-related chronic illness in modern America. Decades of programs and aid have barely scratched the surface. "If we're going to end food insecurity, we have to acknowledge the food system is not built to dismantle that," says Qiana Mickie, a New York City–based food systems consultant who is certified in local food hub management. "Our food and foreign policies are very much still rooted in historical and racial inequity. You can't talk about capitalism in the US without talking about how race really intersects the income and class that speaks to what we do. It's an acknowledgment that it has not really worked for many of us."

The benefits that do get doled out barely cover the cost of cooking a healthy meal, which just widens the meat wealth gap, says Mickie. In 2018 SNAP, the Supplemental Nutrition Assistance Program, formerly known as food stamps, amounted to $68 billion in benefits and administrative costs. But with one in eight Americans participating, or forty-two million people, the money falls short. The average benefit per person pre-pandemic was about $120 a month. It was far from enough. Most SNAP households redeemed three-quarters of their benefits by the middle of the month. Yet this support has spent decades under constant attack.

After years of SNAP getting slashed in congressional budget negotiations, the Biden administration quickly signed an executive order in January 2021 and increased funding by $29 billion. The formal changes announced in August 2021 marked the first funding increase to SNAP since 2006 and the largest permanent spike in the program's six-decade history. Monthly allocations increased by an average of $36 per person, but more aid is still needed.

Nonprofits have filled in the gaps, but not every community is so lucky. My own neighbors, Moonlynn Tsai and Yin Chang, together started a grassroots effort that combats isolation in New York City's elderly East Asian community through food care packages. I've had the honor of watching their nonprofit Heart of Dinner evolve from some of its earliest days in the spring of 2020, when one of my jumbo-size cans of San Marzano tomatoes transformed in their three-hundred-square-foot apartment into hot meals. At least one hundred thousand fresh meals have been served since then. They feed elderly neighbors in need purposefully, sourcing culturally appropriate ingredients and tapping their network of volunteers to pen handwritten notes to include with each meal. But without Heart of Dinner, these neighbors would be largely on their own.

Without access to additional grassroots help, many households must choose between filling calories and nutrition. Processed food is largely cheaper than fresh food. Some nutritious foods are cheap, like dried beans, but often take longer to cook, and convenience wins out. A can of already cooked beans is deemed worth it, even though those beans come with a higher price tag and additives. Access to the dried beans, in that case, isn't enough. Instead, the consumer opts for something processed, which, author Michael Moss explains in his 2021 book, *Hooked: Food, Free Will, and How the Food Giants Exploit Our Addictions*, is formulated with the purpose of making people crave more.

Or the purchasing decision comes down to spending money on food or medication. A diet full of processed foods can lead to serious disease and complicates the management of chronic illness, which is common among households lacking access to healthy food. These households are more likely to have health problems from what they eat. A third of the households served by the nationwide nonprofit food bank network Feeding America have a member with diabetes. Nearly 60 percent include someone with high blood pressure.

As nutrition expert Marion Nestle writes of the federal government's subjugation: "The laws provide just enough aid to keep people from dying on the streets (inconvenient, unsightly) or engaging in outright rebellion (politically problematic), but never enough to live decently. Although ostensibly aimed at relieving hunger, the Poor Laws also had political purposes: keep the destitute off the streets and willing to work for low wages. Today's politicians still use welfare and food assistance for these purposes, but add one more: They gain power by exploiting the poor." Note that nearly half of SNAP recipients are children, who require protein to grow. Nestle goes on to point out that congressional debates about SNAP "focus entirely on how to reduce SNAP enrollments and costs, never on how best to bring people out of poverty. When employees of Walmart and Amazon must rely on SNAP to get by, as many do, we taxpayers enable corporations to perpetuate poverty."

Convenience, Time, and the Problem with Preserved Meats

Gnarly problems are hiding in meat. In 2015, the World Health Organization's international agency for research on cancer ranked processed meats, including ham, bacon, salami, and hot dogs as "group 1" carcinogens, which means there's strong evidence that the foods cause cancer. Red meat like beef, lamb, and pork are "group 2A" carcinogens, classifying the meat as having probable cause. During studies, researchers found that eating fifty grams of processed meat like two slices of bacon or a thick piece of ham was linked to an 18 percent greater risk of colon cancer. Red meat showed increased risk of colon, pancreatic, and prostate cancer. The World Cancer Research Fund also suggests limiting red meat to three times a week and to consume "very little, if any" processed meat.

Processed meat is the most common kind sold in America—more than $17 billion worth sold at retail stores in 2021, according to NielsenIQ. Most sells at fast-food chains, which represent the most common options for eating out in some marginalized neighborhoods. But harmful chemicals that are rarely disclosed or studied are highly prevalent in fast-food meat. Public health researchers at George Washington University found phthalates, known endocrine disrupters commonly used to make plastics soft, as well as replacements called plasticizers that emerged as phthalate use has become restricted in popular fast-food meals. Meat like cheeseburgers and chicken burritos had higher levels of these chemicals.

The USDA has found SNAP households and non-SNAP households purchased similar foods in similar patterns. Meat, poultry, and seafood are the top-purchased category for each. SNAP households spent 23 percent of their benefits on protein, versus 21 percent for non-SNAP homes. Meats like frozen prepared chicken and dinner sausages are more than twice as likely to be purchased by families with SNAP benefits.

A lot of SNAP funds are spent on industrially produced food. Grocers are more likely to accept federal assistance payments than a neighborhood butcher shop, especially chains like Amazon, Walmart, and Aldi, which all take EBT, or Electronic Benefit Transfer, cards. Few craft butchers accept aid-based payments, even though it's possible for these businesses to register. All consumers should have a choice, though the high price of craft meat might mean those limited EBT dollars may not go far.

Lunch meat is the tenth-most-purchased commodity for SNAP households, compared to the seventeenth most popular for non-SNAP households. According to NielsenIQ's data of nationwide retail sales, roughly $13 billion worth of deli meats sold in 2021. The sales data also lays out some important emerging trends: $650 million of sales came from "natural" sources, and nearly $6 billion sold as free of preserving agents nitrates or nitrites.

Brands from Oscar Mayer to Hebrew National are developing no-nitrate-added formulas. But as animal behaviorist Fred Provenza points out in his book *Nourishment*, natural sources of nitrates like celery salt or juice are still chemically the same or similar as synthetic versions, which means they're probably just as likely to be tumor-enlarging carcinogens. The problem with the push to clean up packaged food labels is that some controversial ingredients are just getting replaced with another that works for a clean label claim but still may cause the same problems.

But corporations claim old-school methods aren't efficient for industrial slaughterhouses. Meatpacking plants have gotten used to making extra money selling what would otherwise go wasted, which hinges on using nitrates and other preservatives to make the product formulas last on shelves. They have an incentive to support any use for those scraps, no matter the consequences. That's what makes additive-riddled meat products so problematic. Unless industrial meatpacking ends, this waste will need a home, and millions are already huge fans, despite what's binding them together.

Working through Complicated Feelings about Meat

America's meat supply chain has a fundamental access problem. Thoughtfully produced meat is often too expensive and hard to secure. Yet industrially processed meat is artificially cheap and plentiful where many need convenience. Institutions and decades of policy have encouraged this, which is why it can be overwhelming to source food in this system. It's set up to bend individuals' purchasing to the whim of corporations.

That's why, when I need a guide to what to eat, I look to Sophia Roe. Her key point is simple: "There's no such thing as good or bad food when you're starving. I can tell you right now that I don't agree with factory farming, and I can tell you that a family feeding themselves is not bad." The central Florida native grew up with her mom struggling to feed her. She and her three siblings were sent to foster care when Roe was ten years old, and for the next eight years, Roe lived in twenty different homes. She dropped out of the University of Central Florida and ended up taking a job at a local Vietnamese restaurant. From there Roe bounced to California and Las Vegas, and then culinary school, before becoming a private chef known for healthy, mostly vegetarian dishes. In the years since, Roe, a Black woman of Brazilian, Japanese, and French heritage, has become a critical voice addressing injustice through the lens of food and access.

Brooklyn-based since 2013, the hunger advocate thinks consumers have a lot of power but need to approach supporting brands differently. Roe says she wants to see less canceling and more calling out—focusing on specific problems like plastic use and the responsible manufacturers or corporations. Canceling is lazy, she says, and doesn't do anything meaningful. Making a dent is critical, because injustice permeates the global food system: while 20 percent of US food production is exported overall, according to the USDA, only half a percent of US agricultural exports go to the nineteen countries of the world with the highest levels of hunger.

"It's really important that we humanize these global issues. Climate change. Environment. Farming. We need to distill them down and create a little sedimentary relationship with them. Either it's such a big idea that it gives us paralysis, or we get anxiety and just can't sleep over it," Roe said when she and I spoke in early December 2020.

Roe breaks down these overwhelming problems in her show *Counter*

Space on the VICE channel. Each episode begins with localized news stories at the intersection of food and global politics. The show adopts the raw honesty that Roe has become known for on social media, as well as her brand of realistic optimism. Structural barriers impede progress, Roe acknowledges. That's why she highlights stories that inspire watchers to drive change in their own neighborhoods. "It's going to take a very revolutionary existence to get through and fix a lot of these problems," Roe told me. "Think granularly about fixing these issues. Just because you can't fix world hunger doesn't mean you can't make a difference on your block."

Roe takes the humanizing one step further at the end of each episode, when she cooks a dish inspired by a story she heard and teaches viewers how to make the simple meal at home. Most recipes call for five ingredients or less and feature frozen or canned ingredients. She eats meat and animal products like goat milk on the Emmy-nominated show, because, culturally, that's what happens around the world. She ate meat, for example, after a story that led her to cook Uighur-inspired lamb kebabs. She also adapted some recipes to use mushrooms or tofu instead of the traditional meat.

Roe's plant-heavy cooking all of a sudden featured a fair amount of meat. Before shooting, Roe had barely eaten land animals, dairy, or eggs for a decade, aside from a meal from a host here or there while traveling. Roe was never one to ask what kind of fat was used to cook the beans she ate in Mexico. But when I heard she had decided not to officially limit herself, I felt relief. I also had been struggling with this idea. Living in downtown Manhattan means I have access to some of the most diverse food in the world, and while Rivington Street had just welcomed a great birria taco shop with halal-certified meat, that level of transparency is a rarity on a restaurant menu. I have never liked the idea of restricting where I may eat or what I might order while exploring a new menu based on the protein sourcing alone. Especially if the meal gives me the chance to try food from another culture. I felt grateful to discuss this complex and emotional topic with Roe.

"There's the idea that everybody going vegan will fix the issue. We have to be very mindful with that. Telling everyone in the world they need to go vegan, that's colonization, cultural erasure," Roe said. "We have to be really mindful about these black-and-white didactic answers to these big questions. Hunger, feeding people, is that the question? Feeding people isn't super complicated. But it's also feeding people nutritious and healthy food, also with the planet in mind, also with good farming practices in mind, also with equity, also with fair trade in mind, all the different nuances, it's very complicated."

Roe added: "Very few things are as dichotomous as, do you eat meat or not? I just want to let people know that there's no easy answer. That's okay. We're going to work through it."

Her idea of what's ethical is ever evolving, she says. When I caught up with her in January 2022, that meant eating thoughtfully and locally produced meat sparingly. "I had to look at myself and my own eating habits and at my own carbon footprint, as a vegan who was constantly eating acai bowls and things in plastic, containered milk, and then I have a partner who eats eggs from miles up the block and who killed a deer and has been eating it for the past six months," Roe said. "It's not just meat consumption. It's nuance."

After listening to Roe, I believe that I, too, can work through these conflicting feelings. Her approach makes the what-ifs feel a bit more manageable, and I appreciate the break from what has become an exhausting struggle. Many whom I admire abstain from meat because most pasture-raised meat is inaccessible to the masses. Others choose not to eat meat due to concerns about production harming animals, workers, or the planet. But even with these unsettling factors, extreme restriction makes me deeply uncomfortable. I focus on strict sourcing when the choice is in my control. Otherwise, I prefer to take my own small steps whenever I can. Sometimes that might just mean getting excited over a Sophia Roe recipe for mushrooms tossed in oil and spices and laid out on a sheet pan, topped with herbs sprinkled on top. Meat that fits my standards is rare.

SECTION III

—

ALTERNATIVE CHALLENGERS

CHAPTER 11

Can Climate Crisis Reform Meat?

Demand for good meat is strong, but the supply is weak. There are millions of pounds of meat advertised each year as "sustainable" and a range of ethical and health claims on Instagram ads and grocery store shelves. But the truth is, there's very little US-raised meat that can actually live up to these lofty claims, and there's a big mismatch emerging. More customers are willing to shell out for better meat, even though there's barely enough meat out there that would qualify. Meat from bison that graze on pastures, independent of feedlots, remains among the best that's commercially available.

There's been a boom in bison consumption. According to NielsenIQ, which scans receipts at most of the nation's cash registers, about $200 million of bison meat sells in stores across America each year. That's still a slice of total meat sold, and the majority of bison purchased at grocery stores still visits a feedlot before slaughter. But the trend is positive. Sales of frozen bison meat, which smaller producers often opt for, have skyrocketed: up more than 230 percent in 2021, after two consecutive years of more than 70 percent growth. Fresh bison meat sales have also grown over the past three years. America has about five hundred thousand bison in all. About 10 percent are on public lands. About one hundred thousand bison, mostly from family-owned ranches, are killed each year, compared to one million cattle annually.

The most sustainable and ethical bison producers face more demand than they can supply, which creates a tough balancing act. There's an extremely fine line between pasture raising at scale and overproduction. But producers like the O'Briens of Rapid City, South Dakota–based Wild Idea

Buffalo have been willing to settle on a stable level of output without pushing their operation to grow too much.

In the rolling hills across South Dakota, every slaughter for Wild Idea
Buffalo starts with burning sage and a moment of silence. The smoke goes
around every head in the small crew of workers, as well as the head of the
gun and the barrel that will do the ultimate job. "The Native People use sage
to smudge, to purify," co-owner Jill O'Brien told me, explaining that many
Wild Idea employees are members of the Lakota Nation and other Indigenous groups. "We follow some of their ceremonial practices out of respect,
and also because we believe it."

The animals never have to leave their home—the pastures—or suffer a
long trip jostling inside a truck en route to the slaughterhouse. Wild Idea is
one of just a handful of "field-harvest" operations in the country and show-
cases some of the most ethical kinds of livestock slaughter. Jill and her husband, Dan, have been producing bison meat this way for thirty years. While
Wild Idea is by no means the only bison grazing operation in the country,
it's among the oldest and largest independent operations today.

During a slaughter, a Wild Idea crew of four or five drives up to the bison
herd on the prairie. It might be land that the O'Briens own or that belongs to
one of their partners. An inspector is in the field, watching. The crew travels
out in a car, which eventually stops when nothing but grassy pastures are
within eyesight. Out pops the barrel of a gun, and there's one shot.

As the herd moves away, the hide is sliced off in the grass. A truck pulls
up. The still-warm carcass is then tied up, by the legs, and attached to the
back of the truck and driven to the mobile slaughterhouse in a nearby field.
There, the carcass is cleaned out and hung up to rest before it is cut into
halves, then quarters, then pieces. The entire process takes hours. During
an eight-hour workday, the team can butcher as many as twelve bison. The
long trailer, pulled by a semitruck, houses a simple processing table, knives,
and a cooler. Wild Idea owns one and set up another as a nonprofit harvest
partnership with a group of Lakota bison ranchers. Wild Idea has since
worked with tribal herds, including from the Cheyenne River Reservation,
Pine Ridge, South Dakota, Lower Brule, South Dakota, and Fort Peck,
Montana.

Wild Idea has a herd of one thousand that roams across thirty-five
thousand acres of grassland, compared to a few hundred acres for a typical

pasture-raised operation. That's a lot of land for the meat, especially when considering that Wild Idea's online store is often out of stock of its most popular cuts. Of its total herd, five hundred of these thousand-pound giants are killed each year. Wild Idea's operation claims to impact over three hundred thousand acres of grasslands, including land from other ranchers that Wild Idea manages slaughter for.

"Buffalo have been doing it for 170,000 years. We just try to let them do their thing," Jill told me. "The hands-off approach gives them the room that they need to run, which is a lot. They're not meant to run around in a hundred-acre pasture. They're roamers. They need space."

Jill met Dan while he was running cattle on a small ranch in Rapid City, South Dakota. In 2000, he purchased thirteen orphaned late-summer bison calves. That was the beginning of his switch from cattle to bison. Dan came to Jill, a local chef who grew up on a dairy farm, when he wanted to create some recipes to help market his meat. Jill was impressed. The smell wasn't as strong as other bison meat, which is mostly raised like cattle at feedlots, and this omega-3–rich meat didn't need to be tenderized further. That quality comes from slow growth and years of roaming and foraging for themselves. Bison are old animals compared to cattle, which are slaughtered at about two years old, or hogs, after just six months. Wild Idea's bison are slaughtered at between two and four years old. The O'Briens must choose how to cull their herds in a way that meets voracious consumer demand while ensuring that the overall sustainability of the herd is maintained.

"A business like this is driven by wanting to be part of the solution, not the problem. The dollars in it are very few—and it is built on the backs of those willing to make some sacrifices along the way," Jill explained. "Don't get me wrong, we have everything we need, and it is not a complaint—but duplicating it takes a certain tenaciousness and the help of good folks along the way."

The O'Briens and many other bison ranchers must make these tough decisions in a commodity market dominated by one deep-pocketed force: Ted Turner and his estate. Turner sends some five hundred bison a year to be slaughtered by Wild Idea. The billionaire controls more than half the bison market through his herd, the largest private one in the world. Turner's bison are spread across two million acres. The former CNN mogul is the fourth-largest individual landowner in the country, according to the

Land Report, behind timber barons the Emmersons, fellow TV mogul John Malone, and another West Coast logging family, the Reeds.

Around two-thirds of Turner's bison sold into market ends up as burgers or dishes like bison steaks and ribs at one of the three dozen locations of Turner's restaurant chain, Ted's Montana Grill. The brand also sells meat at the restaurant's butcher shops and views itself as a key gateway for Americans to access bison meat. The rest sells with wholesalers, distributors, other chains, and grocery stores.

Turner's transformation into America's largest bison rancher started in 1976. Within a decade, he purchased his first ranch, in Montana. His iconic Flying D Ranch in southwest Montana came next, followed by another fourteen ranches across South Dakota to Kansas, Nebraska, and New Mexico. A herd of about forty-five thousand bison roam across them all, munching on grasses sprouting up while improving soils with their hooves and manure.

Turner's daughter, Laura Turner Seydel, has closely watched these ranches start to transition from synthetic agriculture to land that's close to rewilded. The bison will move to small patches of a few thousand acres and reinvigorate native grasses, then they let that ground rest and move on to another. A third of the Turner bison herd eats forage solely. Still, two-thirds end up eating grain feed and some grasses on the ranch. No feedlots. "I would be happy if all of them could be finished on grass and shot in the field where they stand," Turner Seydel told me. "But it's a transition period, and cost is a factor. What's evening the playing field right now is the cost of commodities, which is through the roof. Finish your animals in field, compared to having to feed them alfalfa or corn, which have doubled in price? Everything is in flux."

Some of the ranches are transitioning, at different stages. Ranches with good access to water have the best chance of being rehabilitated. But Turner's ranches in Southwestern states like New Mexico may eventually get sold off. Without water, not much can be done. Within a year and a half of one forty-thousand-acre ranch in Montana starting its transition, the ranch, which used to farm alfalfa to feed the animals, sold its hay-processing equipment. The bison have enough to munch on based on what has grown back. Researchers have found double the number of native species and double the amount of plant material in a relatively short amount of time. The ranch stopped irrigating fields to grow alfalfa as the region experienced drought, a rain shortfall, and hot weather. Other farmers in the area took their water allotments. Turner Seydel, who is on the board of Ted's Montana Grill as well as the Turner Foundation and Turner Endangered Species Fund, says the Turner ranch not taking their allotment from Montana's Ruby Red River was the main reason the tributary still had water over the summer of 2021.

When I spoke with Turner Seydel in 2021, I wanted to know what *she* eats. The answer is mostly plants, but when she does consume meat, it's from bison that graze only on the open range. "Even if your animals are grass-finished, but they're dining on a monoculture, you do not have the phytonutrients and the phytochemicals in that meat," Turner Seydel told me. "If they're not eating that, they're really not worth all the devastation that those animals can create to provide you with vitamins and minerals."

The Promising Return of Buffalo

The resurgence of demand for meat from bison that graze on the open range is astonishing and hopeful, given the disappearance of buffalo over the last two centuries. The decimation of the American buffalo is intrinsically linked to the land theft from Native Americans by colonists and then the US government. Before the European colonists arrived, the wild bison population was as high as thirty-five million. By the 1800s, less than half remained. That's when these great animals became extinct in the wild. The last fifteen million were killed in under a decade, hunted down at the government's behest. By 1889, fewer than one hundred survived.

With the extinction came the end to generations of grazing patterns that enriched America's vast plains. What was left was a trail of blood and bones on the American prairies. This mandate to kill off a way of life by hunting the buffalo was just one in a heinous past that has shaped America's agriculture policy for decades, and that has historically ignored Indigenous and Black farmers' contributions to the foundations of sustainable agriculture. Bison were targeted because the government wanted to destroy a means of culture and traditions passed down over generations. The mandate had nothing to do with agricultural policy yet had huge implications for sustainable agriculture. The loss of culture included the loss of a sustainable agricultural practice. Without bison hooves charging across the Midwest's tall grasses, the ecosystem fell apart. The dust bowl that followed was a massive

ecological warning that policymakers and executives have compartmentalized and set aside as modern feedlots have contributed to overgrazing and
pollution.

It didn't have to turn out that way. Generations upon generations kept
herds of wild bison thriving. As a pillar of many Indigenous foodways, these
bison maintained crucial grasslands. Through careful rotations and crisscrossing routes, bison aerated soils and kept pests and invasives under control while encouraging biodiversity. Wildlife in a herd's path grew deeper
roots and stronger stalks. The practice of hunting only what was necessary
and using every scrap kept the overall bison population strong. Sustainability wasn't an afterthought. It was a fundamental part of the forethought,
and not just when it came to bison. Author Charles C. Mann's research
shows Native American tribes did not till the land and repurposed wasted
fish to fertilize soils, which both have inspired tenets of modern sustainable
farming.

Amid widespread destruction without these ideals in place for decades,
a movement has been building. Several tribal nations have been reintro-
ducing buffalo back onto their land while other individual ranchers of
Indigenous descent have been taking on bison herds as personal projects.*

"Our first priority is always to make sure the soil is healthy," bison
rancher Lucille Contreras told me. "We are grass farmers." Contreras, a
member of the Lipan Apache Band of Texas, was launching a website for
her bison meat when I spoke with her in 2021. Getting her pasture-raised
meat to hungry customers was a side hustle. Contreras also spends her
days running a nonprofit, the Texas Tribal Buffalo Project, which educates
on healthy foods made using Indigenous techniques. "As a person who is
enrolled in a tribe that is not federally recognized, we are sometimes still
treated like the little stepkids within the circle of the bigger federally recognized Native American communities, but I am extremely persistent," said
Contreras, whose heritage also includes Mexican descent. "I'm making
little, tiny inroads."

Creating strong markets to sell those bison into will be crucial, and it

---

* Some of the projects to restore bison on tribal lands are aided by donations from one of
Ted Turner's foundations. Turner also donated one of his ranches to the Turner Institute
of Ecoagriculture, which focuses on researching bison and other ecosystems.

works best when businesses can take leftover bits and turn them into premium products. That's how Contreras or a rancher like her could eventually raise bison that ends up selling to a supermarket as steaks while other parts are purchased as an ingredient by a maker like Tanka Bar, a brand of protein bars and other meat snacks made of bison. A batch of the bars takes nine hours to make—mainly because of their long bath in the smoker, which allows the bars to remain free of preservatives.

Big Backers for Bison

Tanka Bar was nearly crushed as it struggled to navigate through bouts of unreliable demand. Founded in 2006 by two members of the Lakota Nation, Mark Tilsen and Karlene Hunter, Tanka Bar aimed to support the struggling Pine Ridge Reservation in South Dakota with a bison protein bar. Unveiled at the 2007 Black Hills Powwow, the original bar was sourced from Native bison ranchers and produced by Native peoples. The goal was to eventually build a 100 percent Native-owned supply chain. But it never happened for Tanka Bar. Other protein bar and jerky competitors backed by venture capital firms flooded grocery store shelves thanks in part to marketing funds and deeper pockets. It became difficult for upstart Tanka Bar to break through.

Then the publicly traded conglomerates entered the market in a big way: in 2015 Hershey acquired antibiotic-free jerky brand Krave for $300 million, followed by General Mills spending $100 million on bar and bone broth brand Epic Provisions, known for sourcing grass-fed bison. Tanka Bar was crowded out. The deep pockets upended the commodity markets while wielding better access to funds to pay grocers for extra charges like slotting fees and other marketing promotions. Tanka Bar fell victim to the dynamics of the overconsolidated grocery industry. According to a National Grocers Association report on buyer power and economic discrimination from 2021, concentration in the grocery supply chain has made "suppliers even more beholden to leverage."

"As manufacturers consolidate, they become more dependent on the largest buyers, who represent a substantial portion of their sales," the report reads. "The dominant grocery retailers are not nearly as dependent on a particular supplier as the supplier is on the retailer. This is because a particular grocery supplier's products generally represent only a small fraction of a retailer's sales, which may encompass tens of thousands of products."

The ramifications in Tanka Bar's market hit quickly. Shortly after the acquisition of Epic in 2016—when Epic had announced sourcing "over 250,000 pounds of regenerative protein" and impacting "millions of acres of grasslands"—the General Mills–backed Epic switched to grain-fed bison and took care of expenses like shelf slotting and marketing fees that Tanka faced. But Tanka still had to compete. Writer Marilyn Noble investigated this critically for the nonprofit food outlet *The Counter*, and her article addressed how General Mills had influenced a market families relied on. After pioneering a new wave of healthy, protein-heavy snacks, Tanka reached distribution in 6,500 stores and $3.5 million in revenue in 2016.

Tanka then suffered layoffs and scrambled to raise funds. In 2017, Tanka Bar used crowdfunding platform WeFunder to secure a little over $120,000. After selling on Whole Foods shelves since 2012, the relationship stopped in 2019. Tanka couldn't keep up with the hard-to-predict demand.

Tanka was almost left for dead when Niman Ranch, owned by poultry conglomerate Perdue, came in with an offer. The operation, originally founded by California rancher Bill Niman (though he hasn't been involved in the modern firm for years), decided it could leverage its assets for the start-up. In exchange for a minority stake, Niman Ranch poured funds into Tanka and helped the firm raise a total of $3.5 million including cash and debt. Tanka then got access to the sales and operational team that built Niman's network of 740 small and independent family ranchers and hired top talent. Dawn Sherman, who grew up in South Dakota and has ancestry in the Lakota, Shawnee, and Lenape nations, came in shortly thereafter in January 2020 to run Tanka as CEO.

"I still can't compete with General Mills. They put in the marketing dollars. I'm spending one dollar, they're spending ten dollars," Sherman told me in 2021. "But we're taking our space and telling our story."

Tanka has made some big compromises by accepting capital from institutional financing sources. But it has yet to result in Tanka achieving its original goal: sourcing entirely Indigenous-raised bison. Tanka's sourcing comes from Rocky Mountain Natural Meats—the largest bison processor in America, which has slaughtered the bulk of Ted Turner's annual herd brought to market since 2002. Rocky Mountain is owned by longtime bison rancher Bob Dineen, who is also an investor in Tanka. Dineen himself is white and does process bison raised on Indigenous-operated ranches. But there isn't a system in place for Rocky Mountain Natural Meats to track whether Indigenous-owned ranches are supplying Tanka Bar. "It doesn't necessarily have to come from any particular ranch or source," Dineen told me. A Native American raised supply, he said, is hard to come by. "We buy from a few different producers that are Native American. There are not very many that are active suppliers to Rocky Mountain. There's going to be a slow slog of getting more Native American ranchers to actively participate in the bison industry."

Operational shifts have led to some success otherwise, however. Tanka is back selling at Whole Foods. But Tanka lost its co-packer and had to scramble, which muted growth. The bars are still sold at one thousand stores. There are clearer bright spots: e-commerce sales are up 200 percent, the same as sales at Costco.

How Cover Crops Really Started

After decades of climate concerns, protecting and improving soil health, biodiversity, and water quality while promoting social and economic equity are on the rise. Strengthening soil health naturally improves the nutrients prevalent in soil, and it also increases the absorption capacity of the soil to store those nutrients. Leah Penniman, the cofounder of Soul Fire Farm in Upstate New York, has written about Dr. George Washington Carver in *Farming While Black: Soul Fire Farm's Practical Guide to Liberation on the Land*, and how Carver, in the late 1800s as a professor at Tuskegee University, was among the first to broadly advocate for the use of cover crops, crop rotation, composting, and biodiversity. "Carver was dedicated to the regeneration of depleted southern soils and turned to legumes, such as cowpeas and peanuts, as a means to fix nitrogen and replenish the soil," Penniman writes. "Carver believed that 'unkindness to anything means an injustice done to that thing,' a conviction that extended to both people and soil."

Penniman explains that Soul Fire Farm plants cover crops for three main reasons: to ready a new field for planting, to help soil recover over winter, and to help crops during the growing season. "Cover crops are plants that we grow not to feed the human community, but rather to alchemize air into soil nutrients, stabilize aggregates, and enhance soil health. At Soul Fire Farm, we also use rye, oats, peas, bell beans, vetch, soybeans, sorghum sundagrass, sunn hemp, triticale, and clover as cover crops. In doing so, we pay homage to ancestor George Washington Carver, who was an early champion of the use of leguminous cover crops to fix nitrogen. He understood that the pink-colored nodules growing out of the roots of beans and peanuts were natural nitrogen factories that should be intentionally cultivated by land stewards."

Carver's work is a strong example of the generations of contributions that farmers in the Black and Indigenous communities have made while building the foundations of sustainable farming practices in America. Yet these tenets have long been ignored or, too often, uncredited. Nearly two centuries later, calls to recenter this work—building sustainability and equity into farming—are being heard. But some fear progress will be stunted unless the broader sustainable agriculture movement rectifies how it has gained steam without generations of racism or the lasting impact of threats of land theft being addressed.

Remedying soil health is necessary if we want a chance to survive on this planet in 2050, or rather, if we want a chance to have a say in how we survive. Evening out the inequity requires a real conversation about land access, farming as a tax shield, generational land grabs, the future of redistribution, the ugly history of racism, the opaque chain of how food goes from farm to fork, and egregious systematic failure. Annual tax breaks for farms and land conservation continue to save wealthy landowners a lot of money. That drives billionaires, a lot of rich non-billionaires, asset managers of pension funds, and other corporate interests to view subsidized, synthetic farms as an asset. A deal may even be a way to hedge their wealth against rising inflation. Few are serious about conservation, and I have yet to see a groundswell line up to hand over deeds to land or otherwise leverage agricultural land wealth in a meaningful way.

Land has been stripped from Black farmers in a number of racist ways. In 1910, 14 percent of farmers were Black. But these farmers were left out of federal help across the board—for example, at the height of the farm crisis in 1984, the USDA doled out loans to 16,000 farmers, but only 209 of those farmers were Black. Nearly 97 percent of Black farmers' land was dispossessed by 2007—aided by preferential lending terms to titles with sole hold-ers and other weaknesses in the legal framework. Black farmers didn't leave wills as often, with land rights spelled out. The global recession then took even more Black farmers out of business. As of the USDA's last survey in 2017, just over 1 percent of all farmers in the United States are Black. More than half of Black farmers are livestock farmers: of the fewer than thirty-five thousand Black farmers in America, as many as 50 percent touch beef cattle.

Carver might be disappointed at the modern-day state of sustainable farming. Cover cropping, for one, isn't as widespread as it should be, though that would be a simple way that commodity farming for livestock feed could become more sustainable, and a strong requirement for any farmer accept-ing subsidies. Well-managed adaptive grazing, which we'll get to, isn't well adopted, either.

Sustainability doesn't have an enforceable definition for whenever it's used on food labels. Neither do any claims of carbon positivity. That makes consumers vulnerable to buying something they didn't intend to, and creates a system where cheating is common. Was synthetic fertilizer used? Did my food cause pollution? There's no easier way to threaten progress than cre-ating a system where insufficient verification is passed off as good enough.

Synthetics and monoculture dominate the US farm landscape, which is why validation and strict standards are so necessary. Since genetically engineered seeds debuted in 1996, adoption has been drastic: 90 percent of American corn, soybeans, and cotton come from patented seeds. A stun-ning 50 percent of all corn comes from just six genotypes. Without clear standards, the same forces that nearly pushed Tanka Bar off the shelf will continue wielding too much unchallenged power.

If meatpacking companies like Tyson, JBS, and Smithfield must con-tinue to have long-term contracts with most of their producers, these cor-porations could use their leverage to take a more active approach on the farming of the ingredients for their livestock's feed. Imagine, commitments with clear and transparent goals set for how meat corporations can impact soil health, due to the massive amount of commodity grain the industry's animals consume. A wide range of varied practices—from planting cover crops to refusing to till soils—could be put to work.

But they have not. The Union of Concerned Scientists, an environ-mental advocacy group, published an analysis in February 2022 that found

Tyson contributes to soil erosion and the loss of biodiversity on the land used to grow the row crops needed to feed its chickens. That land amounts to roughly twice the size of New Jersey.* Tyson, the study found, has the power to influence the farming on 5 percent of the entire nation's corn and soybean acres—a significant portion. But so far, the opportunity hasn't resulted in much. The study estimates that just 5 percent of Tyson's total poultry feed comes from farms with stricter environmental standards.

The concept of prairie strips, is another example, which could roll out immediately and suggests that even synthetically farmed row crops like the kind grown for feed could become more sustainable with some tweaks in the fields. Prairie strips transform as much as 25 percent of a farm's cropland. The area, between 30 and 120 feet wide, then gets rewilded with native grasses and flowers. Pioneering research on the practice earned ecologist Dr. Lisa Schulte Moore a spot among the 2021 MacArthur Foundation Fellows, also known as the genius grant, because the benefits of prairie strips are deeply varied. Prairie strips help control erosion while improving water quality and biodiversity around croplands, even ones with years of chemical use. Crucially, the prairie strips emit less while organic carbon in those soils increases. "I continue to engage farmers, build partnerships, and conduct research and development to remove barriers to the strategic integration of perennials and other forms of continuous living cover in Corn Belt systems," Schulte Moore told me. But without widespread adoption of any scientifically backed techniques, progress will remain limited.

Grass That's Best in Class

Given the clear environmental implications of feedlot fattening, it continues to startle me that corn-fed is still considered necessary for superior taste and flavor. Billionaire Henry Davis' operation in Omaha, Nebraska, relies on corn and feedlots, and he doesn't plan to change that anytime soon. His operation is in the heart of the Corn Belt—and when I asked whether he could see the slaughterhouse being used for cattle raised in more holistic

---

* Tyson doesn't own or farm the land in question. Tyson says it wasn't given the chance to review the study ahead of its publication but will keep working to develop "a path forward." Tyson says it is committed to "helping U.S. row crop farmers maximize profitability, while reducing greenhouse gas emissions and benefiting soil health and water resources."

environments, like systems with managed, adaptive grazing, he was blunt: "How are you defining that?" I took the point, so here's the definition for this book: instead of feeding on commodity corn and soy in CAFOs, cattle could graze in high-stocking densities on grasses, reinvigorating small patches of land and then letting the ground rest.

The best proxy for that on menus and grocery store labels currently is "grass-fed," though it's a stretch due to the variety of where grass-fed meat can come from and how it can be produced. Of the top meat-packers, JBS is the only one to have a large grass-fed division, sold under its Grass Run label. Among the top grass-fed producers in the United States, there's Kansas-based Creekstone, Georgia's White Oak Pastures, and Perdue-owned Panorama Meats. What sells as "grass-fed" can be many different things—from livestock that forage solely on pastures to varying degrees of eating grain at some point in the process. The USDA doesn't have a standard for what "grass-fed" really means. Labels vary, but "100% grass-fed" or "grass-finished" means that animal has eaten solely grass its entire life. Labels that designate how the livestock were raised complicate matters further but offer important distinctions because there are grass feedlots where livestock eat grass pellets and are still kept in confinement. That's why it's important to look for other markers, too, like "free-range" or "pasture-raised." There's also livestock that are finished in the pasture on a mix of grasses and hay, and the intentionally confusing "pasture-raised, grain-finished," which means the animals still end up at a feedlot. Plus, grass-fed animals are allowed to eat grain-based feed anyway, during drought, because grass is nonexistent.

When I talk about good grazing from here on out, I mean livestock that forage grass on an open range for their entire lives and move around in a highly managed rotation. In this process, livestock naturally spread their antibiotic-free manure across the pasture and stomp it into the ground, improving water absorption and soil quality, and avoiding the often-deadly waste lagoons caused by industrial agriculture. In animal behaviorist and author Fred Provenza's 2018 book *Nourishment*, he observes that when livestock can graze naturally on whatever they want, they pick a healthy mix of forage. That gives their meat the phytochemicals crucial to creating, ultimately, a better piece of meat.

"Ratings for grass-fed are inconsistent. Livestock eat different diets during the finishing period and that influences the flavor and biochemical richness of meat and fat to the extent that laboratory analyses can distinguish animals foraging in different landscapes, including feedlots. Among many other phytochemicals, flavonoids, carotenoids, and terpenoids in herbivore diets become part of the flavor of meat and fat," Provenza writes.

"These dietary differences, which are not reflected in the generic label 'grass-fed,' partially explain why grass-fed beef doesn't have consistent flavor or quality. Consumers need more information about the phytochemical richness of a landscape where animals were raised to make an educated guess about the flavor of meat from those animals."

Many chefs and grass-fed advocates argue a grazing diet improves taste. But stalwart meat lovers like Davis claim the corn and the quick fat from that diet are necessary elements for a sizzling piece of steak. American eaters have gotten used to marbling, he argues.

Flavor and quality among what sells as "grass-fed" vary widely. That's for three main reasons. First, what sells in the United States as grass-fed can be produced in many ways, and meat from a grass feedlot tastes different from livestock raised fully on pasture. Second, raising animals is hard, and especially when the farmer is avoiding synthetics and other shortcuts. When animals are stressed, their meat tastes worse. Want better-tasting grass-fed beef? That probably means less-stressed farmers. Third, beef is seasonal, and best in warmer months. Most American producers can't accommodate these last two, which is why many start-ups and suppliers are looking abroad for grass-fed beef.

Many top US suppliers have signed agreements to import grass-fed beef, claiming insufficient taste, price, or a combination of the two among the options from America. Ariane Daguín, the founder and CEO of $130-million-in-sales D'Artagnan, a high-end restaurant distributor of meat based in New Jersey, says she won't source US grass-fed beef, only grain-fed, because in the United States, Angus cattle—whether they are grass- or grain-fed—are slaughtered at eighteen months old and don't have enough fat when the cattle eat only grass. Daguín imports grass-fed cattle from Australia slaughtered at five years old. Domestic grass-fed beef often loses out to imports from Chile, Australia, and New Zealand. Even brands focused on ethical sourcing avoid American grass-fed, including Thrive Market. Those start-ups say the trade-offs of international shipping still net out to a more sustainable bottom line, at a cost that can sell to mass American consumers.

Importing will always be more inefficient than sourcing the same protein locally. But if grass-fed isn't going to be better for the environment, then what's the point of all this? New Zealand–based Silver Fern Farms, a leading producer of 100 percent grass-fed red meat in the United States, has secured third-party certification on 4 percent of its emissions occurring off-farm, with transportation and shipping accounting for just 0.8 percent. But that's not nothing, and it adds up. The other problem is that the industry standard isn't a glowing model of sustainability as it is. American beef still travels a fair distance out of the Midwest to many far corners across the country.

I find myself skeptical that relying on imported meat is the solution to bank on. If all the downward pressure on American farmers and livestock producers eventually bankrupts them, then importing more sustainably produced grass-fed meat to package and sell in America does not seem like a viable answer.

Yet aside from inefficient transportation, this kind of thinking ignores the benefits of thriving regional production that supports a local community, especially one where land has been degraded and needs help. Rural areas have already been gutted by international agribusiness, and if production shifts entirely abroad, a major chunk of the economy may sink.

The Case for American Grazing

More meat doesn't need to be produced. But not all pastureland is suitable for crops, and rotational adaptive grazing is the only chance some soils have at coming back to life. In the Midwest especially, decades of misuse from chemical fertilizers and herbicides have depleted once mineral-rich lands that were carefully managed over generations by Indigenous communities and the extinct wild bison. There's not enough time for nature to solve the problem on its own. It takes five hundred years or more to create an inch of fresh topsoil under natural conditions. Floods and drought, already exacerbated by the early impacts of climate change, make this harder.

That's why I'm going to focus the remainder of this chapter, instead, on adaptive multi-paddock grazing.

In Bluffton, Georgia, at White Oak Pastures, Will Harris, his daughter Jenni, and their families run 3,200 acres of rolling hills with herds of cattle, goats, sheep, and hogs. There are rabbits, chickens, turkeys, ducks, geese, and guinea fowl—ten species of livestock in all. Some of the strongest evidence of degraded soils becoming more fertile after getting some work under hooves comes from White Oak, the largest certified organic farm in Georgia. In his late sixties, Will Harris sports a goatee and usually wears a wide-brimmed hat. His drawl is low and could not be mistaken for anywhere else in the South but his southwestern corner of Georgia countryside. Back when he was first transitioning his great-grandfather's farm away from commodities peanuts and cotton in 1995, Harris was laughed at in many meetings with fellow farmers. But after twenty-five years of soil data, White Oak became ideal to research and scientists began to study fields that had been holistically managed for a range of time periods—twenty years, thirteen years, eight years, five years, three years, one year, and zero years—to measure the effects of the Harris' management on the soil.

"Tyson is highly scalable. White Oak Pastures is not highly scalable. It is highly replicable. Tyson is not replicable," explained Will Harris. "There should be two or three White Oak Pastures in every agricultural county in this nation. But there's not. And there probably won't be, unless consumers demand it."

A landmark life-cycle assessment that analyzed the data comprehensively was released in 2019. Conducted by Quantis and funded by General Mills, which buys some White Oak meat for its Epic Provisions brand, the study confirmed that, based on historical sampling, White Oak's managed fields rose from 1 percent soil organic matter to 5 percent. "Soil organic matter is a key indicator for soil health and among other factors, it influences soil aggregates and nutrient cycling," according to the study. It also notes that White Oak improved in what's known as "aggregate stability," which "indicates how well the soil holds together under rainfall, providing greater resiliency to the landscape." White Oak's aggregate stability increased four times over. A year later, at the end of 2020, a peer-reviewed study analyzed the results and confirmed that White Oak soils have strong levels of carbon—though less than the original researchers initially found. Its grazing practices create a greenhouse gas footprint 66 percent lower than conventional beef, though it's on 2.5 times more land, which is already in short supply. Some scientific research since then has called into question the long-term potential of carbon sequestration. One found that hotter temperatures made soils' carbon storage decline and concluded that global warming will degrade soil carbon more than previously anticipated.

Focusing on carbon can eclipse the fuller picture: that once-degraded soils are now teeming with life. The independent soil scientists who peer-reviewed the study agree. Paige Stanley, a PhD from the Department of Environmental Science, Policy, and Management at the University of California, Berkeley, says she gets frustrated when adaptive grazing systems are compared to industrial systems. Why does it make sense to compare them to a system that has so many externalities and addressable problems?

"The surrounding croplands in Bluffton where Will Harris is, they are being abandoned, essentially. They were monoculture for many years, being rotated between cotton and peanuts. When these lands become available, he buys them and essentially implements multi-species rotation," Stanley said. "A lot of people are really hung up on that piece of the land use it takes. But that land has been degraded. That's really important here."

It's a technique that Stanley explained could be used to make degraded portions of the Great Plains productive. Re-perennializing these out-of-use farmlands already left for dead by the sting of synthetic agriculture would be better for food production and the environment.

"When I hear a lot of 'We'd have to convert all of these lands to be able to use the system globally,' I really push back on that," Stanley said, "because we weren't making any claims about maintaining the same level of meat production. We're saying, this is a system that's doing what they can, producing meat, and a lot of it, while doing all these amazing things to the environment, and that seems like the sweet spot.

"Grazing on these plains are some kind of purgatory middle ground— they are closer to wild than they are industrial, but they're also managed with animals on them, which means that they're not totally wild," Stanley continued. "We're producing food on a landscape that doesn't look like any other kind of agricultural landscape and is pretty damn close to wild but not quite, so we're pissing everybody off with one system without doing it intentionally. We're getting a lot of the ecosystem services that we would get from a native ecosystem. Mind you, the initial tilling of native grassland

and forests causes destruction that we can never restore, but as much as we can get back from those ecosystems is the direction that we should be going. It doesn't have to be perfect."

When I asked Stanley if she's ever seen an estimate or map for the ultimate amount of acreage this could work on, she paused. There are many trade-offs to consider. Plus, poorly managed grazing can degrade land, too.

"To paint with a broad brush, I wouldn't be comfortable doing, honestly," she said, before breaking into laughter. "We don't know, and to be totally honest, anybody who claims that they do know, I would call bullshit."

I laughed too. Fair enough. But a good place to start could be a recent map published by researchers at the University of Vermont outlining America's top twenty nitrogen pollution hotspots representing thirty-seven million acres. Since those are croplands, they'd have to recover through an integrated crop and livestock system, which are more frequently used abroad. Stanley said no land is too degraded to recover, though some soils may never come back entirely. Otherwise, I've continued to look for other analysis that could provide some comps, as we call it in the valuation world.

That brought me to a 2017 report funded by the Center for Stone Barns on the potential of the US grass-fed beef market. In terms of tracking, organic grass-fed is the best label equivalent for what we're after.* There are around 3,900 producers finishing grass-fed cattle in the United States, according to the report, up from around 100 in 1998. They bring to market an estimated 232,000 head of grass-fed cattle for slaughter each year, a tiny portion of the 30 million cattle slaughtered annually in the United States. But what most intrigued me was this paragraph at the bottom of page 41. Rangeland ecologist Allen Williams cited there that increasing the amount of cattle per acre by around a third, coupled with intensive adaptive, rotational grazing, "would accommodate enough grass-finished animals to replace all the grain-finished cattle in the U.S. without using more land." Industry estimates suggest that figure is low—rotational grazing could increase the density of cattle stocked per acre anywhere from 80 percent to 400 percent. To stay reasonable, I'll keep my calculation to a nice and simple one-third increase to the overall US grass-fed market, which is currently pegged at $4 billion—including the $1 billion for meat labeled grass-fed at retail and

---

* Even better if the meat was pasture-raised and the label reads 100 percent.

some $3 billion sold through food service. My estimated total market size for beef that touts its environmental benefits would then be at least $5.3 billion. The maximum could be as much as $16 billion. That top end would actually be substantial—about a quarter of the total industry—but even if it captured 15 percent of the market share, that would be impressive.

Increasing stocking density for pasture-based livestock operations doesn't require more land, which is an important counterargument to the defense that feedlot operations are an extremely efficient use of land. Another potential criticism is that the lifetime of cattle and other livestock would increase, so they'd produce more methane emissions over the course of their lifetime. One 2018 study estimates a completely grass-fed cattle system would increase America's methane emissions about 8 percent annually. Climate and livestock scientists insist that meat production must decrease overall. The same 2018 study found transitioning to an entirely grass-fed system would require the nation's cattle herd to increase 30 percent to one hundred million cattle, though researchers also found that pastureland available can support only about twenty-seven million cattle. But there's a place for meat in supporting degraded lands and the regional food systems they are located in. Bison meat from strong operations is probably the best you can eat, but there's not enough while land use and the challenges of management restrict accessibility.

I am still looking for more balance between land use trade-offs and what could be possible in the United States in terms of the maximum amount of land that is degraded or will be too degraded to use soon. This is already common abroad, where much of the livestock grazing is on marginal land that can't be used for crops—because of low soil fertility, or because it's too rocky.

Whatever grazes would still have to be managed. Implementing proper grazing management is difficult. It would not be as simple as letting a bunch of bison loose to roam. That's why cases of properly managed adaptive grazing are so site-specific: every ecology is different. So far, successful producers have decided to make a change and then have fought to reform—against the financial odds.

CHAPTER 12

Breeding a Better Chicken through Feed and Genetics

Historically, in the meat industry, "innovation" has meant flavor engineering, fillers and gums, and preservatives to extend shelf life. That's why, when a box from Arkansas landed on my doorstep, I found myself eagerly awaiting its contents. Inside were four chickens from Cooks Venture, which made me feel like I could peer into the future, and it might actually be better.

Founder and CEO Matt Wadiak has been figuring out how to breed, at scale, chickens raised without any corn and is even working on a small line of birds fed no corn *or* soy—a whole chicken that costs $20 and ships directly to your home, almost entirely outside the confined and industrialized poultry system. Figuring out the least amount of feed possible that it takes to raise an animal to slaughter weight has been the meat industry's Golden Ticket, which is why cheap corn and soy as a feed have been so popular. But if Wadiak could really produce chickens on feed made from sustainably farmed grains at scale, he'd have a shot at creating a new and fully transparent supply chain that reduces the demand for harmful row crops. It may not actually take that long.

"We're creating shifts that nobody's done in America in fifty years," Wadiak told me in January 2021, when he let me in on his R&D secret. Wadiak is creating a new market for purchasing wheat and says he'll source it only if the wheat qualifies as non-GMO and is farmed with minimal chemical fertilizers and herbicides. Wadiak is adamant that the root systems must stay intact. He says his farmers can grow two nondesiccated wheat crops by harvesting first in spring, mowing the tops off the plants, and then waiting for the second set to come up through the weeds. Wadiak says he'll pay a price about 20 percent above conventional and buy as much as he can get his hands on.

Cooks Venture's first farmer, located in Missouri, hadn't ever mowed two wheat harvests before, which underscores the uphill battle Wadiak faces to build the supply chain from scratch. The system he envisions combines several experimental methods into one: directly drilling the second-harvest seed into the soil, mowing both harvests down without tilling the soil, and then drying the harvest, storing it, and milling it roughly fifty miles away in Missouri. Wadiak thinks that's the key to creating a cash crop, meaning an agricultural product ready to sell into a commodified market instead of getting used on-farm, that's also a cover crop.

Part of Wadiak's drive comes from the anxiety that climate change will only make feed scarcer and more expensive. Between my initial conversation with Wadiak and this book's publication, the price of wheat shot up double digits alongside other grains. It threw Wadiak's planning out of whack, since the farmer Cooks Venture contracted sold off some of the thousand acres of wheat when the commodity prices were at a high.* Access to feed is Wadiak's single biggest concern, especially because, in a better system, breeds grow slower than industrial standards. That would mean they need more feed overall in their lifetime, and feed is already the biggest cost for farmers. While every landscape is different and will restore itself differently, and there's definitely no one approach that will work in preparing farms for stress from climate change, adding wheat into rotations in a system with cover cropping does carry some weight.

Cover crops work within existing row-crop farming to help manage water pollution from farm runoff, but benefits are limited unless land stays covered and untilled. According to the Environmental Working Group, a major 2018 study estimated that cover crops on 217 million acres of cropland—roughly fourteen times all cover crops planted—could bank carbon to offset a relatively small 1.6 percent of US net emissions. Regardless, if mass adoption of cover crops took hold, the crop added into rotation would

---

* Wadiak's economics have gotten a bit more complicated amid the skyrocketing price of commodity wheat. It makes what Wadiak is promising to buy from farmers way more expensive and threatens the scale that the project may be able to achieve.

absorb leftover fertilizer from other seasons. It's expected that there would be meaningful reduction of pollution in the Midwest as well as the Gulf of Mexico, which suffers from an annual dead zone. There's also, of course, the awkward threat that the next dust bowl is around the corner, and cover crops are a natural preventive measure. But so far, just one in twenty acres of Midwestern cropland uses cover crops. Wadiak thinks that might change if a proven market is created for a system where cover-cropping practices are required.

When wheat is harvested in the summer, it makes room for planting a winter annual like clover or other cover crops that can help farmers restore one hundred pounds of nitrogen per acre or more. Alison Grantham, who holds a dual doctorate in ecology and biogeochemistry and is a food systems consultant, told me she worked on a regional project for the Walton Family Foundation, Cooks Venture's Arkansas neighbors. It found the addition of a winter cover crop in the five states in the upper Mississippi River basin reduced pollution 50 to 70 percent. Grantham told me Wadiak's wheat rotation could live up to his hype.

"Why do we have so much corn and soy is probably a question that we should answer before we ask how much wheat we could have," Grantham said. "It's not just about how much we can extract, extract, extract out of the system."

A Better Chicken

The four chickens that showed up at my apartment were a part of the first step in Wadiak's grand plan: figuring out how much carbohydrate could be replaced with corn in the local non-GMO feed that Cooks Venture's breed eats. Wadiak's team of five scientists ran testing on their birds and found that Cooks Venture's specialty breed of chickens could be fed as much as 25 percent cover-crop-harvested wheat without any major changes to how much feed the chickens need overall.* It meant they could start testing with flocks immediately.

These experimental no-corn birds were an integral first piece to the puzzle. Our small apartment features a galley kitchen in which our landlords

---

* Nondesiccated wheat, specifically.

forwent an oven in favor of additional cabinet space beneath our stovetop. While our tabletop Instapot toaster oven sports a rotisserie rig, a quick pre-heat, and impressive air-frying convection, it was hardly the ideal tool for the four-chicken experiment on my hands. It was now showing its limits. How was I supposed to cook four chickens and do a side-by-side tasting? I decided it'd have to be an all-day Sunday nosh, where I'd cook one bird, taste it hot and take notes, and then, hours later, when each bird was cooked and cooled, I'd try them side by side.

Each bird was packaged with a simple stamp on it denoting Test #1 from Test #4:

#1 Control: Single stage feed. Local non-GMO corn/soy
#2 15% nondesiccated wheat to displace corn
#3 25% nondesiccated wheat to displace corn
#4 25% nondesiccated wheat with probiotic to displace corn

I checked a text from Wadiak with the instructions: "In the trial, number 2 and 3 performed best on health and feed conversion ratio, indicating that we can displace corn with cover crop harvest wheat between 15-25% in our line. Now the taste test!"

The plan I devised worked, but it took four shifts over the course of six hours. Bites along the way, as planned. Then I still had to taste, carve, make stock, and clean up. By the time I was sitting down with all the chicken in front of me, I felt like I'd just cooked a marathon Thanksgiving meal and was too tired to eat.

I called Wadiak up a few days later to discuss his own tasting notes. The meat raised with probiotics as an addition, consequently or otherwise, had spongier texture, and took the most feed to make the least amount of meat, compared to the rest of the options. My main note while tasting back-to-back focused on how much juicier the wheat-fed chicken was compared to the corn-fed. I still questioned how this idea—still working within the overall industrial crop system—would not make the same mistakes as past agribusiness giants when scale and demands became more intense.

Cooks Venture plans to have a separate, small line of birds that eat no corn or soy at all. Wadiak says this will allow bigger changes as well as experiments. "We'll have the big knob that we're turning, and the small one.

If you do too much too fast, you run the risk of, you know, not having good health in your animals. That's how you end up changing diet over time."

After the wheat test, Wadiak led a trial for sorghum, often featured in cover-crop rotations. The next ones planned included grains like oats, rye, curnzia, and milo. Then the Cooks team tested two soy alternatives: sunflower and pea. They settled on a feed mix consisting of wheat, sorghum, oats, cowpeas, and sunflower. The soy-free tests, in particular, are a big deal. Traditionally, farmers used meat or fish renders for the protein in feed, so there aren't many historic examples to try out. Wadiak tells me his number one customer service email question is: Do your chickens eat soy? This has completely turned his business on its head. "What are you supposed to eat? There is no chicken that's not grown with soy in America. At all," he says, laughing.

Finding a more sustainable grain to feed his chickens had long been an environmental priority, but Wadiak said it became his top priority from a customer standpoint after he realized the emails were so fanatical and that there was nothing on the market that could satisfy them. In addition to better flavor, more collagen, omega-3s, and maybe even phytonutrients, these chickens could be sold with health claims that have been causing a frenzy. The root cause, it seems, is a *New York Times* best-selling nutrition book called *The Plant Paradox* by Dr. Steven Gundry, which argues you are what you eat. Gundry pushes eaters to avoid intake of "most omega-6 fats, which prompt the body's attack mode, encouraging fat storage and hunger" and "eliminate industrial-farm-raised poultry (including so-called free-range poultry) and livestock (along with their dairy products) and all farm-raised fish, which are fed antibiotics, corn, and beans full of omega-6s and laced with Roundup."

Even industrially produced "free-range" animals contain inflammatory lectin in their meat, Dr. Gundry posits, because they are fed soy and corn. "With certain exceptions, omega-6 fats are inflammatory and omega-3 fats are anti-inflammatory. Corn and soy contain primarily omega-6 fats, while grass is high in omega-3 fats." As with all books that try to tell you how to eat, Gundry's proposed diet should be taken with a grain of salt. Kelly Clarkson was promoting this one, and a doctor at the Cleveland Clinic called it a fad that wouldn't work on everybody. Then the Mayo Clinic cautioned against believing a lectin-free diet could cure any and all autoimmune diseases, which is what this Palm Springs–based and Yale-educated doctor had concluded in his research. There are currently more than twelve thousand reviews on the book's Amazon listing, and Gundry has been well on his way to mainstream success with an Instagram page with more than 200,000 followers, a supplement brand with another 140,000, and a podcast.

Wadiak hopes those voracious consumers end up following him and subscribing to regular shipments from Cooks Venture instead. He says the taste of the meat has been better so far in tests. That excites him, since there's already a bunch of frenzied folks primed to seek out lectin-free foods, and his solution comes with soil benefits. But what Wadiak is proposing—replacing harmful corn and soy farmed for feed with cover-cropped grains—is somewhere between a moon shot and a viable reality. It's expected to require a lot of capital, as Wadiak takes on the consolidated chicken breeding industry at large.

Unwinding Big Chicken's Control of the Genetic Code

Wadiak taught me that the quality of the meat we consume fundamentally depends on two things. The first is the feed the animals consume, which is usually a farmer's biggest cost. The second is the genetics from which the animals are bred, which is predetermined in industrial contracts.

Cooks Venture can uniquely tackle both challenges, in a way that no other company I know of can. Changes to feed cannot fully take place without changes to genetics. Animals need to be able to digest whatever they are eating. Mainstream hatcheries, where chicken growers pick up their birds at just a few days old, have bred generations of chickens to be better suited to the feed they eat, mainly commodity corn. If you want to change the feed, you also must change the genetics. It's admittedly wonky, but the potential is big. If Cooks Venture is a success, it may build a viable alternative for supplying meat at scale, completely outside the industrialized agribusiness system. That said, whatever is built could become its own behemoth.

Most of the nine billion chickens that Americans consume each year—from conventional to free-range to organic and even most locally raised—are the same kind of breed, a Cornish Cross. Almost everyone ends up eating the same kind of chicken, no matter where it's purchased from. There's a big difference in price between conventional and heritage breeds for beef and pork because the genetics have been separated and built into the marketing. For example, America's prized Angus cattle, the most popular kind of beef sold, was brought over from England, where it became known for fatty marbling in the 1870s. But eating chicken is a relative novelty. Modern birds have been bred to grow superfast, which means cheaply. Cornish Cross birds have earned a reputation for breast meat prone to woody textures and tasteless, bland flavor.

In fact, genetics industry experts estimate that 99 percent of all chicken sold in America can trace its lineage back to one of two companies, Tyson-owned Cobb-Vantress and Germany-based and privately held EW Group, a genetics conglomerate that owns American firms Aviagen and Hubbard and is backed by a private billionaire named Erich Wesjohann and his family. These two conglomerates have cornered the $28 billion market selling their breeds since the 1980s. The most common are the Cobb 500 and the Ross 308, both variants of Cornish Cross. These birds are bow-legged and can be sickly so that it's hard for them to leave their houses.

Breeding works like the movie *Back to the Future*: There's a great-grandparent chicken, and then a grandparent, a parent, and then fourth-generation Michael J. Fox. That is the broiler. It takes around two and a half years to complete the cycle. Over time, like Michael J. Fox disappearing from the picture in the movie as he travels back in time, adjustments can be made. Geneticists decide whether to prioritize traits like straighter legs or red tail feathers, and eventually the traits emerge. Within a few weeks, their cousins arrive where they once existed.

A Cornish Cross goes from zero to a harvest weight of six pounds in thirty-five to forty-seven days, unlike Wadiak's birds, which take around sixty days. A heritage breed must spend at least sixteen weeks, or 112 days, maturing before going to market, per industry association standards. The Cornish Cross's quick life span is why those chicken breasts in the grocery store are usually double the size of your fist. Over decades, the birds have been selected to have very large muscle structures, particularly in the breast meat. The breed tends to have vascularized muscle cells and tissues, meaning that a capillary network capable of delivering nutrients to the cells forms inside the tissues. When the chickens drink water, the hydration fills up those cells, and they actually get bigger. That means the labels that claim

5 percent water added are barely scratching the surface. Water is ingrained in the tissue itself, which is not showing up on any label.

There were twenty-six Broiler genetics companies worldwide in 1981, but acquisitions by the two remaining companies have eliminated any meaningful competitors. Aviagen is based in Huntsville, Alabama, but has been owned by different European investors for decades. In 1994, London-based buyout shop BC Partners acquired Aviagen from Nutreco, a Dutch livestock and fish feed processor, for $550 million. Under BC Partners, Aviagen rolled up three firms, including British-based Ross Breeders, for about $150 million, in search of more profits. This is the provenance of the genetics of Aviagen's signature Ross 308, and the entire Ross line, billed as "the world's number one broiler breeder brand." These acquisitions kicked off the genetics industry consolidation. Aviagen soon secured 47 percent market share and then changed hands to global private equity firm Advent International in 2003, which acquired Aviagen for $300 million. EW Group purchased Aviagen in 2005.

Family-owned Perdue, the last broiler integrator in the United States to maintain its own genetics research company besides Tyson, ditched its own breed in 2014 because, according to a Perdue-issued press release, "there are no longer significant advantages to having our own breed . . . it is important that we have the flexibility to select the breeder combination that works best for each specific customer requirement." After the Perdue retreat, EW Group scooped up Hubbard in 2018, then nearly bankrupt with falling sales that hovered at 100 million euros annually. Hubbard was the last American breeder selling slow-growth chicken genetics.

Those two decisions almost completely consolidated the poultry genetics industry, and the effects have been drastic. Heritage lines and slow-growth breeds have been essentially eliminated since. These genetics have commanded a fair amount of poultry farmers' purchases: according to confidential Agri Stats data I got my eyes on, heritage breeds hit 10 percent at Hubbard's peak around 2005, as well as a brief period between 2011 and 2013.

"What happens when EW Group says, 'We've had our fun. Sure, it's a profitable company, but we're just going to sell it to some Chinese corporation,'" Wadiak has wondered. "They can easily do that. Who's preventing that? That could happen tomorrow. What does that do to our ability to feed people globally?"

EW Group, with a bestseller breed through Aviagen that requires less feed than Cobb's, controls roughly half of the global market for poultry genetics. The conglomerate counts annual revenue of more than $3 billion. About 50 percent of broiler genetics in the United States come from EW Group, while Tyson-owned Cobb's market share has roughly the other half. There's concern in the industry that Cobb has not been able to keep up as Aviagen advances. And Tyson hasn't been able to keep up with EW Group.

Despite that, owning part of the genetics business has given Tyson "exceptional leverage" over competitors, according to a 2019 lawsuit from Walmart, which eventually joined the chicken price-fixing class action and sued Agri Stats and eleven chicken processors for price-fixing. Walmart didn't include Tyson in the suit, even though that "exceptional leverage" apparently, per the lawsuit, was used "to mandate compliance with this conspiracy." America's largest meat-packer still came up frequently in the complaint:

"Since a supply of primary breeders is essential to each chicken producer's business, Tyson's ownership and control of subsidiary Cobb-Vantress provides it with exceptional leverage over Defendants and other Broiler producers to mandate compliance with this conspiracy. Tyson can offer Defendants and other Broiler producers the carrot of access to Cobb-Vantress' unique Broiler genetic lines, with desirable qualities like high conversion rates of feed into meat. However, Tyson can also use Cobb-Vantress as a stick against any competitor who Tyson and/or Defendants believe is overproducing chickens by providing such competitors inferior, sick, or an insufficient number of breeder pullets, or withholding breeder pullets altogether that the competitor needs to operate a profitable business."

In early 2021, I reached out to Walmart's chief lawyer, who quickly declined to comment: "Thanks for reaching out but no, we are not able to discuss a pending matter."

I followed up two minutes after his email reached my inbox with two questions I still thought he could answer.

"Is there an understanding of a timeline of when this could see movement in the courts? I understand it was last put on hold in July 2020 due to the pandemic. Why is Tyson not included in the suit (but mentioned throughout the complaint)?"

No response.

Taking a Bite Out of Industrial Meat

Cooks Venture is now hyperfocused on creating alternative genetics and feed, which could fundamentally challenge the existing structure of the poultry industry. That's a monumental task, but Wadiak may just be the founder to take a bite out of industrial chicken. Born in Houston the second of four siblings, Wadiak grew up outside Chicago with his mom and stepdad, an aerospace engineer. Wadiak cooked in restaurants throughout high school, usually clocking in sixty hours a week. He graduated from the Culinary Institute of America in 1999 and moved to California to cook. For two years to supplement his $10 hourly rate, during truffle season he'd fly to Italy over a weekend, pick up a bunch of truffles, and sell it to chefs he'd stop in on layovers in New York and Chicago. Eventually back in New York, Wadiak added in catering for film festivals, which led him to the moneyed and start-up-adjacent world, and he became the chef and ingredient chief in the Blue Apron cofounder trio. He was, as the venture capitalists say, on the rocket ship—responsible for building out Blue Apron's supply chain network of more than 250 somewhat sustainable farmers as chief operating officer, cofounder, and board member. But then the rocket ship ran out of fuel. Wadiak jumped off a month after the meal kit start-up went public in June 2017, going from unicorn darling to one of the worst-performing IPOs in food stock history in a matter of months.

On eight hundred acres in the heart of the Ozark foothills in northwest Arkansas, Wadiak now raises millions of chickens a year—there are 1.3 million moseying around the acres at any given time. Cooks Venture and its hatchery has ten houses for broilers, another ten for experiments, and thirty houses for breeding. During the day, the doors are open, and chickens go in and out when they please. The breeding operation feeds and houses one hundred thousand birds, just for genetics.

Cooks Venture is singularly focused on breeding and disrupting the dominance of the Cornish Cross. The firm is the only vertically integrated chicken producer in the country that has an independent genetics operation—it breeds through selection, not genetic engineering—without ties to Cobb or Aviagen. It's the first company in over fifty years to do that. Many entrepreneurs attempt to build a better mousetrap, but few have as much of a David-and-Goliath battle awaiting them as Wadiak. All his unicorn fundraising and IPO roadshow to meltdown experience may give Wadiak the edge to build Cooks Venture as a competitive alternative at scale. He has a better shot than most at knowing the pitfalls, and the sharks, to avoid.

Wadiak has raised $30 million from investors and another $50 million in debt. His company is valued above $100 million. But will investment from private funders help Cooks Venture bring down the price of producing slow-growth chicken? That's something individual farmers may never be able to do, unfortunately, because scale is needed to combat the industry consolidation. To be sure, Indiana pasture–raised farmer Greg Gunthorp (from Chapter 6) says Cooks Venture coming into the pasture-raised market and bringing down prices with its scale is just as much a part of the market forces that helped drive Gunthorp's chicken production out of business. But investors expect returns, even the more impact-minded investors whom Wadiak has brought on, and that dynamic may continue to drive Cooks Venture to consider lowering its prices.

With few heritage breeds sold nationwide, even most local farms are raising Cornish Cross. Heritage, Wadiak says, has no chance at scale. Wadiak acquired the operation for its heat-tolerant breed, originally developed by Lloyd Peterson, who began experimenting in his garage in 1939 as a twenty-seven-year-old. The breed, called Pioneer, claims stronger legs, bone density, immune systems, and gastrointestinal health, mainly because they're bred to stay alive. The birds have higher collagen, more vibrant omega-3 fatty acids, and more protein per pound. Pioneer birds are also bred to be more resistant to disease while having a higher heat tolerance. Any competitors that might want their own climate-friendly chicken breed are roughly two decades of research behind Cooks Venture. Wadiak says that's why his start-up will one day dominate breeds raised on pasture. His strategy leaves room for licensing out his breed, just like Aviagen and Cobb.

CHAPTER 13

The Dumb Money Driving
the Plant-Based Boom

Horrific impacts from climate change are here: workers dying from heat exhaustion in the field, superbugs and antibiotic resistance, algae blooms and water pollution, biodiversity on a full-fledged retreat. There are countless examples of crumbling infrastructure, from notables like the Texas energy grid failure to errant gas pipeline fires in the Gulf of Mexico. Climate change has created a very real existential threat to the global food system, which, at current scope and scale, uses far too many resources while leaving far too many consequences in its wake. Scientists and researchers have concluded broadly that if the food industry doesn't change, humanity will not meet the goals that scientists have laid out to stymie catastrophic climate impacts. The food system is necessary for humanity's survival, but it also could be its undoing if the current course of action is not radically adapted for what's ahead.

That's why there's not enough time to throw money at the wrong projects. There's not enough time for greed to get in the way.

The problem is, within the food system, there are many potential solutions and an infinite amount of factions with competing interests—all of which think they know the best path forward. Many of these folks live in the emerging universe of alternative meat. There are the techno-optimists and the techno-apologists, the lab-grown meat freaks, the lab-grown meat freaks in favor of rewilding, the mycologists, the plant-based bros chasing Silicon Valley money. I have yet to meet anyone in this industry who says they do not care about climate change. In fact, many say they are personally driven by their product's sustainability and environmental potential.

But it's still all to a certain point. There's a reason Impossible Foods is preparing for a potentially $10 billion public listing, and that neither Impossible nor Beyond Meat is registered as public benefit corporations, a move that would legally inhibit the companies from putting profit over their environmental mission. Half of Impossible's investors come from venture capital firms, and the roster even includes a hedge fund, Viking Global Investors. Backers are no doubt ready for an exit, and they want to get Impossible the best deal.

A sustainability halo helps the cause. That's why it's sometimes hard to differentiate between businesses that say they are doing right by the environment and ones that actually are. There's a fundamental conflict at play. Businesses—even ones set up to be "impact-driven" or "mission-oriented"—still need to profit, and backers expect a return on their initial investment. These economic realities make it difficult for businesses to make decisions that don't drive money to the bottom line, in a system set up to help large-scale, synthetics, and industrial the most. Add to that the pressures of venture capitalists or public shareholders, and decision-making can get muddled further. Might it be too wishful to suggest that business should actually provide net positives for the environment and community? Perhaps, but at minimum the tension remains: Is it possible to increase profits while decreasing environmental impact?

Advertising for brands like Impossible and Beyond hinges on the products' environmental impacts. Impossible claims to use 87 percent less water, 96 percent less land, and 89 percent fewer emissions than beef burgers. Beyond touts 99 percent, 93 percent, and 90 percent, respectively. Given realistic limits for consumption and purchasing behavior, how much could mass commercial adoption actually impact? Despite the hype and fast growth, meat alternatives accounted for 0.2 percent of 2020 grocery meat sales in the United States, according to NielsenIQ. Or, rather, a bite that is still so small that meat industry executives, while on the offensive, are hardly that concerned.

Alternative milks including Silk and Oatly commanded 11 percent of total grocery store milk sales in 2021, which has stoked expectations for meat alternatives to reach a similar share. But there's a long way these ambitious forecasts will have to climb. The US plant-based meat industry had $900 million in 2021 grocery sales, according to NielsenIQ. Barclays expects plant-based will rise to 10 percent of total meat consumption, or $140 billion globally, by 2029. Others expect an even rosier picture. One projection puts sales of alternative meat, eggs, dairy, and seafood products at $290 billion by 2035, according to research by alternative protein investor Blue Horizon Corporation and Boston Consulting Group.

The recent adoption of plant-based alternatives comes after several false starts over the decades, which cannot be discounted. Way back in 1972, the USDA projected 10 to 20 percent of all processed meat would be replaced by soy products by 1980.

Luckily, the World Resources Institute's Richard Waite helped me sketch out potential scenarios—to make sure we don't wake up in 2030 and say, did we waste one of our last chances to get this fixed? Let's be clear that this is not the only way to feed more people on a harsher planet, and much more has to be done in terms of reforestation, fertilizer reduction, and biodiversity restoration to adapt for climate change. But if we're going to look to plant-based meat alternatives as a solution in our future, which many big financial institutions are invested in making happen, I want to know how much is actually needed to impact more than a drop in the bucket.

Waite and I decided to base the scenarios on 15 percent, since that seemed like a reasonable goal but also a bit of a reach. What would happen if plant-based meat by 2030 replaced 15 percent of projected total US meat consumption, and what would happen if meat consumption continued to rise and plant-based meat was tacked on as additional? The last question was, how much plant-based meat would have to sell at fast-food locations to make a difference?

Per estimates, the business-as-usual case has US meat production and consumption rising 9 percent by 2030. The main takeaway from WRI's Waite is that meat production would fall by an estimated 7 percent if plant-based meat captured 15 percent of the meat market by 2030. Waite called the finding "quite meaningful." Since the business-as-usual case has meat production at almost double-digit growth, even a tapering off would be big.

Emissions from food production and their supply chains in this case would fall by 65 million tons of CO_2. Waite says due to the reduced agricultural land demand, the carbon opportunity cost from avoided global deforestation would fall by more than 320 million tons of CO_2. Explained another way, it would be the same as taking approximately eighty million cars, or roughly a quarter of all vehicles in the United States, off the road. If consumption of plant-based meat grew alongside increases to meat purchases, and meat purchases stayed flat instead of growing as the business-as-usual prediction suggests, the environmental benefit would be the equivalent of taking more than fifty million cars off the road. That's the kind of significance that makes me think twice.

How Much More Can We Eat?

Since Impossible launched in 2016, its stated goal has been to lead a revolution that completely replaces animal protein (including milk and fish) by 2035. I first met Impossible's founder, Pat Brown, in September 2019, a month after the nationwide Impossible Whopper launch. He was in New York for the United Nations' Climate Week, and also to launch Impossible into New York supermarkets. When I met him, he was in a tie-dye T-shirt on a makeshift stage inside a soon-to-be-bankrupt Upper West Side location of Fairway Market, where he was more of an outspoken professor than the biohacking tech CEO I expected.

"People have a hard enough time when they're massively overweight to change their diets, much less something that is more abstract like climate change," he said at one point. "The only way to solve it is to figure out a way to enable people to continue to eat all the foods they love without compromising on any deliciousness or nutritional value, but find a way to produce them with a vastly reduced environmental footprint."

A year later, during a one-on-one interview, I pressed further, and Pat Brown told me: "Our mission is to completely replace animals as a food technology by 2035. We didn't just say we'll eventually do it. We said by 2035, because it's incredibly urgent. Part of the reason for saying 2035 is, you know, the concern that the people would think we were bullshitting if we said earlier than that. But I think we can do it faster than that."

Drawing from marketing that refers to each new formula like a software update, he continued: "Look at what happened with digital cameras from the time of the first camera that stored eight pictures to when they were three hundred thousand pixels. There were 0.3 megapixels, it cost a thousand dollars, until the film industry was dead. It was less than a decade. When you have an inherently better technology—even if, at the start, it's still catching up—you know where it's going to end, and the transition can happen very fast. That's why I'm optimistic that it's not going to be until 2035. But I have to be careful about saying that, because people think I'm crazy."

The major meat-packers in the industry doubt Brown (and Ethan Brown, the founder of Beyond Meat, who is unrelated) will be able to substantially take away their market share. Though the meat processors have picked up the trend and are funding their own divisions, venture investments, and acquisitions to stay competitive with meat alternatives. Don't let the marketing around alternative protein lines fool you. The reality is, the brave new world the big meat processors are preparing for does not include shrinking meat sales. If you take it how Tyson's then head of alternative protein, Justin Whitmore, explained it to me, meat-packers like Tyson are preparing for plant-based products to increase profits.

"Plant protein is high-growth, but also a very small base. Our viewpoint is that plant protein will be an option, alongside meat, in the developed world for many consumers, particularly younger consumers," Whitmore explained. "However, we don't see a world where that protein replaces meat to the degree that it changes the shape of that global meat growth that I referenced earlier. That's a part of the new world of eating."

Fast-Food Dreams

Fast-food menus could be a quick way to reduce meat consumption globally and quell climate change. But it's up to consumers. That's the pitch, anyway. And that's really where I began to wonder how much adoption in fast-food locations was even in the realm of possibility, and what is really needed to make an impact on climate. I wanted to focus on fast food because of the lower price points and how quickly just one major chain can change the size and scope of a start-up brand's sales. Fast food still has huge menus full of different options, and there's still a lot of competition. I was curious, was anyone really buying this stuff?

I attempted to find out how a megachain would prepare for a big plant-based deal like this while reporting a *Forbes* magazine feature about Restaurant Brands, the 3G Capital–backed parent company of Burger King, Popeyes, and Tim Hortons. The reporting focused on how the company can be massive—with $5 billion in sales—and still take substantial risks. Becoming the first to test out Impossible Foods at thousands of locations was a big one. McDonald's had been quiet on the subject. Alternative burgers were still a novelty that only a handful of smaller chains, like Carl's Jr., were selling.

I had tasted a few early versions of Impossible's burger—at a food tech conference in Brooklyn's Industry City where I moderated, and years later the 2.0 version at Expo West, the food trade show that's really an annual sample-eating Super Bowl in Anaheim. But I expected the Impossible Whopper to be a little different—it would have the same char-broiled flavors that Burger King's signature item was known for. Unfortunately, a Whopper is not my formerly beloved McNuggets, so I didn't have much nostalgia to compare it to, but I did get to try a regular Whopper alongside the Impossible version. Lucky for Burger King, the Whopper is known for mayonnaise that can hide all manner of sins.

In March 2019, I flew down to Miami to visit the headquarters of Restaurant Brands. Out came an executive smiling wide and holding tight to a special-made tray with a tower of wrapped burgers. The Impossible versions had a bright teal-and-white wrapper to differentiate the meatless meat inside, which was helpful since, side by side, they looked relatively identical. We sat down and broke open some burgers. Cutting each in half and looking up close—and I mean very close, too close for a normal dining setting—you could see differences in the centers of the burgers. Impossible had some more holes in places, but by and large it passed the tests. The classic charred waft? Present. A crisp crust on the burger? Also present. The sesame seeds, pickles, and expected grease? Yup. That all too.

"There's no sacrifice on taste," the executive said at the table, grinning with his Impossible Whopper in hand.

If nothing else, I was amused by the feats of modern food science. It was spongier, for sure, but I was also intrigued by what this window into launching a new menu item was showing me. Mostly, I was struck by how many executives around the building thought it would drive customers to doors. Chains like Burger King, with seven thousand US stores, could provide a quick and easy way for plant-based products to scale. But messing up the first big test could set the entire emerging industry back. All of it meant nothing if customers still didn't buy it.

Early data suggested Impossible's Burger King launch was a win for the chain's overall foot traffic, but less so for the environment. Impossible Whopper sales initially brought new customers into Burger King stores, but all-beef Whopper sales also rose. Despite the Impossible launch, Burger King sales fell short of Wall Street's expectations for the year.

All this made me even more committed to figuring out how much it would really take for plant-based burgers to make a substantial impact. Silicon Valley–backed burgers were suddenly being touted as potentially relieving capitalism from its climate dread with the momentum of a truck hurtling down the highway, but really, plant-based alternatives were still relatively niche—and hardly a major driver of sales. As it turns out, one analyst estimates that Impossible Whoppers are still less than 5 percent of total beef sales at Burger King. That 5 percent is a good proxy for how much it could be at other chains, too, if plant-based alternatives were to replace their meaty counterparts on menus. Lackluster adoption is not going to change anything.

But early backers are hoping they will get a windfall from Impossible's future IPO or acquisition. Most restaurants that sell Impossible's faux-meat products obtain distribution through a licensing agreement. But Impossible, I was told, may have traded minority ownership to the restaurant group, Momofuku, which gave the start-up some of its first validation on diners' plates. That's noteworthy: Impossible and Momofuku have never disclosed any formal stake before, yet chef-founder David Chang has hawked the burger for years, saying in 2016 that he was "genuinely blown away." Chang declined to comment. Momofuku has continued to plant the products in high-profile places: In 2021, Momofuku's Ssäm Bar became one of the first restaurants to serve Impossible's pork alternative, while Chang promoted the start-up in a Hulu series on the future of food. As one Momofuku insider told me, cash proceeds from any Impossible exit or IPO would transform Momofuku's business.

The New Rules of Food Finance

Alternative proteins raised $3.1 billion in 2020, the most ever in the burgeoning industry's history. That breaks down to $2.1 billion for plant-based alternatives, including $700 million for Impossible Foods across two raises,

$335 million for Livekindly, and nearly half a billion between dairy alternatives Oatly and Califia. Otherwise, cell-based meat raised $360 million in 2020, while fermentation start-ups raised a total of $590 million in 2020, including big checks for Perfect Day (which raised $300 million) and Nature's Fynd (which raised an $80 million series B and $45 million in debt). Massive checks continued. Nature's Fynd then raised another round, a series C, that totaled $350 million and valued the start-up at $1.75 billion, followed by NotCo, a Jeff Bezos–backed company run by a young entrepreneur from Chile, which raised $235 million at a $1.5 billion valuation. In 2021, alternative protein start-ups secured a record $3.8 billion in new funding, according to PitchBook.

These big checks are noteworthy because, two decades ago, fewer investors in the food industry had a steadier go of it. Returns for food business exits were expected at around two to five times the initial investment. Publicly traded food conglomerates, pretty much the main acquirers, could pay only so much—for a food brand, one to three times sales for acquisition value was solid. But the climate crisis is emerging at a time when there's been unprecedented funding flowing into the food and beverage industry, igniting investors and previously untapped financial heavyweights from Sequoia Capital to Goldman Sachs. They see food as a new frontier of investment.

The bad news is, they see it as a last frontier of investment, which means big returns are expected. Some founders don't understand when they first start that signing a term sheet means two things. First, those investors expect an exit, one way or another. Second, they expect that exit to come with a return—usually at a multiple of what they invested.

The founders often don't understand what they're getting into. I saw that many times over five years of reviewing the applicants for the 30 Under 30 food and drink list, and it has frustrated me. There's all this financial capital funneling in to solve the "problem" of meat—but there's so much frenzy about how much money investors could make in the process that the entire industry could blow up on greed while Big Meat and its Big Macs kick back and watch the whole thing fizzle out. It seems possible that investors wanting to cash in on the next big thing will ruin one of the last possibilities that exists to prepare for a climate-challenged future.

Not Enough Time to Waste Any Money

Lisa Feria has a phrase for the frenzy to make a profit in food companies: dumb money. Feria grew up in San Juan, Puerto Rico, and came to the United States for a chemical engineering degree. She started working in food at General Mills, got an MBA from the University of Chicago, and then went to Procter & Gamble to learn how to manage profit and loss statements and big research and development budgets. A PETA video exposing the meat industry is what set her off on a journey to pioneer investing in the alternative protein industry—"I had a Matrix blue pill–red pill moment. I couldn't unsee what I had seen." She moved to Kansas City to start one of the first alternative protein investing firms, Stray Dog Capital. Feria stayed in the Midwest to avoid Silicon Valley hype skewing her frame of mind: "Food is not technology. It's not a widget. It's not a Facebook. It can come from every little town in the United States, and the Midwest, as a matter of fact, is the most likely place for it to flourish, because you need manufacturing, you need cooling, you need distribution, logistics. Those tend to be concentrated in areas that are lower-cost."

So far, Stray Dog has backed more than thirty start-ups, including Beyond Meat, Ecovative's MyForest Foods, Miyoko's Creamery, Daring Foods, Kite Hill, as well as a trio of lab-grown start-ups (Israel's Aleph Farms, the Netherlands' Mosa Meat, Silicon Valley's Upside Food). But it wasn't easy. Feria says she spent the first three years just "going through the queue of investments that were in desperate need of funding, and funding them."

"Food wasn't considered very sexy as an investment," Feria shared with me. "We found that there was a death trap in early stage start-ups between pre-seed and seed where there weren't enough investors and these companies weren't getting funded, even really good companies. There wasn't enough money around. They would just hobble from raise to raise and barely make it a year before they needed to do the whole rigmarole again. We found a spot that an investor group needed to cover, in order to keep the whole category moving and grooving. Most of the investors that were present were later-stage investors. Because that's safer. A lot of this dumb money that I see throwing money around tends to be in the later stages.

"These investors, usually individual investors, that want to invest in this cool new thing, they will give money to a lot of these companies that

shouldn't be getting money. What's happening is unnatural," Feria explained. "That's a good example of how investors who don't have a lot of
knowledge in this space will fund companies at early stages and then cause
harm, because those companies would not have gotten funded."

But there's still a scarcity of capital for truly groundbreaking technologies, and distraction has the potential to emphasize the wrong ideas. I
find this powerful when considering how to finance a better food system,
because there's a finite amount of resources as well as capital. These start-
ups are diverting money from other start-ups that could be meaningful
and desperately need the funds, because research and development *does*
take time and *is* expensive. Alternative seafood needs to cannibalize some
of the funding from lab-grown, Feria added, instead of a private investor's
million-dollar check giving a start-up another six months of cash to keep
the lights on while the team isn't making advances.

Yet that logic is often removed from the emerging industry's decision-
making. Investors are terrified of missing deals. Take an example from 2021,
when an alternative protein company had a meeting with a billionaire-
backed investment firm, quickly got an offer with a valuation of over $1 bil-
lion, and within fifteen minutes had fielded a matching offer, negotiated,
and closed the entire round.

"Those companies end up diluting the money in the cash that can go
to other companies," said Feria. "That money doesn't really get allocated
properly, so that's the harm in the dumb money. They don't understand the
category enough to make better bets and then end up overfeeding some that
shouldn't be eating that, and then starving some that really do need that to
get to the next level."

With investors eyeing the plant-based industry, the frenzy has fueled a
boom in start-ups. They don't have your classic founders with an invented
product. A lot of what's getting funded are copycats, perhaps fronted by a
celebrity influencer type, made by a co-manufacturer, with an off-the-shelf
recipe, a label slapped on, and a marketing campaign funded by a few investors. Their crazy valuation multiples are hinging on the hopes of getting
swept up in a consolidation boom. The copycats are here, and so are the
tourists. Many are banking on a consolidation windfall, or private equity
or a food conglomerate like General Mills rolling up a few brands at once.

The losers will go bankrupt, and investors are expecting a bloodbath. So says Marcus Keitzer, who sees nearly every deal opportunity in the emerging industry as alternative protein chief at Germany-based PHW Group, which was one of the first backers of Beyond Meat in Europe. PHW Group originates from the same German company as EW Group, the owner of Aviagen and its poultry-breeding powerhouse. "It's absolutely crazy these days how investors are desperately looking for plant-based platforms in which they can invest," Keitzer told me. "Make no mistake, it's supercompetitive, and it will become even more competitive. You will see a lot of companies go belly-up because it's very competitive."

The investors behind these companies often know it's a riskier business. They are operating under the impression that for every start-up that fails, a big exit will make it all worth it, which is why these start-ups are nothing more than numbers on a spreadsheet. The rounds and valuations are bigger. But it's also led to a higher failure rate than before, a rate that was rising pre-pandemic. Investors who have been backing alternative start-ups the whole time tell me it's now just as common to make a ten-times return as lose money on a company going bust and write off the investment on taxes. These investors are investing for profit, which will cement us on a path toward a bleaker future.

That's a problem given the limited time and amount of resources to fix the food system, which makes me question how much of the $6 billion that alternative protein start-ups have already raised in the last decade will end up wasted, and what would happen if it could go toward a better use before it's too late?

Buyer Beware

It was during the end of Beyond Meat's earnings call to explain its year-end 2020 results that I first heard Ethan Brown, Beyond's founder and CEO, talk about investors expecting consolidation to plow through the plant-based industry sometime soon. The call had been an interesting mix of news: Beyond remained the clear market leader, even while it lost 14 percent of its restaurant and food service sales due to COVID-19 shutdowns. The news was softened by a long-awaited partnership with McDonald's, the largest restaurant chain in the world, for Beyond to develop McDonald's McPlant burger. Brown was optimistic, and then the analyst from Jefferies asked whether Brown expected consolidation in the industry. Brown added: "From the investment community, there's a lot of people that are investing very late in the hope that they can get the next break, and I think that we have established this position." Beyond will be a key consolidator in the industry—and might acquire brands outside its signature products, like in fish or milk.

Beyond Meat's own IPO had driven a lot of hype. Before Beyond Meat went public in May 2019, the previous decade had barely any. But institutional investors, pension funds, and family offices were hungry for public investments that satisfied criteria for "ESG," or environmental, social, and governance criteria. Then Beyond stunned, more than doubling on day one and surging 250 percent within those first few months. It became one of the best-performing public offerings of the pre-pandemic era. A boom of public listings has followed: six food or agriculture companies went public in 2020, followed by twelve in 2021.

But then Beyond's stock crashed. Beyond's meteoric rise came with downsides, and its stock turned into something of a devil's bargain. Beyond Meat quickly became the most volatile food stock on the public markets. The price to pay for cheap and quick access to capital forced Beyond under the microscope of thirsty hedge funds, activist investors, and short shops. Unwanted attention had been drawn to a brand with a mission to make the most sustainable and accessible protein on the planet. There's enough pressure to do that right as it is. Why add short sellers into the mix?

Beyond Meat transformed into one of the most heavily shorted food stocks on the public markets. Short sellers like Citron and ValueWorks have major money to make off volatility. ValueWorks' founder, Charles Lemonides, said that when he started shorting Beyond in October 2021, it had all the makings of the perfect short: the unprofitable company had flipped "from one growth story to another" and would sustain its launches with a marketing push that seemed to take too much. Lemonides described it to me as "a change bank."

"Existing sales weren't profitable. The growth didn't seem to be organic. They had to buy growth. Management seemed to be in turmoil," Lemonides told me. "The valuation was absurd, and it had already lost investor enthusiasm. If you look at the number of people searching on it, it had basically fallen off a cliff."

ValueWorks started its short when the stock was around $110. When we spoke four months later, the price had dropped 40 percent and ValueWorks had made millions. But shorting Beyond can be fickle because the price is so volatile. In January 2021, leading up to announcing a line of codeveloped snacks with Pepsi, a quarter of Beyond's total shares were shorted. The Pepsi joint venture announcement went out on the wire just as the infamous GameStop meme stock surge first started ripping billions from investors shorting GameStop. Suddenly, the news bid up Beyond stock, too—shooting up to a high of $221 per share. This killed a lot of the short positions, which officially speaking were forced to cash out, which is also what happened with GameStop over the same few days. The short positions fell to 11 percent. A big drop, yes, but that's actually still a huge amount of shorts. Most food stocks have less than 5 percent of shares shorted.

The brief break from short sellers didn't last long. Just two months later, the shares shorted had risen to 18 percent, and by January 2022 the Beyond shares shorted rose again, to a third of total stock.

"The issue is the stock market environment is booming and it is creating opportunities for lots of companies to sell stock, whether or not these companies are good investments or not, whether they're mature, proven or unproven," short seller Ben Axler of Spruce Point Capital Management told me after he went public with his Oatly short in July 2021. "The market has an appetite to fund these companies. For us, it's a great market environment. We're seeing all sorts and stripes come public that shouldn't be public."

Some companies that have gone public have no business being public, Axler said. "There's too much capital chasing, too few quality opportunities," he said. "The takeaway is, buyer beware. The food industry, it's very tough. It's very hard to have long, sustained success, even for the global brands."

Dumb Money Has Serious Consequences

Founders like Josh Tetrick will fight to stay relevant. Tetrick is blue-eyed and square-jawed, with the muscular stance of a former linebacker. He played football in college at West Virginia University and even in his early forties retains the charm of a smooth-talking jock.

A few years ago, Tetrick was on the brink of losing control. A messy boardroom battle nearly tanked Tetrick's latest start-up, originally called Hampton Creek. Tetrick's checkered journey remains a prime example of the power that billionaires and deep-pocketed investors wield, and how these hidden forces are shaping the alternative protein industry. That an operator as smooth as Tetrick nearly lost his company should serve as a warning for entrepreneurs everywhere. Yet Tetrick's prevailing in this environment is equally telling.

Tetrick whipped his origin story into a narrative as smooth as the vegan mayonnaise he once sold. Born in Alabama and raised in Philadelphia, Tetrick claims that a childhood of eating junk food led him to seek out vegetarianism and eventually start a company to create planet-friendly food. After transferring to Cornell, he spent a few years going back and forth to sub-Saharan Africa. His LinkedIn banner photo is him surrounded by African children on a soccer pitch. Eventually, Tetrick went to law school and spent ten months at a law firm before parting ways after an op-ed he wrote that criticized industrial farming. After a stint in motivational speaking, where Tetrick often found himself volunteering to give a speech to students, Tetrick linked up with cofounder Josh Balk.

Tetrick had no background in food and had not held down any job for longer than a year. He still secured a meeting with billionaire venture capitalist Vinod Khosla's firm in 2011. But in his pitch, Tetrick hyped up his recipe's ingredients as "close to perfection." The meeting led to a half-million-dollar check.

The investment gave him invaluable access. Whole Foods dispatched a buyer, Errol Schweizer, to fly to San Francisco to meet Tetrick, and Hampton Creek did secure national distribution through Whole Foods distributor UNFI.

A few months later, Hampton Creek issued an email to investors, that the product was the top-selling mayonnaise in Whole Foods. Tetrick declined to comment on the accusations that he mischaracterized Hampton Creek's Whole Foods sales. According to Schweizer, the vice president of grocery between 2009 and 2016, his connection to Khosla was a clear asset to his relationship with Whole Foods.

"I didn't see success, but I couldn't discontinue it. I would have gotten in trouble," said Schweizer. Schweizer recalled a time he was on a phone call where Whole Foods CEO John Mackey threatened to fire executives over not treating a friend of his well. "If something like that had come through John [Mackey] and you'd done your job as the buyer protecting the P&L and your fiduciary responsibilities, but it was a friend of John's, you would have gotten in trouble."

Thanks to the prominent placement in Whole Foods and other help from fresh connections, including investment from Salesforce CEO Marc Benioff and Li Ka-shing's Horizons Ventures, Hampton Creek kept growing—so much so that members of the American Egg Board and its affiliates once joked over email about putting "a hit" on Tetrick, according to a trove of federal emails released in 2016.

But Tetrick was about to learn that dumb money can have serious consequences. His investors had far different plans than he did. One board member quickly encouraged Tetrick to consider planning for a sale to a conglomerate like Unilever. The unexpected exit strategy startled Tetrick. Then, in 2015, investors increased the pressure. Tetrick, meanwhile, was fixated on creating the company's flagship "technology"—a vegan egg. Tetrick had been able to sweet-talk his investors at first, but they were growing impatient. Tetrick fought with investors over putting more budget behind the start-up's signature egg and even more experimental research into lab-grown meat. But investors wanted to see a return, and soon.

Tetrick prepared to protect his power in 2015 while raising a $100 million series D. Some founders might believe in their own vision and ability too much, but all too often they give up huge portions of their companies, welcoming the fox into the henhouse. Tetrick made three key changes to the board's bylaws. The first added more common seats than preferred to the start-up's board, so Tetrick has a better shot at investors not controlling a major decision. He then focused on the mechanism of the quorum and how investors can use it to exploit a time-sensitive decision, like signing a big investment deal that would launch a new product line, or whether an executive should be fired. Those meetings need to happen on short notice, which can be practical or create drama. To remove the chance of an ambush, Tetrick's start-up, now rebranded as Eat Just, requires its board to provide twenty-four-hour notice for big decisions. Third, Tetrick changed his will to create a windfall situation where, if he were to die suddenly, a designated representative would continue to vote in his place. That made Tetrick's presence at the company potentially far more permanent, which didn't sit well with some investors. The board still retained the ultimate power to fire a senior executive, including Tetrick.

Then, in 2016, a *Bloomberg* article hit about a controversial program to buy back mayo from store shelves and falsely disguise the purchases on income statements, which Hampton Creek allegedly ran to inflate sales. Tetrick, backed by an independent investigation, claims it was just 1 percent of his 2014 sales. The revelation launched a Securities and Exchange Commission investigation. The probe ultimately found no wrongdoing.

What followed was even more dramatic: an attempted coup, led by three executives, including the chief technology officer. Their plan was simple: oust Tetrick and turn the company over to investors. The coup team thought Tetrick's dream egg alternative was pointless and that the start-up should instead pivot to operating like a biotech company, in which it would forgo its own brand and identify functional proteins to license out to big food companies. Tetrick debated the idea with the CTO and thought it was just a disagreement. But the executives decided to go to some members of the board to discuss it. Other investors let Tetrick know, and once he uncovered the plot, he fired them.

Some of the board members didn't want Tetrick making any decisions without consulting them first, according to the *Bloomberg* article. Tetrick still pulled it off through an elaborate bait and switch. The three executives were in Majorca, Spain, on a business trip, and instead of flying to their next destination in Germany, Tetrick told them to stay and book a hotel conference room to meet a venture capitalist who was also on the island. But then Tetrick videoconferenced himself into the room with his start-up's human resources team and fired them.

The board members still erupted and demanded Tetrick rehire them. But Tetrick had already leaked the story as his own contingency plan. That's when the board's last four members resigned. Everyone on the board but Tetrick stepped off. The five-year-old start-up went from a five-person board to one.

The pressure for short-term returns eventually became too much. Reflecting, Tetrick said bringing on investors can lead to making "dysfunctional choices." Eventually Tetrick ditched those extra products, and through the six-month process of identifying potential board members, he learned how the Coca-Cola Company manufactured its proprietary flavor as a syrup and used a global network of partners to add the fizz, bottle it, and distribute it. The Coca-Cola network inspired Tetrick because of the chance to "scale and get to profitability a lot faster."

Adopting that vision has helped Eat Just survive. In three years, Eat Just's mung bean egg has grown to forty-four thousand points of retail distribution in North America, along with thousands more in restaurants. The company maintains its own mung bean ingredient manufacturing in the United States, working with companies for manufacturing and distribution in China, South Korea, Singapore, Hong Kong, and South Africa. "My initial instinct was to look at the assets of big ag and say, that's not me. We need to build something entirely different and new and better," Tetrick told me. "But as you remove the label of big ag from it and all the emotions that are associated with animal agriculture, what are we actually talking about here? Very efficient manufacturing facilities. High shear mixers. Tanking equipment. Cold chain distribution. Millions of points of distribution, both in retail and food-service outlets. Tens of thousands of people who are selling into those outlets. That's exactly what I want." Tetrick has been building a foundation that stacks the odds of longevity in his favor.

The founders who survive, like Tetrick, must often pull off crazy feats to stay in power. Tetrick has solidified his own control while other investors, corporate agribusiness firms, and sovereign wealth funds have taken stakes in Eat Just's future. That means the pressure to drive returns will continue, especially as Tetrick pushes his start-up to produce lab-grown meat. Involving billionaires ups the stakes. Extreme expectations become the norm, attracting extreme personalities who often are willing to do whatever it takes to remain in those high-pressure environments.

CHAPTER 14

Will Meatless Meat Actually

Help the Earth?

Plant-based foods have gotten so contorted that the emerging market must also contend with the power dynamics of JBS, the world's largest meat-packer, exerting its muscle. When JBS approaches Wall Street with its IPO, its plant-based businesses will be a testament to what JBS can do when the conglomerate says it cares about sustainability. In 2021, on the Sunday after spending $410 million to acquire Netherlands-based Vivera, Europe's third-largest plant-based company and the largest independent in that market, JBS took out a full-page ad in the *New York Times* to tout its climate goals: "agriculture can be part of the climate solution."

In the United States, JBS has launched a company named Planterra. The JBS connection, CEO Darcey Macken told me in 2020, is "seen as stability" by grocers and others in the industry. "We weren't quite sure how people would react to that connection, but it's been incredibly positive," Macken said. "It's not a sprint. It's a marathon. We keep getting the feedback from JBS saying, how do we build this to be sustainable as the best protein company in the world, not just to win tomorrow? We want to secure the best ingredients. We want to be at the forefront of that and JBS is really helping us get there. Otherwise, if we were a true start-up, we'd be out fundraising right now."

Planterra has accomplished a lot in a short time. The team created a line called Ozo and developed four fresh-ground alternatives, flavored to resemble beef, within five months. The Ozo crumbles launched in the spring of 2020. I had an exclusive story that they would hit shelves just as pandemic panic-buying emptied meat offerings in stores. Within its first year, Planterra had reached two thousand Kroger locations and unveiled a frozen line of nuggets, meatballs, burgers, and Italian breakfast sausage made with mostly organic ingredients. There were no plans to go fully organic and certify the product for consumers.

Macken confided that it's been tough. "Even with the strength of JBS's relationships with the retailers," she told me in 2021, "we're still struggling to get on shelves. That tells you how hard it is for everybody to try to really break through and find that reason to speak to a different consumer."

Hearing how rattled Macken was reminded me that every CEO still has to answer to the owners. Plant-based is on trend, but what about in five years? Will JBS pack up and refocus on something else?

Wait, That's Where It Comes From?

"Impossible Burger and Soy Trends," the subject line read. Inside was a little pitch from a rep for the United Soybean Board, attempting to ride the plant-based-foods wave. And at the crest of that wave, Impossible had announced it was ditching wheat in its formula. The start-up was fully embracing genetically modified soy. I was surprised to see that its formula included the kind of soy known to be grown using chemical herbicides.

"We can no longer in good conscience avoid embracing farming practices used by American farmers on the majority of their cropland, and which our careful analysis has conclusively shown to be safe for consumers and better for the environment than the alternatives—especially when the real alternative is increased livestock production," Impossible's founder and CEO, Pat Brown, wrote in a blog announcing the decision in May 2019.

Experts have debated the issue. The technology behind different kinds of genetically modified organisms has been scientifically proven to be safe, but there's a level of distrust. One of the pioneers of this technology was Monsanto, with its RoundUp Ready seeds and the herbicide, glyphosate, a potential carcinogen.

The claim that genetically modified organisms are better for the environment is debated. Some seeds may be engineered to require fewer inputs for higher yields, but there have yet to be indicators of them making a noticeable difference environmentally. While there are many different GMOs, the kind Impossible buys is commodity soy, which historically has meant that it is grown on these fields treated with the herbicide glyphosate and other kinds of chemical inputs.

Impossible's soy comes from patented seeds, which highlights another underlying issue with genetic modification: it becomes more about patents, intellectual property, trade secrets, monopolies, consolidation, and control of the food system. The system allows for emerging, billionaire-backed start-ups to lay a legal ownership claim to the creation of a protein source billed as a climate solution. Global food security is what's at stake, explained Adrian Rodrigues, who cofounded San Francisco–based investment bank Provenance Capital Group, which manages deals for strictly responsible companies, family offices, and investors. "A lot of the money is going into companies with a patent or intellectual property around a process. That's where you see the money going into highly processed plant-based [food]," Rodrigues told me. "It's perpetuating this system where one organization owns the intellectual property or the rights to production of something and then gets to collect economic rent on it at a global scale."

The United Soybean Board was promoting Impossible's soy use as an unlikely ally, since the closest the organization's farmers usually get to meat is marketing to feed companies supplying the livestock industry. But the announcement came as soybean farmers were seriously hurting from the impacts of the Trump administration's trade war with China, and the soy market was trading at historically low prices; 2019 turned into a terrible year for soybean farmers. The situation turned dire after Impossible's announcement. Flooding across much of the Midwest's farmland pushed back planting times, causing US soybean farmers to lose their title as the world's top soybean producer for the first time in years, to Brazil. But plant-based foods, however small in current volume, provided a shiny path forward. Smithfield and Nestlé followed Impossible and launched plant-based lines containing soy.

That's why the United Soybean Board's unbridled enthusiasm has continued to stick with me. It underscores a key problem with many of the plant-based food brands on the market: working within existing structures, in this instance, supports an extractive system, rubber-stamping a problematic kind of farming responsible for decades of soil erosion, pollution runoff in many rivers, tributaries, and a dead zone in the Gulf of Mexico. Farmers have been at the mercy of a system where subsidies and crop insurance are the end goal, where marginally increasing profits and continually being promised better yields with chemicals that repeat the treacherous cycle are commonplace. Part of what makes Impossible's value proposition so appealing, as the investors say, is that unless Congress dismantles the commodity system, Impossible's main ingredient will probably stay artificially cheap forever, thanks to subsidies.

All this is woven into the subtext of that United Soybean Board pitch. Ever since, I've been obsessed with figuring out if the supply chain of Impossible, or quite frankly of any of these start-ups, could be unwound enough to find actual US farmers who were benefiting from the boom in plant-based foods. I've asked Impossible periodically, inspired by this email, and the answer is always some version of no. Every time, a different rep demurred. For the record, the United Soybean Board couldn't find me a single example of a farmer confirmed to be benefiting, either. When I interviewed Pat Brown in August 2020, I asked then, too. Was Brown hoping to impact farming long term?

"We can trace back our supply chain substantially, although because soy is such a commodity product, we don't source it directly from the farmers," Brown explained. "There are cooperatives, and then they go to the soy processing plants that we buy the soy protein from. We know regionally where it comes from, but we don't know the individual farmers at this point."

Those acres of monoculture play a crucial role in Brown's grand plan. Nearly jumping out of his seat, Brown went on to explain that Impossible's production requires 4 percent of the land that cattle need. "That will have a very complicated set of consequences for farmers, because we're going to need the farmers as much as ever, but we're going to need way less crops and way less land to produce the food supply.

"We're actually looking at alternative crops as the primary source of our ingredients," Brown added. "Most of the crops grown large scale globally are optimized for feeding animals. They are not great crops for making human food. This is why this is such a fun problem. If you think about it, what defines an optimal crop's suitability as a raw material to make efficient foods directly from plants—it is very likely a different set of crops. You can also think about, okay, we'd like to optimize for global food security, and we'd like to have a more diverse set of crops, the massively grown feed crops, than the ones that are dominant in today's industrial system. But the fundamental answer is, if we turn plants directly into efficient foods, we need less crops."

Even though these burgers are technologically enhanced, founders, start-ups, manufacturers, investors, and grocers want to employ plant-forward marketing without accepting that these are still agricultural products. Consumers cannot forget this. The deeper I get with this reporting, the more I return to the idea that our power as consumers is remembering that food, drinks, wine, grain alcohol, weed—all of it comes from the ground. It needs to be grown. Industrialized agriculture has traded natural variation and phytonutrients for chemicals and systematic extraction. It has traded one industrialized food for another. When we forget this, it doesn't register that a pumpkin spice flavor of Kraft Heinz mac and cheese is unnatural. If Beyond and Impossible's founders really do want to create the change they say they desperately want in the food system, that starts with the soil, and a fully transparent supply chain would make it easy for consumers to buy into the vision themselves.

This new economy of plant-based foods holds a lot of promise, in theory, but might the industry be about to massively consolidate and continue propping up problematic commodity systems? As Beyond and Impossible scale, they may end up needing just as much specification and standardization of their ingredients and products as the largest conglomerates and fast-food chains. I wonder whether their purported missions will get distorted and misguided as the industry's top competitors pursue scale. Will the opportunity crumble as competitors attempt to beat each other in a race to the bottom for more grocery store distribution and fast-food deals? If they don't heed the warnings from big meat-packers' centralization, corporatization, and pressure to deliver profits to shareholders in the past fifty years, the rise of plant-based foods could be just as threatened in the future.

At the heart of the long-term issue here is synthetic farmed monoculture, and whether the emerging alternative protein industry will grow within existing commodity systems or attempt to incentivize biodiversity and strong ecological practices throughout its supply chain. As Stray Dog Capital's Lisa Feria told me point-blank: "This monoculture isn't good for the Earth. It is not good from a long-term sustainability standpoint."

If I could speak to a farmer who was seeing a direct boost thanks to Impossible, I'd ask if her fields are any different, and if basic practices like cover cropping or organic inputs are being used. I'd want to see more. It still surprises me how plant-based companies don't detail how their supply chains impact the soil. Improving how their key commodity ingredients are farmed should be a clear part of their sustainability plans long term.

Unlike Impossible, Beyond avoids soy and all GMO ingredients, but it is not organic, meaning its ingredients can be farmed with synthetic fertilizers. While Impossible uses soy, Beyond uses pea protein, which, before 2010, was grown on about 840,000 US acres. Price is more important: according to Beyond, "By sourcing ingredients both domestically and globally, we seek to increase our scale and reduce product costs, with a goal of being able to offer at least one product that underprices animal protein by 2024."

Acres in America grown for peas have increased by nearly a fifth to just under one million acres planted in 2020. Pea protein has even become a multibillion-dollar industry. Not all of that is going to burgers. It's also in vegan yogurts, milks, fortified baked goods and breads, smoothies, and frozen meals.

Chef Sophia Roe is concerned. "Nobody is saying that these ingredients aren't natural," she told me. "Most of these things are toxic just to grow. I don't know if it's good for the planet."

The Limitations, Drawbacks, and Promise of Alternatives

Plant-based products that rely on inputs like soy and pea protein continue to have their limitations, both nutritionally and environmentally. There's already a next generation of alternatives vying for more shelf space and capital. Most of them are utilizing advances in fermentation technology and the decreasing cost of producing microbes required for industrial scale. Some are attempting to use the power of fungi, one of the oldest organisms in our world. While fungi and their roots, called mycelium, can store more carbon than they release, anything that seeks to standardize and industrialize a living thing comes with its own set of trade-offs.

Fermentation has opened up a world of possibility. But everything has a cost, and fermentation relies on cheap sources of sugar for the yeasts to feed on. That feed source is often a by-product of commodity corn called dextrose, or something similar.

That's why I was struck by Meati, the mycelium-based start-up headquartered in Boulder, Colorado, that sources Brazilian organic sugarcane for its fermentation. The crop has a nasty history but can be grown with a low carbon footprint. Sugarcane can thrive on floodplains and poor soils. "Sugarcane can grow on low-cost, marginal lands," Meati founder and CEO Tyler Huggins, who wants eventually to invest in Meati's own source of sugar, told me. "It's the whole system that is going against this idea of adding back to the land, instead of stripping it. There are a lot of subsidies for sugarcane and headwinds against doing the right thing. It's really important that there's economic incentive."

Few founders have followed Huggins. When fermentation-based alternative protein start-ups use corn, the conversion ratio from sugar to protein is still unmatched, compared to how much it takes to feed livestock corn. But the dependency on cheap corn, inherent to fermentation, is a key example of how commodities known to have environmentally problematic farming are still intertwined in the fabric of the emerging industry of alternatives. That's why I am skeptical that alternative protein will ever upend traditional industrial systems. In fact, conglomerates like ADM, the publicly traded grain company founded in 1902, are investing in start-ups like Nature's Fynd and Air Protein. ADM's multibillion-dollar operation is positioning itself to manage fermentation end to end, from sourcing the corn and other inputs necessary to fuel fermentation to leveraging its manufacturing assets and global sales force.

"We have the corn supply to process into dextrose, which gives us the feedstock into our fermentation assets. We've got the fermentation assets already. We've got an outstanding logistics network," explained Ian Pinner, ADM's senior vice president of strategy and innovation. "We've got a sales force and custom application centers in all regions of the world that we can work with customers to see how we can make it applicable to consumer products and ingredients."

Fermentation enables some wacky ideas. Take Air Protein, which is commercializing NASA research that converts carbon dioxide from, yes, the air into an apparently nutritious single-celled organism. It has raised $32 million, including from ADM Ventures, Barclays, and Google's GV, and is led by Lisa Dyson. Ever since Dyson, one of the few Black entrepreneurs in the emerging industry, founded the research a decade ago, she has heard her share of jokes about "air meat." But she says her start-up's faux chicken is nearly ready for customers. She describes the protein as "essentially carbon-negative" and says it would take land the size of Texas to make enough soy protein to equal the output of an Air Protein farm that's the size of Walt Disney World.

"We worked a lot on it and we've hit the commercial metrics that we need to hit in order to be economically attractive at scale," Dyson, a vegetarian since grad school, told me in 2021. "We're attacking the meat problem at a fundamental level. Investors see we start with the elements."

There's also Nature's Fynd, which ADM's venture arm invested in alongside Al Gore's venture fund and Bill Gates. Their capital has funded the commercialization of the Chicago-based start-up's protein source, a fungus named Fy. The mycoprotein, or single-cell protein from fungus, was discovered wild in Yellowstone National Park in 2009 while cofounder and chief science officer Mark Kozubal was a PhD student collecting samples from an acidic hot spring on a grant funded by the National Science Foundation and NASA. Nature's Fynd uses a simple source of sugar along with a wide range of carbohydrates to fuel its fermentation. It can be corn or soy, or something more experimental, like grinding grass into a pulp and acidifying it. Fermentation then helps the fungi grow.

"Think about a soy burger. Or pea protein. You have to extract the protein out of it, with a lot of chemicals involved. It's a complex process. You end up with the protein concentrate, or a protein flour, and once you have that you need to process back a texture and add moisture back," Nature's Fynd CEO and cofounder, Thomas Jonas, told me. "We don't have to do any of these things."

I got my hands on some samples of the Fy-laced breakfast sausage and cream cheese shortly after Nature's Fynd had raised a $350 million series C, led by former WeWork backer SoftBank, over the summer of 2021. It brought the microorganism protein start-up's total funding to more than $500 million and its valuation to $1.75 billion. I immediately texted my dear friend Nadia Bernstein, the PhD flavor historian and award-winning food writer, a picture of what looked like hockey pucks of dog food, and told her we must dine together.

Soon, I was in her home flipping two fake sausage disks, and Nadia was asking aloud a resounding question: Is it supposed to be a better fake, and what makes it better? Fy, which claims to be non-GMO and possible to produce in space, has the official name of *Fusarium strain flavolapis*. I tried to picture the future retail packages sharing that story. Mine was vacuum-sealed with a bare-bones office-printed label. The packages indicated that both products also contained soy. Were there troubles in Fy paradise? We had no idea what flavorings or other additives had been used, other than soy added to the Fy. I suddenly got a little apprehensive that I was slurping down single-cell organisms, disguised as cream cheese on crackers, that had yet to be FDA approved for commercial sale.

"It's just one of the things that flavorists are called upon to do, to make this not taste so pond scummy," Nadia said as she sucked down a spoonful of Fy spread. "Maybe the advantage of this over prior single-cell organisms is that it doesn't have an inherent flavor. The thing that people are looking for, in a sense, is the flavorless protein that can then be flavored."

The Fy in the "original" cream cheese had something in it that tasted a little sweet compared to the sample of chive spread. The sausages—one was maple-flavored, the other original—smelled like Jimmy Dean's finest, and broke apart like similar mystery meat.

"They remind you of the breakfast patties of your childhood. Something you might want for nostalgia reasons, but it has nothing in common with anything you'd get at the local butcher. It smells like we're in a McDonald's for breakfast," said Nadia, who thought the sausages were stronger products than the cream cheeses, though, overall, we remained mostly unimpressed. "There's a lot of vegan breakfast sausage out there."

Fy aside, the more time I spend digesting the alternative protein industry, the more I have come to see fungi as probably the strongest foundation for meatless meat. Start-ups selling reishi and lion's mane powders have blown up, alongside mushroom jerky and more.

"Plants and mushrooms have a long head start on the R&D cycle. Plants have a five-hundred-million-year R&D cycle. Mushrooms have an eight-hundred-million-year R&D cycle," James Joaquin, who cofounded Obvious Ventures with Twitter billionaire Evan Williams, told me. "Lab-grown meat does not even have twenty years in the cycle."

Mycelium, or the living root structures of mushrooms that can be manipulated to grow in certain ways, are a naturally stronger starting point to get to the same texture and feel of a whole cut of meat, Joaquin explained. It's also a flavorless starting point, unlike soy, which has taken generations of research to try to get over the flavor hurdles. It also requires less processing as a protein than soy or pea protein isolate. Since the substrate fed to the fungi is usually cheap, manufacturing costs can stay low. Meati, which makes a faux chicken breast and steak, and MyForest Foods, which makes fake bacon, are at the forefront of mycelium research and its many applications.

"We love the ability to scale and become accessible. The way those two meet is where you can get a product that's cheap enough to manufacture at scale that you can put on a shelf at Target or Costco. We don't want to fund luxury items. We want to fund things that can change," Joaquin added. "The economics of mushrooms are really, really good."

Yet I also struggle with all the fungi optimism. Mushrooms wild in the forest can absorb more carbon than they release, and on a farm they can be a critical part of a circular system because compost, recycled hulls, and hay can be reused as substrate to grow mushrooms. This is also a powerful idea when you think about urban composting waste and creating a local urban food source. Mushrooms take wasted agricultural by-products and transform them into good protein with relatively tiny amounts of water—an average of less than two gallons per pound for button mushrooms. Mushrooms are also one of the most efficient kinds of protein to grow in terms of land use: one million pounds of mushrooms can grow on one acre.

The beauty of mushrooms grown commercially is that they feed on farm waste. According to the USDA's 1897 guide *How to Grow Mushrooms*, a text in my apocalypse digital library, cow manure is the best source to use. But manure, especially horse manure as a by-product of the horse racing industry, is expensive, and there's far more demand for mushroom production than there is a supply of good manure. Modern-day operations also use compost as well as old and often moldy hay and straw that can't otherwise be used. At Pennsylvania State University, Dr. David Meigs Beyer has posited that mushroom farms could transition to using composted urban waste to fight garbage accumulation in cities, or could work with the poultry industry to reuse manure from chicken houses.

But with food, there are always trade-offs, and industrializing mushrooms at scale could still be environmentally harmful. If the substrate isn't wasted or composted, then what is it? I still wondered whether there is any production using nonsustainable feedstock. Turns out, synthetic logs are common in production, and the most popular substrate for shiitake mushrooms in the United States is sawdust, a by-product of the logging industry.

My heart continued to sink as I learned more about commercial mushroom production. Workers, if they don't wear masks, have had a long history of health concerns, mainly from fungal spores and poorly ventilated operations. In industrial settings, the CO_2, which mushrooms emit while naturally growing, adds to air that can be thick with spores. While a farm might have mushrooms grow outdoors on logs, leveraging nature, commercial operations vary greatly.

The energy it takes to run the industrial plants to farm fungi can be considerable, and in one study, mycoprotein manufacturing had the worst environmental impact of all protein sources tested, other than lab-grown meat. That means having a sustainable, renewable energy source to run these kinds of plants is critical. Then there's transportation. In another study of a farm outside Paris, transportation accounted for 31 percent of the climate impacts, even for a locally based network.

MyForest Foods, the Albany-based maker of mycelium bacon, brought me to their production center so I could see mycelium get produced. The industrial warehouses were retrofitted to grow mycelium through a process called solid-state fermentation. The growth chamber was a temperature- and humidity-controlled room that was about forty feet by twenty feet by thirty feet, with twenty-six-foot-tall ceilings and twenty-six beds where the mycelium grows. The system uses machinery from the industrial mushroom-growing industry, coupled with hacks that allow for additional automated processes, like substrate filling into each bed. Each shelf could produce one hundred kilograms of the mycelium ingredient for MyForest Foods' bacon. Every year, the MyForest Foods team has moved into a facility that is ten times larger. By January 2021, when I visited, they had a 100,000-pound capacity upgrade. Under construction was a growth chamber with the capacity to grow millions of pounds of mycelium a year.

When I asked founder Eben Bayer about his plant's energy use, he didn't deny that it is similar to industrial white button mushroom production. MyForest Foods' facilities will use far less if the nation's energy grid electrifies. The single largest source of energy consumption is actually airflow,

Bayer shared, due to the fans used to control humidity and carbon. The second-largest source is the heating and steam to cook the substrate before it ferments.

"It's not free. It's just much better, on an energy basis, than other stuff. It's about fan energy and cooking energy," Bayer explained.

MyForest Foods' core idea is that there are better mushrooms that can't be grown at scale economically or in an industrial format. This is why gourmet mushrooms aren't used as often as meat substitutes except at high-end restaurants, which can afford to spend more per pound.

"Nature actually gives us a lot of what we need. If we can be smarter as humans through using technology, we can probably drastically reduce the impact we're having without drastically reducing our standard of living and, I hope, with food, actually increase people's standards of living and make them healthier."

Before Bayer was a mycelium inventor, he grew up on a farm in Vermont. Every Saturday morning his dad would interrupt *Sesame Street* with a yell for help in their backyard plant, where he and siblings would help process fifty chickens. He says he's killed pigs after keeping them as pets growing up, and describes it as a cultural tradition for the working farm. Bayer also said that he'll never forget how it feels: "It's not fun. It breaks your heart every time you do it."

After leaving the farm, he became a student at Rensselaer Polytechnic Institute and eventually started eating meat. At RPI, Bayer discovered he was a natural inventor, and he created a new domain of materials science known as mycelium materials. After linking up with fellow researcher Gavin McIntyre, Bayer founded Ecovative Design in 2007 as a research company to license technology. Over the years, he has developed items including home-compostable packaging, a product that's now made around the world with licensees, and a vegan leather. But it wasn't until a few years ago that Bayer had a self-described "second awakening" as he realized how mycelium technology could be applied to food. That's when the homesteader who lives off the grid mostly gave up meat.

Bayer spun out MyForest Foods from parent company Ecovative Design in 2018 after deciding to go all in on meatless meat as the next frontier. He purchased an old smokehouse that closed and got to work rehabbing. He started out looking at steaks, chicken breasts, and bacon. The question was, where should they begin? They settled on bacon after a dinner party in 2019 called Feast of the Future where diners sampled a meaty pasta, two kinds of sushi, clams casino, a chicken sandwich, and a BLT. No surprise, America's top-sold cut featured in the BLT was the hands-down favorite.

Bayer had been careful to fundraise over the years. He secured roughly $100 million in 2021 between Ecovative and MyForest Foods. Ecovative was seeded by the family office of former Google CEO Eric Schmidt and the venture arm of 3M. The funds covered far from everything over those years. Bayer and McIntyre once had to go to the bank knowing that the company would be out of money in thirty days and that they had to sign over their houses for half a million dollars of credit. The mortgage put everything on the line: Bayer's house, which he brought me to, is an off-grid paradise that he's meticulously worked on for a decade, complete with a pond that doubles as an ionized battery energy source, gardens, and a guest cabin.

But Bayer waited out the challenges, and alternative protein is finally hot. Bayer got his pick of the checks offered to him. MyForest Foods started out with $7 million in seed funding, including a million-dollar check from Gary Hirshberg, the cofounder of Stonyfield Organics. Hirshberg joined the board in 2020 alongside Stephen McDonnell, the founder of antibiotic-free meat pioneer Applegate.

"We've always been super careful about who we have on the cap table. We live in capitalism, but there are many flavors of investors. I get calls, people are like, 'All the roads seem to point back to you folks.' It's like, 'Where were you eight years ago when we were doing business plan competitions to stay afloat because no one would write us a seed round check?'" Bayer said. "Timing is everything. To survive to the moment where timing is on your side, I'm very grateful for. There's a whole cycle you go through as an entrepreneur where you're awesome, and then you suck. If you survive, you have scars. I made it through the Valley of Death, in that sense, with my company intact and still privately held."

Many founders will not be as lucky as Bayer. The emerging industry of alternative proteins has been set up for only a few start-ups to succeed, while hundreds plied with millions of dollars in funding may eventually combust. Most of those flameouts will have barely impacted the environment before they run out of money and call it quits.

CHAPTER 15

Lab-Grown Power Grab

The running joke in lab-grown meat circles has been that it's all about to happen. It's been the same joke for the past twenty years. That was as much as I wanted to say on lab-grown meat. But a flurry of swift developments convinced me that it merits more immediate discussion, from sovereign wealth funds investing in billion-dollar start-ups to production plants open or in the works in California, Scandinavia, Singapore, and Qatar. Those first-of-their-kind facilities need industrial incubators and bioreactors, which have been in high demand for vaccine production, and large amounts of energy to run at scale.

In December 2020, the Singaporean government, driven by its plan to source 30 percent of food domestically by 2030, approved Josh Tetrick's Eat Just for selling lab-grown chicken nuggets. A few weeks later the nuggets started getting cooked up at 1880, an upscale restaurant in Singapore. A few months later, in 2021, Israel-based MeaTech 3D—a prototype-stage start-up—moved its listing from the Tel Aviv stock exchange to Nasdaq in the United States. It ignited a modern-day space race—Aleph Farms was unveiling its 3D-printed rib eye in Israel, and Eat Just, under the spin-off brand Good Meat, inked a home delivery deal in Singapore. In November 2021, JBS acquired a Spain-based meat start-up called BioTech Foods as part of a goal to raise a $100 million investment in lab-grown meat. Then José Andrés joined Good Meat's board and promised to serve the lab-grown chicken at one of his American restaurants once the government's regulatory approval is completed.

A funding boom has blown these early signals all out of the water: lab-grown meat raised more than $360 million in 2020, 12 percent of total alternative protein funding raised. The most disappointing part is that a lot of the money raised has gone toward start-ups that are developing products for the premium end of the market. The frenzy has driven a lot of the "dumb money" in investments, Stray Dog Capital's Lisa Feria told me. She estimates there are at least 120 cellular agriculture start-ups globally—and more on the way.

"What I would have loved would have been that cellular agriculture had stayed in academia for another five years and then gone to the market. A lot of them are not reinventing the wheel. There's no way that they know that because they don't see each other's information, but I do," Feria said. (I nodded. I do, too.) "I wish that there had been enough funding for things like this to really progress in academia before rolling over to the private market."

Feria is the backer of many of Eat Just's best-funded competitors—Silicon Valley–based Upside Foods, which raised a $186 million series B round in 2020; the Netherlands' Mosa Meats, the original pioneers of the first lab-grown burger; and Israel's Aleph Farms, which has raised nearly $120 million for its rib eye and other steaks. Some estimates peg the total investment figure at $2 billion.

What makes the funding frenzy so laughable is that there's still such a long way to go when it comes to commercialization and price. The economics are out of whack and will threaten lab-grown meat from ever getting off the ground. Industrial chicken sells for under $3 per pound, whereas the same amount of a lab-grown equivalent can cost thousands of dollars to produce.

Finding a sustainable growth medium has been the biggest hurdle to bringing down costs. We all need something to eat. Cells are no different. In lab-grown meat, they feed on what's known as "the growth medium." Finding a synthetic and sustainable source for the growth medium has been a longtime holdup limiting research. Historically, this is where one of the most controversial elements is introduced to the process: fetal bovine serum. The liquid, considered a by-product of the dairy industry, is highly effective for encouraging cells to grow in vitro. But it's also highly unethical. It comes one way only: slaughtering a pregnant cow and draining the fetus's blood. It's also expensive.

Fetal bovine serum is usually only used early in the lab-grown meat process to help spur growth so that production has a bank of cells ready to throw into the bioreactors. Eat Just's Good Meat uses fetal bovine serum and says it's 2 percent of the overall formula. Tetrick calls it "obviously entirely antithetical to why I'm doing this—a burst glass." When the brand started the safety and approval process in Singapore two years ago, it didn't have an alternative. It now claims to have an effective animal-free nutrient—an unspecified mix of amino acids, minerals, and vitamins—to feed its cell banks, which the start-up has updated with regulators. The recipe will change pending Singapore government approval.* There's a race to get rid of animal-based serum across start-ups, but it remains a pricey challenge.

When Eat Just is ready to make a big batch, researchers throw cells into the bioreactor and seal it for roughly fourteen days. Bioreactors are the other pricey part of the process. Bioreactors historically have been used by big pharma (like Merck) to manufacture drugs. That's why publicly traded MeaTech 3D thinks it has a shot at filling in a major blank space: the company is developing the machinery necessary to manufacture cultivated meat at scale—a big need, because most bioreactors currently in use are smaller, which is better for pharma. Bioreactors will have to be much larger to make hundreds of millions of pounds of meat. What's served in Singapore gets made inside a 1,200-liter bioreactor at a Singaporean food research facility. Out of the bioreactor, it takes another three to five days before getting manufactured from a raw ingredient to a nugget. The company must source the bioreactors amid wait lists and competition from the pharma industry, which has been in short supply of bioreactors because they are necessary for vaccine production. Tetrick estimates a factory with ten 250,000-liter bioreactors, like the one Tetrick plans to build in America, could produce 30 million pounds of cultivated meat and would cost as much as $650 million.

Eat Just is taking an estimated loss of millions of dollars a year on production, but it has raised enough money that it can afford to. When the lab-grown nuggets debuted in Singapore, five cost $17, similar to the menu's chicken dishes. At a hawker stall called Mr. Loo's, the cultivated meat, fashioned as Hainanese Curry Rice, sells for a few dollars. "We just decided to price it at that," Tetrick told me. "Our costs still have a long ways to go. We're still not making money by selling the product."

---

* The Good Food Institute says, "Cells are fed an oxygen-rich cell culture medium made up of basic nutrients such as amino acids, glucose, vitamins, and inorganic salts, and supplemented with proteins and other growth factors."

"It is very capital intensive and there's no getting around it," Tetrick added.

Cuts like a steak have a certain chew from the mix of fat and muscle, and replicating a proper steak in a lab is an experimental nightmare. A big challenge is finding the right "scaffolding"—meaning what helps hold up the structure of the lab-grown steak. It's what the cells grow on. Researchers are trying to fill in the cells around the scaffold, from adaptations of 3D printing to fermentation. Think of scaffolding like steel wool, only it's made by ingredients like soy protein. Good Meat's nuggets take this idea but flip it on its head: it's 75 percent lab-derived chicken cells and roughly 25 percent plant protein, which works as the scaffolding.

It's a sign of the bubble in cell-grown meat that there are already an ecosystem of businesses popping up, even without cell-grown meat widely available. MeaTech is one such company that aims to offer an end-to-end system. As an early stage start-up, MeaTech is developing research in two key areas: 3D bioprinting machinery and the serum-free biomass to grow stem cells for beef and chicken. Cofounder and deputy CEO Omri Schanin and I spoke a month before the transferred listing to Nasdaq was complete, and he said the main reason they wanted to enter American markets so soon was because of the potential to fund acquisitions and jump-start deals. His company wants to be the manufacturer for budding biotech founders looking to process their upstart lab-grown meat brands.

"It gives us the opportunity to execute deals," Schanin told me. "The industry doesn't exist at the moment, but it will exist, and everyone wants to take part in it."

MeaTech is backed by billionaire Sheldon Lavin's graying son Steve, who is a top shareholder and served as board chairman until January 2022. Steve is also the vice chairman of his father's meat processor, OSI, as well as the president of a law firm. MeaTech hopes to one day command the scope of OSI. "We are not aiming to compete with OSI Group. This is a very good example of the model. The go-to-market plan there is what we are aiming to do," Schanin told me. "You can turn a building into a meat-growing facility."

Here's how MeaTech claims it works: First, cells are taken from an umbilical cord without harming the animal. Second, a line of cells is developed in bioreactors to create a cell bank—as Matt Wadiak at Cooks Venture would build his breeder flock, which live across thirty chicken houses. Third, there's 3D printing. The cells are split up into different "inks"—but instead of black, cyan, magenta, and yellow, the cells are split up into a fat ink tank and a muscle ink tank. The secret sauce is how to get the ink to fill in correctly and latch on to start growing naturally on the right scaffolding. That's all about finding the right inks that can be filled in around the scaffold the best way. Into the bioprinter! The concoction creates a foundation for a cut of meat like a steak. Then it is placed into an incubator so the cells can grow. Will we call steaks "prints" instead of "cuts" in the future? In MeaTech's hypothetical case, finished prints would then get frozen and shipped out.

Retailers have started showing interest because growing meat from cells in small plants could easily fit into their food supply chain. Costco and Walmart are already getting more involved with their meat supply chain to make sure it's more stable. Different kinds of food companies will want different sizes of capability—and lab-grown meat might one day be able to be grown anywhere, from home countertops to a facility tacked onto a Walmart distribution center.

There's still a risk of foodborne illnesses like salmonella and E. coli, which is why many early stage prototypes rely on antibiotics. Good Meat claims it doesn't use antibiotics, and others say they are actively working to get rid of them from their supply chains. That undercuts Big Meat, because lab-grown start-ups enjoy calling out factory farming for its reliance on antibiotics that fuel resistance globally.

Lab-grown meat also has come under the microscope for its environmental impact, with some researchers questioning whether it could one day really be better. The answer seems to be that lab-grown meat is more sustainable only if the labs and production plants are also run sustainably. That means plants need their own independent energy sources like solar panels or to purchase energy directly from a wind or solar company. But some may be banking on the trend that the grid will eventually be 100 percent carbon pollution–free—which the US government has claimed will happen entirely by 2030. A research study with data from five start-ups and others in the supply chain that was funded by the alt protein industry trade group Good Food Institute claims that if renewable energy is used, in a decade lab-grown meat could have a smaller environmental impact compared to conventional cattle production. It estimates roughly 80 percent fewer carbon emissions, in addition to less land used. A previous study, published in the *International Journal of Life Cycle Assessment*, found that if lab-grown meat uses traditional energy sources at scale, it would be worse than industrial meat production.

A Billionaire's Feast

I've done my own *Supersize Me*–inspired reporting over the years, but when it came to the thought of lining up lab-grown alternatives like Good Meat's chicken nuggets, Upside's chicken breast, and Aleph Farms' rib eye, I was both fascinated with trying to see and smell it in person and completely perturbed by actually eating it. I ended up opting out. There are many complicated moral dilemmas involved when it comes to eating meat. That all got heightened and turned on its head, for me, when contemplating lab-grown meat. Aside from the antibiotics use and fetal bovine serum, lab-grown meat is designed and produced in a sterile environment. There's no chance for Fred Provenza's beloved phytonutrients to exist.

There are also broader ethical implications, says Sikowis Nobiss, of the Plains Cree and Saulteaux nations, who is the executive director of Great Plains Action Society, an Indigenous-led organization focused on climate and agribusiness. "I don't think I could eat it," Nobiss said. "We think rocks are alive. Why wouldn't we think that this thing running in a lab is not alive, and it's basically being grown just for consumption. It never moves. It just sits there and it just grows? I don't think that's okay, and I don't think that's the way to solve the world's problems."

But many of the world's richest men sure do. That includes Bill Gates, who as of May 2022 had the fourth-highest net worth in the world, to a tune of nearly $130 billion. A small fraction of that has been invested in food tech. Gates' shillings can instantly change a market. Gates—an investor in Eat Just and Upside Foods, as well as Impossible Foods, Beyond, Nature's Fynd—thinks rich nations should eat 100 percent synthetic meat. He doesn't think the eighty poorest countries will be eating synthetic meat—a statement that ignores the traditions of pastoralists and Indigenous groups.

Most of Gates' deals are early stage, except some follow-ons in Impossible rounds in 2018 when Impossible raised $189 million, and again in 2019, when Gates personally joined a $300 million roster that included

Jay-Z, Katy Perry, Serena Williams, and her husband, Reddit cofounder Alexis Ohanian. Gates' stake in Impossible is still minority but will probably amount to a tasty exit. Impossible has been eyeing a public market debut, which could value the start-up at $10 billion or more.

Gates and many other Impossible investors don't need the money. But that's not the point. Gates has backed most of these top start-ups and his investments show that he is intent on bringing alternative proteins—from Impossible's heme-and-soy to lab-grown meat—to the masses. His track record shows he tends to accomplish what he sets out to. But Gates is playing both sides. Gates is also the top farmland owner in the country, according to the Land Report. Yet for all the talk of a sustainable revolution, that cropland is mostly farmed as industrially and conventionally as it comes.* Across the more than 250,000 acres traced to Gates' fortune through different shell companies, there's farms that grow potatoes for McDonald's french fries, as well as ones that farm carrots and onions, alongside others that grow commodities like soybeans, cotton, and rice. That history makes it incredibly difficult to imagine an environment where less advantaged farmers decide willingly to transition to better practices when someone who was once the world's richest man may not be embracing the concepts himself. When asked about his farmland investments while promoting his 2021 book *How to Avoid a Climate Disaster* during an Ask Me Anything interview over Reddit, Gates replied: "My investment group chose to do this. It is not connected to climate."

Gates is not a farmer himself. Gates is a businessman. One whose farmland is rented by other farmers, some of them large businesses themselves. According to the National Farmers Union, that's a cause of concern, from pushing up land values to negatively impacting the environment: "For renting farmers, there is no guarantee that they'll be tending the same tract of land in five or ten years. That means there is less incentive to invest the time, money, and energy into implementing practices that protect soil, water, and air quality because they may or may not be around to reap the benefits. Landowners, on the other hand, often don't have any agricultural

---

* Representatives for Gates didn't return my email or calls. Gates' investment firm Cascade told the Land Report in 2021 that it is supportive of sustainable farming but did not elaborate further. Cascade told NBC News that it has invested in a pollinator habitat in Nebraska and "wildlife-friendly trees on dry pivot corners in Florida."

experience and may not understand the importance of protecting natural resources. Consequently, they may be unwilling to sacrifice rental income in order to take marginal land out of production or support lessees' conservation efforts." Gates has some other controversial opinions about farming and the future of food. Over on Reddit, as Gates replied to the farmland question, he added that he's interested in the fuel potential, rather than the food potential, of some agricultural commodities.

"The agriculture sector is important," says Gates, who has been a proponent of genetically modified and patented seeds for years and briefly invested in Monsanto in 2010 before selling the shares amid public scrutiny. "With more productive seeds we can avoid deforestation and help Africa deal with the climate difficulty they already face. It is unclear how cheap biofuels can be but if they are cheap it can solve the aviation and truck emissions."

Whole Foods' former head of grocery Errol Schweizer, who spent fourteen years at the chain, chalks up Gates' investments and overall stake in the future of lab-grown meat as simply "a land grab." It's a monopolistic approach to owning the intellectual property of a key food source. And, he asks, what happens to the farmland assets being subsidized by the government to grow animal feed once lab-grown replacements are commercialized? That doesn't sit well with Schweizer.

"There's a strain of white supremacy from the financiers and developers who are really into it, because you don't have to deal with injustice. But what if those lands were under Indigenous management and stewardship? Because most of those lands were stolen. At its heart, these philosophies are ecofascist and misanthropic," Schweizer said. "They don't have a social analysis or a power analysis. That's why they're so fond of attracting these billionaires and big resources and big names, who they know they can just appeal to them, because they don't need to appeal to social movements who are fighting for justice and equity within this society."

How We Got Here

How did we, all of a sudden, wake up in this brave new world? The first lab-grown burger was unveiled in 2013 by Dutch medical professor Mark Post and his team at Maastricht University. The project reportedly cost

$330,000—just to produce a few burgers for the big reveal. In 2016, Post decided to commercialize it and founded a private start-up called Mosa Meat. It's raised more than $100 million, including a 2020 $85 million series B to build its own manufacturing plant. It is backed by investors, including the corporate venture arm of Merck, billionaire Google cofounder Sergey Brin, billionaire Takeaway.com founder Jitse Groen, Mitsubishi, and others. Upside, with $200 million raised, is the only one with more funding (aside from Eat Just, which earmarked nearly $270 million of more than $800 million specifically for Good Meat). Aleph Farms, founded in 2017, has raised from Cargill. Post told me in 2021 that he's never had a difficult time raising money. His splashy burger reveal had billionaire mouths watering around the world, and the investment officers for the personal holdings of Brin, Google's former moonshot factory chief, funded the 2013 experiment and continued backing him. "I never really asked for them to fund this. I never, up till now, have ever really asked for funding from anybody. People just throw it at me," Post, Mosa's chief science officer, told me. "Public funding is difficult to get for these kinds of projects."

I asked Post what he sees as the endgame. Is it getting acquired by a Tyson? He demurred. "Some things just happen. If you get acquired it may start leading its own life," Post laughed. "Whatever development that happens needs to support the cause. Maybe that's through an IPO, or a very good partner wants to invest a lot of money, or banks, what have you. We want to optimize the chance to transform the meat industry. That's one of the advantages of investors coming to you. We get to choose. We are in a luxury position."

Eat Just's journey in lab-grown meat started formally in 2017 as the start-up's cofounder and CEO, Josh Tetrick, faced the board coup. Part of the disagreement was over the future of Tetrick's lab-grown meat project. Eat Just then acquired two sets of patents, including the patents of the late Willem van Eelen, a Dutch researcher known as the godfather of lab-grown meat, who died in 2015. The acquisitions came from smooth-talking Tetrick finding himself in the right place at the right time. He was speaking at an event, and a stranger came up and offered a connection to the van Eelen family. Tetrick was intrigued and found out that van Eelen's heirs could be open to a sale if the company could give the work new life. There were several others who had been circling, trying to buy the patents, but Tetrick charmed his way to a successful acquisition. (I asked what Eat Just paid, or even a rough estimate, but Tetrick declined.) The deal gave Tetrick's struggling start-up a fresh lease on life.

But it's another of Singapore's lab-grown start-ups and Good Meat's neighbor that stands out. Shiok, launched in 2018, focuses on the niche of lab-grown seafood, and doesn't have to worry about inhumane growth serums. Its CEO, Sandhya Sriram, is one of the few women as well as founders of color in the emerging industry. Born in India and raised in the Middle East, Sriram has been working with stem cells out of Singapore since 2004. She picked her headquarters wisely. Her start-up is closer to commercializing prototypes for lobster and shrimp than many others globally, despite some investors' initial skepticism. Its pilot production plant opened in mid-2021, with construction on a full-scale facility slated for 2022.

After raising $30 million, she continues to fend off investors. Sriram maintains she wants to hit the milestone of having the test production plant fully functioning and at least having submitted paperwork for regulatory approval for sale before raising again. When she does next go raise, it will be a nine-figure round. "The interest is very high. In fact, people are asking us, 'Why aren't you raising?'" Sriram told me in mid-2021. "We are not in need of money. Yes, there's a war chest [mentality] in the industry. Everybody's raising. But you also need to keep in mind that you want to raise money from the right investors."

Lab-grown meat is a moonshot and should be treated as such, with a skeptical eye. The same distraction and economic exclusion that worry me with plant-based foods apply. My best guess is that lab-grown meat might find a place in the future. But without groundbreaking technology that would fundamentally change how much it costs to make a steak from a cell, I'm skeptical that lab-grown meat will find mainstream adoption outside of being used as an ingredient. That's slightly more compelling: consider a 15 percent lab-grown chicken sausage, which gives it all that expected chicken-y flavor (can't rock the boat!) along with supplemented fungi-based ingredients, just as the processed meat industry has been doing for years with fillers like soy.

Up for debate is whether the government should take on some of the capital burden. Each geographic market requires entirely new regulatory approval. Aside from currently selling in Singapore, start-ups, investors, and industry advocates have been lobbying behind the scenes to get lab-grown meat approved for sale in the United States, in addition to Japan, South Korea, Israel, and the European Union. I'm ready to watch a fight unfold when the approval and commercialization of lab-grown meat comes to the United States. Policies like Meatless Mondays in school cafeterias can already stir wild vitriol in some communities. Some zealots are putting pressure on governments and global environmental NGOs to invest in cultivated meat like it's a new space race. Keeping up with the threats of climate change and security concerns are why Good Meat has been courted by sovereign wealth funds in two countries: Singapore and Qatar. Those investments and others like it are driving up the market, pushing the prices up on deals so that investing in most lab-grown start-ups has become inaccessible even to most food venture capitalists. Yet Good Meat will break ground on a second manufacturing facility, in Qatar. The country is expected to become one of the next to approve the start-up's lab-grown chicken for sale. The US is the other big one. Lab-grown meat developers based stateside want that money to be invested in US manufacturing.

That's how lab-grown meat hoards funding from other critical areas, distracting from other potential solutions. Here, yet again, is another example of the system of the future looking to grow via systems of the past. Industrial agriculture gets billions in subsidies annually. It's why it will be difficult, structurally and institutionally, for industrial meat production to change its ways without coming from within. While science funding is commonly provided by federal governments, should lab-grown meat funnel research dollars away when there are understudied areas like antibiotic resistance or biodiversity efforts? The US Department of Agriculture has already cast its vote, creating a National Institute for Cellular Agriculture at Tufts University with a $10 million award announced in 2021.

The closest to commercializing in the United States is Upside Foods, formerly known as Memphis Meats. The start-up opened a fifty-three-thousand-square-foot pilot plant inside a former grocery store in Emeryville, California, at the end of 2021, and it hopes lab-grown meat will be sold in America soon. With all ends of the meat supply chain vying for a slice of the potential profits, Upside has put together an impressive roster of meat-friendly institutional investors, including Tyson and

Cargill. That also includes retailers, even once-celebrated natural grocers. Amazon-backed Whole Foods invested in Upside Foods alongside the chain's founder, John Mackey, in May 2021. After closing the deal, I interviewed cofounder and CEO Uma Valeti, who explained his start-up's strategy with retailers. "Whole Foods is one, but there's a few others that are really interested in launching our product. We certainly want to understand which demographic would really want to be able to get their hands on it," said Valeti, a former cardiologist whose production lab allows neighbors and passersby to peer in through windows. "There is a question of what can be actually supplied because there is going to be a supply-demand mismatch."

Does Open-Source Still Have a Future?

If you're cringing about the technification of meat grown in labs, you're not alone. For what it's worth, until recent years, much of lab-grown meat has been conceptualized as open-sourced, or otherwise free of intellectual property constraints. The potential to be more democratic when adopted at scale makes it far more tantalizing theoretically than venture-backed plant-based food start-ups. I've seen designs for cell-grown meat appliances—fit for the kitchen counter—but I'm not sure that something like that, no matter how much marketing and design, will ever have a home in my apartment. I could envision a world where such an appliance could be a compelling novelty. But maybe you'll have me at the idea of open-source lab-grown burgers (without the antibiotics and fetal bovine serum), if the lab-grown meat is combined with manufacturing and distribution as a public utility (we'll get to that). I can't tell you that I'll enjoy eating it.

To talk more about lab-grown meat's open-source potential, I called up Dr. Robert Chiles, an assistant professor of rural sociology at Pennsylvania State University, who studies democratizing access to more sustainable proteins. He describes his work as challenging society's "deep-rooted assumption that ownership matters in terms of people's reaction and the public's reaction." His research centers on the idea that factory-produced nutrients from cells or yeast could either accelerate socioeconomic inequality or democratize access to food. My question for him: How can we develop a lab-grown agriculture system that works for local communities and is regionally embedded to ensure access and economic opportunity? He told me that what he's found over studying this for years is twofold.

Chiles, who says he is not a big fan of the Great Man Theory of history, contends that "what I'm starting to look at more and more is that, when you have someone coming up with an idea, how they choose to license that or how they choose to organize their business or how they choose to interact with their peers or collaborate can have huge ripple effects. If someone invents something that they have claimed ownership over, it can make a big difference." Chiles explained that some people in the emerging industry are very much interested in open-source. "But they're very interested in principle," Chiles said with a smile. "It's really up to them if they want to start a company and just monetize it. There's a role for open-source, there's a role for proprietary, there's a role for venture capital. For the digital age, sometimes ownership isn't as important as access."

His second point: "My reading of our discipline has generally been skepticism: big is bad. It doesn't matter, big tech or just big globalized. Just everything at these monstrous scales, you have all these problems and unintended consequences. Little people get squished and all these things, which has historically been accurate," Chiles said. "However, when people are constantly reacting to something, rather than creating, you're almost by definition a step behind, and the world is changing at a blistering pace. It's important to think about how these types of tools and techniques and technologies might be leveraged."

Chiles is proud that he comes from a legacy of Black farmers, among the few who persisted amid decades of violence and federal policy that contributed to the mass stripping of land from Black families in agriculture. His mom grew up on a dairy farm, the oldest of seven, and because she was a girl, her parents left the farm to the next-oldest boy, Chiles' uncle. Chiles has since grappled with the cultural implications and the systemic racism of what it means when people talk about saving the family farm. Why talk about saving unprofitable family farms when 30 percent of rural America and much of Detroit doesn't have access to broadband, and health-care costs are still 14 percent of the poorest Americans' income? "Most people don't inherit a farm like my uncle. Most people work on farms as laborers. For me, as tragic as it is when people are forced to sell their land or sell their farm, they have wealth that they can at least rely on, and a lot of people don't have that," Chiles said. "Many farmworkers didn't inherit land. Are they less of a farmer to us, morally? To me, that's offensive, on a number of levels."

Chiles has convinced me that there could be a glimmer of optimism in lab-grown meat after all. If the technology withstands the pressure to get co-opted, it might create greater opportunities for democratization, localization, open-sourcing, and community involvement than the burgeoning plant-based-food industry ever could. That said, few are investing in lab-grown meat start-ups for the future of democratic access to a sustainable protein source. There is major money to be made from this industry and the production of lab-grown meat.

CHAPTER 16

Sourcing Local Alternatives

Chef whites and all, Dan Barber stormed out of the kitchen at the original Washington Square location of his award-winning restaurant Blue Hill. It was the start of winter in 2019 and Barber was walking me through a tasting of the latest in development. I wasn't there for his famous restaurant, but for his freshly formed seed company, Row 7. The start-up had launched a few months earlier out of a research project at Blue Hill's Tarrytown, New York, nonprofit farm, the Stone Barns for Food and Agriculture, to commercialize hybrids of produce bred for flavor. The project was Barber's way of going a bit commercial while still selling certified organic seeds for around $2 more than an heirloom option. Barber's restaurant tasting menu for two could run above $500 before drinks or wine, tip, and tax, but here was a way to create a modern victory garden bursting with flavor for a fraction of the price. Row 7's flagship was a butternut squash called 661. In the months leading up to our meeting, I'd noticed that Row 7 squash was suddenly popping up a lot within a certain affluent but eco-minded bubble. Sweetgreen featured the squash in a limited-edition bowl, as did the dinner for Food Tank's annual summit, where the squash kicked off a vegetarian meal.

Back in his restaurant for my private harvest tasting, Barber brought a roasted squash for me to try and shook his head. It was still not perfect. When stored for grocery stores, the squash didn't hold up and the skin started to deteriorate. "To breed a squash that can have that kind of flavor but also the shelf life of what the industry wants is really the goal," Barber said. At that point, Row 7 had twelve commercial seeds for sale and was working with another forty breeders in early stages around the country.

"It's clear that, for chemical companies, owning the future of food isn't going to work," Barber told me. "We have a serious problem with flavor, nutrition, access, ecological functioning. We need new tools in the toolbox, and we are one that's appealing to deliciousness."

Barber, a visionary to some and an elitist to others, is best known for his Hudson Valley, New York, restaurant on the farm. He is a voice in the chef-driven challenge to the industrialization of food. When Barber in 2000 opened his first restaurant off New York City's Washington Square Park, consolidation in the seed industry was already on the rise as the four largest seed companies—Monsanto, Novartis, Dow Chemical, and DuPont—spread across the nation with their patented seeds that boosted the value of the annual corn and soybean crop. Then, a decade ago, Barber said, he had a conversation with a Monsanto executive on a panel and was stunned when he heard that Monsanto spends $1 million a day on corn research. That fact has been in the back of Barber's obsessive mind ever since. In the years following, consolidation has gotten worse. Then the Big Four in seed became the Big Two. In 2015, Dow Chemical and DuPont laid out a $130 billion megamerger, followed by Bayer announcing it would swallow up Monsanto for $63 billion (and take on all Monsanto's glyphosate lawsuits). Soon after the Bayer-Monsanto merger closed (and dropped Monsanto's more than century-old name), the Dow-Dupont merger then consolidated all its agriculture businesses under a new publicly traded spin-off, Corteva, which debuted in 2019. The consolidation that the seed industry has undergone in just the past few years is a large part of Barber's rallying cry.

"We're on the right side of the fence," he said. "We can feed a lot of people, too, and we can do it with a lot of nutrition, ecological understanding, and sensitivity."

Sounded like a nice thought. Unfortunately, I was skeptical—and asked him point-blank, "As you've been pushing for more yields, how have you protected this company from the same downfalls that those other companies you're talking about have? Something's gotta give . . . ?"

"Well, yes and no," Barber responded. "That's a question that I've been learning over the last ten years. My assumption ten years ago was, if you want good flavor, you have to get very low yield and go to the heirlooms."

I had got him riled up, I realized.

"The answer is, you just tasted it," he continued, raising his voice, explaining how the yield is strong for the squash. "It's especially not true in grains, which you're about to taste. The extent of consolidation of the seed business, it's really been the result of grains, because that is where the seed companies and chemical companies can control the seeds and the farming methods that follow from them. It's a big deal to get into grains."

With that, he turned on his heel and retreated back to the kitchen. In that moment, I was almost miffed—it felt too much like a show. Off to get the Grains! But then, out came barley in a small cast-iron skillet. This is where he got me.

"I'm sorry this is out of the pot," Barber started, laughing as he scraped the bottom in a cackling screech while fluffing up boules of barley. I inhaled deeply and—a little too quickly—grabbed a wide-rimmed metal spoon. I didn't realize it at the time but, thanks to my recorder, know that this was the moment when I started saying "wow" over and over, surprising myself.

Barber quipped while I was in a full-blown barley daze, "Wouldn't you have that for breakfast, lunch, and dinner?"

Wow. Yes, I would. Focused chewing stripped me of all other words. And then—

"Can I have another bite?"

"Double dip!"

"I'm doing it." I grinned.

He let out a sharp breath and continued: "That's just water and salt. Nutrition and flavor, out of this world. Like, what the hell else do you need?"

Another bite and I blinked a few times, a little stunned. I looked at him seriously. Was this *cacio e pepe*? Barber recognized me processing this foreign concept—the silkiness of cream, the toothiness of each boule, and the slight nuttiness in the bite—and chimed in proudly: "People don't even know that barley could taste like this."

Barber said he just simmered the barley with water and a little salt: "I didn't do anything."

"It's nuts," I said definitively.

"It's nuts." He nodded.

What I was eating that day was drastically different from what I could have bought in natural grocery stores. If I'd gone to Whole Foods that night to buy barley, it would have been "meant for a pig, or to be malted for beer," as Barber put it, explaining how it would have been instead diverted to Whole Foods from its distributor, Unfi, from industrial sources. "That's what you're getting at Whole Foods, unless you're buying an heirloom barley," he explained.

I was suddenly seeing Barber and his work in a new light. I've been a Barber skeptic over the years, particularly because both times I'd visited his $258-per-person restaurant tasting before, I'd left with a grumbling stomach and a voice crying out in the back of my head begging to stop at Popeyes or get a dollar slice on the way home. But the barley spoke for itself. I could picture myself excited to eat that barley every day, and the crop actually could do some good on farms. Barley is an ancient crop, and it can grow almost anywhere. It is a good crop to add into a rotation on a farm because it can cover and help with erosion, especially for organic farmers. Barley is beneficial in nearly every way, according to the USDA: it's a fast-growing grass that discourages weeds from growing and adds nitrogen to the soil, thanks to its long roots. Barley has also been known to help with everything from protecting cotton plants from dust blowing in Arizona to protecting carrots and onions from wind damage to protecting potatoes from soil pathogens and even improving the fungus that grows around soybean roots. The environmental benefits, combined with better flavor and nutrition, are the trifecta that Barber is after: "This is the ticket. You have got to get it through the flavor. You have got to have the demand. The farmers who are growing these pathetic rotations of corn and soybeans use all these chemicals to intervene. If they could have the diversity to make their system more resilient, they would do it. But they need the demand for the diversity." The crazy part is that, so far, the breeds seem to prove that the better the flavor, the stronger the nutrition.

That's easy to get excited about. But just when I started holding my breath for an outlandish statement, like that this barley could change the world, Barber went back to playing a good, skeptical New Yorker: "I'm not sitting and saying we can solve the food system," he said. "We're talking about chefs being a part of the answer, because if chefs aren't a part of the answer, flavor, and therefore nutrition, because they're one and the same things, tend to fall way down the scale."

That's when he pointed out the clarified, yellow fat. "One thing you may notice," he started. "See all that? That's fat on the barley. Yeah, that's the good fat. That's all the fats that you want in your body." Then he told me about the moment in the kitchen when a sous-chef started seeing all this yellow fat seep out and exclaimed, "It's like meat!" They came to the idea that they could grind it. He left the barley for me as he quickly turned back to grab another dish from the kitchen.

He returned with a sausage made 70 percent from this magic grain, supplemented 30 percent with heritage pork. I could picture it sold through Baldor, at the refrigerated sausages rack at Whole Foods or Erewhon, maybe moonlighting at Cervo's or Dimes Market in my neighborhood. Barber knew he knocked it out of the park: "What if Joe Six Pack Dude, who's eating sausage three times a day, seven days a week, would give up 70 percent of the meat to eat that?"

He had clearly come to a potentially viable solution to reshape part of the food system from the small produce farm up.

Stuffed with these sausage slices, I was in a musing mood, and asked how else Barber had seen the industry evolve in his two decades of owning a restaurant. I sat back and waited for him to laugh in my face. After a pause, he said, "Look, when I started this restaurant twenty years ago, I swear to God, I had to have steak and some variety of meat. Those very things are actually the sign of the death of a restaurant that's old-school and out of fashion today."

It's so much more important than not being trendy. Barber's point was that chefs and other food media personalities have the once-in-a-century opportunity to shape the future of what we eat. And that includes the emerging plant-based-food industry. David Chang was the first to welcome the Impossible Burger to his later panned and closed Nishi in 2016. It's an event Impossible still talks about because it brought them a certain caché, to be leveraged later on when they made the real push into restaurants, and specifically fast-food chains. There is an alternative way for chefs to embrace trends without selling out via a corporate partnership. As the trendsetters, chefs can demand better-tasting and more highly nutritious ingredients be used in faux burgers, sausages, and other products, setting the example from their own kitchens first. In turn, this would create a steadier and stronger market for these ingredients, helping sway farmers to invest in growing another crop like barley or mushrooms.

In Barber's vision for the future, where local farms and regional producers thrive, there's a fresh approach to terroir through seed breeding: "You can respect and honor it by changing it and updating it, and you can update it by regionalizing it, growing different kinds of barley for different regions, so that chefs in the Pacific Northwest shouldn't be growing necessarily this barley in the same way barley's been grown in the South. It should be different, because the environments are different. It's different because the culture is different. That's where the excitement and food comes in. But it has to start with the seed. That's the bare minimum."

I had been seeing that kind of thinking already playing out on menus across the country, though it was rare, and I brought up a mind-blowing meal from a few months before at Mister Jiu's. It was the most lucid I've ever felt while dining. At the same time the meal was a whimsical reflection of personal coming of age through chef-owner Brandon Jew's heritage, but also firmly rooted in geographic history, time, and place, with dishes that are distinctly representative of San Francisco's Chinatown, such as sourdough scallion pancakes. I was quite fond of Jew's take on Cantonese-style charcuterie. Barber nodded along with me. Regional seeds bred for flavor could put teeth behind a new kind of farm-to-table movement that holds way more meaning than one that's just about what's in season.

"What is it about this restaurant, in this place, that gives me a sense of the place that connects to its history or its environment or culture that I can't get at home? That's called the experience of eating," Barber said. "It's not about one-size-fits-all. The seed has to follow that. Unless you think that the seed of the future is going to be to look back two hundred years and find a variety to repatriate, that may be part of the conversation, but it's not the end of the conversation. It's really the beginning of it."

A Historic Tofu Shop

It's rare that someone like Dan Barber spoon-feeds me the best barley of my life. It's more common for my husband, Nick, and me to eat simply at home. Sometimes that means tofu, especially if my sister Emery is coming over. When we do, it's from down the block, at Fong On, which opened on Division Street in 2019 and has roots as the oldest family-run tofu shop in New York City. I am lucky that Fong On is my version of locally sourced fresh tofu. I don't even have to cross any major intersections to get there.

The Eng family has been making tofu since 1933, when owner Paul Eng's grandfather first learned the recipe shortly after immigrating and started a fresh tofu shop in New York City's Chinatown. That spot was called Fong Inn Too, and it closed in 2017 amid rising rents and demand for fresh tofu waning. A shame for all of us. It was one of the last two fresh tofu shops in Manhattan's Chinatown. Restored as an homage to that history, today when you walk into the tiled shop, there's fresh tofu, soymilk, homemade tea, and sweet pudding. The fresh tofu is made in the back in stainless-steel trays. The tofu is pressed to get all the excess water out, which also binds the curds together. Fong On uses a small pneumatic press, while Eng's grandfather's shop used stones and body weight.

Sometimes I'll make chef Sophia Roe's recipe for tofu styled as ground beef. It's perfect for lettuce season in my urban garden, where there's only ever a few leaves ready to go at a time. All I do is break up Fong On's soft tofu with a spatula or my hands and, per Roe's instructions, season it heavily and bake until crispy. Then I wrap the pieces inside a just-cut lettuce leaf.

Growing Mushrooms Inside Restaurants, Grocery Stores, and at Home

Like all protein, mushrooms need a substrate to grow. In livestock, it's the feed. In lab-grown meat, it's the growth serum. For mushrooms, it depends on the species, but all it takes is the correct spores for a strain to meet the substrate they like to grow on, like a log or wood chips or coffee grounds, and a little water and, boom. Complex mycelium of crisscrossing proteins.

An exploratory mission brought me to a town house in the Bushwick section of Brooklyn. In February 2020 I met Andrew Carter and Adam DeMartino there. The friends from the University of Vermont moved to New York City and started out growing mushrooms in a storage container. They eventually pivoted to selling an entire growing system (because mushrooms need a certain temperature and humidity, and also release a lot of CO_2 as they generate). These growing machines could plug in at restaurants and grocery stores like the Whole Foods in Williamsburg. As they showed me around the headquarters of Smallhold, I saw all the elements of a normal New York City start-up: desks with computers, some stacked with papers, books, notebooks, and binders. Takeout from lunch and a little breakroom kitchen. Then we made our way to the mushroom production floor in the basement. DeMartino turned around on the stairs with a huge grin as smells of earth and faded blue light started to illuminate a glowing ring around his face.

The duo had figured out how to commercialize the perfect environment for fungi, which grows completely differently than plants. Smallhold's system just gives fungi all the elements necessary for the best chance at nature making it easy. It was working out pretty well. Smallhold's modulated tanks tinted blue stay between 90 to 100 percent humidity and 60 to 80 degrees, depending on the type of mushroom growing.

I was gazing upon varieties of oysters, lion's mane, reishi, and others. These mushrooms were blooming under the blue lights off the bags filled with sawdust. It's the ultraviolet light that told the mycelium to fruit. Everywhere I looked, more mushrooms were jutting off the sides of growing bags. As I peered into one of the shelves filled with reishi, a winding and prickly-looking mushroom that's dark brown—a mix of caps and branch-like sticks topped with a white tip—Carter explained the process.

"In reality it's more like animals," Carter, Smallhold's CEO, stated, pointing out the different parts of the reishi. "The mycelium, the white stuff, is digesting this sawdust, kind of like an external digestion process like your stomach does. Then it's breathing in oxygen and releasing CO_2."

I had only ever seen reishi in a manufactured powdered form, the kind popular in $12 elixirs, and I was surprised to realize the entire mushroom was the whole brown and white cactus-like shape. Carter went on. "Reishi, you can be artistic with it. You give it too much CO_2 and it'll grow an antler," he said, explaining the branches poking out that I had seen topped in white. "When you give it oxygen, then it starts to raise the cap like it's doing right here, and that'll start to fill out."

Smallhold's model shunts that energy cost down to whoever buys its machines. Those customers must pay to run them. Which is why, a few weeks later, when the pandemic hit New York City, many of Smallhold's restaurants with visible growing systems, including a restaurant a few blocks away from my apartment (the other direction from the tofu shop), had to terminate their deals and get their growing machines turned off when many restaurants shut down. Growing sustainable gourmet mushrooms within reach became a luxury they couldn't afford. As the machines were delivered back to the Smallhold town house, Smallhold lost half its revenue. Carter and DeMartino were turning off the farms of countless customers, including their first. But as they braced for an unknown future, Smallhold started selling its extra mushrooms and mushroom growing bags on the side. They were just plastic bags with the substrate already inoculated, like what grows inside the tanks that I saw at the town house. But they were offering an at-home version at a pop-up for around $10 a bag. For at least five pounds of mushrooms, all you had to do was cut X's around the bag, spray two to three times each day, and wait for the fungi to grow.

The Smallhold cofounders had been prepared for this apocalyptic moment for the food industry. They're both futurists. Smallhold's early investor pitches touted how the tech-enabled farms could be used in refugee camps, like Syrians who grew mushrooms while escaping the devastating civil war. Carter even has an old bike called the Beast, which he created as the ultimate get-out-of-the-apocalpyse mode of transportation. Except when the pandemic hit, Carter and DeMartino stayed in their community and helped hospitality workers feed themselves, when many were scared they wouldn't be able to. When I followed up with them a few weeks later, from what felt like a lot more than a river away, it was refreshing to hear their shock, tempered with a mix of long-awaited dread and a fresh calm.

"The entire company has actually been built around some future where people will turn inward and you'll need to grow local food and you'll need a supply chain that's based around more resilience," DeMartino told me during that particularly dark and rainy pandemic day in the spring of 2020. "History repeats itself. Look at World War Two. What happens when shit hits the fan on a global scale? People turn inward. There's nationalistic tendencies. But then they also look to their local community for support in ways that they hadn't before. What happens when we have entered into the brave new world? When we are no longer science fiction. It's the reality. What happens when a globalized world turns inward?"

They shipped out fifteen mushroom bag deliveries that day. Those were the days when I could peer out our window and see the easternmost corner of Canal Street almost entirely empty. At all times. The only traffic on the streets was delivery workers on bikes, including a few carrying mushroom grow bags from Smallhold.

"Knowing that the population is increasing beyond the carrying capacity, it doesn't make someone want to eat." Carter paused. "We don't tell that story. But now we're in this place where supply chains are being strained. I wouldn't say that Smallhold is creating a new victory garden or anything, but the concept is similar. You have people that are concerned about their food security."

I bought a few bags, oyster and lion's mane varieties, excited I could finally try this out myself and trust the spores. A few months before, I had bought some sketchy spores off the internet that got moldy before I could inoculate the inside substrate, which I don't recommend! These Smallhold bags were more manageable, with fully colonized mycelium ready to fruit. Think about mycelium another way: it's the living organism, the tree, and the mushroom blossoms from that as the fruit. As I cut X's into the bags and sprayed those areas, I was telling the mycelium to concentrate on fruiting in those specific spots. In a matter of days, tiny mushrooms started to pop through. I didn't have the blue lights or the humidity or the temperature controls but, mystified by mushrooms, I sat in awe and stared at the bags: it still worked.

The buds of oysters and furry lion's mane started popping out, and every day the process of spraying down the bags at several points gave me a moment of Zen. The simple acts of repetition were refreshing. I woke up excited to see how big they had grown each day, what had popped out overnight, what cap had morphed or bent. There came a point when the bags were on fire and we couldn't cut them off quick enough.

Soon we were eating mushrooms. A lot. We munched on mushrooms over toast, mushrooms over pasta, mushroom pizza, and warm mushroom salad topped with a bacon vinaigrette (sorry, vegans). The texture of some was a bit woody—this was my first try, after all, and in those early batches, I was so fascinated by how big the fungi grew each night that I didn't cut the shrooms off early enough. But others were tender and full of umami. I wish I could tell you they had a distinct Manhattan terroir and tasted of subway sweat in the summer, dollar slice and Mr. Frosty all in one. But the only terroir those mushrooms had was that of pandemic mouse infestation, some pollution, and grime tracked in from the bottoms of our shoes. But they were mine! And I loved them!

Smallhold survived the pandemic on its mushroom grocery sales and expanded to Texas at the end of 2020. Supermarkets like Whole Foods were flocking to Smallhold for their mushrooms, which customers could trace back to Smallhold's own production for retail or even visibly watch grow in stores. Customers bought mushrooms faster than buyers expected in 2020.

Historically, eight hundred million pounds of mushrooms are produced in the United States every year. Many of them are button mushrooms. The portobellos you see at the store are the same mushroom, only grown for more days. But commercializing something so wild takes an imprecise mix of bravado, artistry, and luck. White button mushrooms are the easiest to industrialize, and the industry is based in Pennsylvania, where more than 60 percent of the country's fresh mushrooms come from.

A Beacon amid Ruin

Other fungi, like Japan's prized matsutake mushroom, are nearly impossible to reproduce. That's why, when they turned up in the 1990s in the swaths of clear-cut forests in California's Cascade range, it was wild that the National Forest Service estimated that their value was as much as the timber itself. These shockingly adept mushrooms had transformed the wreckage of a so-called scalable and industrial system (forestry) and created a nonscalable economy in its wake, writes Anna Lowenhaupt Tsing in her highly recommended book *The Mushroom at the End of the World*. The book is about how mushrooms can be a beacon amid ruin. The first living thing to emerge after the atomic blast of Hiroshima, it's been said, was a matsutake mushroom. Pointing to the moment in 1991 when the Soviet Union collapsed and thousands of Siberians reportedly ran to the woods to forage, Tsing writes that "the uncontrolled lives of mushrooms are a gift—and a guide—when the controlled world we thought we had fails." Mushrooms, she writes, can serve as an everyday reminder of "the conditions of precarity, that is, life without the promise of stability."

Tsing's work has been striking to me for years, but it's prescient especially because of the emphasis on mushrooms and other mycoproteins—a single-cell protein from fungus—as a so-called clean option in the squabble to lead the alternative protein revolution. On top of that, back to Tsing's point, the capital boom is trying to commercialize and standardize something that is beautiful and mystical in its wild form.

The sobering thought struck me when Seth Goldman, the founder of Honest Tea and chairman of Beyond Meat, explained to me why he launched his own plant-based brand in 2021—an organic mushroom jerky called Eat the Change. Goldman, a vegan, quipped to me that the start-up wouldn't pose any problems for him personally, even though he has a non-compete clause with Beyond Meat, because his start-up's mushroom-based product is decidedly less processed than any sold by Beyond Meat. "I had to design the company so that I'd never be in competition with Beyond Meat," Goldman said. "So one of the things we're about is food in its native form."

When I speak with founders like Goldman, or other young founders branding other competitive mushroom jerky, I ask them about how they are building these industrial supply chains. How are you improving the mushroom production process—because we're fools to pretend that not every food is extractive. How are safety and health conditions improving for workers? Is there equity? These are mostly insular family-run operations. The exciting part of the mushroom funding boom is that the capital could go to some potentially impactful supply chains. These founders are usually sourcing directly with a mushroom operation, yet these companies could eventually build their own plants. But the funds raised may just go to targeted ads on Instagram and a few hires.

Big money is getting pumped into the alternative challengers competing to replace factory-farmed meat. But what we're left to decide between, online and on shelves, too often falls short. Finding alternatives supported by locally based and economically viable supply chains remains the best route.

SECTION IV

———

MAXIMIZING WHAT WE'VE GOT

CHAPTER 17

An Independent Slaughter

I'd already spent a few hours helping my friend Phil Haynes slaughter chickens when it happened. One of the birds I held by the feet as Phil sliced its neck jumped out of the stainless-steel death trap it was stuck in headfirst. The bird was one in a lineup next to a dozen other cones filled with chickens bleeding out from their throats. I had just watched the chicken throw its legs up in a last-ditch attempt at survival. It managed to make air. The big fella landed legs up on the floor, blood gushing out with its heartbeat every few seconds. It flailed and kicked. I stood there, less than a foot away, unable to move. I had been fine holding the chicken as Phil sliced with one fast motion. The weathered feet were soft and cold. I had to admit, I was rooting for this one, even though I knew his fate was sealed. It was a chicken with its head half cut off, dangling as it writhed on the blood-splattered floor.

I had found my line. And crossed it. Phil immediately saw me freeze and swooped in, picking up the chicken by its feet. He slid the bird back into the cone. It kept kicking.

Phil eventually cut the neck fully off. I waited a second and let myself take a deep breath before pulling the bird and his neighbors out of the cones and dumping them into the scalder. I pressed a big red button, and the birds sank into the 140-degree water below. Then we reloaded the cones as the other birds stayed submerged. This dance all took place within a tight but workable 240 square feet. After a batch of birds got scalded in the boiling water for around forty-five seconds, I picked up as many as I could at once, usually two or three, and dropped them into a circular machine with pegs sticking out. The device looks like an industrial kitchen–size colander, if it was stuffed with a convex hawk shield for tiny dogs. The birds get tossed around inside so their feathers come off. Then the freshly plucked chickens slide through an opening in the wall connected to a conveyer belt on the other side, down to the evisceration room. We worked quickly. No other choice. There's no time to spare during a two-day slaughter of 350 chickens with a crew of eight.

Replicability and Carversville's Steady Funding

At a party a few years ago at a friend's apartment in New York's Nolita neighborhood, I was catching up with my pal Phil, who had taken the train down from Tarrytown, where he was managing the rangeland program at Chef Dan Barber's Stone Barns Center for Food and Agriculture. Over on his Instagram account @hogboi, he had been chronicling the daily lives of many of his pigs, including his favorite, Persimmon, an adorable three-hundred-pound mom of a litter with reddish spots. Over the years I had loved the updates on how Persimmon was doing, how big she was smiling in the sunshine. Naturally, I inquired about how Persimmon was, but this time his face fell.

"We ate her," he said quietly.

It was her moment, he said, but it still was hard. Phil makes the best pâté I've ever had, has always been very direct about the past lives of what he eats, and Persimmon had the best life possible for a pig on a farm in America. I shouldn't have been surprised, but the sudden turn of my simple catchup chitchat horrified me. Then I recognized the feeling of shame and I wanted to explore it. My discomfort only grew when I thought about why I was sad, and how I had eaten a bacon-and-egg sandwich from the neighborhood bodega that morning, which no doubt had far worse ingredients.

Soon after that, Phil joined a Pennsylvania farm that raises cattle and hens on pasture to supply Philadelphia soup kitchens with restaurant-quality ingredients. There are none of Phil's beloved pigs at Carversville Farm Foundation, but he gave that up in exchange for some room to explore his skills not just as a livestock farmer but also in the slaughterhouse. He kept one of his favorites from Persimmon's litter, named Cinnamon, at a friend's nearby farm. At twenty-seven years old, he moved to Bucks County for the opportunity Carversville was offering him: the chance to design an on-farm poultry plant from scratch with a full bank account behind it. To give himself a little extra job security, he laid it out for someone left-handed, at his height.

It's the centerpiece of a two-hundred-acre nonprofit farm that includes much more: egg layers, thousands of pounds annually of organic produce, and mushrooms growing on logs in the woods. My tour of Carversville taught me that on a farm, mushrooms can be added to the operation at relatively low cost. Inoculated logs can grow in wooded or shady areas. All that's needed in addition is the water and any shading, tarps, or structures to organize the logs around. It's a low-maintenance way to diversify a farm's harvest.

Carversville's mostly flat fields are an organic operation that's nearly zero waste. All the feathers, coagulated blood, and guts discarded during a poultry slaughter go back into the compost pile to feed Carversville's soils, which have been depleted after being farmed continuously for three hundred years. Steers rotate through the pastures, followed by groups of chickens, turkeys, and geese in mobile coops. More than 90 percent goes to Philadelphia's soup kitchens. The last 10 percent is sold out of Carversville's website and at its on-farm store—local pickup only.

The nonprofit has long-term and steady funds backing it, which frees it from the pressures of fundraising and paycheck-to-paycheck accounting that forced other lofty operations to fail in the past. Carversville's deep pockets belong to a retired entrepreneur who built one of the top firms for background checks and employee screening services for the finance and health-care industries. According to the *Bucks County Courier Times*, co–executive director Tony D'Orazio describes himself as "an accidental entrepreneur." As a student in the 1980s at Temple University, he "participated in anti-war protests at the General Electric nuclear missile plant in King of Prussia and other defense contractors elsewhere in the country." The son of a master carpenter then got a job as a consultant with accounting firm KPMG, and he commuted to New York City from his home in Philadelphia every day on Amtrak. He decided to strike out on his own after a random attack one evening in 1989 when a fellow commuter punched D'Orazio in a fit of rage on an overcrowded train. He started his firm, Vertical Screen, in 1991, maxing out credit cards for financing and answering the phone with different voices to pretend he had more employees in the early days. In 2013, he and his wife, Amy, cofounded the farm as a foundation.

The benevolence of well-intentioned rich people is not a replicable model. But there's still much to learn from its idealized operations—among the best that money can buy. No expense was spared, which I appreciate, since the cause (hunger in Philadelphia) is at a critical inflection point. That's why I wanted to work a slaughter at Carversville. I wanted to test the theory that local meat in its purest form is better for the climate and ethically superior for both worker conditions and animal welfare.

My First Slaughter Day

Carversville's poultry plant has windows that overlook rows of produce and fields of chickens clucking in grass. Inside are two rooms: where there's killing and where there's eviscerating. Both are overwhelmingly bright, with a lot of plastic and metal, so every crevice can get power-washed at the end of a long slaughter session. Volunteering at day one of a forty-eight-hour Carversville poultry slaughter in August 2020, we spent eight hours killing and disemboweling 350 pasture-raised Cornish Cross chickens. We started at eight a.m. The next day, after the birds chilled overnight, we focused on plucking out any errant feathers and deciding how many to donate whole and how many as packs of butchered breasts and thighs. Then we vacuum-sealed, packaged, and stashed them in the freezers.

I started out in the evisceration room—the second part of the slaughter-house, where the group crowds together around stainless-steel work sinks and cuts out the lungs, liver, and guts from each chicken. There were four people at my workstation, just a few inches apart. Some could slice and pull out the intestines and guts in one quick motion. My boning knife slid onto my finger and broke through my gloves with a single slice during my first chicken. I got a small cut that started to bleed. So I quickly washed up, threw new gloves on, and got back to work. I finally got the rest of the guts out in another ten cuts. At least.

Slaughter work is highly skilled. I burst only one gallbladder, which is one of the worst things that can happen, because if a gallbladder's toxic liquid gets on the meat, or anyone else's, that meat could be ruined. As the dark organ exploded all over my gloved hand, its dark green ink oozed out. Luckily, the gallbladder was already out of my bird, my seventh that morning. The meat was safe. I just had to contain the situation. I rushed to the sink to shed my gloves, wash up, and start again. Again. When I got back, the dark green ink was still in the sink below the station I was working at. I watched it slowly creep closer to the drain. I was ready for relief, the toxic adulterant almost taken care of, and the embarrassment almost over. But then, just as the liquid reached the drain, the farm's tattooed produce manager working across from me at the long sink station broke one, too. A minute later, he broke another.

Farm manger Steven Tomlinson noticed the trend, nodded to me, and whispered: "Solidarity."

These chickens were heavy. At least to me. I had barely worked out or walked beyond five blocks of my neighborhood in months. The big ones were six pounds. I started feeling it in my shoulders and neck almost immediately as I held the bird with one hand up its cavity and worked the knife in my other. Aside from the squawks coming from the other room, the evisceration room was quiet and the pace was quick. The fuzzy, harmonic guitars of a psychedelic rock band I couldn't quite make out hummed in the background, providing a calm, if not slightly trippy, ambiance. Tomlinson broke the silence every once in a while to keep the pressure on, especially when he saw sloppy cuts or fat dangling.

"We want it to be the best quality going to soup kitchens," Tomlinson reminded us, to nods all around. "They never have enough meat."

The 10:30 a.m. break came just as my knees were starting to wobble. I went outside to sit on the slaughterhouse's stoop and drink some water. When I looked up, Phil was grinning wide. He was covered in blood, splatters as high as his face, caked on up to his elbows. He had been working solo in the kill room, where I was going next. I was doing the second part of the process first—post-kill.

Tomlinson walked over to us outside the plant and asked me if I was learning what I had hoped.

"I'm trying to understand how an on-farm slaughter operation like this can be financially viable," I replied, "and I want to know if there's a way to make this profitable and replicable elsewhere."

Tomlinson looked at me, a city rat that he had graciously welcomed to his farm from a pandemic epicenter, and smiled. Slaughtering at Carversville doesn't help them keep costs low, that's for sure, he said, and they still must send the cattle out, per regulations.

"It comes down to why we want to do this," Tomlinson replied, explaining how it stresses animals less not to travel off-farm. This way, Tomlinson explained, he and the team know exactly how the kill was done—apparently with the utmost reverence, which I was about to see. Tomlinson was clear: taking control of their own slaughter wasn't the best financial choice. Still, this nearly circular operation was extremely efficient, which, for me, pokes another hole in the industrial mantra that operations need to be optimized within half a cent to be viable.

After catching a nod from someone else closer to the plant door, Tomlinson turned to us, and we knew it was time to get back to work. Too much talk. I walked behind Phil as we entered his domain, a kill floor one person can run all alone. We had four crates of live chickens to get through during this second shift.

As they chirped and squawked loudly, I half yelled over the roar to Phil to ask if he usually says anything before he starts. I instantly felt naïve. He shook his head as he started grabbing a bird by its feet. Immediately, the bird got stuck headfirst into one of a dozen stainless-steel cones stationed on the wall, lined up next to each other barely an inch apart. We were off. Once the chicken was secure, Phil made two incisions and slit its neck to let the blood drain out. The stainless-steel rig included a sink underneath the cones. That meant less mess. As the chicken's heart pumps some of its last beats, the rest of the blood pours out. The sink catches most of it.

Phil quickly grabbed more birds and dropped them into open cones, lining them up—twelve in a row. I followed his lead. When birds tried to squirm and flap their way out of the cones, Phil asked me to hold their feet as he cut. The goal was to cut as little as possible, in a swift motion, to not prolong the pain. We registered that the job was done when the bird's butthole stopped twitching. That's when Phil knew to cut the head clean off. The heads fell into a sink full of blood thickening around other chicken heads.

At times I found myself holding two sets of feet at once, arms extended wide, with my legs in a split stance, as blood drained down from the necks across the line in front of me. The chickens kicked their feet. But the kicking always stopped, and then I would pull the birds out of the cones and place them in the boiler, feeling like Nicolas Cage in *Mandy*, in too deep to go back.

The birds got scalded before getting tossed around a machine that spins the dead birds and sheds most of the feathers easily. Phil then reloaded the cones. We fell into a rhythm, continuing to move the birds from the cones into the scalder, and then defeathering machine, until there were no chickens left. The chirps and squeaks echoing in my ears suddenly stopped.

By one p.m., we started an initial cleanup before breaking for lunch. It didn't hit me what I'd just helped with until I was cleaning the stainless-steel wall caked with blood. The sink that caught all the blood as the chickens drained out of their necks had coagulated blood two inches thick and chicken heads stuck in the Jell-O. I was tasked with cleaning it out, so I spent a while grabbing errant heads by the handful and dumping them all into the bucket slated for the compost pile. It was quite the Lady Macbeth moment, only my hands were filled with chicken heads covered in chunks of dark blood. I wanted to laugh, but instead I was sweating for the first time in six months and kept it moving. I had a big task ahead.

I eyed the pile of wet feathers that had accumulated in the corner of the slaughterhouse, behind the defeathering machine, and found there was a mountain to be moved. The sweat was dripping off me as soon as I started shoveling it down. I never want to see wet feathers again. I scratched at the corners to get the wet last few where they had gotten stuck. Anything I couldn't reach in the back corners I hit with the hose, and each and every feather eventually drained toward me. The feathers joined the compost, too. I felt accomplished. At least it was worth it.

As perspiration beads slid off my face, I realized how rare what I had just experienced was in the grand scheme of American chicken slaughters. Not because of the blood, but because of the cleaning, which I now think might be the most important part for an on-farm chicken plant. Usually, the people who raise the livestock don't also do the slaughter, and after animals are processed into meat, plant workers go home. A separate cleaning crew shows up, usually overnight, to deep-clean the facility. Do the managers know what it is like to regularly clean up a pile of wet feathers? They probably get immediately sucked down a stainless-steel drain, completely out of sight. When these processes are mechanized and sterilized, we lose the gravity of the situation, and the humanity. These feathers were on a live being just a few hours before. If we're not even acknowledging that, what else is being sterilized in our food system? In this case, the feathers and saving every last drop that's usable for compost are the final loop to close the cycle and prevent waste—while compost remains one of the best ways an on-farm plant can give nutrients back to its soils.

I thought about that as I recovered from the shoveling and heavy breathing. I took a break and rested on my shovel.

"Phil, do you ever want to run your own farm again?" I asked. He hadn't been more than a few inches from his daily organic certification log all day, and he clearly did well with the responsibility. He was writing details in the boxes when he looked up to respond. During his first year out of college, Phil had tried farming with his brother, only growing produce, and stopped the next season.

"It's broken," he told me. "Here I get to learn and do it my way." But he smiled, and I knew he wouldn't like being managed for long. Aside from Phil's desire for independence, hired hands on farms get a raw deal. Carversville is a nonprofit, but if it were for profit, workers would still be at a top-down organization, likely without equity or profit-sharing. Farmworkers can also make meager wages in exchange for housing, often in suboptimal conditions. Sure enough, within a year Phil was already back to envisioning his next move, and decided to become the agricultural director at another nonprofit, this time back in New York's Hudson Valley, called Sky High Farm.

Pearl of Wisdom: Don't Forget the Oyster

The next day, I was back in my smock, rubber boots, gloves, and mask at eight a.m. for what I thought might be a nightmare. Maybe it was because of the scene from that terrible Nicole Kidman and Tom Cruise movie, *Far and Away*, in which Kidman plays an Irish immigrant plucking chicken feathers at a Boston factory. I had to watch it in college, and that scene has been stuck in my brain ever since. Would I ever be able to look at feathers again? I spent almost the entire day standing hunched over a stainless-steel table like a diamond handler working with a magnifying glass. I had tweezers, slightly larger than the kind I have on my sink at home, and a bucket of water full of floating in-grown chicken feathers. I meticulously scoured every bird for unappetizing bits and entrails left over. Every once in a while, I got a shooting shoulder pain from the precarious position. Phil inspected every bird before packaging, vacuum-sealing and boxing the meat in the freezers.

Phil's apprentice, Sarah Savannah Knight, a former executive sous-chef at the Four Seasons in Baltimore, was helping him cut the biggest birds into packages of certain cuts like breasts. But Phil got impatient. After he inspected some of her thighs and found the oysters missing, he called her out. The oyster is widely thought to be the most tender piece of poultry. It's what I split with Nana first when carving my Thanksgiving turkey.

"Leaving flavor on the table," he said as he shook his head. Tension cut through the crisp slaughterhouse air.

Knight, who decided to explore livestock handling after being furloughed during the pandemic, responded: "Restaurant butchering is prettier." This was common style, she retorted, so how would he prefer she cut them? "I was falling back on my muscle memory," recalled Knight, who was trained to break down chickens for a restaurant service in a way that didn't take extra time to slice around the oyster, which probably would have gotten trimmed off anyway to maintain a uniform look.

"I came into farming because I knew there was something about my industry that needed to change, and I wanted to learn how to raise animals well and what it is to take care of the land," Knight later told me. "That swagger that chefs walk around with all the time? I dropped it at the door and had a student-like mindset."

There are multiple ways to butcher chicken. But Phil came over, visibly annoyed, and whipped out his boning knife. With a fresh bird, he made exactly six separate cuts and let the knife grind between the joints and bone effortlessly. First a clean cut to the breast, then two slices following along the edges of the muscle. He found the joints instantly and cut through with ease. I've never seen someone break down a chicken so seamlessly, especially in silence. The crew watched, eyes bugging out and mouths agape under our masks. The entire show took less than thirty seconds. Nothing else was said, but every thigh included the oyster for the rest of the day.

I just focused on my work: plucking and dipping the feathers into a cup of water to get them off my tweezers. Plucking, dipping, plucking, dipping. By the end of the two days, the joints in my fingers were sore. Sometimes they creaked a little. With every twinge, I was reminded how meatpacking is one of America's most injury-prone industries.

CHAPTER 18

Bracing

Burn it down. Start from scratch. A full reset. These echoes are starting to compound. And while I'm here for that energy, and I feel the anger it stems from, when it comes to the food system, there needs to be a dash of reality, too. There simply isn't enough time to start from scratch, and large food and agriculture companies have four major reasons to contribute: hard assets, capital, a ready workforce, and scale.

Amid stalled international collective action, business cannot be ignored. Whether we like it or not, within a capitalist society, market-driven opportunities might be our best way to enact changes on the scale required to meet climate threats. But that can only really exist in a competitive market that functions fairly. Industrial meat production needs to drastically change, but we also don't have the time to start over completely.

There's a lot at stake. Status quo food production will seal our apocalyptic fate. The UN's 2021 IPCC report shows the planet already has had damage from fossil fuels and industrialized livestock production at levels "irreversible for centuries to millennia." Expect more flooding, monsoons, sea level rise, and tropical storms, along with ice caps melting, drought, harsher winters, blight, superbugs, and more antibiotic resistance. While many disasters are already here, an even more severe future awaits us all.

Stronger biodiversity, more holistic systems that don't erode soils or pollute environments, safer workplaces, true cost accounting, equitable businesses, localized ownership, and investments that stay in their communities—these are just a few of the solutions that could add flotation to the sinking ship. Existing structures need to change.

Solutions need to address hunger, and the myriad of logistical, economic, nutritional, social, and cultural facets of this systemic issue. Preparedness should be a fundamental part of any business design moving forward. Is it greedy to expect that this system create less stress for the animals, as well as better products nutritionally?

The future needs to have more equitable and accessible financial tools so change can be accelerated. My years tracking billionaires and valuing their assets taught me that equity is the most important piece of the puzzle—especially for food. Most of the billionaires in food and agribusiness get there from overwhelming ownership of a private company. Commodities-based systems often seek out vertical integration and overall concentrations of wealth and power over time. The counter to this is a business model that incorporates employee equity and profit-sharing (from co-ops to employee stock ownership plans). Ownership is power. Independent livestock farmers and "mission-driven" brand founders alike go up against an industrialized and commoditized system, which is not going to retreat willingly. Equity is one of the most powerful pieces of leverage that challengers can have.

The institutions that have historically given out small business loans, nondilutive grants, or research-based awards have been uneven. Diverse founders have historically been denied access to finance, compared to their white counterparts. Many that are able to break through and turn over equity to secure capital are then locked into venture capitalist expectations and funding cycles. There need to be stronger structures in place to fund and support businesses while evening out power spread among different stakeholders (from workers to suppliers to retailers to customers).

My hope is that more adaptive financial tools and structures can successfully accelerate change. All solutions will be limited without a living wage, or better, universal access to a basic income, job guarantees, and just health care and housing. Any lack of transparency and accountability will also limit any progress. I believe the best-case scenario will have layers of solutions on top of each other—a patchwork stitched together via overlapping farms and distribution networks and supply chains, each thriving on their own level. There must be regulators and policymakers at work. What needs to thrive most in these systems is the community-based organizations—be it a version of collective farms or a public food sector or a network of local canneries or all of it—linked together with many other neighbors. That's the modern-day late-capitalist equivalent of the pack of buffalo moving together into a storm, which Tanka Bar CEO Dawn Sherman told me she thinks about often.

"Buffalo face the storm," Sherman explained. "They walk toward the storm. That's just an internal thing that they know to do: if they face a storm and continue walking, eventually they will emerge. It may be tough and you're going to get all that rough snow, wind, everything that comes at you."

But, Sherman said as a relaxed smile broke out, "you will break through the storm."

The Only Alt Protein Start-Up That's a Public Benefit Corporation

Colorado-based mycelium start-up Meati has decided to go the extra distance in its quest to commercialize a sustainable alternative to chicken breast, steak, and jerky. In addition to buying organic sugarcane to feed its fermentation during production described earlier, Meati is sourcing fully home-compostable packaging for its first home deliveries, meaning the composting worms I keep on my terrace could eat it all and then nourish my garden. CEO and cofounder Tyler Huggins, a thirty-seven-year-old dual doctor of philosophy and civil and environmental engineering, says he doesn't want to compromise on any crucial aspects of building his ideal climate-friendly business. But scaling up Meati's production as vertically integrated will be an expensive challenge, especially with strict ethical guardrails in place. It's why, early on, Huggins registered Meati as a public benefit corporation, which will help protect his vision as the start-up conducts fundraising rounds from investors or if it ever pursues going public.

"Our impact isn't just to our shareholders," Huggins, who grew up eating mostly game in Montana with a bison-ranching dad, explained to me. "It's something that investors are getting more familiar with."

Becoming a public benefit corporation is among the strongest tools a founder can use to put teeth behind "mission-driven" marketing language. But there are few examples of putting those teeth to real work. Public benefit corporation registration "will get us towards a more just form of capitalism," according to Rose Marcario, the former CEO of Patagonia who is an investor serving on Meati's board.

"Will it take a long time for the public markets to come around? I hope not. Some food companies have done it, but there's overall still a lot of progress to be made," added Marcario. "The larger plant-based food companies, you know their names, they're using GMOs. They're imprisoned by pesticides and chemical fertilizers. It's unnatural. It brings on gut health issues. It doesn't taste good. It's highly processed."

It's hard to know what to look for as a consumer who wants to shop ethically in a late-capitalist system. Public benefit corporations rarely highlight the achievement on their labels, but companies that are certified with a similar set of standards, called B Corps, are usually proudly labeled so. There's annual third-party verification that a certified company balances profits with its impact on workers, environment, community, and customers. An amendment to a business's governing documents solidifies that the board of directors must balance purpose with profit, but certification standards can be hard to enforce.

B Corp–certified businesses can doubly register as a public benefit corporation, which changes how corporate law can impact the business. A public benefit corporation is still the same taxwise as a C or S Corp. The registration was originally designed to help protect businesses going public. Being a public benefit corporation legally expands the responsibilities of board members not to maximize shareholder value, but rather to benefit the public. It no longer requires justification of creating shareholder value while considering environmental and social impacts.

Public benefit corporations have sharper legal teeth than a certified B Corp. They are an option in over half the country. Others are working on adding their own registration. It can give a fledgling start-up a backbone—legally compelling a founder and management team to do the right thing instead of pushing for growth, mainly to benefit private investor funds and their demands for returns. I've been encouraged in recent years by the number of food companies that have registered or become certified.

It was Matt O'Hayer, the founder of pasture-raised egg brand Vital Farms, who first told me about the real reason he wanted his young company to register as a public benefit corporation in 2016. Up until this point, I had gathered through my reporting that many brand certification claims were nothing more than vanity. But that changed after O'Hayer explained to me how it works. Our journey started on an egg-layer farm in Paris, Texas, then led to O'Hayer flying us back to Austin on the tiny airplane version of the DeLorean with doors that swing up nearly ninety degrees to open, and, after arriving in one piece, ended at his Austin headquarters sitting in his boardroom. O'Hayer, a friend of John Mackey's who no doubt benefited from the access, was at the head of the table and shook his head. He then said, straight-faced: "Let's say that if the company was ever for sale, you don't have to sell to the highest bidder. With shareholder rights under common law, shareholders can say, 'Well, you should have sold to those guys that offered a higher price.' When you are a benefits corporation, we actually could do something that's more beneficial to society and to our other stakeholders."

Signing away rights to register the company as a public benefit corporation was an example of Vital Farms' shareholders putting their money where their mouths were. They had to approve changes that gave them less power. The decision mattered—especially three years later, when Vital Farms went public. Roughly thirty minutes after the IPO in August 2020, O'Hayer joined me on *Forbes*' Instagram for a live chat, and as soon as I asked him about registering as a benefit corporation again, he quickly replied: "Every company should be a benefit corp.

"I would recommend it. It changes the attitude," he said. "I was a lifelong entrepreneur who had started dozens of companies. I was always looking for the exit. When I first heard about conscious capitalism and B Corps, I realized, instead of looking for an exit and looking to get rich, I could build a company where I'm focused on the stakeholders: employees, customers, vendors, shareholders, environment, community. We give them equal attention. It makes it so much more fun than working on just profit all the time."

Consumers are starting to seek out companies like this, and so are employees. But it's hard to pull off, especially if investors and board members must agree to give up rights. John Foraker, a natural food industry legend who built up Annie's, told me that he always tried to get that brand to switch over, but multiple efforts over the years failed. He tried in the year and a half before taking Annie's public in 2012. After General Mills acquired Annie's in 2014, he tried a few more times. Foraker recalled the momentum starting to shift when Silk maker WhiteWave, which had registered as a public benefit corporation, was acquired by French dairy giant Danone in a landmark 2016 deal for $12.5 billion, including debt.

"I could never get my board to do it. It was always a huge regret for me,"

Foraker told me. "I wanted to be a benefit corp because it was what the company stood for and the lesson I learned then was that it was too early. There weren't any benefit corps that had ever gone public, at least that we were aware of. There was a lot of fear in our investor base that it would somehow taint an offering and the people on the buy side wouldn't really get it."

But he's since gotten his chance. After leaving Annie's, Foraker cofounded Once Upon a Farm, a baby food maker and kids' snacking brand, with actor Jennifer Garner and two others. In March 2021 it registered as a public benefit corporation, and Foraker was proud. "Finally the corporate governance structure is catching up to where consumers and brands have been for years. People were buying Annie's as much because they loved the mac and cheese but also for the values that were built into the company over time. Embedding that into your corporate structure in a very legal way is an important affirmation, and there are consumers looking for it now," Foraker said. "Down the road, it puts us in a better position relative to activist investors and the like who might sue us and say, 'Hey you're not following the core principles of making money. Your corporation is supposed to make money and that's the only thing that matters.' We know that's not the case."

When I first heard Vital Farms was going public in 2020, I was surprised. Then I felt naïve, and wondered how far being a public benefit corporation would really take the egg company. Vital Farms went public during another boom on the public markets. It is expensive to go public, and if Vital Farms had wanted to save money, it would have avoided the traditional IPO. Special-purpose acquisition listings flourished in 2021 because they cut those expenses to a fraction. At least SPACs make the process a little more egalitarian, despite the majority of them resting on somewhat absurd financial footing. By 2021, the boom had food investors cashing in like it was 1999. But this decade doesn't have time for a rally followed by a bust, a global recession setting everything back, while limiting future investment in climate change solutions for protein.

"Whether it's a traditional IPO or an SPAC, there's more appetite than ever before for exits," S2G chief investment officer Sanjeev Krishnan told me in 2021. "That's not something I would have anticipated two years ago."

Why could that accelerate change? Krishnan sees the boom of exits as a big positive. "Innovation travels very slowly from the lab to the farm to the shelf. Part of that is the industry structure of the food system," Krishnan added. "In many parts, it's an oligopoly. You've got tanker ships, not speed-boats. The more speedboats that go public, they can be more nimble, agile, focused on their niche. That will build an ecosystem of faster and more innovative companies. That ultimately provides people more choice and challenges a lot of the incumbents to make changes."

Being publicly traded gives shareholders certain rights that board members must adhere to, like maximizing financial returns for shareholders. Going public also comes with the pressure to continually grow and meet expectations for each quarterly earnings report. Big food investors have come to expect steady returns, margin accretion, share buybacks, and dividends.

Most of the valuations are off the charts, considering that many food start-ups spending a lot on research and development are unprofitable. That's why these companies are prime targets for short sellers. As Beyond short seller Charles Lemonides, the founder of ValueWorks, told me: "When there's enthusiasm, everything goes up. When troubled times happen, some things get really, really cheap. Some of those agri-tech companies will prove to be real and some of them will prove to have been investment opportunities for Wall Street to make money. Knowing which turn out to be which will be part of the hard job."

"We're in the early days in the damage," Lemonides added. "The bloom is off the rose."

More short sellers or activist investors are coming. "There will be some money to be made on the short side with trends like more plant-based and sustainable agriculture," short seller Siggy Eggert, the CEO of Philadelphia-based Grizzly Research who doesn't have a position against either Beyond Meat or Oatly, told me. "You can sell this concept to investors and package everything nice, but the underlying company is not actually doing the things to the degree they thought they were doing. A lot of times you find in the very good industries that you want to be invested in that the companies that end up on the public markets are the lower quality of the bunch."

Maybe it's more likely that Tyson, JBS S.A., or Pilgrim's Pride will attract some short-seller interest, considering how late these companies have been to start mitigating risks and formalizing their own climate preparedness plans. Short sellers so far have not been as drawn to big meat companies. Tyson had about 1 percent of stock shorted in January 2022, while the share of Beyond Meat stock short was more than 30 percent. When I asked

German-born Eggert why more short sellers hadn't targeted traditional meat firms, he laughed.

"A lot of what I see in the farming industry is disgusting to me and I really dislike it," said Eggert, citing high antibiotics use and animals in confinement. "It is, though, I'm afraid, part of our reality, part of the world and the American way. It's all protected from the consumers to the politicians. Everybody is on board with that system continuing to work like the past. That's something that I'm concerned about, but as a short seller, there's not a lot of economic occasions for my criticism of that because other investors will say, 'That's how the world is, congratulations, buddy.' "

Short sellers, demanding hedge funders, or other activist investors complicate the operations of companies that should be devoted to adapting their portion of the food supply for climate change while keeping costs down. Yet if you're scoffing that these kinds of threats rarely happen, consider what went down at French dairy giant Danone, a publicly traded company with a North American division that is the largest registered public benefit corporation in the world. But Danone started attracting unwanted attention by activist shareholders by underperforming compared to competitors. After several months, its longtime CEO and chairman was ousted. While sales had declined almost 7 percent, Danone still had delivered 2020 net profits of $2 billion, at a margin of 8.3 percent, compared to 7.6 percent in 2019. The pressure continued. Danone's incoming leadership has been strict. In 2021, Danone-owned Horizon Organic cut contracts with eighty-nine dairies on the East Coast in favor of bigger operations across the country.

This is an example of why many believe food companies should not be publicly traded. Should an entity with the stated goal of feeding as many people as possible, as accessibly, nutritiously, sustainably, and ethically as possible, waste energy and resources on quarterly earnings, short sellers, activist investors, or worse? More and more, I think benefit corporation status is a crucial counterweight for any publicly traded company claiming to be "mission-driven." It's far from perfect, but if the public benefit corporation Danone North America and its CEO were targeted by activist investors directly, perhaps the ouster could have been prevented.

When it comes to alternative proteins that claim to be funding a better future, privately held Impossible Foods and Eat Just are not public benefit corporations, and on the public markets, neither is Beyond Meat. I find that telling. None of them are certified B Corps, either. Marcario says it's unsurprising. Look at the products, she says, made with pesticides and synthetic fertilizers. "That's not good for the planet. Whether it's good for investors and scales and makes them a lot of money, I can't comment on that," Marcario said. "Even though it's plant-based, it doesn't mean it's good for the planet if it's using bad agricultural practices."

B Corps are rare on the public markets. Aside from Vital Farms, I don't know of any publicly traded food companies that are also registered public benefit corporations. I also recognize that Beyond Meat paved the way for a lot of investors when it went public, as well as many future food listings. I understand Ethan Brown's would-be argument that you can do only so much. But as a writer, this is where I ask for shareholders and founders alike to do better, especially if they really are claiming to be "mission-driven."

Beyond will continue to face tension from being publicly traded. Throughout 2020 and 2021, the share of short positions ebbed and flowed between 10 and 30 percent of total shares trading. Those are huge percentages that will continue to attract unwanted attention. I mentioned Beyond's situation to John Foraker, of Annie's and Once Upon a Farm, and an investor in Meati. It was a few weeks since the Danone CEO ouster, two months since Beyond's stock surged with short sellers alongside Robinhood-fueled meme stock GameStop, and three months before post-IPO Oatly would start getting attacked from its own nagging activist short seller. I asked Foraker if he thought it was fair that Beyond's Ethan Brown had a lot to contend with as a "mission-driven" founder. Foraker replied: "It is really challenging to keep your eye on the horizon when you have all those distractions, especially the shorts and all that coming in. There is a tug-of-war for sure that's out there."

Provenance Capital Group cofounder Adrian Rodrigues explained that public benefit corporations are a step in the right direction, but ultimately fall short. Rodrigues said a public benefit corporation still may not be penalized for choosing profits, while at least the B Corp certification has the third-party organization B Labs "on you all the time." Rodrigues prefers stronger ownership structures, such as steward ownership, which features an "asset lock" that prevents the proceeds from a sale from being privatized. He's also fond of perpetual purpose trusts, a noncharitable firm set up around a core principle. "Biological systems don't always fit neatly into a VC fund or private equity," Rodrigues told me. "Having different capital providers which can better align with the time horizon and return expectations is really what our sweet spot is."

Titans of Alternative Finance

I doubt traditional financial institutions will combust anytime soon, and I'm eager to track how family offices, private wealth, and pensions repurpose their trillions in assets under management for sustainable goals, not greenwashed ones. To that end, the Securities and Exchange Commission is expected to start requiring climate and environmental impact disclosures in public filings, which might be the least the agency can do. But I'm more encouraged by alternative financial tools that spread out equity and address mistakes that have already been made. I hope some of those trillions will be put to work in this design.

Take the concept of loans financed by communities, for communities. I spoke with Cornelius Blanding, the executive director of the Federation of Southern Cooperatives and the Land Assistance Fund, an organization of co-ops and credit unions for Black farmers and landowners across the South, to talk through the implications for Black livestock farmers. The federation was created more than fifty years ago directly out of the civil rights movement in 1967 when twenty-two organizations—agricultural cooperatives, credit unions, worker cooperatives, housing cooperatives—came together in solidarity to leverage their collective power. The concept of a credit union was a foundational part of the civil rights movement. Back in the late 1960s and early 1970s, one of the federation's early organizers, Charles Black, would hold meetings with groups about their challenges around finances. On the spot, he would call for folks to pull out money from their pockets and put it on the table. "That would be the start of a spark," Blanding explained to me. "People just pool their resources. In the Black community, still to this day, some people still do that, they just call them saving clubs." What makes credit unions formal is the federal recognition from the National Credit Union Administration. Modern community-based credit unions are often housed in churches, post offices, and municipal buildings.

"We believe in local ownership, local control, and local governance,"

Blanding said. "We think that's the solution to many problems of our nation." Blanding's organization is owned and governed by the membership. Credit unions have a field of membership. Sometimes it's for a profession, like teachers. In agriculture, Black farmers who belong to a credit union are usually part of a geographic-based credit union, like a credit union in a Mississippi zip code that happens to have a lot of chicken producers living there.

The USDA's American Farm Service Agency is known as the industry's lender of last resort, Blanding says. When Blanding came to the federation close to three decades ago, he started out working on a revolving loan fund and developing business plans and packaging for small farmers and landowners. It was during the years leading up to the landmark 1999 class-action lawsuit *Pigford v. Glickman*, which asserted the USDA had discriminated against Black farmers over credit for decades and had failed to respond to complaints. The case led to a settlement of about $100 million, followed by a $1.25 billion settlement for a second class of impacted farmers in 2010, a money pool that still barely scratches the surface.

"Getting financing and credit has always been a need," Blanding said. "Having access to credit is extremely important, however sometimes extremely scarce. Many times, it is exploitative. For us, it's about building these financial cooperatives, these credit unions, these community development banks so that people own and control the financial resources in their community."

Credit unions aside, there's a lot of historic evidence that suggests creativity when it comes to financial tools and securities can be a bad thing: Michael Milken's junk bonds, commercially backed securities creating a housing crisis, cryptocurrency's energy-use problem—I could go on but I won't. But could there still be a hope for financial tools to be used as weapons for progress?

I've heard about an alternative to traditional small business loans—private loans tied to company revenue—but have yet to see it used in any major food deals. I'm intrigued, though, because it would align loan payback schedules with cash flow without turning over equity. That could be key for seed or early stage start-ups, or long-term family businesses that don't want to be tied to jam-packed growth and an exit within a few years. The concept comes from the oil and gas industry, which has used these kinds of loans for years. Not only do they not have to give away equity, but the structure aligns the return with the actual cash flow of the companies. That's a lot healthier for them, especially when they're getting started.

Another idea is more creative and extreme. RePlant Capital's loans were designed to financially incentivize farming that supports soil health. The loans help farmers while they spend three years embarking on (and paying for) the organic certification process, during which they can sell only into commodity markets.

RePlant cofounder Don Shaffer, who heads up the debt side of the firm, previously attempted to tie loans to soil health improvements while deploying some $250 million in loans to more than two hundred impact companies at his past firm. But he "never quite got there."

Shaffer realized the loan could work as part of a strategy that also includes equity investing and partnerships with big food companies. That's since become a key strategy for rePlant, as it deploys $200 million of its flagship $250 million fund on soil health loans. The firm's other two cofounders fill in there. David Haynes, a venture capitalist, runs the firm's equity strategy. Robyn O'Brien, a former hedge funder who became a consumer advocate after an epiphany over her son's allergy, heads up partnerships with corporations contracting farmers including Danone North America and Anheuser-Busch InBev. The recipients are barley farmers growing for big beer, but also some independents, like White Oak Pastures in Bluffton, Georgia. When owner Will Harris decided he needed to take out $2 million in 2020 to build a new distribution center for White Oak's online store, he turned to rePlant.

Lastly, there are loans from crowdfunding. When I think about the future system that really has a shot at taking on industrialized production, I get excited about crowdfunding. I'm not talking about kick-starter campaigns. I'm talking about a formal raise with the Securities and Exchange Commission, through a platform like WeFunder, Republic, or Kiva, which are popular among food brands and farms.

There are consumers who want to see better food out there—and want to have an active stake in that fight, while regulators are helping open that opportunity up to more people. Most founders have overlooked crowdfunding as an avenue, but it has become a viable option. In March 2021, the Securities and Exchange Commission raised the limit that can come from nonaccredited investors—from $1 million to $5 million.

Many founders talk about small business loans as an alternative route—but we know that comes with privilege: financial institutions, local banks, and lending firms are systemically racist. Especially in agriculture. On top of that, young entrepreneurs may have student loans or a tough credit score, and might not be able to take on debt. Some venture capital firms in food therefore offer young founders sky-high valuations. The founders, in turn, give too much equity away in their business while not fully understanding that selling that portion of their start-up is already requiring an exit—expected at multiples of what the investors paid.

Most food companies, independent restaurants, or farms should not have growth rates and returns like a tech start-up. But they should have access to capital, and crowdfunding keeps voting control for founders while leveraging loyal brand advocates.

Federal regulations until this point have prevented anyone from privately soliciting wealthy people with an investment idea: it had to be a formal invitation. Crowdfunding creates opportunity for normal folks to invest. The "nonaccredited" piece is important, because being "accredited" by a bank means it's certified that they have more than $200,000 in gross income for the past two years, or $1 million in net assets. These accredited investors are the kind of rich people who can personally invest in monetary funds run by private investment houses. Up until this point, there has not been enough incentive for a founder to spend the money and time to raise from average folks who wouldn't qualify as accredited. In a world of Airbnb, Wikipedia, and social media, the idea that a founder is limited to privately pitching rich people they have a direct contact with is anachronistic and undemocratic.

But platforms like WeFunder are digitally powering these transactions and opening them up to anyone a founder can email or connect with on LinkedIn. Investors are sent an offering—it could be a private or public link—and they can invest via the platform, which takes a fee off the top (for WeFunder, the rate is 7.5 percent). Maybe some on that list are among a business's most loyal customers—and offering them the chance to put skin in the game and invest could transform them into lifelong brand ambassadors. Consider that many could invest—and could come out with a nice return—who would have rarely gotten a chance before. This strategy is no doubt riskier, but the opportunity is compelling.

WeFunder, a public benefit corporation itself, says fifty-five food and beverage companies have used its platform, including certified B Corp Tanka Bar's crucial fundraise in Chapter 11, an upcycled bacon jam, a start-up building two high-tech hog barns outfitted with manure filtration technology that creates a dry fertilizer, a third-generation family fishing operation in California with a seventy-five-year-old seventy-foot boat, and a bone broth soup brand. About 20 percent of WeFunder's companies have historically been from the food industry, while 22 percent of funding in 2020 went to women-founded businesses. That's compared to 3 percent of venture capital money, and the platform can still do way better to promote diverse start-ups. Black founders got more than 4 percent of funding, compared to 1 percent of venture funding overall.

There's also Kiva, a nonprofit that doesn't charge a fee to crowdsource loans up to $15,000, which is popular among small farmers. Kiva US has funded more than $40 million in loans since its launch, of which more than 8 percent went to small farms and 25 percent to food or beverage, like food trucks or small restaurants. Five vendors at the Oakland Farmers Market have even taken a Kiva loan. "We don't require a big track record. A lot are entrepreneurs starting off on their own—and need equipment or seed," explained Kiva's Rohit Agarwal. "It's patient. Even if you miss a payment, it's not like someone is coming after you. Kiva continues to follow up, but it's a very different follow-up than traditional. It's more understanding to eventually pay it back."

Universal Access to Food and Its Champions

Jose Luis Vivero Pol is a Spanish economist based out of Cameroon with the World Food Programme. He has wiry dark hair pulled back in a ponytail and scruff around the edges of his mouth. When I video-called him up in the spring of 2021, he was wearing a layered knit sweater and talked to me as he drank a glass of white wine. He was explaining why he felt so strongly that the idea of universal food access and food as a human right should be adopted before climate change worsens.

If a government declared such an idea, it would put food on the same level as education and health care. In many ways, food is more fundamental than either. Like the coexistence of private and public schools or hospitals, a new public food chain could be funded by the state or federal government. Maybe it could repurpose some of the subsidies that have been helping consolidated agribusiness for decades. It would take food out of the commodity system while still working within the confines of market demand—an enticing thought.

The markets have been co-opted. But providing total access to food, like a public utility, could secure a supply of food without relying on corporations and billionaires. The idea has been taking hold, in different forms: in May 2021, US senators unveiled a bill that would make school lunch free for all, while the United Nations was promoting the idea of universal access to food in its "resilience" track for its Food Systems Summit. In 2021, West Virginia policymakers recently proposed adding a "right to food" to the state's constitution, while Maine's House of Representatives overwhelmingly voted for a similar measure. While discussing hunger at the Forbes Future of Food Summit in 2021, I thought it might be a good time to poll the audience: Do you believe in the right to food? I was happily surprised by the results: 69 percent voted yes, 22 percent responded no, and 9 percent said they needed to know more. The right to health care is commonly understood. Why should food, which is arguably a more necessary resource for human existence, be any different? Universal food access would only give communities a foundation to withstand crisis in dignity.

José Andrés says he's a fan, too. "The system that is clear right now is, everybody is going to know you are in need. Anybody can be having a hard time," Andrés told me. "Let's create systems that don't shame anybody."

Vivero Pol, for one, is not optimistic about the future, even if universal food access or food utilities are adopted. "We are fucked," he told me. "I'm waiting for the next crack. The next crisis. There will be revolutions. A lot of people will die. We may have another pandemic that is really lethal. If you read history, that's the only way that civilizations die. Ours will die as well. We are at the end. We are now in the final part of our civilization. We enjoyed the best part of it. The eighties and nineties. Civilizations take many generations to collapse."

"Climate change will distort everything," he added solemnly.

I try to stay optimistic, but it's hard. These experts, even the intentionally provocative ones like Vivero Pol, make a strong case for doom. I find hope when I hear more about how Vivero Pol and others have strategized about how to get universal access to food to work within our economic reality. Remember John Ikerd, the hog economist from Chapter 2? He thinks the future is structuring food companies and retailers as public utilities like how the energy grid, sewers, and water delivery are managed. Ikerd's idea is called a Community Food Utility. It's another application of the same concept of universal food that Pol talks about. It puts food into the public sector and makes it a human right.

It has taken Ikerd a long time to arrive there. After growing up on a small dairy farm in southwest Missouri, he worked his way through the University of Missouri, and in between his bachelor's and master's he spent three years at a local slaughterhouse, which happened to be one of the largest in the country. Back in academics, he spent the first half of his thirty-year career as a traditional agriculture economist. He helped start the hog industry in North Carolina and worked with big feedlots in western Oklahoma. Ikerd stopped advocating for growth at all costs around the farm crisis of the mid-1980s, when land values tanked, exports halted, commodities crashed, farmers defaulted on billions in loans, and a string of suicides rattled the industry—all while Wall Street's merger mania continued without a hitch.

Ikerd's system would shift current federal and state funding for industrial farming to supporting the purchasing directly of farmers, and their risks when transitioning to more sustainable practices. Community Food Utilities would create deeper community connections than current federal assistance programs and could have programs for in-person local markets or food boxes delivered at home. Ikerd posits that a Community Food Utility could be set up as a vertical cooperative with a board of directors that includes local ranchers and growers, consumers, processors, distributors, taxpayers, and local officials.

In Ikerd's design, the Community Food Utility still seems amorphous to me, and a long way off because it creates an entirely fresh alternative value chain. I'm rooting for another project inspired by it, which applies the ideas in a way that could be put to action within the complex network of existing bureaucracy.

Bronx-born, Austin resident Errol Schweizer, who is a fourteen-year veteran of Whole Foods and the chain's vice president of grocery between 2009 and 2016, started researching the idea of "a public food sector" after the 2021 blackout in Texas when a winter snowstorm devastated the state's power grid. Without heat and water in most places, more than one hundred died. Schweizer and his family were without water for a week. That's when he started thinking about why the city of Austin didn't have its own emergency response department that could operate as a publicly owned food distribution system to make sure residents are fed in times of crisis. "I come at this from being a retailer. It still needs to be framed around meeting demand. Supply chains don't come into existence naturally. They respond to the power of purchase orders," Schweizer told me. "Individual responsibility for me is very much a function of the development of the supply chains and there needs to be some way to aggregate that demand, and mandate purchasing standards. So much of the value and power is off the farm."

The concept of voting with your dollars is "a false Messiah," Schweizer said. The grocery industry manufactures the demand for the products it sells. Common operational norms like slotting fees or free product that supplier brands must pay to stay on store shelves limit what brands can afford to sell in some grocery chains. Supplier brands shell out roughly $225 billion or the equivalent in free product annually, lining the bottom lines of consolidated grocery chains. "It's weighted towards those with privilege and access, and narrowly defines social change in the realm of individual responsibility and choice. Choice is important, but not if it's mediated by exchange values, not if it's mediated by the price or the location where you can shop," Schweizer said. "A public food sector functions outside of these conversations because it's in the notion of rights instead of transactions. Retailers manufacture demand. They advertise."

Schweizer has been drumming up support for a program within Austin's city government and elsewhere, and it has given me a host of ideas. Here's one: Could each region have its own locally run plant or warehousing set up? Yes, and maybe the food utility could be structured by zip code so it overlaps with credit unions.

Rebuilding as a Solidarity Economy

When Harlem-based consultant Qiana Mickie envisions the future she wants to eat in, she pictures a food system built around a solidarity economy. A concept that first emerged in the 1990s in Latin America and Europe, the solidarity economy, in theory, could add a level of measured scale to community-based solutions.

The foundation of a BIPOC-centered solidarity economy could take the form of a food hub. A food hub is a network of independent farmers, producers, and purveyors that cuts costs and handles the logistics of delivering food to customers. Some are consumer-facing and sell to folks at home, while others coordinate wholesale orders for institutional accounts like hospitals and nursing homes, which need stronger access to local and fresh food. Food hubs, also known as local food directories, are marketplaces for independent farmers, producers, and purveyors. There are more than two hundred food hubs nationwide, according to the USDA. Think of them as a way for local food businesses to collectivize the logistical side of retail and marketing, like a buying group for local food. Food hubs are a key facet of America's $6 billion local food network, as is community-supported agriculture. Paying a farmer up front for a share of a future season's haul, often in exchange for a weekly or monthly box of what's been harvested, would contribute to the strength of a neighborhood's food security.

"We need to start building and supporting alternative models that do have impact," Mickie told me. "The solution is lifting up those and then countering when people say, 'Well, that's just one way' or 'That's not scaled.' We need climate resiliency. We need an economic viability, and we need genuine diversity on an economic, environmental, and regional scale."

Bringing scale to the food hub is key. The journey of Common Market, a nonprofit aggregator and distributor of local farm foods, proves that. The operation scales regional food by investing in infrastructure like refrigerated trucks and warehouses. Access is also democratized: Common Market sells mainly to anchor institutions like hospitals and nursing homes that serve at-risk populations for diet-related illness. Founded by Haile Johnston and Tatiana Garcia Granados, Common Market has expanded since it first launched out of a food pantry in North Philadelphia in 2003. It took five years and $1.7 million of annual sales for Common Market to reach financial self-sufficiency. Common Market's network has since extended throughout the mid-Atlantic, Georgia, and Texas. The goal is to launch chapters in most of the country's largest metropolitan areas over the next ten years.

While Common Market isn't a crisis provider, its services have been a foundation of community when a catastrophe hits. As Texas farmers and ranchers prepared for the freezing storm Uri in February 2021, Common Market linked up with José Andrés' World Central Kitchen and purchased as much local produce as it could fit in its twenty-one-thousand-square-foot warehouse in Houston. Common Market then distributed seventeen thousand boxes of food while connecting Austin's public school system with its beef rancher to make sure children in need were fed.

Food hubs, buying groups, and CSAs are decades-old structures. Community-supported agriculture has been utilized since the early 1900s, when advocates like Tuskegee University's Dr. Booker T. Whatley began publicizing the benefits of customers helping farmers plan ahead for their season. Then, in the 1960s and '70s, Whatley pushed farmers left out of federal aid to adopt shares to save more profits for their farms. The concept continues to lend power to Black- and Indigenous-led organizations, including Soul Fire Farm in Upstate New York, which offers produce sold as "solidarity shares." Yet one key difference that must evolve with a solidarity economy, Mickie said, is addressing workers: "In food hubs, we can't continue to just focus on the supply chain, without focusing on what's been inequitable about the labor."

Meat has a role to play in the solidarity economy, Mickie added: "As people want to shift to different alternatives, and there's real reasons for that, we still will have animals on our planet. We still need animals on the planet. Some people are going to still want a meat-based source."

The biggest hurdle is getting land in the hands of BIPOC entrepreneurs and farmers. Amid generations of stolen land as well as the rising value of acres and gentrification, buying a farm isn't cheap. About 40 percent of all US farmland is rented. But collectivizing a farming operation is one way to spread resources and bridge the gaps. The ultimate goal would be for a farm to create its own regional economy. Self-sustaining yet local in spirit, that farm would have some scale and levels of vertical integration. The farming collective could have farming operations for a variety of items (livestock, eggs, produce, mushrooms), a slaughter and further processing division, a direct-shipping consumer business, and a sales and marketing arm. This model, crucially, has the logistics of retail built in. Think White Oak Pastures in scope, but worker-owned and -led.

A Major Gap I Still See

Contract manufacturing is what makes the food industry run. Most are opaque private companies where worker treatment is hidden but should not be ignored. Small family-run plants passed down over the generations specialize in areas as specific as jerky or sports beverages. Or they can be as big as OSI, the global manufacturer for McDonald's as well as Impossible Foods that is owned by Illinois billionaire Sheldon Lavin, described in Chapter 2. If I had money to invest in the future of food gold rush, it'd be here, in the shadowy world of contract manufacturing.

Far more private contract manufacturers will need to open to support alternatives. Especially among emerging alternative proteins, a lot of the money flowing to start-ups to make their own production plant is for only one key part of ingredient processing. Remember that these technified foods are ultraprocessed. Ingredients still need further processing, and then the ingredients must still be formulated into products that people like eating. These last two parts of the process are the real gold mine, and where communities should quickly look to draw a line in the sand.

No one yet owns the means of production at scale. This part of the supply chain has barely started to form. When I asked ADM chief strategy and innovation officer Ian Pinner about what parts of the so-called downstream process he predicted more companies needed to be involved with, Pinner explained to me that it's vast and underestimated. "You've identified very well that there's bottlenecks and there's going to be emerging investments," Pinner said. "It could be that each one of these companies has to have their own bespoke manufacturing capabilities once it's coming out of fermentation. That's an area that's going to be short of capacity, because you're going to be building new capacity for every new technology."

Manufacturing at this level is where all the headaches are, from an operational and financial perspective, Riana Lynn of Journey Foods told me. The processing plant is where most of the profits come from, and it's also the key to the development of more nutritious products and more sustainable packaging. "It's all driven by the profit margin," Lynn said. "Our unhealthy foods have a higher profit margin. We are figuring out a way to really unlock the cost behind the scenes to really accelerate it."

Just as alternatives getting commercialized will need a full ecosystem of contract manufacturers to transform technified ingredients into food, less-processed, fresh food needs a little help getting dressed into forms convenient to cook and eat. Think about the networks of local butchers, smokehouses, and canneries in the 1900s. There are ways of preserving food and making more valuable products out of the bits. Repurposing scraps left over from meat processing could allow independent producers to become profitable or even self-sustaining.

"There's a lack of infrastructure around handling fresh, seasonal foods," natural foods industry pioneer Hans Taparia, the founder of Asian-inspired entrée and side dish brand Tasty Bite, told me. Instead of industrialized systems of manufacturing, Taparia, who took Tasty Bite public before food conglomerate Mars acquired it in 2017, wants to see more companies embrace supply chains utilizing seasonal and local ingredients.

What's really needed are commercial kitchens, where brands could make fresh food in large quantities and have access to ten ovens, large walk-in freezers for storage, and production lines for packaging and sealing. That describes the layout of Mosaic Foods' commissary in Woodland Park, New Jersey, which makes ten thousand frozen meals like kale mac and cheese, coconut chickpea curry, and verde pozole a week. When one of Mosaic's copackers closed in 2020, Mosaic had trouble finding another facility that could cook and freeze food. Usually a facility can offer only one method or the other. So CEO Matt Davis decided to open his own. "The plants have very set equipment that can only do certain things," Davis said. "To make meals that cost $3.99, the supply chain developed has huge capital, lots of inertia in a negative way, lots of barriers to entry. It's hard to make new or better products."

When it's time to fill up a plate, six workers set up a lunch line to dose out each part of the meal. Then the dish runs through the production line, where it's film-sealed. Lids are placed by hand, as are boxes packed and folded. This kind of production grows into another facility after it becomes harder to make the dish in a bigger format, and it's easier to just start running a second operation concurrently. "The immersion blenders only get so big," Davis adds. "At that point, you need to get another facility. The kicker is, are you already profitable at the first one?" It's easier because Mosaic doesn't have meat to deal with. If a business cooks meat, there's a higher cost of operating. A USDA inspector is required on-site to open and close the facility every day and sign off on all the meat.

Products that offer some convenience are in high demand, like premade meatballs, sausages, or precooked carnitas, with meat raised ethically. Shared kitchens and other infrastructure can help farmers or other local purveyors process and package these often higher-value products. Meatballs and sausages can help farmers avoid selling their meat at commodity prices and can even be some of the highest-margin products that they can sell. But many farmers are so tired at the end of a harvest that they understandably end up cutting up the animal into quarters and selling it quickly.

If only a network of local producers and purveyors could take up the torch. Qiana Mickie agrees. Local infrastructure for livestock producers to cook and package products is a key missing link in making local food systems profitable and viable. Creating lasting impacts wouldn't cost much. "We have the information and we have the evidence. What we don't have are the facilities and shared space where multiple people can leverage that at their business's scale," Mickie told me. "It's just crazy to me to be in a space where we're trying to meet so many intersecting issues of inequity, and have to prove it one hundred percent, and then in another realm, people are playing with stem cells and getting two hundred million dollars. We literally feed people and want to do it better. Can we get a hundred thousand dollars?"

When I Eat Meat and How I Buy It

I limit the meat I eat out these days but make exceptions for places where I know which processors and distributors are used. Sourcing can be murky, which is why it's best to know this rule: the vast majority selling to restaurants, corporate cafeterias, and chains are industrial and commoditized. It's an unfortunate generalization that holds true even at the best barbeque haunts in America, especially in Texas, where more corn-fed fat means a juicer brisket. That's why I jumped at the chance to visit Blue Hill at Stone Barns in Tarrytown, New York, in May 2021 for a pop-up led by pitmaster Bryan Furman. The former welder launched a barbeque catering business before leading Atlanta's hot spot B's Cracklin' BBQ. He was there to build a menu around the bounty of Blue Hill's nonprofit farm, Stone Barns, and its four hundred acres of forest, hills, and fields of produce and flowers. It was a rare chance to taste pasture-raised heritage hog breeds—fed lacto-fermented spent brewer's grain, expired dairy, and waste from the farm and restaurant—prepared by a barbeque legend.

The pulled pork came out on a red-and-white-checkered-sheet-lined tray, along with two cheddar-jalapeño-stuffed sausages and fresh hot sauce. Sides prepared by Furman's mom, Almeta Benjamin, were bountiful, including hoe cakes, hash and rice, fermented pickles, grilled asparagus, and bites of bunched lettuces wrapped in herbs. The vegetarian meal we also ordered came with two skewers of oyster mushroom slices, a large glazed carrot, and four grilled scallions. The spread was such a treat, and as a first meal dining out after vaccination, it was also a somewhat reasonable yet celebratory splurge at $75 per person. It was far less expensive (and far tastier) than what I've spent on a lot of other corn-fed barbeque after waiting in line in the Texas heat.

At home, I'll cook meat if I know where the meat was slaughtered and how the animal was raised. I'm an eater who will try anything, but my meat must come from somewhere I trust. When I cook, I like to work with cuts that aren't commonly used. I don't shy away from marrow bones and oxtail, chicken livers or guanciale. My favorite part is the cheek. A signature dish is my own variation of a stew my dad used to make growing up. I go back and forth on whether yellow tomatoes and pork cheeks or beef cheeks with an onion-jammy, red wine reduction performs best. I prefer to buy direct whenever possible—be that from a local food hub or the online store of a farm like White Oak Pastures—because the producer keeps more of the profit.

That might be why online retailers and subscriptions for better meat have recently exploded. The internet and social media have provided a whole new world for entrepreneurs, in addition to independent farmers, to reset traditional corporate supply chains. More meat is being sold online than ever before.

But meat sales extend from Instagram to Instacart. Many investors have begun to see it as a place to make a buck. A proliferation of subscription box services—like ButcherBox, which is a certified B Corp—source directly and ship to homes nationwide. Food subscription boxes as an industry have raised about $100 million in funding annually since 2016, according to

PitchBook, and nearly $300 million in 2021. Online grocery marketplaces, meanwhile, have raised $20 billion since 2016. Start-ups secured nearly $6 billion in funding in 2021 alone.

The forces pushing customers online to these marketplaces have been driven by what I've heard described several times as "the disappointment of Whole Foods." In the aftermath of the chain's acquisition by Amazon for $13.7 billion in 2017, the natural foods chain has standardized some distribution while moving away from sourcing at nearby farms and other local suppliers. During a summer 2021 visit to the Union Square location of Whole Foods with a private equity investor, we laughed at the cases of White Claw piled high in the meat department, a few steps away from pastured, no-antibiotic, thick-cut bacon. A decade ago, we never would have found hard seltzer or a beverage with a similar ingredient profile, with industrial flavors often made from a by-product of petroleum production, in Whole Foods. Another private equity investor in an online grocery competitor put it to me this way: "The Amazon destruction of Whole Foods has created white space for new competitors."

One of those online grocers, filled with executives who previously worked at Whole Foods, is Thrive Market. The start-up has a clear opportunity to take market share, while subscriptions fund free donated memberships to those who cannot afford it. Among the former longtime Whole Foods buyers working on sourcing at Thrive are chief merchandising officer Jeremiah McElwee and meat chief Michael Hacaga. They say there are constant challenges and ravenous competitors, backed by even more ravenous investors, nipping at their feet, waiting for their next mistake.

The investor interest in meat subscription boxes is driving the emerging sector to become a commodity game that's all about paying the lowest prices possible for the meat itself and paying high rates to acquire customers through social media channels. That creates a lot of churn—meaning, customers who eventually unsubscribe. The start-ups that engage in this behavior are probably not that interested in driving systemic supply chain change. It's more about building the customer list and making the start-up the most attractive business it possibly could be, to court a short-term flip. "Free bacon for life, that sounds really great, but it also doesn't sound like you're trying to make money," Thrive's McElwee laughed while explaining the situation to me. "Sometimes it's nuts seeing some of the ways we are getting undercut. But we're not in this for how fast can we grow our customer list and sell to Amazon. That was never the point. Watching some of these fly-by-night folks come in and just try to scale as fast as they can, it's frustrating, but we have to do us." The problem is, this is the same ads market that independent producers with far fewer resources than even White Oak Pastures must compete with. The investor funding and pressure to make returns quickly are driving up the market not just for Thrive Market but also for those completely independent and trying to go it alone online.

I don't like that my dollar is being co-opted with every financing round or rumor that the company might go public, as Thrive Market was even said to be exploring in 2021, to the tune of $2 billion. I buy only pastured or grass-fed products. Local meat isn't always better for the environment, nor is it always ethically superior for workers' safety, equity, or animal welfare. But it is important to invest in food distribution that has the shortest distance to reach us at home from the farm. I try to source where I know my producers are going the extra distance in each of these categories.

I try not to be known as the CSA's resident food nerd, but I do my best to find out about all aspects of the livestock's raising and slaughtering. That's why, if I'm buying meat and it doesn't come from my friend Phil Haynes, it's probably from my local community-supported agriculture share's partner network, called Lewis Waite. Acting as a food hub, as Qiana Mickie walked us through, the marketplace shares costs among local small-scale producers to get their goods to customers. I pick up my preorder whenever I get my CSA. Lewis Waite sells not only beef, pork, lamb, and poultry—and pastured, antibiotic-free turkey around Thanksgiving—but also a delightful variety of specialty items. There's the fresh yogurt from Berle Farm, which uses glass jars printed with the names of the cows and other highlights from its operation, like its solar panels. I've checked out the mix of butters and cheeses and have made fried chicken with buttermilk that runs out of stock almost as quickly as the few pints of ice cream that go up for sale every month. I've sourced everything from locally jarred summer tomatoes to lentil soup mix to mushrooms to Hudson Valley–dried spices, and even organic pantry items like Worcestershire and soy sauce. I relish browsing through the constantly changing online offerings.

Yet, as much as the seasonal produce beckons me, I avoid farmers' markets. About eight thousand exist in America, and many are rife with hidden costs and inequity. Roughly $1 billion worth of food sells annually at farmers' markets nationwide. There's a reason farmers' markets command such a tiny percentage of overall food sales—compared to more than $1 trillion spent on food in America annually. Producers share the brunt of the cost of selling to farmers' markets. To start, there's the travel, staffing, prep, and farmers' market fees. Foot traffic barely made it worth it prepandemic.

Farmers' markets remain far from viable as a go-to-market strategy for a farm or local food maker to sustainably rely on. That's why consumers should not view farmers' markets as the best way to support their favorite farmers with a dollar vote.

There are also lasting questions about how workers are treated at the operations that farmers' markets support. There's still exploitation on many of these farms. Few workers at those pretty farmers' market booths also have health insurance. Many of those farmers work eighty-hour weeks while being left out of broader worker rights like overtime pay or a fixed workday.

"Because of our insistence on independence and our failure to cooperate more closely, we're being outsold at the grocery store by a factor of 400 or more. Accounting for on-farm, food hub, restaurant, and other non-market sales does little to affect the scale of this imbalance," Chris Newman, a Black and Indigenous farmer who owns Virginia-based Sylvanaqua Farms, wrote in 2019. "Farmers' markets and other 'local' outlets punch well above their weight in terms of social and cultural value, but this is fooling us into believing we're making more of an impact than we actually are, and that a rapidly consolidating food system backed by venture capital, entrenched interests, and the world's wealthiest corporations will somehow be displaced by the romance of neoliberal peasant farming."

A perhaps extreme thought: farmers' markets should mainly exist as a crucial access point to fresh produce and nonindustrial meat in marginalized zip codes. Federal assistance payments cover just 2 percent of total farmers' market purchases. Increasing access doesn't always increase adoption, especially when prices still aren't accessible, but democratizing access to farmers' markets could be a start. Otherwise, a clearer place in the future for farmers' markets would be in high-trafficked tourist areas where it makes profit-loss sense to participate in them, or where local tourist boards can fund infrastructure and logistics costs. That would be a meaningful way for tourists to sample local purveyors and support a variety of business owners and farms. But long-term residents with a modicum of access have no excuse for not forging deeper economic relationships with the local farmers growing their food.

For that reason, it's even rarer that I'm in a supermarket, and I'm definitely not buying meat from any. I'll admit I've been known to enjoy a grilled tenderloin from Costco at a summer party. But I try to make a habit of going the distance now, which is a major privilege. I aim to stick to that, since traditional grocery might be one of the most margin-hungry sectors in the food industry. Chains have been squeezed for the past decade amid consolidation and regional bankruptcies, and that's translated into more pressure on producers.

What about a grocery store that focuses its operations on sourcing fresh foods that are minimally processed? That's the model of Basics Market in Oregon. The four-store chain was founded by Chuck Eggert, who previously founded Pacific Foods, which was acquired by Campbell Soup Co. for $700 million in 2017. I'd shop there. Prices are discounted compared to similar items at a Whole Foods—including meat and poultry. Basics sources directly from a network of local and organic farms and sells the bounty fresh. Within a couple days of the expiration date, they either freeze the food or use it in the commissary while cooking the prepared foods sold there. That's how Basics Market's model is replicable: the business manages the losses on items and makes sure inventory is managed as tightly as possible. As a result, profit margins are strong.

I do enjoy checking out local cooperative grocers, though I don't have one where I belong close by. Co-op grocery stores offer their members access to food from locally sourced supply chains, often outside industrial distribution. At some, members are required to work a shift at the register or volunteer at the organization, as I do with my neighborhood CSA. I appreciate that kind of mandate, because the experience gives more people a window into all that goes into getting food to kitchens around the country. Still, in two hundred years, the co-op system has not been able to scale or meaningfully impact industrial production.

My attitude these days usually is, if it's not meaningful, why bother? I could drive myself crazy in all the details, second-guessing every food purchase and menu decision, but it's not worth the stress. There's a certain freedom in knowing just how meaningless voting with your dollar can be.

What matters far more is how we take part in our own communities. Regional food systems must be strengthened, in preparation for short-term crises as well as the protracted doom of climate change.

Taking an active role in your eating future can start as simply as working a shift at your CSA or co-op. Even that suggestion exposes another crucial choke point: access here really means free time, which is a major privilege and barrier to entry for many. But there is a deep world to dive into, for those who are energized and ready. From advocating for local policy changes to setting up regional infrastructure like canneries, commissary kitchens, and other small-scale processing, there is a lot of work to be done.

Actions that create collective impacts are the foundation of a food system that's more democratic, healthier, and safer. A fundamental restructuring of the meat industry is necessary. We've been served up a raw deal. While meat corporations spend the coming decades testing their limits, it's time for transformative change to take hold.

Afterword: Implosion

In Central Nebraska's Hall County, the Wood River curves for ten miles past farmland, ranches, and neighboring small towns. By the time the river winds toward the city of Grand Island, the river approaches a JBS plant with the capacity to kill 1.4 million cattle every year. There, on a thirty-two-degree January day in 2024 with flurries falling from the cloudy sky, a wastewater lagoon snapped. A manhole on the east side of the lagoon was destroyed and propelled to a parking lot downhill. At least two million gallons of sludge unleashed in a wave—pooling to more than an inch in the parking lot and on nearby streets, and gushing far beyond. The sludge flowed downstream into the Wood River, as well as into an unnamed tributary of the river. Once JBS realized, contractors built a dam. But it was too late. Sludge dripped from burst pipes as trucks and cars plowed through the mess, spreading bacteria elsewhere.[*]

In the days following, dead and dying fish washed up on a riverbed near a street crossing over the Wood River. Wastewater and sludge were floating along with the odor-emitting current. The plume of likely antibiotic-filled sludge even made it eighteen miles away to the Platte River, where more fish died. Water tested positive for e. Coli bacteria across four different sites, as well as chloride, ammonia, and other chemicals.[†‡§]

Concerns over contaminated water got so bad that the local board of

---

[*] According to the inspector's report, "The discharged material from the anaerobic lagoon on the city street must be removed immediately and is a violation."

[†] Nebraska does not require testing for antibiotics during incidents.

[‡] The inspector's report noted that "the water in the tributary is very turbid and black with solids visible in the water. The discharge into the tributary is a violation."

[§] The Wood River intersects with the Platte River, which is an offshoot of the Missouri River.

commissioners sent a letter to JBS—worried that roughly twenty properties' wells and a nearby lake had been tainted. Regulators had been citing the facility with at least one violation a month, according to the letter, which firmly stated, "The noncompliance issues are exceedingly far too frequent and need to be addressed." As the largest employer in the area, JBS had to take accountability. Its plant manager responded, promising to replace the "failed" lagoon, test water at eight sites, and make other improvements: "We recognize that a reactive position, while critical, is not enough."

Infrastructure is crumbling, and communities caught in the crosshairs are forced to beg for Band-Aids. Yet we're in this mess because corporations responsible like JBS have been ignoring their own environmental damage. The Grand Island lagoon failure's state inspector found "extensive erosion" in several other places around the lagoon, according to the state report, which indicated that "the leak had taken place over an extended time period." Upon examining soil erosion around other parts, other leaks were found still flowing.*

Cracks like these are spreading, as short-term thinking limits our future. It takes a lot to change, and we're losing time. Yet America's meat production is growing. As is consumption. During the hottest year ever recorded in 2023, I experienced power outages from energy infrastructure pushed to the brink, with meat and other provisions going bad while defrosting inside freezers, as cattle across America's heartland died from extreme heat and lack of water. It was only a taste of the coming climate crisis.

I know just how terrifying these lagoons, and what they represent, can be. Smithfield, America's largest pork producer, agreed to let me visit one of its biggest lagoon-style pits with a bubble on top, called an in-ground digester, in eastern North Carolina. Its bubble was football-field-size and used to capture methane seeping out of all the brown muck. Since I understood the noxious fumes that come off these operations are dangerous and how common it is for farmers to die after accidentally falling in, I was shocked when one of the employees told me they often go on top of the balloon. When he then dared me to go up, I decided I had to, for the sake of being taken seriously. I put on a safety vest that Smithfield employees promised

---

* According to the inspector's report, "The discharge from the lagoon was not reported to the department and is a violation."

would catapult me out of danger. I was even assured the one I was wearing was similar to the kind backcountry skiers don to protect themselves from avalanches. I looked up at the massive bubble I was about to climb atop. I gulped and then slowly started trekking up the thick rubber. It bellowed gently in the breeze. I stood up at the peak for a few moments, holding myself steady as I looked around. It was serene, almost. If I didn't let myself look deep enough.

Farther afield, I could see another open-air manure lagoon and the antibiotic-filled brown stream flowing from a pipe into it, along with a complex crisscrossing network of pipelines in the distance that connect the waste to the plant and the methane to the energy grid. As I peered down, clutching the straps of my sludge-avalanche harness, I understood the full magnitude of the shitstorm that's brewing. Just like that methane-filled balloon I balanced on, the meat industry is built upon a pile of toxic slop, and the precarity of the foundation is getting worse. The biggest companies like JBS and Tyson are eating away at their own futures by prioritizing short-term profits over the environment. They're ignoring the threats, even as alarm bells sound off. Loudly. Every day we inch closer toward the abyss I was staring down at the top of that balloon—where soils and waterways are so polluted they stop producing nutritious food, where livestock can't survive due to drought and extreme heat, where antibiotic-resistant illnesses have little chance of a cure, and where those left behind must fight for the scraps.

A more stable foundation—that's designed to survive climate crisis, not make it worse—is desperately needed. Yet far too little is still being done to jump-start that transformation. JBS and Tyson have put in serious time and money toward making the situation even worse. All the while, crucial infrastructure keeps breaking, and it's harder than ever to combat the meat industry's environmentally devastating status quo. Fake meat start-ups have wasted even more time and resources, when there's not enough going around as it is. Many of the challengers promising to produce protein way more sustainably that brought me hope, like pasture-raised chicken brand Cooks Venture and mushroom farmer Smallhold, have flamed out in full-on implosions that underscore how spectacularly these businesses can quickly erase the good they've set out to accomplish. That's why change cannot be rushed, yet it must accelerate. Time is running out.

Among America's largest meat companies, none has claimed to be as good for the climate as JBS. But there are major issues with that marketing. JBS is one of America's largest sellers of grass-fed beef, and its supply is the world's largest. Yet a lot of the animals are raised at feedlots that still cause significant environmental damage. JBS is also among America's largest sellers of imported beef allegedly tied to deforestation in the Amazon, which eliminates a chance to negate greenhouse gas emissions with every branch snapped. After repackaging the meat on US soil, it's offered to restaurant chains, supermarkets, and school cafeterias. These are just a few of the business practices JBS has been looking to cement through an initial public offering on the New York Stock Exchange.

The public listing has dredged up fresh allegations of environmental damage. Critics of the IPO insist it would greenwash how JBS has directly and indirectly contributed to climate-worsening devastation, including deforestation in Brazil's Amazon. Representatives of the Parakanã community, for example, allege that JBS illegally exploited the Apyterewa Indigenous Territory near the rainforest by buying cattle raised on cleared acres, according to a complaint over the IPO sent to the Securities and Exchange Commission. Amid pushback to the listing, the New York attorney general also filed a lawsuit against JBS USA for misleading consumers about its environmental impact. The lawsuit alleges that JBS saw sustainability claims as a key way to target climate-conscious consumers and remain competitive, but that the company had not even calculated its own greenhouse gas emissions when making the public promise that it would achieve net-zero greenhouse gas emissions by 2040. There was no way JBS could have actually known whether it could reduce its emissions to net zero by 2040.[*†] Yet the claim was used frequently when discussing the business's prospects and its coming IPO.

---

* Prior to New York's lawsuit, two independent advertising review boards had found that JBS should stop using the phrase, both of which JBS appealed.

† JBS's "net zero by 2040" talking point was not discussed in *Raw Deal*. It seemed implausible at best, especially considering how much JBS was also publicly planning to increase production. The only mention is in a footnote on page 83, as a response to allegations. The representative for JBS cited the climate goal as a canned response prepared for critics to claim JBS had invested in being a good employer.

Despite all the alleged environmental deception, JBS will continue to earn millions in federal contracts selling meat for soldiers, public school lunches, and others. Agriculture Department Secretary Tom Vilsack wrote, in a letter obtained by POLITICO through the Freedom of Information Act, that the department had considered suspension or debarment following the guilty plea by the Batista family's holding company J&F in 2020, but ultimately decided against it because taking out such a big supplier from a highly concentrated market could increase prices. Let's be clear: As JBS's US IPO has been on hold amid allegations of environmental damage, why won't the USDA opt for another contractor? Securing cheap meat wins out again. And the at least $176 million that JBS has earned in federal contracts since 2020 also indicates the funnel won't be slowing down. How much of their proceeds from those contracts will go toward changes that lessen the impact on the environment? Money spent on lobbyists pushing for policies that would make it easier to ignore climate concerns is far more likely.

At JBS, what the Batistas want is what goes. When JBS completes its New York Stock Exchange listing, the deal is expected to help the family greatly.* They'll make more money while being ushered back into the realm of the business elite. According to documents filed, the imminent public offering would help the Batista family solidify their control. The proposed trans-action includes the chance to convert their common shares to preferred. Those shares would come with voting power—as much as 84 to 91 percent. It would drastically limit the future influence of minority shareholders, while forever linking the Batistas to their meat empire, much as the Tyson family has insulated its shares. While JBS prepares for the listing, the board has even taken the opportunity to bring back as full directors the billionaire brothers Joesley and Wesley Batista, previously jailed for their part in the major bribery ring.† Wesley Batista's son Wesley Batista Filho, at the time a thirteen-year-long JBS employee at thirty-one years old, also moved into

---

* The offering, announced in July 2023, has been delayed twice—first at the end of 2023, then again in February. The company says it still expects to go public in 2024.

† Both Joesley and Wesley Batista ended up serving Brazilian sentences of about six months, starting in September 2017 and lasting until February and March 2018. In October 2020, the US Department of Justice reached its settlements. J&F pled guilty to US foreign brib-ery charges and agreed to pay $128.25 million in criminal fines. The firm also agreed to an additional $27 million to the Securities and Exchange Commission. Wesley and Joesley Batista also had to pay $550,000 each for their SEC violations.

the role of JBS USA CEO. As he took the job his father had when JBS acquired its first American meat plant back in 2008, Batista Filho formalized his position as next in line to take over the family business—ensuring there likely will be a Batista at the helm well into 2030, and even possibly in 2040.

Back in Brazil, even with more scrutiny of Amazon deforestation, the Batistas have been thriving. With Luiz Inácio Lula da Silva elected again as Brazil's president, the family has returned to favor. Joesley and Wesley Batista were even part of a delegation traveling with Lula to China. Then Lula visited a JBS plant in Brazil set to become the first to ship meat to China under a new trade agreement. That changing tide is the political backdrop for the legal battle the Batistas have waged as they fought to slash how much they had to pay of their massive $3.2 billion fine in Brazil—even though their US plea deals were officially lenient because of the hefty fines already on the family. Brazil's Supreme Court decided to end J&F's fines in December 2023. J&F confirmed that "the payment of the fine's installments are suspended as the fine calculations are rectified."

These developments only add to the questionable portrait of what the Batistas care most about. They have demonstrated a willingness to greenwash for their own gain, while seeming barely concerned over climate change beyond the halo it can provide their mega-meat-packer. Since the Batistas are far from going away, these priorities won't change. That could hurt a lot more than just buyers and eaters of JBS meat. JBS's slaughterhouses, for example, remain one of the main options for independent grass-fed producers who sell on the open market in the US, as well as in South America and Australia. The Batistas' influence runs deep. That's what challenger start-ups are up against and what is really holding back progress, as time to make the crucial changes needed to eat through the climate crisis with dignity slips away.

Tyson has been embroiled in scandal while the pressure to increase profits, after years of unprecedented gains, has collided to overshadow new threats to environmental and human health.* As profits dropped over 2023, Tyson

---

* Scandals that include John R. Tyson—the son of Tyson's chairman John H.—getting arrested in November 2022. The thirty-two-year-old fourth-generation heir, who had been Tyson's chief financial officer for a month, ended up in a stranger's bed. After she found

closed eight plants, impacting about 1,100 employees.* Tyson also laid off more workers, including an estimated 250 at a poultry factory in Wilkesboro, North Carolina, as well as 10 percent of its corporate workforce. Amid that chaos, Tyson abandoned antibiotic-free farming.

Just eighteen days before Tyson announced reversing its policy, the US Agriculture Department made its own big reveal. As *Raw Deal* reported, a lot of meat that has been labeled as being raised without antibiotics actually wasn't. Evidence has pointed to at least some instances of fraud—knowingly or otherwise. With that pressure to act, the USDA decided to end its decades-long system of relying mostly on affidavits signed by the companies. A multistep plan to sample and test livestock is helping the government verify that meat sold as "antibiotic-free" actually is what it claims.

That's why Tyson's sudden switch requires further examination. Only six years prior, Tyson had proudly pushed the entire chicken industry to follow its lead and go antibiotic-free—specifically for the sake of doing its part to quell the threat of a public health crisis from the spread of antibiotic resistance. But then, just before the 2023 Fourth of July holiday break, America's largest chicken producer slid in some news: Tyson went back to using antibiotics on its two billion chickens. The caveat is that Tyson says it won't give animals antibiotics used to treat sick humans and will stick to ionophores, a class given to animals. But using antibiotics like ionophores still creates antibiotic resistance to medically important drugs through a phenomenon known as coresistance, where resistance genes to multiple drugs are linked together on the same piece of DNA. It's not as bad of a driver as using drugs like tetracyclines, but its negative consequences are only starting to be understood. Antibiotics like these still remain in waterways and soil, which spreads resistance and can make farmland less productive.

Administering antibiotics on overcrowded farms helps Tyson's bottom line. Antibiotics help produce more chickens—bigger and quicker—and are

---

him there, asleep, Fayetteville, Arkansas, police officers arrested John R. He apologized a few days later during a quarterly call to discuss earnings—his first since being promoted to CFO. He settled with the city of Fayetteville. John R. pleaded guilty to the charges of public intoxication and criminal trespass, agreeing to a $150 fine for each charge. Tyson's board continued their support, but in June 2024, he was arrested again, this time for drunk driving, and Tyson suspended him.

* Layoffs continued into 2024: in March another 1,200 employees lost their jobs as Tyson shut down a pork plant in Perry, Iowa.

force-fed whether the birds are sick and need them or not. Prior to Tyson's change, signals were already concerning. Sales of antibiotics used in meat production have been swinging back to highs not reached in years, according to the latest data from the Food and Drug Administration. In 2022, sales increased 4 percent.

The threat of antibiotic resistance should be more frightening than what's already transpired from America's worst-ever outbreak of avian flu. The deadly virus had been raging—killing a record seventy-nine million birds in 2022 and 2023. Because chickens are packed in so closely, the disease spreads quickly. The outcome—quarantine zones and mass killings of infected birds—is not all that dissimilar to what could happen if an antibiotic-resistant superbug multiplied on a factory farm and then started to really spread. Adding antibiotics to farms only increases those odds. Meanwhile, avian flu has mutated. Dairy cows in Texas and Kansas marked the first time the virus had ever infected cattle. Then a Texan dairy worker in contact with infected cattle caught the strain. It's fatal in humans in more than half of reported cases, according to the Centers for Disease Control.

Tyson's abandonment is chilling. There's "a new norm" in the industry with "ripple effects" that could drag other producers back, too, says Dr. Lance Price, the founding director of George Washington University's Milken Public Health School's Antibiotic Resistance Action Center. A cascade has started, and major brands have thrown up their hands, pretending to forget they can demand change. Panera ended its antibiotic-free pork and turkey as it prepared for its own initial public offering. Chick-fil-A also stopped serving antibiotic-free chicken at its $6.4 billion chain.

"Tyson feels like they need to go back to this crutch to keep their animals healthy," Price said. "Why don't you just raise them in a cleaner house and do other things to control infections, rather than just dosing them with constant levels of drugs that will eventually lead to resistance?"

Resistance is spreading and could easily create a major mess. But I didn't think I'd be writing about Tyson unleashing more threats at the expense of the future of humanity and the environment, or the implosion that came next.

Across Arkansas on nineteen farms in November 2023, more than one million chickens were killed. Stuck inside their houses, doors and windows

closed, the birds were sprayed and immersed in a deadly foam. The cacoph-
onous hum of clucking stopped. Suddenly, each house was silent.

That waste wasn't from a large meat-packer, but the remnants of Cooks
Venture as its business came to a screeching halt. Cooks Venture deteri-
orated rapidly. The decline started well before founder Matt Wadiak got
pushed out as CEO and board director in August. The business was losing
money too quickly.

Cooks Venture's dream was big. Maybe too big for the constraints of
the modern meat industry and how financing it works. Wadiak wanted to
do it all. It wasn't just breeding and hatching slower-growth yet more heat-
tolerant chicks, and feeding and raising them on Cooks Venture's farm,
and then bringing the meat to retailers. That would have already been a lot.
Wadiak then led trials to drastically alter what his chickens ate, and, in the
quest to get corn and soy out of their diet and encourage less monoculture
farming, he experimented with contracting farmers to grow wheat, and
even growing wheat as a cover crop that's still harvestable. That's while
going after mass-market scale and proclaiming to be combating climate
change.

All that sapped Cooks Venture of money. (Though switching to an
alternative feed based on the grain Milo did end up providing some cost-
savings.) To be fair, Wadiak's big dreams are what the investors had agreed
to back, and the board voted for the strategy at multiple junctures along
the way, too. But raising so much, giving up equity to investors at times in
unfavorable deals, and inviting all that investor influence put Wadiak at a
disadvantage because he couldn't scale naturally without the fundamentals.
The push to fundraise could have been avoided if the business was profitable. But that was still a long way away, and that big of a business—with an
estimated $50 million in annual revenue from slaughtering 170,000 chick-
ens per week—needs a lot of cash to run. The constant pressure to keep the
chickens fed and the machinery running drained the cash pile. Plants also
get finicky, especially if machines must be redesigned to fit the anatomical
differences of an alternative breed. Let alone funding Wadiak's moon shots.
The $150 million raised wasn't enough.* All torched. A massive amount of
money got squandered.

---

* Including $50 million in debt refinancing.

Mismanagement may be at the root of that. Customers loved the chicken, but there were troubles delivering. After securing a contract, the business often had issues supplying enough chicken. More equipment to package the meat would have helped, but machinery is expensive. While overpromising and underdelivering, the company struggled to execute. Some retailers, like Meijer, backed out. Other deals were questionable. One of its largest contracts was with Trader Joe's, which rarely lets suppliers use their own branding and sold "Heirloom Whole Chicken" so low—around $20 a bird in my New York City neighborhood—that profit was improbable, some former executives claim. As the orders grew, they became so big they became hard to fill. The financially unsustainable decision created losses. Accounts at Texan grocer H-E-B and mid-Atlantic chain Giant Eagle were break-even, but total volume probably would have had to double to get to full profitability.

Wadiak, always chasing the next deal, thought he had it under control. But a labor shortage hit the business hard. As did the increasing cost of feed, thanks to inflation and commodity market swings from Russia's invasion of grain powerhouse Ukraine. Cooks Venture could have survived longer if it raised more money, and Wadiak almost put a deal together. But the lead investor backed out just before Wadiak could close the round, and then two more investors revoked their deals, too. Profitability would have given Wadiak actual power after he had given up too much equity. But it was too late. In the three months after Wadiak exited, panic set in. The board hired the next CEO, John Niemann, who had spent twenty years at Cargill and wasn't looking for a job when the board approached him. Inspired by the business's climate goals, Niemann agreed without understanding how serious the financial situation was. He made some progress solidifying the business, but it wasn't quick enough. He and the board had trouble raising more, and existing investors couldn't inject enough to get over the hurdles of how much the business was burning through each week. The business could barely cover the cost to feed its birds and its workforce's payroll. The death spiral started.

By mid-November, the business was a shell of what Wadiak had dreamed it could be. The board decided investors would stop funding the business and immediately start closing it down by canceling contracts with growers as well as deals to supply customers. Niemann disagreed with the abrupt approach and resigned the next day. Cooks Venture's operations in Arkansas and Oklahoma then shut down. Around five hundred employees were laid off. With no slaughterhouse running, farmers under contract to raise chickens for Cooks Venture were an afterthought. Cooks Venture couldn't afford to feed the birds. The business could have done one more run and sold the last of the chicken online. But its web store, where 20 percent of customers bought its chicken, closed. Then the state government of Arkansas had to kill the birds.

The shutdown is a huge loss. The birds were bred with climate change in mind: stronger birds that could take higher temperatures and better withstand extreme weather. Cooks Venture fed millions. They were ingesting protein made by an independent operator that was attempting to create a real and significant alternative to mass-produced chicken, addressing structural issues and corporate consolidation from the hatchery to the slaughterhouse. Families relied on the meat. Those customers aren't going away.

Cooks Venture's farmers aren't going away, either. At least two farmers have said the shutdown put their farms at risk. A group of fifty farmers gathered claiming Cooks Venture owes them thousands each. Cooks Venture had been trying to be different from big poultry contractors like Tyson and JBS-owned Pilgrim's Pride, and had even helped some of the farmers with investments. Yet the farmers were still left holding the bag.

Wadiak never learned from previous mistakes. But there's not enough time left to avoid confronting the hard lessons head-on. Blue Apron, the business Wadiak cofounded with two others, combusted after over-raising, overexpanding, and trying to do too much, too quickly. Cooks Venture followed along the same path and flamed out before it could hit the scale it was building toward.

The failure will sting for a long time. After Cooks Venture filed for Chapter 7 bankruptcy in April 2024, Pitman Family Farms, the privately held owner of Mary's Free-Range Chicken, acquired the remaining assets. But Cooks Venture didn't have to end this way. Cooks Venture needed to come from a position of strength, especially because the meat industry is unforgiving. Challengers to the status quo are not dealt with benevolently, and while consolidation makes it harder, if the strength of Cooks Venture had spoken for itself, not much could have been done to push the brand out of the market.

Wadiak let his dreams get the best of him without focusing on the fundamentals. The lesson is clear: trying to fast-grow a company of slow-growth chickens doesn't make sense. The soils all over in need of repair—and the environmental proof of concept that Cooks Venture was working toward—have lost out the most. It's a setback for every eater who wants to see good meat truly accessible. But former Cooks Venture employees told me they still think businesses producing good meat can work. The gap is real, and the need is very much there. Cooks Venture shouldn't be the last chance to attempt to create meaningful change at scale.

If the $150 million that Cooks Venture blew through sounds like a lot, consider the billions of dollars more that have been wasted in the fake meat industry—at a crucial juncture when there's not a moment to spare. The boom that *Raw Deal* detailed and the subsequent bust that it predicted have tarnished the promise of many meat alternatives. Start-ups raised $1.6 billion in 2023, according to industry group Good Food Institute's analysis of PitchBook data, and have secured nearly $16 billion in all over the past decade. A lot of that is gone. In 2023, PitchBook tracked at least fifty-two companies that got acquired or went out of business. Investors, loan officers, and banks have been burned. In the rubble left behind, there's less willingness to dole out cash for climate friendly foods. Nearly 70 percent less money flowed into alternative protein start-ups than in 2022, according to PitchBook's tracked US deals. In 2023, plant-based deals dropped more than 40 percent. Investors are scampering away. But they have capital that is still very much needed, albeit elsewhere.

Time is of the essence. Some companies are trying to interrogate their supply chains to make sure every ingredient is sustainable, and not just the cheapest option. But that tends to require a self-sustaining stream of profits and a commitment to push for more. Both are lacking at most start-ups. The best of these brands could limit the damage being inflicted on the environment, and, if adopted by enough people, eating these challengers instead of meat would reduce some of the worst drivers of environmental issues, like methane emissions and water pollution. Instead, the fake meat industry has been pushed to the brink.

It has sure been a bloodbath, as the remaining start-ups navigate consumers who have tried their food or a competitor's, and often never purchased another fake meat again. A major casualty was Impossible's founder and original CEO Pat Brown, who envisioned the start-up while on sabbatical from Stanford's biochemistry department and got pushed out of the company. His replacement, Peter McGuinness, told me he cut back on research spending so Impossible could lead the collapsing sector onward. McGuinness, formerly of billionaire-owned yogurt maker Chobani, which prevailed through its own season of copycats, knows well that shelf space lost may not come back for years. Or ever. During our interview in March 2024, McGuinness took aim at the small brands. Together, he pointed out, Impossible and Beyond Meat, along with their two old-school plant-based competitors, Morningstar and Gardein, control about half the plant-based industry's total sales. Around 150 start-ups are trying to edge each other out for the rest. "These tiny companies don't have great food," McGuinness told me. "Ten of these companies go out of business every other month."

Even Beyond is at risk. If Beyond goes bankrupt, all climate-friendly foods could take a hit. Especially challengers looking for the help of financial institutions in the future. The disappointment of Beyond's financial picture has already caused many to call the company a canary in a coal mine. The problem is twofold. Beyond's debt swelled past $1.1 billion in 2021—and those loans are coming due in 2027. As debt inches up, Beyond's cash has dwindled. From more than $700 million on hand, cash fell to $300 million in 2022 and then further to $190 million in 2023. The owners of Beyond's debt could force a pay-up or a renegotiation. The debt holders would have to agree, and a deal might come alongside a cash infusion from a new stockholder. But a dark savior cloaked as a white knight could come to the rescue. That's why, as sales have fallen and profitability has struggled, short sellers have been swarming. Beyond became the most shorted stock across the entire stock market in November 2023—with more than 42 percent of total shares owned by short sellers. High levels of shorts, when most food companies have at most single digits, has continued. As of June 2024, 38 percent of Beyond shares were shorted—the most among any food stock. The cratering of Beyond's stock price hasn't helped the pile-on, either. There's been a five-year slide from Beyond's post-IPO run-up and all-time-high of $234 in July 2019, which gave the start-up a market value of

$14 billion. Beyond's price has more recently hovered around $6 per share. The problem with all this is simple. While Beyond eaters wait to see what's in store for the company, they're getting short-changed. With so much money going to pay off debts and deal with the headaches of short sellers and other struggles of a publicly traded company, not enough is left over for drastic transformation.

Competitors not as lucky as Beyond have been liquidating. Some brands have been rolled into others. Most didn't make their own food and paid to slap their label on a manufacturer's recipe. Not enough people enjoyed what they were eating to buy more. The big retreat also includes large companies, like Smithfield, which launched a line of soy-based links, ground faux-meat, and meatballs that shuttered by January 2023. Yet the biggest flameout was at JBS, which shut down its non-GMO plant-based brand Planterra after just two years on shelves.

Planterra had been selling at Kroger and Albertsons and was about to launch at Costco and Target. But in October 2022—just after Wesley Batista Filho was promoted to head up JBS global operations, on his way to securing the role of CEO of JBS USA—he decided the business wasn't worth it anymore.* Its 189,000-square-foot factory in Denver, where more than one hundred employees worked, closed. Everyone, including Planterra CEO Darcey Macken, who was one of the only women to report directly to Batista Filho, got fired. JBS could have made some money by selling Planterra, which Macken and her executive team owned their own equity in. Instead, the state-of-the-art plant has sat unused for months—as a crude testament to the power the Batista family wields, and how they can pull back on anything at JBS that doesn't suit them at any moment.

Maybe less money going around will give founders pushing boundaries for the right reasons a moment to breathe, and that could be what's best for the future of these foods. Investors pushing for returns helped unravel another company that brought me hope, mushroom grower Smallhold. The pressure squelched the growing business, which increased access to gourmet varieties of carbon-sequestering fungi. Prior, these kinds of mushrooms were almost nonexistent at scale. What transpired is a cautionary

---

* JBS still has an $8.5 billion plant-based brand, Seara, in Brazil that ranks among its most profitable divisions.

tale. Smallhold had a $95 million valuation at its peak, according to Pitch-Book, backed by more than $30 million raised. But the business sacrificed profitability for the sake of bringing its mushrooms across the country. Expanding its grow warehouses ended up costing the company direly. Smallhold's expensive mega-farm in Los Angeles was built all at once, instead of modularly as demand increased, like its other farms had been constructed. A quarter of Smallhold's monthly expenses were going toward leases. The network was built fast but still took time to fully utilize the cost of the spaces. The rent for its farms plus all the tech-backed machinery (which Smallhold's pitch to investors of tech-grown mushrooms hinged on) cost way too much. Especially for something that grows without help in shady parts of the woods. Investors were initially excited about the technology, but then Smallhold got caught in the crosshairs as investor attitudes toward all that money spent on infrastructure changed. In the end, Smallhold was a viable business that was bogged down by strategic mistakes and pandering to a flawed business model, one set up for failure by investors looking for big returns at any cost.

The business was unprofitable but could have gotten closer to profitability by going after more shelf space. Higher-margin products like the mushroom pesto it launched just before running out of cash are a peek into what should have become a powerful brand with an authentic and environmentally friendly farming origin story. But as investors pushed for more, the business couldn't deliver. In February 2024, a minority shareholder, Monomyth, acquired the shares of another investor, Sage Hill Partners, and secured more than 90 percent ownership. Once Monomyth took control of the board, the former chief operating officer of Burger King Brazil was hired as interim CEO. Smallhold's cofounders—CEO Andrew Carter and chief innovation officer Adam DeMartino—abruptly resigned. The business was headed toward Chapter 11 bankruptcy, and the incoming team's bankruptcy plan looked to trim employees' severance packages and paid-time off. About one hundred employees were laid off, as Smallhold cut off contracts with its partner farmers. With bankruptcy restructuring, there's hope that some production will get revived. The business is currently purchasing mushrooms from other suppliers and reselling them, allegedly at a loss, to maintain the brand's shelf space at stores like Whole Foods. I'm still bullish on mushrooms, but whatever Smallhold becomes won't be the same. The future of Smallhold lies with what can be salvaged of its farming network.

That's the case for the future of the entire food supply, too. Farmers are *it*, whether they are raising animals for meat or growing plants or fungi. Without them, we wouldn't eat, but farmers have been pushed out of a seat at the table too many times. That's especially true when looking at alternative proteins. Products created to supposedly withstand years of climate crisis continue to barely address how their ingredients get farmed, or how they will continue to be raised amid hotter temperatures and extreme weather. Instead, the moneymaking opportunity has been too tantalizing. The boom and bust have translated into serious time, money, and resources wasted.

In the short amount of time left to enact real change, we will find out whether these not so healthy and not so environmentally (or financially) sustainable faux-meats will suck up the last funding out there for themselves and eventually waste even more. Many farmers could have done much more with just a slice of the money that's gone toward fake meats. Those funds could have set soils around the country on a far better path forward than what Beyond and Impossible have accomplished by purchasing monoculture-farmed commodity ingredients from large suppliers unwilling to change. From JBS-backed Planterra's shutdown to challenges at Beyond, Smallhold, and many more, lessons must be absorbed. The attention captured by creating climate-friendly foods must not be thrown away.

Lab-grown meat may be blowing its shot, too, after getting introduced to American diners with fanfare over the summer of 2023. At chef Dominique Crenn's Michelin-starred Bay Area restaurant Bar Crenn, lab-grown chicken from start-up Upside Foods was served—barely visible. It sat underneath a pile of edible flowers as a romantic fog unfurled, thanks to dry ice. A chili aioli topped it off. Upside was sold as part of a $150 six-course tasting menu, and briefly later à la carte for $45 a plate. Just 112 sold in all.

In Washington, DC, at chef José Andrés's restaurant China Chilcano, lab-grown chicken from Good Meat came out of the investor's kitchen marinated in a sauce of anticucho and served with Peruvian-inspired potatoes and aji amarillo chimichurri.* It was offered in August and September on the restaurant's $70 tasting menu. Good Meat claims it didn't track how many it sold in DC.†

Whatever got purchased was done at a big loss to each business's bank accounts. People who tried the cells may never see a point in their lifetimes when producing these proteins is a profitable business. So far, despite the much-hyped demand, there's not enough money to keep lab-grown meat regularly on dinner tables. A billionaire can, of course, still sponsor an event. (Though not in Florida.)

The economic realities long ignored by founders and investors have begun to haunt the start-ups. Lab-grown meat has pulled in more than $3 billion in the past five years. But it's still billions of dollars away from real size or scale. Some businesses have shuttered. Others have struggled. Eat Just and its lab-grown spinoff Good Meat, last valued in 2017, according to PitchBook, at $1.25 billion, is cash-strapped. If CEO Josh Tetrick can't reach profitability, Eat Just and Good Meat may not have a future. Profits are still a long way away, though Tetrick has been promising it's close for years. "All alternative protein companies, certainly us, need to obsess over getting to break-even," said Tetrick, who has raised more than $900 million, of which $200 million has been earmarked for Good Meat. "If we're so reliant on external capital, that creates real vulnerability."‡

So, naturally, the Batistas to the rescue. Despite shuttering its US plant-based business, JBS is investing in lab-grown. JBS acquired 51 percent of Spain-based BioTech Foods in 2021, and a little over 40 percent of the deal's $100 million was earmarked to build a factory. The commercial-scale project broke ground in the pintxos mecca San Sebastián, and when it opens, JBS claims it will be the world's largest cultivated meat plant. Time will tell if this thread ends like many others in JBS history.

The Batistas are among many billionaires and wealthy financiers who

---

* That's according to media reports, which these presentations were clearly made to influence. I held off on trying it. At minimum, I wanted to be paying for the true cost of the protein—and it was clear that such an opportunity was never going to happen.

† The total of faux-chicken sold by Good Meat in Singapore tops two thousand, Good Meat claims.

‡ Break-even means generating sufficient gross margin dollars to cover operating burn.

stand to gain a lot from lab-grown meat. That's made their interest in these novel proteins biased. And it may be why there's still little being done to use this technology to address accessibility to healthy protein. Or concerns over the energy use, since large (and quite expensive) factories need to be built to turn all those cells into digestible muscles. Or the additional antibiotic resistance caused by the lab-grown meat sector's reliance on antibiotics. The technology may never live up to its full potential. Worse, it may waste the last money and time left to figure out how to produce enough good meat, before climate crisis sets in even more.

For far too long, the meat industry's top businesses have prioritized profits over the environment, workers, farmers, communities near production, and animals. All of us—meat eaters, pescatarians, vegetarians, vegans, and everyone else—are hurt in the process. As are the generations to follow. The blaring alarms cannot continue to be ignored.

Even though eating sustainably is under threat, we cannot be deterred. B-Corp certification is still a solid first step to figure out which companies are trying their best to produce with integrity. But there are limitations. When it comes to the environment, the certification does not require companies to provide enough information about the suppliers behind their raw materials. The Regenerative Organic certification addresses that while prioritizing soil health alongside fair labor and sourcing standards.

When analyzing businesses that sell food, I've learned that equity is everything. Consider the lofty goals of Smallhold with its rapid expansion westward, and Cooks Venture's trials to feed chicken wheat. These ideas initially seemed important enough for a trade-off, like selling a stake for a funding injection. But the businesses took on too much. Every company that made me briefly wonder whether raising money could be worth it ended up failing—not just at the lofty goals, but at the entire business. The funding clouded the vision. At the expense of the environment.

The top question I get asked is what brings me hope. With the bankruptcy of Smallhold and Cooks Venture, there's real reason for concern. But whenever I feel the spirit of community connection working hand in hand to build a better model, one that's replicable, where maintaining equity, control, and power is a key part of the equation, I am filled with optimism.

The urgency is not lost on me. Time has been wasted. As has a lot of money—tied to a lot of investors, banks, debt holders, and other financial institutions that may not be as willing to back ideas for good meat in the future. My hope is that those who really want a stake in the future of our food supply rise up and take back control—and are more protective of their investment deals and more focused on the business foundation as they get the next chance. It may be one of the last.

Acknowledgments

I have so much gratitude to share with so many who helped me along this book-writing journey.

I'm a firm believer that you're either on the bus or you're off the bus. But finding the right people can be a challenge. I owe so much to the champion of this project, Stephanie Hitchcock. Thank you for being on the bus with me! You got me from Day One. And, of course, thank you to my agent, Tess Callero, for driving the bus, and always listening to my ideas.

To my family: Nick, you are my rock, and my design guru, and reluctant technology chief, and so much more. We are in it together, forever, and I love you. Mom, what an eye! I'll always love that we finish each other's sentences. Without your crucial input, these words would not have worked nearly as well. Damian, who knew your 5 a.m. wake-up habit would come so in handy? What a wild work ethic that you made me think was normal. Thank you for that. And, Emery, the bread was always there when I needed it. You're the Big Tree to me. To my Nana and Pops, thank you for believing in me. To Ingrid, and the many mothers in my life, your support has pushed me forward. And to my family of twelve years and counting, Jeanne, Tom, Carol, Matt, and many more, thank you for opening your hearts to me.

To my research team, I am so indebted to you. Natalie Robehmed, thank you for your constant grace. Your help on this project meant so much to me and I will always look up to you. Justin Birnbaum and Margherita Beale. you jumped at all the challenges and kept me sane, thank you!

Thank you to everyone on the Simon & Schuster Atria team of editors, copy editors, marketers, and more who helped me so much. Special thanks to Claire Sullivan for the badass cover.

There are so many sources whose time and energy brought this book to life. I'd like to extend a deep thank-you to each and every one, from the longtime sources to the ones I crossed paths with while reporting this book. I've done hundreds of recorded interviews for this book, and many more that were not recorded. I so appreciate everyone who spoke with me along the way. Thank you for sharing your truth. A special thank-you to Phil Haynes, for bringing me inside all of your farming, slaughterhouse, butchering, and cooking adventures. Plus, major appreciation to the many analysts and data providers who helped me pinpoint numbers, including NielsenIQ and PitchBook, to the transcription service Otter, and my translator Marco de Souza.

To all the lawyers I've interviewed: I like reading through thousands of pages of legal documents more than the average journalist. But I still want to give a special nod to all the lawyers who took the time out to go over facts of different cases, theory, and strategy with me—on the record, on background, and off the record. And a special thank you to Grant Lachman, Aaron Davis, and Michael Lundholm for all the pro bono legal advice. And to Debbie Reperowitz for my first briefcase!

To the friends who I laugh with and the friends who I cry with, thank you for supporting me through this book-writing process. A few special shout-outs to Isabel Johnson for the unconditional understanding, Diana Marinaccio for the tough love, Margot Wilsterman for being there for the dry-heaves, Karlee Fidler for always being down to take a reporting road trip with me, Nora Princiotti for always chanting with me, Nadia Bernstein for all the dissecting of what's on the plate, Louisa Burnwood-Taylor for the ill-fated food lab adventure. To Eddie Mele for concocting the Sloppy G with me in Nolita, and for always having a great apartment.

To the wonderful folks at Little Canal, and Mel, for the neighborhood cheer.

To *Forbes*, for teaching me so much about business and for countless opportunities. Luisa Kroll, your mentorship, inspiration, and support have pushed me to reach higher than I ever thought I could. Michael Noer, thank you for encouraging me at your favorite dive bar to write a book while I could. Bob Ivry, thank you for accepting me and running with it. To Randall Lane, for the constant motivation. To my former wealth team pod mates, and especially Jen Wang, Maddie Berg, and Noah Kirsch, I'll always remember our late nights *too* fondly. To Sue Radlauer, for being a delight and an inspiration and always so giving. To the copy desk and what's left of it (hi Suzanne O'Neill!) so much love to you for making my words so much better. And to all my friends at the Forbes Union and the News Guild—solidarity! Keep standing tough.

To *The GW Hatchet* and its insatiable crew of journalists, for giving me space to experiment and explore reporting, writing, and editing. Support independent journalism, on campus and beyond. To my inspiring professors in college, including Steven Roberts, Michael Shanahan, Frank Sesno, David Fallis, David Joachim, and many others. And a special thank-you to Steven and Cokie Roberts, who inspired my parents to believe they could raise their children interfaith. I may not have been here if *From This Day Forward* had never been published. But, then again, I may not have been here if a lot of things had not happened.

To Mrs. Grant, Dr. Murray, Dean Sluyter, Madame Castaldo, and Madame Jordan at Pingry, and Ms. Wisniewski, Mrs. Bowden, and Mrs. Springmeyer at Harding, thank you for going above and beyond while teaching me.

To everyone who read this book, and is still reading this book, thank you from the bottom of my heart.

Notes

INTRODUCTION

1 In quick succession, fourteen, "America's Meatpacking Facilities Practicing Safe Reopening to Ensure a Stable Food Supply." USDA, May 8, 2020. https://www.usda.gov/media/press-releases/2020/05/08/americas-meatpacking-facilities-practicing-safe-reopening-ensure.

1 To a halt, Reynolds, Kim, Charles E. Grassley, Joni K. Ernst, and Mike Naig. Letter to Mr. Vice President Mike Pence and Members of the Coronavirus Task Force. "Letter on Covid-19 Impact to Pork Production." U.S. Senate - Jodi K Ernst. U.S. Senate - Jodi K Ernst, April 27, 2020. https://www.ernst.senate.gov/public/_cache/files/acb98e95-8fea-48a1-b9ed-cba0cdba8d64/395806428144EEDED927DD44CD5A6433.updated-2020-covid-pork-letter-1-.pdf.

1 An anonymous lawsuit, "RCWA & Jane Doe v. Smithfield." Public Justice Food Project. Public Justice Food Project, December 3, 2020. https://food.publicjustice.net/case/rcwa-jane-doe-v-smithfield/.

2 "Food supply chain is breaking," "A Delicate Balance: Feeding The Nation And Keeping Our Employees Healthy." Tyson. *The New York Times*, April 27, 2020.

2 Record-breaking profits, Deese, Brian, Sameera Fazili, and Bharat Ramamurti. "Recent Data Show Dominant Meat Processing Companies Are Taking Advantage of Market Power to Raise Prices and Grow Profit Margins." The White House, December 10, 2021. https://www.whitehouse.gov/briefing-room/blog/2021/12/10/recent-data-show-dominant-meat-processing-companies-are-taking-advantage-of-market-power-to-raise-prices-and-grow-profit-margins/.

2 Drafted by, House of Representatives Select Subcommittee on Coronavirus Crisis. Rep. *"Now To Get Rid Of Those Pesky Health Departments!" How The Trump Administration Helped The Meatpacking Industry Block Pandemic Worker Protections*. House of Representatives Select Subcommittee on Coronavirus Crisis, May 12, 2022. https://coronavirus.house.gov/sites/democrats.coronavirus.house.gov/files/2022.5.12%20-%20SSCC%20report%20on%20Meatpacking%20FINAL.pdf.

2 Betting pool, "Tyson Foods Completes Waterloo Investigation (Press Release)." Tyson Foods, December 16, 2020. https://www.tysonfoods.com/news/news-releases/2020/12/tyson-foods-completes-waterloo-investigation.

3 Adopt more humane livestock practices, Grandin, Temple. "Assessment of Stress during Handling and Transport." Oxford University Press, January 1, 1997. https://academic.oup.com/jas/article-abstract/75/1/249/4637218.

3 More than a half century, Grandin, Temple. "Observations of Cattle Behavior Applied to the Design of Cattle-Handling Facilities." *Applied Animal Ethology* 6, no. 1 (January 1980): 19–31. https://doi.org/10.1016/0304-3762(80)90091-7.

3 Adopt more humane livestock practices, Grandin, Temple. "Objective Scoring of Animal Handling and Stunning Practices at Slaughter Plants." *Journal of American Veterinary Medical Association* 212 (1998): 36–39. https://www.grandin.com/references/scoring.ab.html.

4 Big is not bad, Grandin, Temple. "Temple Grandin: Big Meat Supply Chains Are Fragile."

Forbes, May 3, 2020. https://www.forbes.com/sites/templegrandin/2020/05/03/temple
-grandin-big-meat-supply-chains-are-fragile.

5 Third-ranked world emitter of greenhouse gases, Environment, UN. "Promoting
Sustainable Lifestyles." UN Environment Program. United Nations. Accessed April
12, 2022. https://www.unep.org/regions/north-america/regional-initiatives/promoting
-sustainable-lifestyles#:~:text=Globally%2C%20if%20food%20waste%20could,3.3%20
billion%20tons%20of%20CO2.

5 Scratching the surface, Hendrickson, Mary K., Phillip H. Howard, and Douglas H. Con-
stance. "Power, Food and Agriculture: Implications for Farmers, Consumers and Communities." Pp. 13–61 in *In Defense of Farmers: The Future of Agriculture in the Shadow of
Corporate Power*, edited by J. W. Gibson and S. E. Alexander. Lincoln, NE: University of
Nebraska Press, 2019.

5 Backed up, 170,000, "The Tragic Impact of COVID-19 on U.S Hog Farmers The Need
to Euthanize (Press Release)." NPCC.org. National Pork Producers Council, May 8,
2020. https://nppc.org/wp-content/uploads/2020/05/euthanasia-fact-sheet-FINAL-5
-8-20.pdf.

5 At risk, 10 million, Reynolds, Kim, Charles E. Grassley, Joni K. Ernst, and Mike Naig.
Letter to Mr. Vice President Mike Pence and Members of the Coronavirus Task Force.
"Letter on Covid-19 Impact to Pork Production." U.S. Senate - Jodi K Ernst. U.S. Senate - Jodi K Ernst, April 27, 2020. https://www.ernst.senate.gov/public/_cache/files
/acb98e95-8fea-48a1-b9ed-cba0cdba8d64/395806428144EEDED927DD44CD5A6433
.updated-2020-covid-pork-letter-1-.pdf.

5 Cyberattack, nine, JBS USA, LLC. "Media Statement: JBS USA Cybersecurity Attack." GlobeNewswire News Room. JBS USA, LLC, May 31, 2021. https://www.globe
newswire.com/news-release/2021/05/31/2239049/0/en/Media-Statement-JBS-USA
-Cybersecurity-Attack.html.

5 Cresting in profits, Deese, Brian, Sameera Fazili, and Bharat Ramamurti. "Recent Data
Show Dominant Meat Processing Companies Are Taking Advantage of Market Power
to Raise Prices and Grow Profit Margins." The White House. The United States Government, December 10, 2021. https://www.whitehouse.gov/briefing-room/blog/2021/12
/10/recent-data-show-dominant-meat-processing-companies-are-taking-advantage-of
-market-power-to-raise-prices-and-grow-profit-margins/.

5 Twice as high as the average analyst's estimate, Mano, Ana. "Update 2-Brazil's JBS, World's
Top Meat-Packer, Posts Better-than-Expected Results." Reuters, August 13, 2020. https://
www.reuters.com/article/jbs-results/update-2-brazils-jbs-worlds-top-meat-packer
-posts-better-than-expected-results-idUSL1N2FF2I9.

6 Uncompetitive markets, Deese, Brian, Sameera Fazili, and Bharat Ramamurti. "Recent
Data Show Dominant Meat Processing Companies Are Taking Advantage of Market
Power to Raise Prices and Grow Profit Margins." The White House, December 10,
2021. https://www.whitehouse.gov/briefing-room/blog/2021/12/10/recent-data-show
-dominant-meat-processing-companies-are-taking-advantage-of-market-power-to
-raise-prices-and-grow-profit-margins/.

6 Shipments abroad, "S&P's Panjiva Data on Meatpacker Exports; Emailed to Chloe Sorvino." New York: New York, February 18, 2021.

6 COVID-19 slaughterhouse deaths, Douglas, Leah. "Mapping Covid-19 Outbreaks in
the Food System." Food and Environment Reporting Network. Food and Environment
Reporting Network, September 8, 2021. https://thefern.org/2020/04/mapping-covid-19
-in-meat-and-food-processing-plants/.

7 All greenhouse gas emissions annually, a third, Crippa, M., Solazzo, E., Guizzardi, D. et
al. "Food systems are responsible for a third of global anthropogenic GHG emissions."
Nat Food 2 (2021): 198–209. https://doi.org/10.1038/s43016-021-00225-9.

8 No chance at stymieing catastrophic environmental change, *Climate Change 2021: The
Physical Science Basis. Contribution of Working Group I to the Sixth Assessment Report
of the Intergovernmental Panel on Climate Change.* Masson-Delmotte, V., P. Zhai, A. Pi-
rani, S., L. Connors, C. Péan, S. Berger, N. Caud, Y. Chen, L. Goldfarb, M. I. Gomis,
M. Huang, K. Leitzell, E. Lonnoy, J. B., R. Matthews, T. K. Maycock, T. Waterfield,
O. Yelekçi, R. Yu, and B. Zhou (eds.). Cambridge University Press. In Press.

8 Contributing scientists, 700, *Climate Change 2021: The Physical Science Basis. Contribution of Working Group I to the Sixth Assessment Report of the Intergovernmental Panel*

on Climate Change. Masson-Delmotte, V., P. Zhai, A. Pirani, S., L. Connors, C. Péan, S. Berger, N. Caud, Y. Chen, L. Goldfarb, M. I. Gomis, M. Huang, K. Leitzell, E. Lonnoy, J. B., R. Matthews, T. K. Maycock, T. Waterfield, O. Yelekçi, R. Yu, and B. Zhou (eds.). Cambridge University Press. In Press.

8 Overhaul its operations, "Overview of Greenhouse Gases: Methane Emissions." Environmental Protection Agency. Accessed September 4, 2021. https://www.epa.gov/ghgemissions/overview-greenhouse-gases#methane.

8 All fossil fuels, Clark, Michael A., Nina G. Domingo, Kimberly Colgan, Sumil K. Thakrar, David Tilman, John Lynch, Inês L. Azevedo, and Jason D. Hill. "Global Food SYSTEM Emissions Could PRECLUDE Achieving the 1.5° And 2°c Climate Change Targets." *Science* 370, no. 6517 (2020): 705–8. https://doi.org/10.1126/science.aba7357.

8 Lobbying for climate-related issues, at least $200 million, Lazarus, O., McDermid, S. & Jacquet, J. "The climate responsibilities of industrial meat and dairy producers." *Climatic Change* 165, 30 (2021). https://doi.org/10.1007/s10584-021-03047-7 https://s18798.pcdn.co/ceap/wp-content/uploads/sites/11111/2021/04/CEAP_Research_Brief_5.pdf

9 Should eat only synthetic meat, Gates, Bill. *How to Avoid a Climate Disaster: The Solutions We Have and the Breakthroughs We Need.* London: Allen Lane, 2021.

10 Reducetarians, Kateman, Brian. *Meat Me Halfway: How Changing the Way We Eat Can Improve Our Lives and Save Our Planet.* Prometheus Books, 2022.

12 Farm-to-table movement, Pollan, Michael. *The Omnivore's Dilemma: A Natural History of Four Meals.* Detroit: Thomson, 2007.

12 Local food . . . percent of total agricultural output, Johnson, Renée. "The Role of Local and Regional Food Systems in U.S. Farm Policy." Congressional Research Service, 2016. https://sgp.fas.org/crs/misc/R44390.pdf

CHAPTER 1

17 John W. Tyson, "Arkansas Business Hall of Fame: John Tyson." Arkansas Business Hall of Fame. Walton College. University of Arkansas. Walton College of Business, 2019. https://walton.uark.edu/abhf/john-tyson.php.

17 Moved into raising chickens, "John Tyson." The Sam M. Walton College of Business. University of Arkansas. Accessed January 31, 2022. https://walton.uark.edu/abhf/john-tyson.php.

17 Demand started soaring, "U.S. Chicken Industry History." National Chicken Council. Accessed January 22, 2022. https://www.nationalchickencouncil.org/about-the-industry/history/.

17 A rarity in American diets, Ritchie, Hannah. "Per Capita Meat Consumption in the United States." Our World in Data, 2017. https://ourworldindata.org/grapher/per-capita-meat-usa?country=~USA.

17 Strong sales, Waite, Richard. "2018 Will See High Meat Consumption in the U.S., but the American Diet Is Shifting." World Resources Institute, January 24, 2018. https://www.wri.org/insights/2018-will-see-high-meat-consumption-us-american-diet-shifting.

17 Over budget, $15,000, "Our History." Tyson Foods. Accessed January 22, 2022. https://www.tysonfoods.com/who-we-are/our-story/where-we-came-from/our-history.

17 Publicly traded company, Schwartz, Marvin. *Tyson: From Farm to Market.* University of Arkansas Press Series in Business History, Vol. 2. Fayetteville, Arkansas: University of Arkansas Press, 1991.

17 The majority of voting power, "Shareholders Win Unprecedented Support for Reforms at Tyson Foods." International Brotherhood of Teamsters, February 19, 2021. https://www.prnewswire.com/news-releases/shareholders-win-unprecedented-support-for-reforms-at-tyson-foods-301231757.html.

17 Prospect Farms, "Tyson Foods Celebrates 50 Years of North Little Rock Plant's Operation." Tyson Foods, April 25, 2018. https://www.tysonfoods.com/news/news-releases/2018/4/tyson-foods-celebrates-50-years-north-little-rock-plants-operation.

18 Ocomo Foods, "In 1972, We Acquired Ocoma Foods, Virtually Doubling Our Size! #TBT." Facebook. Tyson Foods, September 10, 2015. https://www.facebook.com/TysonFoods/photos/in-1972-we-acquired-ocoma-foods-virtually-doubling-our-size-tbt/868487646540088/.

18 Dropped out of college, "The Forbes 400: Donald John Tyson; Barbara Tyson." *Forbes*, October 22, 1990.

18 "Grow or die," McFadden, Robert D. "Donald J. Tyson, Food Tycoon, Is Dead at 80." *The New York Times*, January 6, 2011. https://www.nytimes.com/2011/01/07/business /07tyson.html.

18 Dozens of other commodities-based businesses, Broehl, Wayne G. *Cargill: Going Global*. Hanover: Dartmouth College, 1998.

18 An agribusiness conglomerate, Broehl, Wayne G. *Cargill: From Commodities to Customers*. Hanover N.H.: Dartmouth College Press, 2008.

18 Grain became a mere third of the business, Tamarkin, Bob. "What—and Who—Makes Cargill So Powerful?" *Forbes*, September 18, 1978.

19 Luter family, Koselka, Rita. "$ Oink, $ Oink." *Forbes*, February 3, 1992.

19 Joseph Luter III, J., T. "Pig Out." *Forbes*, December 1, 1986.

19 Acquiring more competitors, Waltz, Lynn. *Hog Wild: The Battle for Workers' Rights at the World's Largest Slaughterhouse*. Iowa City, Iowa: University of Iowa Press, 2018.

19 Cut carcasses into massive sections, Sorvino, Chloe. "Why Steakhouses Are Obsessed with Beef from This 97-Year-Old Family Business." *Forbes*, October 9, 2017. https:// www.forbes.com/sites/chloesorvino/2017/10/03/henry-davis-greater-omaha-beef -steakhouse/.

19 Boxed beef, "The Meatpacking Revolution: 1950–1974." The Meatpacking Revolution. University of Nebraska Lincoln. Accessed January 22, 2022. http://netwagtaildev.unl.edu /nebstudies/en/1950-1974/beef-state/the-meatpacking-revolution/.

19 IBP, "About IBP: Trusted Excellence." Tyson Fresh Meats. Tyson Foods Inc. Accessed January 22, 2022. https://tysonfreshmeats.com/our-brands/ibp-trusted-excellence-brand /about.

19 A ripple effect, Grain Inspection, Packers and Stockyards Administration, Azzeddine M. Azzam, and Dale G. Anderson. "Assessing competition in meatpacking: Economic history, theory, and evidence" 1996. https://citeseerx.ist.psu.edu/viewdoc/download ?doi=10.1.1.457.1087&rep=rep1&type=pdf.

20 The introduction of chicken as a mainstream source of protein, Ritchie, Hannah. "Per Capita Meat Consumption in the United States." Our World in Data, 2017. https:// ourworldindata.org/grapher/per-capita-meat-usa?country=~USA.

20 Subsidized agribusiness, "Agricultural Act of 1970." Agricultural Act of 1970 Pub. L. No. 91-524, 84 Stat. 1358. The National Center for Agricultural Law Research and Information University of Arkansas, under Cooperative Agreement No. 58-8201-4-197 with the United States Department of Agriculture, National Agricultural Library, 1970. https:// nationalaglawcenter.org/wp-content/uploads/assets/farmbills/1970.pdf.

20 Crop insurance, "Crop and Livestock Insurance." USDA. Accessed January 31, 2022. https://www.usda.gov/topics/farming/crop-and-livestock-insurance.

20 Disaster payments, "Disaster Assistance Programs." Farm Service Agency. USDA. Accessed January 31, 2022. https://www.fsa.usda.gov/programs-and-services/disaster -assistance-program/index.

20 Tax credits, Vilsack, Tom. "Earned Income Tax Credit Can Help Rural Families." USDA, February 21, 2017. https://www.usda.gov/media/blog/2016/01/29/earned-income-tax -credit-can-help-rural-families.

20 Tax credits, "Tax Credits and Agricultural Assessments." Department of Agriculture and Markets. New York State. Accessed January 31, 2022. https://agriculture.ny.gov/land -and-water/tax-credits-and-agricultural-assessments.

20 Depreciation allowances, van der Hoeven, Guido. "Depreciation Deductions for Farm Businesses: An Introduction." Center for Agricultural Law and Taxation. Iowa State University, June 6, 2020. https://www.calt.iastate.edu/taxplace/depreciation-deductions -farm-businesses-introduction.

20 Depreciation allowances, "Tax Reform Changes to Depreciation Deduction Affect Farmers' Bottom Line." Internal Revenue Service, 2018. https://www.irs.gov/newsroom /tax-reform-changes-to-depreciation-deduction-affect-farmers-bottom-line.

20 Relaxing antitrust regulations, Baldwin, William L. "Efficiency And Competition: The Reagan Administration's Legacy in Merger Policy." *Review of Industrial Organization* 5, no. 2 (1990): 159–74. http://www.jstor.org/stable/41798306.

20 Ushered in an open season, Special to the *New York Times*. "Big Change in Antitrust Law

Urged." *The New York Times*, January 16, 1986. https://www.nytimes.com/1986/01/16 /business/big-change-in-antitrust-law-urged.html.

20 Mergers and acquisitions, Lipartito, Kenneth, and David B. Sicilia. "Constructing Corporate America: History, Politics, Culture." Oxford Scholarship Online, 2004. https://doi .org/10.1093/acprof:oso/9780199251902.001.0001.

20 Gwaltney of Smithfield, $34 million, Koselka, Rita. "$ Oink, $ Oink." *Forbes*, February 3, 1992.

20 Television ads featuring, Goydon, Raymond. "Is Frank Perdue Chicken?" *Forbes*, November 4, 1984.

20 Opened its first chicken restaurant, Perdue TV Advertisement. Perdue Chicken TV Commercial (1982). USA: Perdue TV Advertisement, 1982. https://www.youtube.com /watch?v=IfyEM.

20 Pressure to create cheaper, Wolf, Robert. "Farming as a 'Scientific Business.'" *The North American Review* 285, no. 2 (2000): 43–48. https://www.jstor.org/stable/25126443.

20 "Get big or get out," "Leaders in Agricultural Policy A Conversation with Earl Butz (02 /1993)." YouTube. Purdue Ag Econ, October 11, 2019. https://www.youtube.com/watch ?v=46G831BReDs.

20 Farm crisis of the 1980s, Atkinson, Sue Ann. "The Farm Crisis of the 1980s in Iowa: Its Roots and Its Inner Workings." Iowa State University Digital Repository, 1999. https:// doi.org/10.31274/rtd-180813-7470.

20 Bank failures, "History of the 80s—Lessons for the Future: Chapter 8: Banking and the Agricultural Problems of the 1980s." *An Examination of the Banking Crises of the 1980s and Early 1990s* Vol. 1. FDIC. Accessed January 23, 2022. https://www.fdic.gov /bank/historical/history/.

21 Went public, Thornton, Gary. "Pilgrim's Pride Turns 60." WATTPoultry, July 1, 2009. https://www.wattagnet.com/articles/1853-pilgrim-s-pride-turns-60.

21 Sanderson Farms, "The Sanderson Story—Celebrating 70 Years of Sanderson Farms." Sanderson Farms, January 5, 2018. https://sandersonfarms.com/blog/sanderson-story -celebrating-70-years-sanderson-farms/.

21 Occidental Petroleum, Woutat, Donald. "Oxy May Realize $1 Billion on Complex IBP Stock Deal: 49% of the Meat Packer Would Be Offered to Public, Then the Firm Would Pay Its Parent a $960-Million 'Dividend.'" *The Los Angeles Times*, August 20, 1987. https://www.latimes.com/archives/la-xpm-1987-08-20-fi-3439-story.html.

21 Branches of family heirs, "The Forbes 400: Cargill/MacMillan." *Forbes* no. 1983 Fall, Special Issue, 1983.

21 Joined the chicken company, "Joseph Grendys." *Forbes*. Accessed January 22, 2022. https://www.forbes.com/profile/joseph-grendys/.

21 Bought out his mentor, Harris, Melissa. "Inside Billionaire Joe Grendys' Chicken Empire." *The Chicago Tribune*, October 24, 2014. https://www.chicagotribune.com/business /ct-confidential-chicken-billionaire-1026-biz-20141024-column.html.

21 Chicken nugget production and other popular foods, "About Us." Koch Foods, November 4, 2020. https://kochfoods.com/our-company/about-us/.

21 Soared to new heights, Leonard, Christopher. *The Meat Racket: The Secret Takeover of America's Food Business*. New York: Simon & Schuster, 2017.

21 Doubled in size, Holly Farms, "The Forbes 400: Donald John Tyson; Barbara Tyson." *Forbes*, October 22, 1990. Tyson.

21 The vast majority were acquired, "Our History." Tyson Foods. Accessed January 31, 2022. https://www.tysonfoods.com/who-we-are/our-story/where-we-came-from/our -history.

22 A flurry of competing offers, Maynard, Therese H. *Mergers and Acquisitions: Cases, Materials, and Problems*. New York: Aspen Publishing, 2021.

22 IBP agreed to $3.2 billion, Deogun, Nikhil. "Tyson Tops Smithfield In Fight to Acquire IBP." *The Wall Street Journal*, January 2, 2001. https://www.wsj.com/articles /SB978375589200846006.

22 Another crucial bidding war, Reuters Staff. "Tyson Foods Says Wins Bidding War for Hillshire Brands." CNBC, June 9, 2014. https://www.cnbc.com/2014/06/09/tyson-to -acquire-hillshire-brands-for-63-a-share-in-cash.html.

22 Hillshire Farms, 71 percent premium, De la Merced, Michael J. "After a Short, Furious Battle, a Rich Offer for Hillshire." DealBook. *The New York Times*, June 9, 2014.

https://dealbook.nytimes.com/2014/06/09/after-a-short-furious-battle-a-rich-offer-for-hillshire/.

22 American acquisition spree, Blankfeld, Keren. "All You Can Eat." *Forbes*, May 9, 2011. https://www.forbes.com/sites/kerenblankfeld/2011/04/21/jbs-the-story-behind-the-worlds-biggest-meat-producer/.

22 First US deal, J&F Participações S.A., Swift & Company, and HM Capital. "Hm Capital Partners Llc And &F Participações S.A., Of Brazil, Sign Definitive Agreement Under Which J&F Will Acquire Swift & Company." EXV99W1-SEC. Securities and Exchange Commission, May 29, 2007. https://www.sec.gov/Archives/edgar/data/1199114/000095013407012518/d47138exv99w1.htm.

23 National Beef, Reuters Staff. "Brazil's JBS to Buy U.S Beef Company." Reuters, March 5, 2008. https://www.reuters.com/article/us-brazil-jbs/brazils-jbs-to-buy-u-s-beef-company-idUSN0454263520080305.

23 Triggered regulators' concerns, Press Release #09-146, Office of Public Affairs. "Department of Justice Statement on the Abandonment of the JBS/National Beef Transaction." The United States Department of Justice, September 16, 2014. https://www.justice.gov/opa/pr/department-justice-statement-abandonment-jbsnational-beef-transaction.

23 Pilgrim's Pride went bankrupt, JBS purchased majority ownership, Spector, Mike, Lauren Etter, and Alastair Stewart. "Brazilian Giant JBS Agrees to Buy Pilgrim's Pride." *The Wall Street Journal*, September 18, 2009. https://www.wsj.com/articles/SB125310503697015705.

CHAPTER 2

24 The first fresh hamburger meat supplier to McDonald's, Sorvino, Chloe. "Meet the Secretive Billionaire Who Makes McDonald's McNuggets, Burger King's Impossible Whoppers and More." *Forbes*, September 21, 2020. https://www.forbes.com/sites/chloesorvino/2020/09/21/meet-the-secretive-billionaire-who-makes-mcdonalds-mcnuggets-burger-kings-impossible-whoppers-and-more/.

24 Years as an independent, Lavin, Sheldon. "Sheldon Lavin on Professional Tales." Medium, December 12, 2019. https://medium.com/@sheldonlavin/sheldon-lavin-5ac8ef02a984.

24 Remained active in the business, Lavin, Sheldon. "A Century of Innovation at OSI Group." Medium, September 25, 2019. https://medium.com/@sheldonlavin/a-century-of-innovation-at-osi-group-5706d72dcd0f.

24 Make a full-time commitment, Lavin, Sheldon. "The Sustainability Vision of Sheldon Lavin, CEO of OSI Group." Medium, December 11, 2019. https://medium.com/@sheldonlavin/the-sustainability-vision-of-sheldon-lavin-ceo-of-osi-group-2619db3ab73b.

25 A third of the company's ownership, Lavin, Sheldon. "A Century of Innovation at OSI Group." Medium, September 25, 2019. https://medium.com/@sheldonlavin/a-century-of-innovation-at-osi-group-5706d72dcd0f.

25 Meat baron, Sorvino, Chloe. "Meet the Secretive Billionaire Who Makes McDonald's McNuggets, Burger King's Impossible Whoppers and More." *Forbes*, September 21, 2020. https://www.forbes.com/sites/chloesorvino/2020/09/21/meet-the-secretive-billionaire-who-makes-mcdonalds-mcnuggets-burger-kings-impossible-whoppers-and-more/.

25 The past fifty years, Goldberg, Ray A., and Harold F. Hogan. OSI Group. Boston, MA: Harvard Business School, 2001.

25 One of the world's largest contract manufacturers, with a network of sixty-five plants in eighteen countries, "Locations." OSI Group, May 26, 2021. https://www.osigroup.com/locations/.

25 Gained control of the business, Goldberg, Ray A., and Harold F. Hogan. OSI Group. Boston, MA: Harvard Business School, 2001.

25 Told the Meat Hall of Fame, "Hall of Famers: Sheldon Lavin." Meat Hall of Fame Winners Bios. BNP Media/National Provisioner, 2013. https://www.provisioneronline.com/meat-industry-hall-of-fame/hall-of-fame-winner-bios#L.

25 Amick Farms, "Company Timeline-OSI." OSI Group, January 8, 2021. https://www.osigroup.com/about-us/company-timeline/.

25 A large shareholder of Marfrig, "Lavin in Meat Industry Hall of Fame." Prepared Foods. BNP Media, July 3, 2013. https://www.preparedfoods.com/articles/112885-lavin-in-meat

-industry-hall-of-fame#:~:text=July%201%2FAurora%2C%20Ill.,many%20of%20 the%20world's%20leading.

25 To trade publicly in the United States, Renaissance Capital. "Israeli Cultured Meat Tech Developer MeaTech 3D Sets Terms for $25 Million US IPO." Nasdaq, March 5, 2021. https://www.nasdaq.com/articles/israeli-cultured-meat-tech-developer-meatech-3d -sets-terms-for-%2425-million-us-ipo-2021-03.

25 Transferred its listing, "MeaTech 3D Initiates Process to Voluntarily Delist Its Ordinary Shares from the Tel Aviv Stock Exchange." MeaTech 3D Ltd.,May 3, 2021. https://www .prnewswire.com/il/news-releases/meatech-3d-initiates-process-to-voluntarily-delist -its-ordinary-shares-from-the-tel-aviv-stock-exchange-301282230.html.

25 To Nasdaq, "MeaTech 3D Ltd.. Reports First Half 2021 Financial Results and Recent Business Developments." MeaTech 3D Ltd., August 16, 2021.

25 One of the largest individual shareholders, "MeaTech 3D Ltd. Form 6-K Filed on Aug-09-2021." S&P CapitalIQ. Securities and Exchange Commission, August 9, 2021. https://www.capitaliq.com/CIQDotNet/Filings/DocumentRedirector.axd?document Id=1426622658&activeText=2846856&activityTypeId=4581&activity ObjectId=639249393.

25 Hopes to manufacture, MeaTech 3D Ltd. "Amendment No. 1 to Form F-1 MeaTech 3D Ltd." Securities and Exchange Commission, March 5, 2021. https://www.sec.gov /Archives/edgar/data/1828098/000117891321000919/zk2125695.htm.

26 Net worth, "Sheldon Lavin." *Forbes.* Accessed January 22, 2022. https://www.forbes.com /profile/sheldon-lavin/.

26 Third-generation Tyson patriarch, "John Tyson." *Forbes.* Accessed January 22, 2022. https://www.forbes.com/profile/john-tyson/.

26 Chicago's chicken titan, "Joseph Grendys." *Forbes.* Accessed January 22, 2022. https:// www.forbes.com/profile/joseph-grendys/.

26 Omaha beef packer, "Henry Davis." *Forbes.* Accessed January 22, 2022. https://www .forbes.com/profile/henry-davis/.

26 Batista brothers, "Joesley Batista." *Forbes.* Accessed January 22, 2022. https://www.forbes .com/profile/joesley-batista/.

26 Batista brothers, "Wesley Batista." *Forbes.* Accessed January 22, 2022. https://www.forbes .com/profile/wesley-batista/.

26 Acquired Smithfield through his Chinese conglomerate WH Group, "Wan Long." *Forbes.* Accessed January 22, 2022. https://www.forbes.com/profile/wan-long/.

26 Cable mogul turned bison rancher, "Ted Turner." *Forbes.* Accessed January 22, 2022. https://www.forbes.com/profile/ted-turner/.

26 Minneapolis *Star Tribune* owner "Glen Taylor." *Forbes.* Accessed January 22, 2022. https://www.forbes.com/profile/glen-taylor.

26 Concentrated animal feeding operation, Hribar, Carrie. "Understanding Concentrated Animal Feeding Operations and Their Impact on Communities" (2010). https://www .cdc.gov/nceh/ehs/docs/understanding_cafos_nalboh.pdf.

26 Subsidized, Gurian-Sherman, Doug. "Direct and Indirect Subsidies to Cafos." *CAFOs Uncovered: The Untold Costs of Confined Animal Feeding Operations.* Union of Con- cerned Scientists, 2008. http://www.jstor.org/stable/resrep00054.8.

26 Spend their last few months getting much bigger, Hribar, Carrie. Rep. "Understanding Concentrated Environmental Health Animal Feeding Operations and Their Impact on Communities." Accessed September 6, 2021. https://www.cdc.gov/nceh/ehs/docs /understanding_cafos_nalboh.pdf.

26 Often squeezed close together, Grandin, Temple. "Evaluation of the Welfare of Cattle Housed in Outdoor Feedlot Pens." *Veterinary and Animal Science* 1–2 (2016): 23–28. https://doi.org/10.1016/j.vas.2016.11.001.

26 A bunch of other animals, Grandin, Temple. "Welfare Problems in Cattle, Pigs, and Sheep that Persist Even Though Scientific Research Clearly Shows How to Prevent Them." *Animals: an open access journal from MDPI* vol. 8, 7 124 (July 20, 2018). doi:10.3390/ani8070124.

26 Small towns, "Understanding Concentrated Animal Feeding Operations and Their Impact on Communities." US Centers for Disease Control. Accessed January 22, 2022. https://www.cdc.gov/nceh/ehs/docs/understanding_cafos_nalboh.pdf.

26 Dotting Iowa, Nebraska, and Colorado, The Cattle Feeders Hall of Fame. Accessed January 31, 2022. http://www.cattlefeeders.org/inductees/.

26 Closer to where the corn was grown, Butcher, Allan, Nancy Easterling, Larry Frarey, Kristin Gill, and Heather Jones. "Livestock and the Environment: Emerging Issues for the Great Plains." *Conservation of Great Plains Ecosystems: Current Science, Future Options* (1995): 365–90. https://doi.org/10.1007/978-94-011-0439-5_22.

26 Forced other smaller plants to close, Ikerd, John. "The Corporatization of Animal Agriculture." University of Missouri, April 24, 2020. https://www.johnikerd.com/post /the-corporatization-of-animal-agriculture.

26 An acquisition frenzy, Domina, David A. and C. Robert Taylor. "Restoring Economic Health to Beef Markets: prepared for the Joint U.S. Department of Justice and U.S. Department of Agriculture/GIPSA Public Workshop on Competition Issues in the Livestock Industry." August 27, 2010.

27 Simultaneously forcing meat-packers to supersize their plants, Ward, Clement E. "A Review of Causes for and Consequences of Economic Concentration in the U.S. Meatpacking Industry." *Current: Agriculture, Food and Resource Issues, A Journal of the Canadian Agricultural Economics Society* (2002): 1–28. www.cafri.org.

27 Because they could drive away competition, Ikerd, John. "The Corporatization of Animal Agriculture." University of Missouri, April 24, 2020. https://www.johnikerd.com /post/the-corporatization-of-animal-agriculture.

28 American meat output then increased more than twofold, "Meat Production, 1961 to 2018." Our World in Data. Accessed January 31, 2022. https://ourworldindata.org /grapher/meat-production-tonnes?tab=chart&country=~USA.

28 Cheaper meat prices, Domina, David A. and C. Robert Taylor. "Restoring Economic Health to Beef Markets: prepared for the Joint U.S. Department of Justice and U.S. Department of Agriculture/GIPSA Public Workshop on Competition Issues in the Livestock Industry." August 27, 2010.

28 Major declines in feed costs, Becker, Geoffrey S. "Livestock Feed Costs: Concerns and Options" (2008). https://digital.library.unt.edu/ark:/67531/metacrs10763/m1/1/high _res_d/RS22908_2008Jun30.pdf.

28 From government subsidies, Howard, Philip. "Corporate Concentration in Global Meat Processing: The Role of Feed and Finance Subsidies." *Global Meat: Social and Environmental Consequences of the Expanding Meat Industry* (2019): 31–53. https://doi.org /10.7551/mitpress/11868.003.0011.

28 Remains crucial to JBS's strategy, Sorvino, Chloe, and André Nogueira. Interview with JBS USA CEO André Nogueira. Personal, November 19, 2020.

28 The Amazon rain forest has been clear-cut away, Mano, Ana. "Brazil's JBS Bought 301,000 Cattle from 'Irregular' Farms in the Amazon, Audit Finds." Reuters, October 7, 2021. https://www.reuters.com/business/sustainable-business/brazil-audit-finds-32 -jbs-cattle-amazon-state-irregular-farms-2021-10-07/.

28 The Amazon rain forest has been clear-cut away, Mano, Ana. "Update 1-Brazil Audit Finds 32% of JBS Cattle in Amazon State from 'Irregular' Farms." Reuters, October 7, 2021. https://www.agriculture.com/markets/newswire/update-1-brazil-audit-finds-32-of -jbs-cattle-in-amazon-state-from-irregular-farms.

28 The Amazon rain forest has been clear-cut away, Mano, Ana. "Brazil's JBS Bought 301,000 Cattle from 'Irregular' Farms in the Amazon, Audit Finds." Reuters, October 7, 2021. https://www.reuters.com/business/sustainable-business/brazil-audit-finds-32-jbs -cattle-amazon-state-irregular-farms-2021-10-07/.

28 "The reality of all sizes of plants," Sorvino, Chloe, and André Nogueira. Interview with JBS USA CEO André Nogueira. Personal, November 19, 2020.

29 Cattle feedlots had also declined, Bullard, Bill. "Under Siege: The U.S. Live Cattle Industry." *South Dakota Law Review* 58, no. 3 (2013): 560–610.

29 Some six thousand feedlots went out of business, Domina, David A. and C. Robert Taylor. "Restoring Economic Health to Beef Markets: prepared for the Joint U.S. Department of Justice and U.S. Department of Agriculture/GIPSA Public Workshop on Competition Issues in the Livestock Industry." August 27, 2010.

29 A capacity of more than a thousand cattle per day, Bullard, Bill. "Under Siege: The U.S. Live Cattle Industry." *South Dakota Law Review* 58, no. 3 (2013): 560–610.

29 Captured a record amount of the industry's profits, Aherin, Dustin. "The Case for Capacity: Can the US Beef Industry Expand Packing Capacity?" Rabobank Research: Food & Ag. Rabobank, October 2020. https://research.rabobank.com/far/en/sectors /animal-protein/the-case-for-capacity.html.

29 Estimated the operating income for packers, Sorvino, Chloe, and Dustin Aherin. Interview on cattle markets' need for added capacity with Rabobank's Dustin Aherin. Personal, January 13, 2021.

29 Beef has become a huge driver for the business, Sorvino, Chloe, and Peter Galbo. Interview with Bank of America's Tyson analyst Peter Galbo. Personal, January 29, 2021.

29 The dividend that Tyson pays out quarterly to its shareholders, "Tyson Dividend History." Nasdaq. Accessed January 22, 2022. https://www.nasdaq.com/market-activity/stocks/tsn /dividend-history.

29 Dividend yield, "Dividends at JBS." JBS. JBS S.A. , November 23, 2021. https://ri.jbs.com .br/en/shareholder-information/dividends/.

29 JBS spent, Tyson had enough cash to repurchase, "Addressing Concentration in the Meat-Processing Industry to Lower Food Prices for American Families." The White House, September 8, 2021. https://www.whitehouse.gov/briefing-room/blog/2021/09 /08/addressing-concentration-in-the-meat-processing-industry-to-lower-food-prices -for-american-families/.

30 Masked gunmen kidnapped purveyors, UPI. "Increased Price of Meat Brings A Second Kidnapping in Rome." *The New York Times*, June 17, 1976. https://www.nytimes .com/1976/06/17/archives/increased-price-of-meat-brings-a-second-kidnapping-in -rome.html.

30 Otis, John. "Venezuela's Deepening Crisis Triggers Mass Migration into Colombia." NPR, February 20, 2018. https://www.npr.org/sections/parallels/2018/02/20/587242391 /venezuelas-deepening-crisis-triggers-mass-migration-into-colombia.

30 Zuñiga, Mariana, and Cardiff Garcia. "Why Are Venezuelans Starving?" NPR, March 20, 2019. https://www.npr.org/sections/money/2019/03/20/705267066/why-are-venezuelans -starving.

30 " 'We Are like a Bomb': Food Riots Show Venezuela Crisis Has Gone beyond Politics." *The Guardian*, May 20, 2016. https://www.theguardian.com/world/2016/may/20/venezuela -breaking-point-food-shortages-protests-maduro.

30 Meat production has contracted, Otis, John. "Economic Crisis Rattles Venezuelan Cattle Ranchers." NPR, July 26, 2019. https://www.npr.org/2019/07/26/745536166/economic -crisis-rattles-venezuelan-cattle-ranchers.

30 Venezuelans who remain in the country can't afford to buy meat, "As Venezuelans Go Hungry, the Military Is Trafficking in Food." NPR, January 9, 2017. https://www.npr .org/sections/thesalt/2017/01/09/508986586/as-venezuelan-go-hungry-the-military-is -trafficking-in-food.

30 Protests, Greenberg, Doris. "Meat Price Relief Asked of Anderson in Plea by Mayor." *The New York Times*, June 14, 1947. https://timesmachine.nytimes.com/timesmachine/1947 /06/14/87538954.html?pageNumber=1.

30 Protests, Van Gelder, Lawrence. "Some Prices Cut by Meat Boycott." *The New York Times*, April 6, 1973. https://timesmachine.nytimes.com/timesmachine/1973/04/06/99139986. html?pageNumber=1+https%3A%2F%2Fwww.nytimes.com%2F1948%2F03%2F21% 2Farchives%2Fstrikers-score-rise-in-meat-prices-here.html.

30 Toppling of the Democratic party's sixteen-year control of Congress, Rude, Emelyn. "Election History: When Meat Determined American Politics." *Time*, August 30, 2016. https://time.com/4471656/the-beefsteak-election/.

30 Worker strikes, "Miners on Strike over Meat Dearth." The Associated Press. *The New York Times*, May 18, 1945. https://timesmachine.nytimes.com/timesmachine/1945/05 /18/305589882.html.

30 Tom Hayes, Sorvino, Chloe, and Tom Hayes. Interview with Tyson CEO Tom Hayes. Personal, November 2017.

31 Profit, a new record, Press Release. "Strong Fourth Quarter Propels Tyson Foods to Record Year." Tyson Investor Relations, 2017. https://ir.tyson.com/news/news-details/2017 /Strong-Fourth-Quarter-Propels-Tyson-Foods-to-Record-Year/default.aspx.

31 A low priority, "New Financial Modelling on Climate Shows Billions of Dollars at Risk

in the Meat Sector." FAIRR. Farm Animal Investment Risk and Return, March 12, 2020. https://www.fairr.org/article/new-financial-modelling-on-climate-shows-billions-of -dollars-at-risk-in-the-meat-sector/.

31 Business-as-usual model, "The Future of Food and Agriculture—Alternative Pathways to 2050." Supplementary material. Rome. 64 pp. Licence: CC BY-NC-SA 3.0 IGO. FAO, 2018. http://www.fao.org/3/CA1564EN/CA1564EN.pdf

31 Not likely to give up future gains willingly, "MEAT: OECD-FAO Agricultural Outlook 2020–2029." OECD. United Nations FAO, July 16, 2020. https://www.oecd-ilibrary.org /sites/29248f46-en/index.html?itemId=%2Fcontent%2Fcomponent%2F29248f46-en#s notes-d7e27170.

31 Sustainability-minded model, "The Future of Food and Agriculture—Alternative Path-ways to 2050." Supplementary material. Rome. 64 pp. Licence: CC BY-NC-SA 3.0 IGO. FAO, 2018. http://www.fao.org/3/CA1564EN/CA1564EN.pdf.

31 Harder to keep delivering on growth, McLeod, A., ed. "World Livestock, 2011: Livestock in Food Security" (2011).

31 Harder to keep delivering on growth, "Major Gains in Efficiency of Livestock Systems Needed." FAO, December 14, 2011. http://www.fao.org/news/story/en/item/116937 /icode/.

31 Climate change continues to test systems of production, Alexandratos, Nikos, and Jelle Bruinsma. "World Agriculture: Towards 2015/2030." *FAO Agricultural Development Economics Division*, June 2012. https://doi.org/10.4324/9781315083858.

31 2050 global production levels, "The Future of Food and Agriculture—Alternative Path-ways to 2050"(2018). https://www.fao.org/3/CA1564EN/CA1564EN.pdf.

31 "The future is bright," Sorvino, Chloe, and Andre Nogueira. Interview with JBS USA CEO André Nogueira. Personal, November 19, 2020.

32 Projections are still based on imperfect trends, Ritchie, Hannah, and Max Roser. "Meat and Dairy Production." Our World in Data, August 25, 2017. https://ourworldindata.org /meat-production.

32 China and Brazil are expected to lead the surge in meat consumption, Alexandratos, Nikos, and Jelle Bruinsma. Rep. "World Agriculture Towards 2030/2050: The 2012 Revision." United Nations FAO: Agricultural Development Economics Division, June 2012. http://www.fao.org/3/ap106e/ap106e.pdf. ESA Working Paper No. 12-03.

32 "One of the strongest determinants," Ritchie, Hannah, and Max Roser. "Meat and Dairy Production." Our World in Data, August 25, 2017. https://ourworldindata.org /meat-production.

32 Generations of traditions, Rammohan, A., Awofeso, N., & Robitaille, M. C. (2011). "Addressing Female Iron-Deficiency Anaemia in India: Is Vegetarianism the Major Obstacle?" *ISRN Public Health*, 2012.

32 Plan years in advance for increased consumption, "Major Gains in Efficiency of Live-stock Systems Needed." FAO (Press Release). United Nations FAO, December 14, 2011. http://www.fao.org/news/story/en/item/116937/icode/.

32 Meat consumption per capita in the United States, "Livestock, Dairy, and Poultry Out-look." USDA Economic Research Service, January 19, 2021. https://www.ers.usda.gov /webdocs/outlooks/100263/ldp-m-319.pdf?v=3825.2.

32 Beef has dropped by around half . . . poultry consumption has doubled, Bentley, Jeanine. "U.S. Per Capita Availability of Red Meat, Poultry, and Seafood on the Rise." USDA Economic Research Service, December 2, 2019. https://www.ers.usda.gov /amber-waves/2019/december/us-per-capita-availability-of-red-meat-poultry-and-sea food-on-the-rise/.

32 U.S. per capita beef consumption, Ritchie, Hannah, and Max Roser. "Meat and Dairy Production." Our World in Data, August 25, 2017. https://ourworldindata.org/meat -production.

32 The average American consumes, Ritchie, Hannah, and Max Roser. "Meat and Dairy Production." Our World in Data, August 25, 2017. https://ourworldindata.org/meat -production.

32 "The demand side of the equation," Apostolatos, Alessia, and Chloe Sorvino. Interview with HSBC's Alessia Apostolatos on JBS. Personal, March 19, 2021.

CHAPTER 3

33 The cattle trial of the century, one of the most widespread examples of manipulating the cash markets in beef history, *Pickett v. Tyson Fresh Meats, Inc.* (C.A. No. 96-A-1103-N, No. 04-12137-D, June 15, 2004).

33 The price of cattle on the cash market, McEowen, R. A., N. E. Harl, P. C. Carstensen, and S. E. Stokes. Brief of Amici Curiae in the United States Court of Appeals for the Eleventh Circuit. *Pickett v. Tyson Fresh Meats, Inc.* (C.A. No. 96-A-1103-N, No. 04-12137-D, 2006, June 15, 2004).

33 Thirty-five days in federal court, Carnes. "Pickett v. TYSON FRESH Meats, Inc." Legal research tools from Casetext, August 16, 2005. https://casetext.com/case/pickett-v -tyson-fresh-meats-inc.

33 After outbidding Smithfield, Barboza, David, and Andrew Ross Sorkin. "Tyson to Acquire IBP in $3.2 Billion Deal." *The New York Times*, January 2, 2001. https://www .nytimes.com/2001/01/02/us/tyson-to-acquire-ibp-in-3.2-billion-deal.html.

33 Depressed the prices paid for cattle between 1996 and 2004, a value of more than $2 billion, Sorvino, Chloe, and C. Robert Taylor. Interview about Pickett with C. Robert Taylor. Personal, November 10, 2021.

33 Benefited from lower prices overall, Taylor, C. R. "The Simple Arithmetic of Captive Supply," Organization for Competitive Markets Newsletter, September 2005.

33 Jury awarded the class-action group $1.28 billion, "Pickett v. Tyson Fresh Meats, Inc., 315 F. Supp. 2D 1172 (M.D. Ala. 2004)." Memorandum Opinion Strom, Senior District Judge. US District Court for the Middle District of Alabama - 315 F. Supp. 2d 1172 (M.D. Ala. 2004). Justia Law, April 23, 2004. https://law.justia.com/cases/federal/district-courts /FSupp2/315/1172/2404061/.

33 The victory was short-lived, Callicrate, Mike. "Pickett v. IBP: Judge Rules to Allow Testimony BY Plaintiff's Experts: Experts Will Testify in the Most Significant Cattle Industry Trial since the 1920's." January 17, 2011. https://nobull.mikecallicrate.com/2003/04/16 /pickett-v-ibp-judge-rules-to-allow-testimony-by-plaintiffs-experts-experts-will-testify -in-the-most-significant-cattle-industry-trial-since-the-1920s/.

34 Declined to hear, Peck, Clint. "U.S. Supreme Court Dumps Pickett v Tyson." Beef Magazine. Beef Magazine, April 6, 2006. https://www.beefmagazine.com/cowcalfweekly /US-Supreme-Court.

34 A run-in, Sorvino, Chloe, and Mike Callicrate. Interview with Mike Callicrate. Personal, January 18, 2021.

34 Owns a meat market in Colorado Springs, "Retail Store." Ranch Foods Direct. Accessed September 6, 2021. https://ranchfoodsdirect.com/retail-store/.

34 "About." Mike Callicrate, October 28, 2013. https://nobull.mikecallicrate.com/about/.

35 Founded at a kitchen table in Fort Wayne, Indiana, "Company History." Agri Stats, Inc. Accessed November 12, 2021. https://www.agristats.com/history.

35 Facilitating collusion, Sorvino, Chloe, and Peter Carstensen. Interview about Agri Stats with Peter Carstensen. Personal, August 10, 2021.

35 Anonymized data, WALMART INC.; WAL-MART STORES EAST, LP; WAL-MART STORES ARKANSAS, LLC; WAL-MART STORES TEXAS, LLC; WAL- MART LOUISIANA, LLC; SAM'S WEST, INC.; SAM'S EAST, INC., v. PILGRIM'S PRIDE CORPORATION; KOCH FOODS, INC.; JCG FOODS OF ALABAMA, LLC; JCG FOODS OF GEORGIA, LLC; KOCH MEAT CO., INC.; SANDERSON FARMS, INC.; SANDERSON FARMS, INC. (FOOD DIVISION); SANDERSON FARMS, INC. (PRODUCTION DIVISION); SANDERSON FARMS, INC. (PROCESSING DIVISION); HOUSE OF RAE-FORD FARMS, INC.; MAR- JAC POULTRY, INC.; PERDUE FARMS, INC.; PERDUE FOODS, LLC; WAYNE FARMS, LLC; O.K. FOODS, INC.; O.K. FARMS, INC.; O.K. INDUSTRIES, INC.; PECO FOODS, INC.; HARRISON POULTRY, INC.; FOSTER FARMS, LLC; FOSTER POULTRY FARMS; CLAXTON POULTRY FARMS, INC.; MOUNTAIRE FARMS, INC.; MOUNTAIRE FARMS, LLC; MOUNTAIRE FARMS OF DELAWARE, INC.; AMICK FARMS, LLC; CASE FOODS, INC.; CASE FARMS, LLC; CASE FARMS PROCESSING, INC.; and AGRI STATS, INC. (Case 5:19-cv-05100-TLB May 24, 2019).

36 The Department of Justice investigated the business, 385,000 pages of documents, IN RE BROILER CHICKEN ANTITRUST LITIGATION This document relates to: All

Actions MEMORANDUM IN SUPPORT OF DEFENDANT AGRI STATS, INC.'S MOTION FOR PROTECTIVE ORDER (Case: 1:16-cv-08637 Document #: 895 May 18, 2018).

36 The Packers and Stockyards Act of 1921, "Packers and Stockyards Act, 1921." Agricultural Marketing Service, Fair Trade Practices Program, Packers and Stockyards Division May 2021. USDA, May 2021. https://www.ams.usda.gov/sites/default/files/media /PSAct.pdf.

36 A proposal to amend the Packers and Stockyards Act, Sorvino, Chloe, and Peter Carstensen. Interview about Agri Stats with Peter Carstensen. Personal, August 10, 2021.

36 Best financial performance, IN RE BROILER CHICKEN ANTITRUST LITIGATION: MEMORANDUM IN SUPPORT OF DEFENDANT AGRI STATS, INC.'S MOTION FOR PROTECTIVE ORDER (Case: 1:16-cv-08637 Document # 895 May 18, 2018).

36 The target of lawsuits, IN RE BROILER CHICKEN ANTITRUST LITIGATION This document relates to: All Actions MEMORANDUM IN SUPPORT OF DEFENDANT AGRI STATS, INC.'S MOTION FOR PROTECTIVE ORDER (Case: 1:16-cv-08637 Document #: 895 May 18, 2018).

36 Sysco, *Sysco Corporation v. Tyson Foods, Inc. et al.* (CASE #: 1:18-cv-00700 January 30, 2018).

36 Walmart, WALMART INC.; WAL-MART STORES EAST, LP; WAL-MART STORES ARKANSAS, LLC; WAL-MART STORES TEXAS, LLC; WAL- MART LOUISIANA, LLC; SAM'S WEST, INC.; SAM'S EAST, INC., v. PILGRIM'S PRIDE CORPORA TION; KOCH FOODS, INC.; JCG FOODS OF ALABAMA, LLC; JCG FOODS OF GEORGIA, LLC; KOCH MEAT CO., INC.; SANDERSON FARMS, INC.; SANDERSON FARMS, INC. (FOOD DIVISION); SANDERSON FARMS, INC. (PRODUCTION DIVISION); SANDERSON FARMS, INC. (PROCESSING DIVISION); HOUSE OF RAEFORD FARMS, INC.; MAR- JAC POULTRY, INC.; PERDUE FARMS, INC.; PERDUE FOODS, LLC; WAYNE FARMS, LLC; O.K. FOODS, INC.; O.K. FARMS, INC.; O.K. INDUSTRIES, INC.; PECO FOODS, INC.; HARRISON POULTRY, INC.; FOSTER FARMS, LLC; FOSTER POULTRY FARMS; CLAXTON POULTRY FARMS, INC.; MOUNTAIRE FARMS, INC.; MOUNTAIRE FARMS, LLC; MOUNTAIRE FARMS OF DELAWARE, INC.; AMICK FARMS, LLC; CASE FOODS, INC.; CASE FARMS, LLC; CASE FARMS PROCESSING, INC.; and AGRI STATS, INC. (Case 5:19-cv-05100-TLB May 24, 2019).

36 Chick-Fil-A, *Chick-Fil-A, Inc., v. Agri Stats, Inc., et al.* (Case: 1:20-cv-07205 Document #: 1 December 4, 2020).

36 Target, *Target Corporation, v. Agri Stats, Inc., et al.* (Case: 1:20-cv-07191 Document #: 1 December 4, 2020).

36 White Castle, *White Castle Purchasing Co. v. Tyson Foods, Inc. et al.* (1:2020cv06179 October 16, 2020).

36 Aldi, *Aldi, Inc., v. Agri Stats, Inc., et al.* (Case: 1:20-cv-06904 Document #: 1 November 20, 2020).

36 Cracker Barrel, *Cracker Barrel Old Country Store, Inc. et al. v. Tyson Foods, Inc. et al.* (1:2020cv06201 October 19, 2020).

36 Wawa, *Wawa, Inc. v. Tyson Foods, Inc. et al.* (1:2020cv05259 September 4, 2020).

36 Kraft Heinz, KRAFT HEINZ FOODS COMPANY, vs. AMICK FARMS, LLC; TYSON FOODS, INC.; TYSON CHICKEN, INC.; TYSON BREEDERS, INC.; TYSON POULTRY, INC.; PILGRIM'S PRIDE CORPORATION; JCG FOODS OF ALABAMA, LLC; JCG FOODS OF GEORGIA, LLC; KOCH MEAT CO., INC.; KOCH FOODS, INC.; SANDERSON FARMS, INC.; SANDERSON FARMS, INC. (FOOD DIVISION); SANDERSON FARMS, INC. (PRODUCTION DIVISION); SANDERSON FARMS, INC. (PROCESSING DIVISION); HOUSE OF RAEFORD FARMS, INC.; MAR- JAC POULTRY, INC.; MAR-JAC POULTRY MS, LLC, MAR-JAC POULTRY AL, LLC, MAR-JAC POULTRY AL/MS, INC, MAR-JAC POULTRY, LLC, MAR-JAC HOLD-INGS, INC., PERDUE FARMS, INC.; PERDUE FOODS, LLC; WAYNE FARMS, LLC; GEORGE'S, INC.; GEORGE'S FARMS, INC.; SIMMONS FOODS, INC.; SIMMONS PREPARED FOODS, INC.; O.K. FOODS, INC.; O.K. FARMS, INC.; O.K. INDUS-TRIES, INC.; PECO FOODS, INC.; HARRISON POULTRY, INC.; FOSTER FARMS, LLC; FOSTER POULTRY FARMS; NORMAN W. FRIES, INC. d/b/a CLAXTON POULTRY FARMS, INC.; MOUNTAIRE FARMS, INC.; MOUNTAIRE FARMS, LLC;

MOUNTAIRE FARMS OF DELAWARE, INC.; CASE FOODS, INC.; CASE FARMS, LLC; CASE FARMS PROCESSING, INC.; and AGRI STATS, INC (Case: 1:20-cv-02278 Document #: 14 May 21, 2020).

36 Pleaded guilty and agreed to pay $107 million, "Pilgrim's Announces Agreement with DOJ Antitrust Division." Pilgrim's Pride Investor Relations. Pilgrim's Pride Corporation, October 14, 2020. https://ir.pilgrims.com/news-releases/news-release-details/pilgrims-announces-agreement-doj-antitrust-division.

36 Pilgrim's chicken sales, *United States of America v. Pilgrim's Pride Corporation* (Case 1:20-cr-00330-RM Document 58 Criminal Action No.: 20-cr-00330-RM February 23, 2021).

36 Agreed to set aside about $220 million, "Tyson Foods, Inc. 2021 Current Report 8-K." Tyson Foods Item 8.01 Other Events. SEC EDGARf, January 19, 2021. https://sec.report/Document/0000100493-21-000002/.

37 McDonald's, McDONALD'S CORPORATION, vs. PILGRIM'S PRIDE CORPORATION; KOCH FOODS, INC.; JCG FOODS OF ALABAMA, LLC; JCG FOODS OF GEORGIA, LLC; KOCH MEAT CO., INC.; SANDERSON FARMS, INC.; SANDERSON FARMS, INC. (FOOD DIVISION); SANDERSON FARMS, INC. (PRODUCTION DIVISION); SANDERSON FARMS, INC. (PROCESSING DIVISION); HOUSE OF RAEFORD FARMS, INC.; MAR-JAC POULTRY, INC.; PERDUE FARMS, INC.; PERDUE FOODS, LLC; WAYNE FARMS, LLC; SIMMONS FOODS, INC.; SIMMONS PREPARED FOODS, INC.; O.K. FOODS, INC.; O.K. FARMS, INC.; O.K. INDUSTRIES, INC.; HARRISON POULTRY, INC.; FOSTER FARMS, LLC; FOSTER POULTRY FARMS; NORMAN W. FRIES, INC. d/b/a CLAXTON POULTRY FARMS, INC.; MOUNTAIRE FARMS, INC.; MOUNTAIRE FARMS, LLC; MOUNTAIRE FARMS OF DELAWARE, INC.; CASE FOODS, INC.; CASE FARMS, LLC; CASE FARMS PROCESSING, INC.; and AGRI STATS, INC. (Case: 1:21-cv-04354 Document #: 1 August 16, 2021).

37 Supplied some data to the beef industry, *Kenneth Peterson and Richard Kimble, v. Agri Stats, Inc., Jbs Usa Food Company Holdings, Tyson Foods, Inc., Cargill, Inc., and National Beef Packing Company* (CASE 0:19-cv-01129-JRT-HB April 26, 2019).

38 JBS became the first to settle, In re Cattle and Beef Antitrust Litigation Class Action (Defendants: JBS USA Food Company Holdings, Tyson Foods, Inc., Cargill, Inc., and National Beef Packing Company) (CASE #: 0:20-cv-01319-JRT-HB June 6, 2020).

38 Devastated prices paid to ranchers, Grassley, Chuck. "Grassley Testimony at Judiciary Hearing on Beefing Up Competition in Meat Supply Chain." Prepared Statement by US Senator Chuck Grassley (R-Iowa) Ranking Member, Senate Judiciary Committee. Senate Judiciary Committee, US Congress, July 28, 2021. https://www.judiciary.senate.gov/grassley-at-judiciary-hearing-on-beefing-up-competition-in-meat-supply-chain.

38 Capturing more of the consumer dollar, "Price Spreads from Farm to Consumer." USDA ERS - Price Spreads from Farm to Consumer. Accessed September 7, 2021. https://www.ers.usda.gov/data-products/price-spreads-from-farm-to-consumer/price-spreads-from-farm-to-consumer/.

38 Plant closures, RANCHERS CATTLEMEN ACTION LEGAL FUND UNITED STOCK-GROWERS OF AMERICA; WEINREIS BROTHERS PARTNERSHIP; MINATARE FEEDLOT INC; CHARLES WEINREIS; ERIC NELSON; JAMES JENSEN d/b/a LUCKY 7 ANGUS; and RICHARD CHAMBERS AS TRUSTEE OF THE RICHARD C. CHAMBERS LIVING TRUST on Behalf of Themselves and All Other Similarly Situated, v. TYSON FOODS, INC.; TYSON FRESH MEATS, INC.; JBS S.A.; JBS USA FOOD COMPANY; SWIFT BEEF COMPANY; JBS PACKERLAND, INC.; CARGILL, INCORPORATED; CARGILL MEAT SOLUTIONS CORPORATION; MARFRIG GLOBAL FOODS S.A.; NATIONAL BEEF PACKING COMPANY, LLC; and JOHN DOES 1-10; (Case: 1:19-cv-02726 Document #: 1 April 23, 2019).

38 Plant in Cherokee, Iowa, Hardy, Kevin. "Held 'Hostage' by Tyson: An Iowa Town's Dilemma." *Des Moines Register*, July 16, 2016. https://www.desmoinesregister.com/story/money/business/2016/07/08/held-hostage-tyson-iowa-towns-dilemma/86449400/.

39 Refused to lease the plant to competition, Hardy, Kevin. "'No Hard Feelings': Tyson Finally Agrees to Leave Empty Iowa Factory as New Meat Processor Opens Shop." *The Des Moines Register*, September 19, 2018. https://www.desmoinesregister.com/story/money/business/2018/09/19/tyson-foods-cherokee-iowa-plant-iowa-food-group-moves-justin-robinson-pork-beef-chicken-processing/1356962002/.

39 Amended its deed with a requirement, confirm the amount harvested was not violating its agreement with Tyson at least every three months, Cherokee County, Iowa Recorder. Trustee Special Warranty Deed for former Tyson Plant, by Mark Murphy, Recorder. 1850, Cherokee, Iowa: County Recorder, 2018.

39 Artificially depressed by, RANCHERS CATTLEMEN ACTION LEGAL FUND UNITED STOCKGROWERS OF AMERICA; WEINREIS BROTHERS PARTNER-SHIP; MINATARE FEEDLOT INC; CHARLES WEINREIS; ERIC NELSON; JAMES JENSEN d/b/a LUCKY 7 ANGUS; and RICHARD CHAMBERS AS TRUSTEE OF THE RICHARD C. CHAMBERS LIVING TRUST on Behalf of Themselves and All Other Similarly Situated, v. TYSON FOODS, INC.; TYSON FRESH MEATS, INC.; JBS S.A.; JBS USA FOOD COMPANY; SWIFT BEEF COMPANY; JBS PACK-ERLAND, INC.; CARGILL, INCORPORATED; CARGILL MEAT SOLUTIONS CORPORATION; MARFRIG GLOBAL FOODS S.A.; NATIONAL BEEF PACKING COMPANY, LLC; and JOHN DOES 1-10; (Case: 1:19-cv-02726 Document #: 1 April 23, 2019).

39 Vukina, Tomislav, and Porametr Leegomonchai. "Oligopsony Power, Asset Specificity, and Hold-up: Evidence from the Broiler Industry." *American Journal of Agricultural Economics* 88, no. 3 (2006): 589–605. https://doi.org/10.1111/j.1467-8276 .2006.00881.x.

39 Mark Lauritsen, Sorvino, Chloe, and Mark Lauritsen. Interview with UFCW's Mark Lauritsen on meat-packer power. Personal, July 2020.

40 Represents over 250,000 meatpacking workers at companies like JBS, Tyson, and Cargill, "UFCW, Cargill, Announce COVID Vaccine Rollout for Meatpacking Workers across the Midwest Still at Risk of Virus Exposure on Frontlines of Pandemic." The United Food & Commercial Workers International Union, March 1, 2021. https://www.ufcw.org /press-releases/ufcw-cargill-announce-covid-vaccine-rollout-for-meatpacking-workers -across-the-midwest-still-at-risk-of-virus-exposure-on-frontlines-of-pandemic/.

40 A fundamental reason, "Packing and Processing." The United Food & Commercial Workers International Union, August 19, 2021. https://www.ufcw.org/who-we-represent /packing-and-processing/.

41 Entered the grocery industry, "Our History." Walmart Corporate. Accessed September 7, 2021. https://corporate.walmart.com/our-story/our-history#:~:text=1988,is%20 named%20chief%20executive%20officer.

41 Gobbled up, Matsa, David A. "Competition and Product Quality in the Supermarket Industry." The Quarterly Journal of Economics, Volume 126, Issue 3 (August 2011): 1539–91. https://doi.org/10.1093/qje/qjr031.

41 More than 50 percent of grocery sales in forty-three metropolitan areas, as well as more than 70 percent across thirty-eight regions, Stacy Mitchell. "Walmart's Monopolization of Local Grocery Markets." Institute for Local Self-Reliance, June 2019. https:// ilsr.org/wp-content/uploads/2019/06/Walmart_Grocery_Monopoly_Report-_final _for_site.pdf.

41 Annual grocery revenue is more than double that of its next-biggest competitor, "Buyer Power and Economic Discrimination in the Grocery Aisle: Kitchen Table Issues for American Consumers." The National Grocers Association, 2021.

41 Dominance wherever it expands, "Walmart to Create Angus Beef Supply Chain." Corporate Walmart Newsroom. Walmart, April 24, 2019. https://corporate.walmart.com /newsroom/2019/04/24/walmart-to-create-angus-beef-supply-chain.

41 The retailer's share rose the most, "Ending Walmart's Rural Stranglehold: A Plan to Rebuild Rural America's Food Supply Chain with the Revival of Rural Economies for Workers, Ranchers and Farmers by Reinvigorating the Marketplace and Reining in Walmart's Anti-Competitive Practices." UFCW, 2010.

41 Slaughterhouses retained, "Price Spreads from Farm to Consumer." USDA ERS. Accessed September 7, 2021. https://www.ers.usda.gov/data-products/price-spreads-from -farm-to-consumer/price-spreads-from-farm-to-consumer/.

41 While the retailer's share has swelled, so has the meat-packers', Sorvino, Chloe, and Ashley Murdie on behalf of USDA. Meat volume estimates / USDA Economic Research Service. Personal, April 22, 2021.

41 Unprecedented buying power over the packers, "Ending Walmart's Rural Strangle-

hold: A Plan to Rebuild Rural America's Food Supply Chain with the Revival of Rural Economies for Workers, Ranchers and Farmers by Reinvigorating the Marketplace and Reining in Walmart's Anti-Competitive Practices." UFCW, 2010.

42 Muscle to work in new ways, "Buyer Power and Economic Discrimination in the Grocery Aisle: Kitchen Table Issues for American Consumers." The National Grocers Association, 2021.

42 Hard for them to renegotiate, Apostolatos, Alessia, and Chloe Sorvino. Interview with HSBC's Alessia Apostolatos on JBS. Personal, March 19, 2021.

42 The online grocery market, Sorvino, Chloe, and Marc Wulfraat. Interview about meat, Walmart, and Amazon. Personal, April 20, 2021.

42 Coming from Walmart, Apostolatos, Alessia, and Chloe Sorvino. Interview with HSBC's Alessia Apostolatos on JBS. Personal, March 19, 2021.

42 Amazon's network of warehouses and distribution centers, Sorvino, Chloe, and Marc Wulfraat. Interview about meat, Walmart, and Amazon. Personal, April 20, 2021.

43 Cost data is essential for testing for market power, Sorvino, Chloe, and C. Robert Taylor. Interview on Pickett trial and monopsony issues with Auburn University's C. Robert Taylor. Personal, January 22, 2021.

43 Concentration of power, "Meat Packers as Grocers." The New York Times, August 17, 1919. https://www.nytimes.com/1919/08/17/archives/meat-packers-as-grocers-one-complaint-is-that-big-five-has-used.html.

44 Investigated the Big Five, Virtue, G. O. "The Meat-Packing Investigation." The Quarterly Journal of Economics 34, no. 4 (1920): 626. https://doi.org/10.2307/1885160.

44 Could have been said about modern times, Ward, Clement E. "A Review of Causes for and Consequences of Economic Concentration in the U.S. Meatpacking Industry." Current Agriculture, Food and Resource Issues 281 3 Marketing 2002 2002-01-06 CAFRI: Current Agriculture, Food and Resource Issues Journal Article10.22004/ag.econ.45696.

44 Could have been said about modern times, Ward, Clement E. "Economics of Competition in the U.S. Livestock Industry." 2010. https://www.justice.gov/atr/page/file/1075121/download.

44 Nothing was broken up then, Virtue, G. O. "The Meat-Packing Investigation." The Quarterly Journal of Economics 34, no. 4 (1920): 626. https://doi.org/10.2307/1885160.

44 Nothing was broken up then, Aduddell, Robert M., and Louis P. Cain. "The Consent Decree in the Meatpacking Industry, 1920–1956." Business History Review 55, no. 3 (1981): 359–78. https://doi.org/10.2307/3114129.

44 The eggs have been scrambled, Sorvino, Chloe, and Seth Bloom. Interview with antitrust lawyer Seth Bloom on breaking up meat-packers. Personal, February 18, 2021.

44 Introduced stricter rules for trying cases involving issues of monopoly and monopsony, "Senator Klobuchar Introduces Sweeping Bill to Promote Competition and Improve Antitrust Enforcement." Press Office of US Senator Amy Klobuchar, February 4, 2021. https://www.klobuchar.senate.gov/public/index.cfm/2021/2/senator-klobuchar-introduces-sweeping-bill-to-promote-competition-and-improve-antitrust-enforcement.

44 Scrutinizing the acquisition, Cargill, Sanderson Farms, and Continental Grain. "Cargill and Continental Grain Company to Acquire Sanderson Farms for $203 per Share in Cash and Create a Leading U.S. Poultry Company." Cargill, August 9, 2021. https://www.cargill.com/2021/cargill-and-continental-grain-company-to-acquire-sanderson-farms.

44 Third-largest poultry processor, "Sanderson Farms 10-K Filed 12/21/21 for the Period Ending 10/31/21." Securities and Exchange Commission, December 21, 2021. https://seekingalpha.com/filings/pdf/15438095.

44 Try to break up big meat-packers retroactively, Sorvino, Chloe, and Seth Bloom. Interview with antitrust lawyer Seth Bloom on breaking up meat-packers. Personal, February 18, 2021.

44 The FTC has power, Kreisle, Nicholas. "Price Effects from the Merger of Agricultural Fertilizer Manufacturers Agrium and Potashcorp." SSRN Electronic Journal (2020). https://doi.org/10.2139/ssrn.3664047.

44 Prefer the market to solve these problems, Sorvino, Chloe, and Peter Carstensen. Interview with Peter Carstensen on consolidation and the future of meat. Personal, March 22, 2021.

44 Failed to address these anticompetitive harms, American Beverage Licensees, Energy Marketers of America, National Association of Convenience Stores, National Association of Truck Stop Operators, National Community Pharmacists Association, National Grocers Association, Organic Farmers Association, and Protect Our Restaurants. Letter to Lina Khan, Federal Trade Commission. "Main Street Competition Coalition Letter To Lina Khan, Federal Trade Commission on Retail Consolidation." October 28, 2021.

45 A producer's union or a bargaining co-op, Sorvino, Chloe, and Peter Carstensen. Interview with Peter Cartensen on consolidation and the future of meat. Personal, March 22, 2021

45 One-sided new contract, McClendon, Trina. "Testimony of Trina McClendon, Trinity Poultry Farm, Magnolia, Mississippi, January 19, 2022 Hearing 'Reviving Competition, Part 5: Addressing the Effects of Economic Concentration on America's Food Supply'." January 19, 2022 Hearing "Reviving Competition, Part 5: Addressing the Effects of Economic Concentration on America's Food Supply." House Judiciary Committee Subcommittee on Antitrust, Commercial, and Administrative Law , January 19, 2022. https://docs.house.gov/meetings/JU/JU05/20220119/114345/HHRG-117-JU05-Wstate-McClendonT-20220119.pdf.

45 Buying groups, Carstensen, Peter C. "Buyer Cartels Versus Buying Groups: Legal Distinctions, Competitve Realities, and Antitrust Policy." *William & Mary Business Law Review* 1 (2010). https://scholarship.law.wm.edu/wmblr/vol1/iss1/2.

CHAPTER 4

46 Her home in Box Elder County, CARMENLITA BUSBY, v. SWIFT BEEF COMPANY, a foreign corporation, d/b/a SWIFT & COMPANY TRADE GROUP, d/b/a SWIFT GLOBAL USA, d/b/a E. A. MILLER, d/b/a JBS USA (Case 1:14-cv-00009-DB Document 2 February 3, 2014).

46 Beef slaughterhouse in Hyrum, "Hyrum JBS/Swift Workers Stand up for Voice on the Job." The United Food & Commercial Workers International Union. UFCW, November 20, 2008. https://www.ufcw.org/press-releases/hyrum-jbsswift-workers-stand-up-for-voice-on-the-job/.

46 A series of mishaps, CARMENLITA BUSBY, v. SWIFT BEEF COMPANY, a foreign corporation, d/b/a SWIFT & COMPANY TRADE GROUP, d/b/a SWIFT GLOBAL USA, d/b/a E. A. MILLER, d/b/a JBS USA (Case 1:14-cv-00009-DB Document 2 February 3, 2014).

46 Among the highest for occupational rates of injury, "When We're Dead and Buried, Our Bones Will Keep Hurting." Human Rights Watch, April 7, 2021. https://www.hrw.org/report/2019/09/04/when-were-dead-and-buried-our-bones-will-keep-hurting/workers-rights-under-threat.

47 Nearly twice as likely to get hurt and fifteen as likely to contract a job-related illness, "When We're Dead and Buried, Our Bones Will Keep Hurting." Human Rights Watch, April 7, 2021. https://www.hrw.org/report/2019/09/04/when-were-dead-and-buried-our-bones-will-keep-hurting/workers-rights-under-threat.

47 Among the most dangerous jobs in America, United States Department of Labor. "Meatpacking—Overview." Occupational Safety and Health Administration. Accessed November 12, 2021. https://www.osha.gov/meatpacking.

47 A high risk of developing serious, United States Department of Labor. "Meatpacking—Hazards and Solutions Occupational Safety and Health Administration. Accessed November 12, 2021. https://www.osha.gov/meatpacking/hazards-solutions.

47 Amputated after his smock sleeve got caught, Kupper, Amanda. Letter to JBS Foods, Inc, dba Swift Beef Company. "JBS Foods Letter From OSHA August 2021." U.S. Department of Labor Occupational Safety and Health Administration, August 17, 2021. https://aboutblaw.com/Zm6.

47 Falling into a vat containing toxic chemicals, Release Number 21-1742-DEN. "US Department of Labor cites JBS Foods Inc. for repeated safety failures after worker's death at Swift Beef's Colorado facility." Occupational Safety and Health Administration. US Department of Labor, September 28, 2021. https://www.osha.gov/news/newsreleases/region8/09282021.

47 Exposed daily to hazardous chemicals, an increased risk of lung cancer, bacterial in-

fections, United States Department of Labor. "Meatpacking—Hazards and Solutions." Occupational Safety and Health Administration. Accessed November 12, 2021. https://www.osha.gov/meatpacking/hazards-solutions.

47 Management ignored her complaints of retaliatory harassment, Another coworker accused her of faking injuries, CARMENLITA BUSBY, v. SWIFT BEEF COMPANY, a foreign corporation, d/b/a SWIFT & COMPANY TRADE GROUP, d/b/a SWIFT GLOBAL USA, d/b/a E. A. MILLER, d/b/a JBS USA (Case 1:14-cv-00009-DB Document 2 February 3, 2014).

48 Groped her, restrained her, and attempted to kiss her, CARMENLITA BUSBY, v. SWIFT BEEF COMPANY, a foreign corporation, d/b/a SWIFT & COMPANY TRADE GROUP, d/b/a SWIFT GLOBAL USA, d/b/a E. A. MILLER, d/b/a JBS USA (Case 1:14-cv-00009-DB Document 2 February 3, 2014).

48 A filthy vermin-infested room, CARMENLITA BUSBY, v. SWIFT BEEF COMPANY, a foreign corporation, d/b/a SWIFT & COMPANY TRADE GROUP, d/b/a SWIFT GLOBAL USA, d/b/a E. A. MILLER, d/b/a JBS USA (Case 1:14-cv-00009-DB Document 2 February 3, 2014).

48 Given the option to return to the gut bin or go home,CARMENLITA BUSBY, v. SWIFT BEEF COMPANY, a foreign corporation, d/b/a SWIFT & COMPANY TRADE GROUP, d/b/a SWIFT GLOBAL USA, d/b/a E. A. MILLER, d/b/a JBS USA (Case 1:14-cv-00009-DB Document 2 February 3, 2014).

48 Fired, CARMENLITA BUSBY, v. SWIFT BEEF COMPANY, a foreign corporation, d/b/a SWIFT & COMPANY TRADE GROUP, d/b/a SWIFT GLOBAL USA, d/b/a E. A. MILLER, d/b/a JBS USA (Case 1:14-cv-00009-DB Document 2 February 3, 2014).

49 A group of seventeen Black employees from a plant, JIMMY MITCHELL, LASHAUNDA § BOYD, CARLA BROOKS, ANTOINETTE § BROWN, CHRIS BURNS, RICHARD § HEARN, KRISTI KING, CHERYL LANE, § CRYSTAL LANE, CARLA MASON, § DONTRAIL MATHIS, MARANDA § MCCULLOCH, KEYON MITCHELL, § TIERNEY MITCHELL, DELORES § MORGAN, DOMINIQUE SMITH AND § MICKEY WISE, § §, § v. § § PILGRIM'S PRIDE CORPORATION § JBS USA HOLDINGS, INC. (Case 5:15-cv-00019-JRG Document 1 February 18, 2015).

49 Miscarried, JIMMY MITCHELL, LASHAUNDA § BOYD, CARLA BROOKS, ANTOINETTE § BROWN, CHRIS BURNS, RICHARD § HEARN, KRISTI KING, CHERYL LANE, § CRYSTAL LANE, CARLA MASON, § DONTRAIL MATHIS, MARANDA § MCCULLOCH, KEYON MITCHELL, § TIERNEY MITCHELL, DELORES § MORGAN, DOMINIQUE SMITH AND § MICKEY WISE, § §, § v. § § PILGRIM'S PRIDE CORPORATION § JBS USA HOLDINGS, INC. (Case 5:15-cv-00019-JRG Document 1 February 18, 2015).

50 A settlement was reached, JIMMY MITCHELL, LASHAUNDA § BOYD, CARLA BROOKS, ANTOINETTE § BROWN, CHRIS BURNS, RICHARD § HEARN, KRISTI KING, CHERYL LANE, § CRYSTAL LANE, CARLA MASON, § DONTRAIL MATHIS, MARANDA § MCCULLOCH, KEYON MITCHELL, § TIERNEY MITCHELL, DELORES § MORGAN, DOMINIQUE SMITH AND § MICKEY WISE, § §, § v. § § PILGRIM'S PRIDE CORPORATION § JBS USA HOLDINGS, INC. (Case 5:15-cv-00019-JRG Document 1 February 18, 2015).

50 A plant in Enterprise, Alabama, Robyn Place v. PILGRIM'S PRIDE, CORPORATION, and JAMIE HOLMES, (Case 1:11-cv-00606-WKW-SRW Document 1 July 28, 2011).

51 Her abuser was fired for stealing chickens, Robyn Place v. PILGRIM'S PRIDE, CORPORATION, and JAMIE HOLMES, (Case 1:11-cv-00606-WKW-SRW Document 1 July 28, 2011).

51 In violation of the Sherman Antitrust Act, *Jien, et al. v. Perdue Farms, Inc., et al.* (Case 1:19-cv-02521-SAG Document 384-2 October 16, 2020).

52 Webber, Meng, Sahl and Company, *Jien, et al. v. Perdue Farms, Inc., et al.* (Case 1:19-cv-02521-SAG Document 384-2 October 16, 2020).

53 A similar method to Agri Stats, "Jien, Et Al. V. Perdue Farms, Inc., Et Al." Cohen Milstein. Accessed September 7, 2021. https://www.cohenmilstein.com/case-study/jien-et-al-v-perdue-farms-inc-et-al.

54 Two years in a row, *Jien, et al. v. Perdue Farms, Inc., et al.* (Case 1:19-cv-02521-SAG Document 590 October 16, 2020).

54 Among America's most vulnerable, *Jien, et al. v. Perdue Farms, Inc., et al.* (Case 1:19-cv-

02521-SAG Document 590: THIRD AMENDED CONSOLIDATED COMPLAIN; February 22, 2022).

54 At the federal poverty level, "'When We're Dead and Buried, Our Bones Will Keep Hurting.'" Human Rights Watch, April 7, 2021. https://www.hrw.org/report/2019/09 /04/when-were-dead-and-buried-our-bones-will-keep-hurting/workers-rights-under -threat.

55 A period of record-setting industry profits, "Jien, Et Al. V. Perdue Farms, Inc., Et Al." Cohen Milstein. Accessed September 7, 2021. https://www.cohenmilstein.com/case-study /jien-et-al-v-perdue-farms-inc-et-al.

58 Undermines the ordinary functioning of the market, Sorvino, Chloe, and Peter Carstensen. Interview about Agri Stats with Peter Carstensen. Personal, August 10, 2021.

58 Filed for Chapter 11 bankruptcy, Chasan, Emily, and Bob Burgdorfer. "Pilgrim's Pride Exits Bankruptcy under JBS Deal." Reuters. Thomson Reuters, December 28, 2009. https://www.reuters.com/article/us-pilgrimspride/pilgrims-pride-exits-bankruptcy -under-jbs-deal-idUSTRE5BR2O820091228.

58 Swooped in to acquire a majority of shares, Spector, Mike, Lauren Etter, and Alastair Stewart. "Brazilian Giant JBS Agrees to Buy Pilgrim's Pride." The Wall Street Journal. Dow Jones & Company, September 18, 2009. https://www.wsj.com/articles /SB125310503697015705.

58 Strictly adhered to ranges deduced from Agri Stats, *Jien, et al. v. Perdue Farms, Inc., et al.* (Case 1:19-cv-02521-SAG Document 384-2 October 16, 2020).

58 Renegotiated its collective bargaining agreement, *Jien, et al. v. Perdue Farms, Inc., et al.* (Case 1:19-cv-02521-SAG Document 384-2 October 16, 2020).

59 Unions and their members were not able to obtain the Agri Stats reports themselves, "Jien, Et Al. V. Perdue Farms, Inc., Et Al." Cohen Milstein. Accessed September 7, 2021. https://www.cohenmilstein.com/case-study/jien-et-al-v-perdue-farms-inc-et-al.

59 Organized with UFCW, *Jien, et al. v. Perdue Farms, Inc., et al.* (Case 1:19-cv-02521-SAG Document 384-2 October 16, 2020).

59 Shave labor costs down, Sorvino, Chloe, and Mark Lauritsen. Interview with UFCW's Mark Lauritsen on meat-packer power. Personal, July 2020.

CHAPTER 5

60 He found President Michel Temer, Exhibit 8: Annexes to Plea Bargain Agreements. Annex 9: "Joesley Batista—Facts Directly Supported By Special Elements of Evidence— Michel Temer" as translated in *J&F Investimentos S.A., v. Baker & Mckenzie LLP, Trench Rossi E Watanabe Advogados* (No. 2018 CA 002569 M - The Superior Court for the District of Columbia Civil Division September 10, 2018). Declaration of Ana C. Reyes In Support of Baker & McKenzie LLP's Motion To Dismiss.

60 A key conspirator was about to be sentenced, Brooks, Brad. "Former Brazil House Speaker Cunha Sentenced to 15 Years for Graft." Reuters, March 30, 2017. https://www .reuters.com/article/us-brazil-corruption-cunha/former-brazil-house-speaker-cunha -sentenced-to-15-years-for-graft-idUSKBN1712DX.

60 Potential risk of whistleblowing, Exhibit 8: Annexes to Plea Bargain Agreements. Annex 9: "Joesley Batista—Facts Directly Supported By Special Elements of Evidence—Michel Temer" as translated in J&F Investimentos S.A., v. Baker & Mckenzie LLP, Trench Rossi E Watanabe Advogados (No. 2018 CA 002569 M - The Superior Court for the District of Columbia Civil Division September 10, 2018). Declaration of Ana C. Reyes In Support of Baker & McKenzie LLP's Motion To Dismiss.

61 Taking care, important, *The Edge of Democracy*. Brazil: Netflix, 2019. https://www.imdb .com/title/tt6016744/.

61 Eduardo Cunha and his fixer, Exhibit 8: Annexes to Plea Bargain Agreements. Annex 9: "Joesley Batista – Facts Directly Supported By Special Elements of Evidence – Michel Temer" as translated in J&F Investimentos S.A., v. Baker & Mckenzie LLP, Trench Rossi E Watanabe Advogados (No. 2018 CA 002569 M - The Superior Court for the District of Columbia Civil Division September 10, 2018). Declaration of Ana C. Reyes In Support of Baker & McKenzie LLP's Motion To Dismiss.

61 Favorably reform meat export regulations, Exhibit 8: Annexes to Plea Bargain Agreements. Annex 5: "Joesley Batista – Eduardo Cunha and Lucio Funaro / Ministry of Ag-

riculture" as translated in *J&F Investimentos S.A., v. Baker & Mckenzie LLP, Trench Rossi E Watanabe Advogados* (No. 2018 CA 002569 M - The Superior Court for the District of Columbia Civil Division September 10, 2018). Declaration of Ana C. Reyes In Support of Baker & McKenzie LLP's Motion to Dismiss.

61 Transferring ownership of an Agusta helicopter that Joesley had owned, Exhibit 8: Annexes to Plea Bargain Agreements. Annex 6: "The Lucio Funaro Current Account" as translated in *J&F Investimentos S.A., v. Baker & Mckenzie LLP, Trench Rossi E Watanabe Advogados* (No. 2018 CA 002569 M - The Superior Court for the District of Columbia Civil Division September 10, 2018). Declaration of Ana C. Reyes In Support of Baker & McKenzie LLP's Motion To Dismiss.

61 Negotiate their own plea agreements, "J&F Investimentos S.A. Pleads Guilty and Agrees to Pay over $256 Million to Resolve Criminal Foreign Bribery Case." The United States Department of Justice, October 15, 2020. https://www.justice.gov/opa/pr/jf-investimentos -sa-pleads-guilty-and-agrees-pay-over-256-million-resolve-criminal-foreign.

61 Truthful cooperation to spare them from jail time, Bautzer, Tatiana, and Joel Schectman. "JBS Brothers Test Dealmaking Skills in Brazil Plea Deal Showdown." Reuters, May 19, 2017. https://www.reuters.com/article/us-brazil-corruption-jbs/jbs-brothers-test -dealmaking-skills-in-brazil-plea-deal-showdown-idUSKCN18F2LQ.

61 Was not disclosed to shareholders, Securities and Exchange Commission. "In the Matter of J&F INVESTIMENTOS, S.A. JBS, S.A. JOESLEY BATISTA WESLEY BATISTA: ORDER INSTITUTING CEASE-ANDDESIST PROCEEDINGS PURSUANT TO SECTION 21C OF THE SECURITIES EXCHANGE ACT OF 1934, MAKING FINDINGS, AND IMPOSING A CEASEAND-DESIST ORDER." Securities Exchange Act of 1934 Release No. 90170 / October 14, 2020 Accounting And Auditing Enforcement Release No. 4189 / October 14, 2020 Administrative Proceeding File No. 3-20124. Securities And Exchange Commission, October 14, 2020. https://www.sec.gov/litigation/admin /2020/34-90170.pdf.

61 Securities and Exchange Commission. "In the Matter of J&F INVESTIMENTOS, S.A. JBS, S.A. JOESLEY BATISTA WESLEY BATISTA: ORDER INSTITUTING CEASE-AND-DESIST PROCEEDINGS PURSUANT TO SECTION 21C OF THE SECURITIES EXCHANGE ACT OF 1934, MAKING FINDINGS, AND IMPOSING A CEASE-AND-DESIST ORDER." Securities Exchange Act of 1934 Release No. 90170 / October 14, 2020 Accounting and Auditing Enforcement Release No. 4189 / October 14, 2020 Administrative Proceeding File No. 3-20124. Securities and Exchange Commission, October 14, 2020. https://www.sec.gov/litigation/admin/2020/34-90170.pdf.

62 Three dozen other incidents of bribery, Exhibit 8: Annexes to Plea Bargain Agreements. Annex 1 to 38 as translated in J&F Investimentos S.A., v. Baker & Mckenzie LLP, Trench Rossi E Watanabe Advogados (No. 2018 CA 002569 M - The Superior Court for the District of Columbia Civil Division September 10, 2018). Declaration of Ana C. Reyes In Support of Baker & McKenzie LLP's Motion To Dismiss.

62 Letter to Chloe Sorvino and Alessia Apostalatos. "RE: Talking JBS? // Some Follow Ups." April 21, 2021.

62 Public listing remains, Sorvino, Chloe. "With a Banner 2020 behind It, Meat Giant JBS Sets Sights on U.S. IPO." Forbes. Forbes Media, March 25, 2021. https://www.forbes .com/sites/chloesorvino/2021/03/25/with-a-banner-2020-behind-it-meat-giant-jbs -sets-sights-on-us-ipo/.

62 Recording was leaked, Jardim, Lauro. "Dono Da Jbs Grava Temer Dando Aval Para Compra De Silêncio De Cunha." O Globo, May 23, 2017. https://oglobo.globo.com/politica /dono-da-jbs-grava-temer-dando-aval-para-compra-de-silencio-de-cunha-21353935.

62 First attempt, "Brazil: Brazil JBS Raises $1.2 Billion From Debenture Issue," TendersInfo, February 2, 2010. https://www.ft.com/content/99df2c89-6c66-39ee-a007-e342ea9cb78e.

62 We wouldn't have made the deal, Depoimento De Joesley Batista Sobre o BNDES e Guido Mantega. YouTube. Ministério Publico, 2017. https://www.youtube.com/watch?v= DHO1grczWCI. Joesley Batista is interviewed by Ministério Publico representatives Eduardo Pelela and Sérgio Bruno Fernandes at the headquarters for Brazil's Attorney General. Translated for Chloe Sorvino by Marco de Souza.

63 Meat was booming across Brazil, Blankfeld, Karen. "All You Can Eat." Forbes, May 9, 2011. https://www.forbes.com/sites/kerenblankfeld/2011/04/21/jbs-the-story-behind-the -worlds-biggest-meat-producer/?sh=494713477e82.

64 Bribed his way in, *Depoimento De Joesley Batista Sobre o BNDES e Guido Mantega*. YouTube. Ministério Publico, 2017. https://www.youtube.com/watch?v=DHO1grczWCI. Joesley Batista is interviewed by Ministério Publico representatives Eduardo Pelela and Sérgio Bruno Fernandes at the headquarters for Brazil's Attorney General. Translated for Chloe Sorvino by Marco de Souza.

64 Securing a meeting with Guido Mantega, Exhibit 8: Annexes to Plea Bargain Agreements. Annex 1: "Joesley Batista–BNDES" as translated in J&F Investimentos S.A., v. Baker & Mckenzie LLP, Trench Rossi E Watanabe Advogados (No. 2018 CA 002569 M - The Superior Court for the District of Columbia Civil Division September 10, 2018). Declaration of Ana C. Reyes In Support of Baker & McKenzie LLP's Motion To Dismiss.

64 Exhibit 8: Annexes to Plea Bargain Agreements. Annex 1: "Joesley Batista–BNDES" as translated in J&F Investimentos S.A., v. Baker & Mckenzie LLP, Trench Rossi E Watanabe Advogados (No. 2018 CA 002569 M - The Superior Court for the District of Columbia Civil Division September 10, 2018). Declaration of Ana C. Reyes In Support of Baker & McKenzie LLP's Motion To Dismiss.

64 BNDES first wrote the company, "Friboi E Electrolux Têm APOIO Do Bndes Para AMPLIAR Empregos e PRODUÇÃO." BNDES. Accessed September 7, 2021. https://www.bndes.gov.br/wps/portal/site/home/imprensa/noticias/conteudo/20041215_not947.

64 Operating since 1952, "The BNDES." BNDES. Accessed September 7, 2021. https://www.bndes.gov.br/SiteBNDES/bndes/bndes_en/Institucional/The_BNDES/.

64 How to leverage BNDES money, "Corporate Profile." JBS, June 26, 2020. https://ri.jbs.com.br/en/jbs/corporate-profile/.

64 The pitch, *Depoimento De Joesley Batista Sobre o BNDES e Guido Mantega*. YouTube. Ministério Publico, 2017. https://www.youtube.com/watch?v=DHO1grczWCI. Joesley Batista is interviewed by Ministério Publico representatives Eduardo Pelela and Sérgio Bruno Fernandes at the headquarters for Brazil's Attorney General. Translated for Chloe Sorvino by Marco de Souza.

64 That's when the journey to internationalize JBS started, *Depoimento De Joesley Batista Sobre o BNDES e Guido Mantega*. YouTube. Ministério Publico, 2017. https://www.youtube.com/watch?v=DHO1grczWCI. Joesley Batista is interviewed by Ministério Publico representatives Eduardo Pelela and Sérgio Bruno Fernandes at the headquarters for Brazil's Attorney General. Translated for Chloe Sorvino by Marco de Souza.

65 Purchased Argentina's largest beef producer and exporter, Barreto, Elzio. "Brazil's JBS-FRIBOI to Buy Swift for $225 Mln." Reuters, May 29, 2007. https://www.reuters.com/article/us-swift-friboi/brazils-jbs-friboi-to-buy-swift-for-225-mln-idUSN2930167420070529.

65 BNDES ended up lending, Exhibit 8: Annexes to Plea Bargain Agreements. Annex 1: "Joesley Batista–BNDES" as translated in J&F Investimentos S.A., v. Baker & Mckenzie LLP, Trench Rossi E Watanabe Advogados (No. 2018 CA 002569 M - The Superior Court for the District of Columbia Civil Division September 10, 2018). Declaration of Ana C. Reyes In Support of Baker & McKenzie LLP's Motion To Dismiss.

65 Mantega and his fixer earned a 4 percent commission, J&F Investimentos S.A., v. Baker & Mckenzie LLP, Trench Rossi E Watanabe Advogados (No. 2018 CA 002569 M - The Superior Court for the District of Columbia Civil Division September 10, 2018). Declaration of Ana C. Reyes In Support of Baker & McKenzie LLP's Motion To Dismiss.

65 Got a better offer from banks, *Depoimento De Joesley Batista Sobre o BNDES e Guido Mantega. YouTube.* Ministério Publico, 2017. https://www.youtube.com/watch?v=DHO1grczWCI. Joesley Batista is interviewed by Ministério Publico representatives Eduardo Pelela and Sérgio Bruno Fernandes at the headquarters for Brazil's Attorney General. Translated for Chloe Sorvino by Marco de Souza.

65 We didn't have enough money to make the purchase, *Depoimento De Joesley Batista Sobre o BNDES e Guido Mantega*. YouTube. Ministério Publico, 2017. https://www.youtube.com/watch?v=DHO1grczWCI. Joesley Batista is interviewed by Ministério Publico representatives Eduardo Pelela and Sérgio Bruno Fernandes at the headquarters for Brazil's Attorney General. Translated for Chloe Sorvino by Marco de Souza.

65 Closing would be contingent on whether BNDES money came through, *Depoimento De Joesley Batista Sobre o BNDES e Guido Mantega*. YouTube. Ministério Publico, 2017. https://www.youtube.com/watch?v=DHO1grczWCI. Joesley Batista is interviewed by Ministério Publico representatives Eduardo Pelela and Sérgio Bruno Fernandes at the

headquarters for Brazil's Attorney General. Translated for Chloe Sorvino by Marco de Souza.

66 Pushed it through, Exhibit 8: Annexes to Plea Bargain Agreements. Annex 1: "Joesley Batista – BNDES" as translated in J&F Investimentos S.A., v. Baker & Mckenzie LLP, Trench Rossi E Watanabe Advogados (No. 2018 CA 002569 M - The Superior Court for the District of Columbia Civil Division September 10, 2018). Declaration of Ana C. Reyes In Support of Baker & McKenzie LLP's Motion To Dismiss.

66 That's when the operation took off, *Depoimento De Joesley Batista Sobre o BNDES e Guido Mantega*. YouTube. Ministério Publico, 2017. https://www.youtube.com/watch?v=DHO1grczWCI. Joesley Batista is interviewed by Ministério Publico representatives Eduardo Pelela and Sérgio Bruno Fernandes at the headquarters for Brazil's Attorney General. Translated for Chloe Sorvino by Marco de Souza.

66 The worst-performing company in the American beef market, Swift, twelve plants, could slaughter twenty-three thousand cattle a day, Blankfeld, Karen. "All You Can Eat." *Forbes*, May 9, 2011. https://www.forbes.com/sites/kerenblankfeld/2011/04/21/jbs-the-story-behind-the-worlds-biggest-meat-producer/?sh=494713477e82.

66 Paid $225 million in cash and assumed $1.2 billion in debt, "CONCENTRATION IN AGRICULTURE AND AN EXAMINATION OF THE JBS/SWIFT ACQUISITIONS HEARING BEFORE THE SUBCOMMITTEE ON ANTITRUST, COMPETITION POLICY AND CONSUMER RIGHTS OF THE COMMITTEE ON THE JUDICIARY UNITED STATES SENATE ONE HUNDRED TENTH CONGRESS SECOND SESSION." May 7, 2008. https://ia802905.us.archive.org/27/items/gov.gpo.fdsys.CHRG-110shrg45064/CHRG-110shrg45064.pdf.

66 At least $362 million of BNDES funds, Tribunal de Contas da Uniao (T.C.U.) (Federal Court of Accounts), TC 034.930/2015-9, April 26, 2017 (Brazil). https://securities.stanford.edu/filings-documents/1060/JS00_01/2018829_r01c_17CV04019.pdf.

66 Wesley interviewed three hundred Swift workers, Blankfeld, Karen. "All You Can Eat." *Forbes*, May 9, 2011. https://www.forbes.com/sites/kerenblankfeld/2011/04/21/jbs-the-story-behind-the-worlds-biggest-meat-producer.

67 In a joint operation with two Brazilian pension funds, "Shareholder Profile: Batista Family Fights to Stay atop JBS as Scandals Deepen." Debtwire, an Acuris Company, March 28, 2018. https://s3.eu-west-2.amazonaws.com/acuris-live/Debtwire%20Shareholder%20Profile%20Batista%20family%20fights%20to%20stay%20atop%20JBS%20as%20scandals%20deepen%20(JBS%20SA).pdf.

67 Added about 1.5 billion pounds of fresh beef processing to JBS USA operations, the largest cattle feedlot operation in America, "Smithfield Foods and JBS S.A. Announce Agreement to Sell Beef Processing and Cattle Feeding Operations To JBS." Smithfield: EX-99.1 4 dex991.htm Press Release. Securities and Exchange Commission, March 5, 2008. https://www.sec.gov/Archives/edgar/data/91388/000119312508047703/dex991.htm.

67 Intended purchase price, "Complaint." The United States Department of Justice, June 30, 2015. https://www.justice.gov/atr/case-document/complaint-137.

67 One of the few modern times when a beef packer's size and scope have been challenged so directly, "CONCENTRATION in Agriculture and an Examination of THE JBS/SWIFT ACQUISITIONS: Committee on Judiciary." Internet Archive. Government Publishing Office, May 7, 2008. https://archive.org/details/gov.gpo.fdsys.CHRG-110shrg45064.

67 Question the connection with BNDES, "CONCENTRATION IN AGRICULTURE AND AN EXAMINATION OF THE JBS/SWIFT ACQUISITIONS HEARING BEFORE THE SUBCOMMITTEE ON ANTITRUST, COMPETITION POLICY AND CONSUMER RIGHTS OF THE COMMITTEE ON THE JUDICIARY UNITED STATES SENATE ONE HUNDRED TENTH CONGRESS SECOND SESSION." May 7, 2008. https://ia802905.us.archive.org/27/items/gov.gpo.fdsys.CHRG-110shrg45064/CHRG-110shrg45064.pdf.

68 Batista replied, "CONCENTRATION IN AGRICULTURE AND AN EXAMINATION OF THE JBS/SWIFT ACQUISITIONS HEARING BEFORE THE SUBCOMMITTEE ON ANTITRUST, COMPETITION POLICY AND CONSUMER RIGHTS OF THE COMMITTEE ON THE JUDICIARY UNITED STATES SENATE ONE HUNDRED TENTH CONGRESS SECOND SESSION." May 7, 2008. https://ia802905.us.archive.org/27/items/gov.gpo.fdsys.CHRG-110shrg45064/CHRG-110shrg45064.pdf.

68 Officially filing an antitrust lawsuit, "Justice Department Files Lawsuit to Stop JBS S.A.

from ACQUIRING NATIONAL Beef Packing Co." Justice Department, October 20, 2008. https://www.justice.gov/archive/atr/public/press_releases/2008/238382.htm.

68 Substantially increase the incentive, "Complaint: U.S. and Plaintiff States v. JBS S.A. and National Beef Packing Company, LLC." File 08CV5992. The United States Department of Justice, October 20, 2008. https://www.justice.gov/atr/case-document/complaint-137.

69 An opportunity to buy chicken breasts, *Depoimento De Joesley Batista Sobre o BNDES e Guido Mantega.* YouTube. Ministério Publico, 2017. https://www.youtube.com/watch ?v=DHO1grczWCI. Joesley Batista is interviewed by Ministério Publico representatives Eduardo Pelela and Sérgio Bruno Fernandes at the headquarters for Brazil's Attorney General. Translated for Chloe Sorvino by Marco de Souza.

69 Another major deal made possible by BNDES's funding, Securities and Exchange Commission. "In the Matter of J&F INVESTIMENTOS, S.A. JBS, S.A. JOESLEY BATISTA WESLEY BATISTA: ORDER INSTITUTING CEASE-ANDDESIST PROCEEDINGS PURSUANT TO SECTION 21C OF THE SECURITIES EXCHANGE ACT OF 1934, MAKING FINDINGS, AND IMPOSING A CEASEAND-DESIST ORDER." Securities Exchange Act of 1934 Release No. 90170 / October 14, 2020 Accounting and Auditing Enforcement Release No. 4189 / October 14, 2020 Administrative Proceeding File No. 3-20124. Securities and Exchange Commission, October 14, 2020. https://www.sec.gov /litigation/admin/2020/34-90170.pdf.

69 A milestone, "A BNDESPAR Subscreverá Até US$ 2 Bilhões De Debêntures DA JBS." BNDES. The National Bank for Economic and Social Development, December 22, 2009.   https://www.bndes.gov.br/wps/portal/site/home/imprensa/noticias/conteudo /20091223_jbs.

69 Deposited into a US bank account, $55 million, "J&F Investimentos S.A. Pleads Guilty and Agrees to Pay over $256 Million to Resolve Criminal Foreign Bribery Case." The United States Department of Justice, October 15, 2020. https://www.justice.gov/opa/pr /jf-investimentos-sa-pleads-guilty-and-agrees-pay-over-256-million-resolve-criminal -foreign.

69 Debt load quickly fell, "SECURITIES EXCHANGE ACT OF 1934 RELEASE No. 90170," October 14, 2020. https://www.sec.gov/litigation/admin/2020/34-90170.pdf.

69 Total JBS S.A. revenues came from the United States, 70 percent, Blankfeld, Karen. "All You Can Eat." *Forbes*, May 9, 2011. https://www.forbes.com/sites/kerenblankfeld/2011 /04/21/jbs-the-story-behind-the-worlds-biggest-meat-producer/?sh=494713477e82.

69 Wesley Batista, CEO of JBS and chairman of the board for Pilgrim's, Joesley Batista, CEO of holding company J&F and a member of Pilgrim's board, Securities and Exchange Commission. "In the Matter of J&F INVESTIMENTOS, S.A. JBS, S.A. JOESLEY BATISTA WESLEY BATISTA: ORDER INSTITUTING CEASE-ANDDESIST PROCEEDINGS PURSUANT TO SECTION 21C OF THE SECURITIES EXCHANGE ACT OF 1934, MAKING FINDINGS, AND IMPOSING A CEASEAND-DESIST ORDER." Securities Exchange Act of 1934 Release No. 90170 / October 14, 2020 Accounting and Auditing Enforcement Release No. 4189 / October 14, 2020 Administrative Proceeding File No. 3-20124. Securities and Exchange Commission, October 14, 2020. https://www .sec.gov/litigation/admin/2020/34-90170.pdf.

69 One day if I need it I'll tell you, *Depoimento De Joesley Batista Sobre o BNDES e Guido Mantega*. YouTube. Ministério Publico, 2017. https://www.youtube.com/watch?v= DHO1grczWCI. Joesley Batista is interviewed by Ministério Publico representatives Eduardo Pelela and Sérgio Bruno Fernandes at the headquarters for Brazil's Attorney General. Translated for Chloe Sorvino by Marco de Souza.

69 Whenever Mantega was owed money, J&F Investimentos S.A., v. Baker & Mckenzie LLP, Trench Rossi E Watanabe Advogados (No. 2018 CA 002569 M - The Superior Court for the District of Columbia Civil Division September 10, 2018). Declaration of Ana C. Reyes in Support of Baker & McKenzie LLP's Motion to Dismiss.

70 Who the ultimate beneficiaries were, *Depoimento De Joesley Batista Sobre o BNDES e Guido Mantega. YouTube.* Ministério Publico, 2017. https://www.youtube.com/watch ?v=DHO1grczWCI. Joesley Batista is interviewed by Ministério Publico representatives Eduardo Pelela and Sérgio Bruno Fernandes at the headquarters for Brazil's Attorney General. Translated for Chloe Sorvino by Marco de Souza.

70 Need you to make these donations, *Depoimento De Joesley Batista Sobre o BNDES e Guido Mantega. YouTube.* Ministério Publico, 2017. https://www.youtube.com/watch

?v=DHO1grczWCI. Joesley Batista is interviewed by Ministério Publico representatives Eduardo Pelela and Sérgio Bruno Fernandes at the headquarters for Brazil's Attorney General. Translated for Chloe Sorvino by Marco de Souza.

71 Only with a blank stare, Exhibit 8: Annexes to Plea Bargain Agreements. Annex 1: "Joesley Batista–BNDES" as translated in J&F Investimentos S. A., v. Baker & Mckenzie LLP, Trench Rossi E Watanabe Advogados (No. 2018 CA 002569 M - The Superior Court for the District of Columbia Civil Division September 10, 2018). Declaration of Ana C. Reyes In Support of Baker & McKenzie LLP's Motion to Dismiss.

71 Bombarded with demands, Fernando Pimentel, Exhibit 8: Annexes to Plea Bargain Agreements. Annex 1: "Joesley Batista–BNDES" as translated in J&F Investimentos S.A., v. Baker & Mckenzie LLP, Trench Rossi E Watanabe Advogados (No. 2018 CA 002569 M - The Superior Court for the District of Columbia Civil Division September 10, 2018). Declaration of Ana C. Reyes In Support of Baker & McKenzie LLP's Motion to Dismiss.

71 Asked Joesley to find Pimentel, Exhibit 8: Annexes to Plea Bargain Agreements. Annex 1: "Joesley Batista–BNDES" as translated in J&F Investimentos S.A., v. Baker & Mckenzie LLP, Trench Rossi E Watanabe Advogados (No. 2018 CA 002569 M - The Superior Court for the District of Columbia Civil Division September 10, 2018). Declaration of Ana C. Reyes In Support of Baker & McKenzie LLP's Motion to Dismiss.

71 Running out, *Depoimento De Joesley Batista Sobre o BNDES e Guido Mantega. YouTube.* Ministério Publico, 2017. https://www.youtube.com/watch?v=DHO1grczWCI. Joesley Batista is interviewed by Ministério Publico representatives Eduardo Pelela and Sérgio Bruno Fernandes at the headquarters for Brazil's Attorney General. Translated for Chloe Sorvino by Marco de Souza.

72 Stadium contract, Exhibit 8: Annexes to Plea Bargain Agreements. Annex 1: "Joesley Batista – BNDES" as translated in J&F Investimentos S.A., v. Baker & Mckenzie LLP, Trench Rossi E Watanabe Advogados (No. 2018 CA 002569 M - The Superior Court for the District of Columbia Civil Division September 10, 2018). Declaration of Ana C. Reyes In Support of Baker & McKenzie LLP's Motion To Dismiss.

72 Someone we'd kill before he makes a plea bargain, *The Edge of Democracy.* Brazil: Netflix, 2019. https://www.imdb.com/title/tt6016744/.

72 A series of shell companies, maintained accounts there, "SECURITIES EXCHANGE ACT OF 1934 Release No. 90170," October 14, 2020. https://www.sec.gov/litigation/admin/2020/34-90170.pdf.

73 A $1.5 million Manhattan apartment, Securities and Exchange Commission. "In the Matter of J&F INVESTIMENTOS, S.A. JBS, S.A. JOESLEY BATISTA WESLEY BATISTA: ORDER INSTITUTING CEASE-ANDDESIST PROCEEDINGS PURSUANT TO SECTION 21C OF THE SECURITIES EXCHANGE ACT OF 1934, MAKING FINDINGS, AND IMPOSING A CEASEAND-DESIST ORDER ." Securities Exchange Act of 1934 Release No. 90170 / October 14, 2020 Accounting and Auditing Enforcement Release No. 4189 / October 14, 2020 Administrative Proceeding File No. 3-20124. Securities and Exchange Commission, October 14, 2020. https://www.sec.gov/litigation/admin/2020/34-90170.pdf.

73 Dropped off himself, Exhibit 8: Annexes to Plea Bargain Agreements. Annex 1: "Joesley Batista – BNDES" as translated in J&F Investimentos S.A., v. Baker & Mckenzie LLP, Trench Rossi E Watanabe Advogados (No. 2018 CA 002569 M - The Superior Court for the District of Columbia Civil Division September 10, 2018). Declaration of Ana C. Reyes In Support of Baker & McKenzie LLP's Motion To Dismiss.

73 Fake invoices as cattle purchased, Agusta helicopter, Exhibit 8: Annexes to Plea Bargain Agreements as translated in J&F Investimentos S.A., v. Baker & Mckenzie LLP, Trench Rossi E Watanabe Advogados (No. 2018 CA 002569 M - The Superior Court for the District of Columbia Civil Division September 10, 2018). Declaration of Ana C. Reyes in Support of Baker & McKenzie LLP's Motion to Dismiss.

73 A slush fund for the Batistas, Securities and Exchange Commission. "In the Matter of J&F INVESTIMENTOS, S.A. JBS, S.A. JOESLEY BATISTA WESLEY BATISTA: ORDER INSTITUTING CEASE-ANDDESIST PROCEEDINGS PURSUANT TO SECTION 21C OF THE SECURITIES EXCHANGE ACT OF 1934, MAKING FINDINGS, AND IMPOSING A CEASEAND-DESIST ORDER." Securities Exchange Act of 1934 Release No. 90170 / October 14, 2020 Accounting and Auditing Enforcement

Release No. 4189 / October 14, 2020 Administrative Proceeding File No. 3-20124. Securities and Exchange Commission, October 14, 2020. https://www.sec.gov/litigation /admin/2020/34-90170.pdf.

73 Dividend payments by Pilgrim's, Securities and Exchange Commission. "In the Matter of J&F INVESTIMENTOS, S.A. JBS, S.A. JOESLEY BATISTA WESLEY BATISTA: ORDER INSTITUTING CEASE-ANDDESIST PROCEEDINGS PURSUANT TO SECTION 21C OF THE SECURITIES EXCHANGE ACT OF 1934, MAKING FINDINGS, AND IMPOSING A CEASEAND-DESIST ORDER." Securities Exchange Act of 1934 Release No. 90170 / October 14, 2020 Accounting and Auditing Enforcement Release No. 4189 / October 14, 2020 Administrative Proceeding File No. 3-20124. Securities and Exchange Commission, October 14, 2020. https://www.sec.gov/litigation/admin/2020 /34-90170.pdf.

73 BNDES ownership of JBS, BNDES press. "A BNDESPAR Subscreverá Até US$ 2 Bilhões De Debêntures DA JBS." BNDESPAR, December 22, 2009. https://www.bndes.gov.br/wps /portal/site/home/imprensa/noticias/conteudo/20091223_jbs.

73 BNDES and related pension funds, "SECURITIES EXCHANGE ACT OF 1934 Release No. 90170," October 14, 2020. https://www.sec.gov/litigation/admin/2020/34-90170.pdf.

73 Toward the Swift acquisition and others at the time, "TCU Aponta INDÍCIOS De Irregularidade EM Aporte Do BNDES Na JBS." G1. Accessed September 7, 2021. https:// g1.globo.com/economia/noticia/tcu-aponta-indicios-de-irregularidade-em-aporte-do -bndes-na-jbs.ghtml.

73 Helped JBS acquire Smithfield Beef and feedlot operation Five Rivers Cattle, "Shareholder Profile: Batista Family Fights to Stay atop JBS as Scandals Deepen." Debtwire, an Acuris Company, March 28, 2018. https://s3.eu-west-2.amazonaws.com/acuris-live /Debtwire%20Shareholder%20Profile%20Batista%20family%20fights%20to%20stay% 20atop%20JBS%20as%20scandals%20deepen%20(JBS%20SA).pdf.

73 Up to $2 billion in collateralized debt, Securities and Exchange Commission. "In the Matter of J&F INVESTIMENTOS, S.A. JBS, S.A. JOESLEY BATISTA WESLEY BATISTA: ORDER INSTITUTING CEASE-ANDDESIST PROCEEDINGS PURSUANT TO SECTION 21C OF THE SECURITIES EXCHANGE ACT OF 1934, MAKING FINDINGS, AND IMPOSING A CEASEAND-DESIST ORDER." Securities Exchange Act of 1934 Release No. 90170 / October 14, 2020 Accounting and Auditing Enforcement Release No. 4189 / October 14, 2020 Administrative Proceeding File No. 3-20124. Securities and Exchange Commission, October 14, 2020. https://www.sec.gov/litigation /admin/2020/34-90170.pdf.

74 Didn't end with those original Brazilian plea agreements, J&F Investimentos S.A., v. Baker & Mckenzie LLP, Trench Rossi E Watanabe Advogados (No. 2018 CA 002569 M - The Superior Court for the District of Columbia Civil Division September 10, 2018). Declaration of Ana C. Reyes in Support of Baker & McKenzie LLP's Motion to Dismiss.

74 Accidentally sent audio recordings of incriminating conversations to the prosecutor's office, Langlois, Jill. "A Recording Accidentally Attached to an Email Is the Latest Twist in the World's Biggest Corruption Scandal." *Los Angeles Times*, September 6, 2017. https:// www.latimes.com/world/mexico-americas/la-fg-brazil-corruption-tapes-20170905 -story.html.

74 Arrested on charges of insider trading, Exhibit 9. "Federal Public Prosecution Office – Supreme Court Requested Termination of Plea Bargain Agreement - December 2017" as translated in J&F Investimentos S.A., v. Baker & Mckenzie LLP, Trench Rossi E Watanabe Advogados (No. 2018 CA 002569 M - The Superior Court for the District of Columbia Civil Division September 10, 2018). Declaration of Ana C. Reyes In Support of Baker & McKenzie LLP's Motion to Dismiss.

74 Arrested on charges of insider trading, Exhibit 10. "Supreme Court Termination of Plea Bargain Agreement - February 2018" as translated in J&F Investimentos S.A., v. Baker & Mckenzie LLP, Trench Rossi E Watanabe Advogados (No. 2018 CA 002569 M - The Superior Court for the District of Columbia Civil Division September 10, 2018). Declaration of Ana C. Reyes In Support of Baker & McKenzie LLP's Motion to Dismiss.

74 Sold shares of JBS at a high Exhibit 10, "Supreme Court Termination of Plea Bargain Agreement - February 2018" as translated in J&F Investimentos S.A., v. Baker & Mckenzie LLP, Trench Rossi E Watanabe Advogados (No. 2018 CA 002569 M - The Superior

Court for the District of Columbia Civil Division September 10, 2018). Declaration of Ana C. Reyes In Support of Baker & McKenzie LLP's Motion to Dismiss.

74 Made a profit in the financial markets, J&F Investimentos S.A., v. Baker & Mckenzie LLP, Trench Rossi E Watanabe Advogados (No. 2018 CA 002569 M - The Superior Court for the District of Columbia Civil Division September 10, 2018). Declaration of Ana C. Reyes in Support of Baker & McKenzie LLP's Motion to Dismiss.

74 Market sell-off, Exhibit 10. "Supreme Court Termination of Plea Bargain Agreement - February 2018" as translated in J&F Investimentos S.A., v. Baker & Mckenzie LLP, Trench Rossi E Watanabe Advogados (No. 2018 CA 002569 M - The Superior Court for the District of Columbia Civil Division September 10, 2018). Declaration of Ana C. Reyes In Support of Baker & McKenzie LLP's Motion to Dismiss.

74 The advice they got from Brazil's then attorney general on how to negotiate their plea deals, J&F Investimentos S.A., v. Baker & Mckenzie LLP, Trench Rossi E Watanabe Advogados (No. 2018 CA 002569 M - The Superior Court for the District of Columbia Civil Division September 10, 2018). Declaration of Ana C. Reyes in Support of Baker & McKenzie LLP's Motion to Dismiss.

74 The jewel in their crown, Langlois, Jill. "A Recording Accidentally Attached to an Email Is the Latest Twist in the World's Biggest Corruption Scandal." *Los Angeles Times*, September 6, 2017. https://www.latimes.com/world/mexico-americas/la-fg-brazil-corruption -tapes-20170905-story.html.

75 Interviewing the Batistas in Brazil, Brito, Ricardo. "U.S. Justice Officials Quiz Shareholders of Brazil's JBS." Reuters, December 7, 2018. https://www.reuters.com/article/us-jbs -corruption/u-s-justice-officials-quiz-shareholders-of-brazils-jbs-idUSKBN1O62C4.

75 Several lawmakers requested investigations, US Senators Marco Rubio (R-FL) and Bob Menendez (D-NJ), United States Senate Committee on Foreign Relations. "Sens Menendez and Rubio Request Committee on Foreign Investment in the United States Review Transactions of Brazilian Meat-Processing Conglomerate." United States Senate Committee on Foreign Relations Newsroom, October 8, 2019. https://www.foreign.senate .gov/press/ranking/release/sens-menendez-and-rubio-request-committee-on-foreign -investment-in-the-united-states-review-transactions-of-brazilian-meat-processing -conglomerate.

75 Rosa DeLauro (D-CT), Sorvino, Chloe, and Rosa DeLauro. Interview with Rep. Rosa DeLauro. Personal, March 15, 2021.

75 Allowed to join and participate in J&F board meetings without voting rights, "Brazil Judge Allows Batista Brothers to Attend Board Meetings at Family Company." Reuters, March 28, 2020. https://www.reuters.com/article/brazil-jbs/brazil-judge-allows-batista -brothers-to-attend-board-meetings-at-family-company-idUSL1N2BL00H.

75 Allowed to rejoin the companies they control as part of management, "Brazilian Appeals Court Authorizes Batista Brothers to Go Back to JBS Parent J&f." Reuters, May 26, 2020. https://www.reuters.com/article/us-jbs-corruption/brazilian-appeals-court-authorizes -batista-brothers-to-go-back-to-jbs-parent-jf-idUSKBN23231I.

75 Pled guilty to US foreign bribery charges and agreed to pay, "J&F Investimentos S.A. Pleads Guilty and Agrees to Pay over $256 Million to Resolve Criminal Foreign Bribery Case." The United States Department of Justice, October 15, 2020. https:// www.justice.gov/opa/pr/jf-investimentos-sa-pleads-guilty-and-agrees-pay-over-256 -million-resolve-criminal-foreign.

75 An additional $27 million, $550,000 each for SEC violations, cooperating in any ongoing and future investigations, "SECURITIES EXCHANGE ACT OF 1934 Release No. 90170." October 14, 2020. https://www.sec.gov/litigation/admin/2020/34-90170.pdf.

75 Shareholder entity J&F and the Batista brothers, "Ownership and Corporate." JBS, August 18, 2021. https://ri.jbs.com.br/en/esg-investors/corporate-governance/ownership -and-corporate/.

76 The Chickenshit Club, Eisinger, Jesse. *The Chickenshit Club: Why the Justice Department Fails to Prosecute Executives.* New York: Simon & Schuster, 2018.

76 Considering that the Batistas are trying to, Megale, Bela. "J&F Tenta Suspender Pagamento De Parcela De R$ 344 Milhões De Acordo De Leniência." *O Globo*, December 8, 2021. https://blogs.oglobo.globo.com/bela-megale/post/jf-tenta-suspender-pagamento -de-parcela-de-r-344-milhoes-de-acordo-de-leniencia.html.

76 Bad behavior, Sorvino, Chloe, and Kevin Hourican. Interview with Sysco CEO Kevin Hourican. Personal, March 24, 2021.

76 Continued to serve as directors, *Raul v. Nogueira de Souza et al.* (IN THE UNITED STATES DISTRICT COURT FOR THE DISTRICT OF COLORADO January 10, 2018).

76 Renominated to the board, "Pilgrim's Pride Corporate NOTICE OF ANNUAL MEETING OF STOCKHOLDERS To Be Held April 29, 2016." Def 14a. Accessed September 7, 2021. https://www.sec.gov/Archives/edgar/data/802481/000080248116000056/ppc _2015proxy.htm.

77 Pilgrim's subsequent annual report, "Pilgrim's Pride Corporation Form 10K." Document, 2016. https://www.sec.gov/Archives/edgar/data/802481/000080248117000010/ppc -2016x12x25x10k.htm#s3064B0A208D0549F8A557639A164A7CD.

77 The 2017 proxy statement, renominated Joesley and Wesley, "Pilgrim's Pride Corporation NOTICE OF ANNUAL MEETING OF STOCKHOLDERS To Be Held April 28, 2017." Document, April 28, 2017. https://www.sec.gov/Archives/edgar/data/802481 /000080248117000026/ppc_2016proxy.htm.

77 Would have been material, did not disclose the reasons to shareholders, *Raul v. Nogueira de Souza et al.* (IN THE UNITED STATES DISTRICT COURT FOR THE DISTRICT OF COLORADO January 10, 2018).

77 Failed to disclose his knowledge of any bribes paid during an internal audit, Securities and Exchange Commission. "In the Matter of J&F INVESTIMENTOS, S.A. JBS, S.A. JOESLEY BATISTA WESLEY BATISTA: ORDER INSTITUTING CEASE-ANDDESIST PROCEEDINGS PURSUANT TO SECTION 21C OF THE SECURITIES EXCHANGE ACT OF 1934, MAKING FINDINGS, AND IMPOSING A CEASEAND-DESIST ORDER." Securities Exchange Act of 1934 Release No. 90170 / October 14, 2020 Accounting and Auditing Enforcement Release No. 4189 / October 14, 2020 Administrative Proceeding File No. 3-20124. Securities and Exchange Commission, October 14, 2020. https://www.sec.gov/litigation/admin/2020/34-90170.pdf.

CHAPTER 6

78 A dozen lawmakers asked antitrust regulators to investigate JBS plant acquisition, Lee, Michael, Steve Daines, John Barrasso, Mitt Romney, John Thune, M. Michael Rounds, Chris Stewart, et al. "7.29.2020 Letter to DOJ - RE: Proposed Acquisition of Mountain States Rosen by JBS USA Holdings, Inc." Mike Lee, Senate, July 29, 2020. https://www .lee.senate.gov/_cache/files/e462cbb9-0546-4cea-b28b-2eb1a7ee926b/7.29.2020-msr -letter-to-doj.pdf.

78 Concerned representatives, Lee, Michael, Steve Daines, John Barrasso, Mitt Romney, John Thune, M. Michael Rounds, Chris Stewart, et al. "7.29.2020 Letter to DOJ - RE: Proposed Acquisition of Mountain States Rosen by JBS USA Holdings, Inc." 7.29.2020 letter to DOJ . Mike Lee, Senate, July 29, 2020. https://www.lee.senate.gov/_cache/files /e462cbb9-0546-4cea-b28b-2eb1a7ee926b/7.29.2020-msr-letter-to-doj.pdf.

78 Considering calling it quits, Sorvino, Chloe, and Greg Gunthorp. Interview with Greg Gunthorp. Personal, February 22, 2021.

80 Repealed for beef and pork, Vilsack, Tom. "Statement from Agriculture Secretary Tom Vilsack on the Country of Origin Labeling Requirements for Beef and Pork." USDA Newsroom Press Release Release No. 0345.15. U.S. Department of Agriculture, December 18, 2015. https://www.usda.gov/media/press-releases/2015/12/18/statement -agriculture-secretary-tom-vilsack-country-origin-labeling.

80 Opened up US beef markets, "Livestock and Meat International Trade Data." USDA ERS. Livestock and Meat International Trade Data. Accessed September 7, 2021. https:// www.ers.usda.gov/data-products/livestock-and-meat-international-trade-data/.

80 Raided three JBS plants in Brazil, Haynes, Brad, and Sergio Spagnuolo. "Brazil Police Raid BRF and JBS Meat Plants in Bribery Probe." Reuters, March 17, 2017. https://www .reuters.com/article/us-brazil-corruption-food/brazil-police-raid-brf-and-jbs-meat -plants-in-bribery-probe-idUSKBN16O1LH.

80 Halting all imports, "USDA on Tainted Brazilian Meat: None Has Entered U.S., 100 Percent Re-Inspection Instituted." USDA, March 22, 2017. https://www.usda.gov /media/press-releases/2017/03/22/usda-tainted-brazilian-meat-none-has-entered-us -100-percent-re.

80 Abscesses, visible blood clots, lymph nodes "FINAL REPORT OF AN AUDIT CON-DUCTED IN BRAZIL JUNE 10 - 28, 2019 EVALUATING THE FOOD SAFETY SYS-TEMS GOVERNING RAW AND PROCESSED MEAT PRODUCTS EXPORTED TO THE UNITED STATES OF AMERICA." Brazil 2019 Foreign Audit Report. Food Safety and Inspection Service United States Department of Agriculture, December 13, 2019. https://www.fsis.usda.gov/sites/default/files/media_file/2020-08/brazil-far-2019.pdf.

80 Denied at the border, "Perdue: USDA Halting Import of Fresh Brazilian Beef." USDA, June 22, 2017. https://www.usda.gov/media/press-releases/2017/06/22/perdue-usda-halting-import-fresh-brazilian-beef.

80 To determine whether it was safe to restart beef imports from Brazil, "FINAL REPORT OF AN AUDIT CONDUCTED IN BRAZIL JUNE 10–28, 2019 EVALUATING THE FOOD SAFETY SYSTEMS GOVERNING RAW AND PROCESSED MEAT PROD-UCTS EXPORTED TO THE UNITED STATES OF AMERICA." Brazil 2019 Foreign Audit Report. Food Safety and Inspection Service United States Department of Agri-culture, December 13, 2019. https://www.fsis.usda.gov/sites/default/files/media_file/2020-08/brazil-far-2019.pdf.

80 Leaking pipes attracting flies, poor trash collection, failing to prevent brain tissue leakage, "FINAL REPORT OF AN AUDIT CONDUCTED IN BRAZIL JUNE 10 - 28, 2019 EVALUATING THE FOOD SAFETY SYSTEMS GOVERNING RAW AND PRO-CESSED MEAT PRODUCTS EXPORTED TO THE UNITED STATES OF AMERICA." Brazil 2019 Foreign Audit Report. Food Safety and Inspection Service United States Department of Agriculture, December 13, 2019. https://www.fsis.usda.gov/sites/default/files/media_file/2020-08/brazil-far-2019.pdf.

81 Have increased, "Livestock and Meat International Trade Data." USDA ERS. Livestock and Meat International Trade Data. Accessed September 7, 2021. https://www.ers.usda.gov/data-products/livestock-and-meat-international-trade-data/.

81 Brazil claimed hoof-and-mouth disease was eradicated, Verdélio, Andreia. "Brazil De-clared Free from Foot-and-Mouth Disease with Vaccination." Agência Brasil, May 24, 2018. https://agenciabrasil.ebc.com.br/en/economia/noticia/2018-05/brazil-declared-free-foot-and-mouth-disease-vaccination.

81 Calls to ban all Brazilian beef, Bullard, Bill. "Cattle Group Supports Legislation Suspend-ing Brazilian Beef Imports; Says More Legislation Needed." Ranchers-Cattlemen Action Legal Fund United Stockgrowers of America, November 19, 2021. https://www.r-calfusa.com/cattle-group-supports-legislation-suspending-brazilian-beef-imports-says-more-legislation-needed/.

81 Institute a ban on all Brazilian beef, Congress.gov. "Actions - S.3230 - 117th Congress (2021-2022): A bill to require the establishment of a working group to evaluate the food safety threat posed by beef imported from Brazil, and for other purposes." November 17, 2021. https://www.congress.gov/bill/117th-congress/senate-bill/3230/actions.

81 A record amount of meat, Rochas, Anna Flávia. "US Is Brazil's Top Beef Buyer in No-vember." Meatingplace, December 13, 2021. https://www.meatingplace.com/Industry/News/Details/102478.

81 Addressing concerns that the labels are voluntary, "USDA Announces Efforts to Promote Transparency in Product of the USA Labeling." USDA, July 1, 2021. https://www.usda.gov/media/press-releases/2021/07/01/usda-announces-efforts-promote-transparency-product-usa-labeling.

81 Unveiled a bill to reinstate the labels for beef, Congress.gov. "S.2716 - 117th Congress (2021-2022): American Beef Labeling Act of 2021." September 13, 2021. https://www.congress.gov/bill/117th-congress/senate-bill/2716.

82 Their stake in the world's largest meat processor, "Joesley Batista: Real Time Net Worth." Forbes. Accessed November 29, 2021. https://www.forbes.com/profile/joesley-batista/.

82 Their world's largest meat processor, "Wesley Batista: Real Time Net Worth." Forbes. Accessed November 29, 2021. https://www.forbes.com/profile/wesley-batista/.

82 Using funds meant to help US farmers hurt by the trade war with China, Sommerfeldt, Chris. "Trump Administration Showers Brazilian Crooks with $62M Bailout Money Meant for Struggling U.S. Farmers." New York Daily News, June 13, 2019. https://www.nydailynews.com/news/politics/ny-trump-administration-bailout-farmers-brazilian-criminals-20190516-6rdb3ithvfec7fttem7qrny54y-story.html.

82 Perdue, Sorvino, Chloe, and Sonny Perdue. Interview with Secretary Sonny Perdue at Forbes Ag Tech. Personal, June 27, 2019.

82 Called out JBS, Office of Federal Contract Compliance Programs. "US LABOR DEPARTMENT'S LAWSUIT ALLEGES HIRING DISCRIMINATION AT FEDERAL CONTRACTOR'S BEEF-PROCESSING PLANT IN CACTUS, TEXAS." Complaint seeks back wages, jobs for applicants from JBS USA: Release Number 16-0173-DAL. US Government Department of Labor: Office of Federal Contract Compliance Programs, December 9, 2016. https://www.dol.gov/newsroom/releases/ofccp/ofccp20161213.

82 Agreed to pay, \$4 million, CONSENT DECREE AND ORDER: IN THE MATTER OF OFFICE OF FEDERAL CONTRACT COMPLIANCE PROGRAMS, UNITED STATES DEPARTMENT OF LABOR v. JBS USA and SWIFT BEEF COMPANY, Administrative Complaints filed in Case No. 2015-OFC00001 and Case No. 2017-OFC-00002 (2018).

82 Settle the allegations, Reid, Trevor. "JBS USA to Pay Back Wages, Hire Applicants to Settle Discrimination Allegations in Two Actions." *Greeley Tribune*, May 28, 2020. https://www.greeleytribune.com/2018/11/15/jbs-usa-to-pay-back-wages-hire-applicants-to-settle-discrimination-allegations-in-two-actions/.

83 An entire investigation and hearing process, Sorvino, Chloe, and John Edwards. Interview with lawyer John Edwards on procurement contracts. Personal, March 26, 2021.

83 Supporting shady businesses, Sorvino, Chloe, and Rosa DeLauro. Chloe Sorvino interviews Rep. Rosa DeLauro. Personal, March 15, 2021.

83 Shady businesses with taxpayer dollars, Sorvino, Chloe, and Rosa DeLauro. Interview with Rep. Rosa DeLauro. Personal, March 15, 2021.

83 Take over the meat supply quickly, rely on a production system, Sorvino, Chloe, and Rosa DeLauro. Chloe Sorvino interviews Rep. Rosa DeLauro. Personal, March 15, 2021.

84 Russia-affiliated hackers, "Five Affiliates to Sodinokibi/Revil Unplugged." Europol, November 12, 2021. https://www.europol.europa.eu/newsroom/news/five-affiliates-to-sodinokibi/revil-unplugged.

84 Russia-linked hackers, "Ukrainian Arrested and Charged with Ransomware Attack on Kaseya." The United States Department of Justice, November 8, 2021. https://www.justice.gov/opa/pr/ukrainian-arrested-and-charged-ransomware-attack-kaseya.

84 Paid a randsom, Nair, Aishwarya, and Chris Reese. "Meatpacker JBS Says It Paid Equivalent of \$11 Mln in Ransomware Attack." Reuters. Thomson Reuters, June 10, 2021. https://www.reuters.com/technology/jbs-paid-11-mln-response-ransomware-attack-2021-06-09/.

84 Al Almanza, "JBS Names Former U.S. Department of Agriculture Deputy under Secretary for Food Safety as Global Head of Food Safety and Quality Assurance." GlobeNewswire News Room. JBS USA, LLC, August 3, 2017. https://www.globenewswire.com/news-release/2017/08/03/1072011/0/en/JBS-Names-Former-U-S-Department-of-Agriculture-Deputy-Under-Secretary-for-Food-Safety-as-Global-Head-of-Food-Safety-and-Quality-Assurance.html.

84 Former Speaker of the House John Boehner and former SEC chairman Harvey Pitt, "JBS USA Appoints Independent Advisory Board of Government, Regulatory & Business Experts." GlobeNewswire. JBS USA, August 29, 2017. https://www.bloomberg.com/press-releases/2017-08-29/jbs-usa-appoints-independent-advisory-board-of-government-regulatory-business-experts.

84 A former Federal Trade Commission antitrust regulator, "JBS USA Names Kevin Arquit Chief Legal Officer." GlobeNewswire News Room. JBS USA, LLC, April 20, 2021. https://www.globenewswire.com/en/news-release/2021/04/20/2213211/17532/en/JBS-USA-Names-Kevin-Arquit-Chief-Legal-Officer.html.

84 Threat of the federal government rescinding its contracts, Sorvino, Chloe, and André Nogueira. Interview with JBS USA CEO Andre Nogueira. Personal, November 19, 2020.

84 A budget request committee hearing, VIDEO: Agriculture Department Fiscal Year 2022 Budget Request. Agriculture Department Fiscal Year 2022 Budget Request. C-SPAN, 2021. https://www.c-span.org/video/?510823-1%2Fagriculture-department-fiscal-year-2022-budget-request.

85 A December 2021 payment through Build Back Better, "PURCHASE AWARD DESCRIPTION FY2022 PCA : 12-3J14-22-B-0099-0001." The Department of Agriculture (USDA), December 21, 2021. https://portal.wbscm.usda.gov/irj/go/km/docs/wbscm

procurement/AMS-Livestock/2021/12-DEC/Bid%20Invitations%20(Solicitations)/12
-3J14-22-B-0099-0001-PCA/12-3J14-22-B-0099-0001-PCA.pdf.

85 How taxpayer dollars are being used, Sorvino, Chloe, and Tim Gibbons. Interview with
Missouri Rural Crisis Network's Tim Gibbons. Personal, August 4, 2021.

85 An American IPO continues to be a goal, Sorvino, Chloe. "With a Banner 2020 behind
It, Meat Giant JBS Sets Sights on U.S. IPO." *Forbes*, March 25, 2021. https://www.forbes
.com/sites/chloesorvino/2021/03/25/with-a-banner-2020-behind-it-meat-giant-jbs
-sets-sights-on-us-ipo/.

86 There may be a shift that has to happen in the industry, Apostolatos, Alessia, Carlos
Laboy, and Chloe Sorvino. Interview with HSBC's Alessia Apostolatos and Carlos Laboy
on JBS. Personal, March 19, 2021.

86 Have questions, Laboy, Carlos, and Alessia Apostolatos. Rep. *HSBC Global Food & Agribusiness Coverage*. HSBC Bank, October 15, 2020.

86 Investigate any firm owned or controlled by Wesley and Joesley Batista, Rubio, Marco,
and Bob Menendez. "Rubio, Menendez Urge CFIUS to Review Brazilian Meat-
Processing Conglomerate in Interest of Safeguarding U.S. Economic, National Security
Interests." U.S. Senator for Florida, Marco Rubio. U.S. Congress, August 13, 2021.
https://www.rubio.senate.gov/public/index.cfm/2021/8/rubio-menendez-urge-cfius
-to-review-brazilian-meat-processing-conglomerate-in-interest-of-safeguarding-u-s
-economic-national-security-interests.

86 Still a family affair, "Board, Council and Committees." JBS Corporate Governance. JBS
Investor Relations, November 25, 2021. https://ri.jbs.com.br/en/esg-investors/corporate
-governance/board-council-and-committees/.

86 A lot of uncertainty, Sorvino, Chloe, and Brian Weddington. Interview with Moody's
Brian Weddington on JBS USA. Personal, March 16, 2021.

87 Why would anybody trust, Sorvino, Chloe, and Marion Nestle. Interview with Marion
Nestle on JBS. Personal, August 16, 2021.

87 A fiduciary duty to our stockholders, Nestle, Marion, and Kerry Trueman. *Let's Ask
Marion: What You Need to Know about the Politics of Food, Nutrition, and Health*. Oakland, CA: University of California Press, 2020.

CHAPTER 7

89 One of two slaughterhouses in the United States initially approved to ship to China,
Sorvino, Chloe. "Why Steakhouses Are Obsessed With Beef From This 97-Year-Old
Family Business." *Forbes*, October 23, 2017. https://www.forbes.com/sites/chloesorvino
/2017/10/03/henry-davis-greater-omaha-beef-steakhouse/.

91 The distinction used to be rarer, Maples, Josh. "Record Level of Prime Grading." Progressive Cattle. Progressive Publishing, September 23, 2020. https://www.progressivecattle
.com/news/industry-news/record-level-of-prime-grading.

91 While driving around, Sorvino, Chloe. "Why Steakhouses Are Obsessed With Beef
From This 97-Year-Old Family Business." *Forbes*, October 23, 2017. https://www.forbes
.com/sites/chloesorvino/2017/10/03/henry-davis-greater-omaha-beef-steakhouse/.

92 Small operation on the exchange floor grew slowly, "Our Story." Greater Omaha Packing
Co., November 4, 2020. https://greateromaha.com/our-history/.

93 They would get shut out, Sorvino, Chloe, and Henry Davis. Interview with Greater
Omaha Packing owner Henry Davis. Personal, March 12, 2021.

95 Still get benefits of operational efficiencies, Sorvino, Chloe, and Peter Carstensen. Interview with Peter Carstensen on consolidation and the future of meat. Personal, March
22, 2021.

96 If there weren't any plants bigger than Greater Omaha, Sorvino, Chloe, and Henry
Davis. Interview with Greater Omaha Packing owner Henry Davis. Personal, March 12,
2021.

96 Just as smart for producers in a remote region to pool their resources, Sorvino, Chloe,
and Bill Niman. Interview with California rancher Bill Niman. Personal, July 2020.

97 Bring prices down and reduce potential profits, Sorvino, Chloe, and Dustin Aherin.
Interview on cattle markets' need for added capacity with Rabobank's Dustin Aherin.
Personal, January 13, 2021.

97 Producing some five million cattle, "2020 State Agriculture Overview for Oklahoma."
USDA/NASS 2020 State Agriculture Overview for Oklahoma. Accessed September 7,

2021. https://www.nass.usda.gov/Quick_Stats/Ag_Overview/stateOverview.php?state=OKLAHOMA.

97 Small beef and bison slaughterhouse from scratch, Shaw Duty, Shannon. "Construction Continues on Nation's First-Ever Meat Processing Facility." Osage News, August 5, 2020. http://osagenews.org/en/article/2020/08/05/construction-continues-nations-first-ever-meat-processing-facility/.

97 If we could just complete the chain, Sorvino, Chloe, James Weigant, Chris Roper, and Jann Hayman. Interview with representatives of Osage Nation on new meatpacking plant. Personal, January 11, 2021.

97 Access to traditional and otherwise whole foods, "Traditional Animal Foods of Indigenous Peoples of Northern North America." Centre for Indigenous Peoples, Nutrition and Environment. Accessed March 1, 2022. http://traditionalanimalfoods.org/mammals/hoofed/page.aspx?id=6136.

98 Put up economically, Garcia, Tatiana, Chris Roper, Karen Washington, Amy Wu, Chloe Sorvino, and Elena Seeley. "Technology and Innovation Can Bolster Food Security." Food Tank and the Refresh Working Group, February 6, 2021. https://foodtank.com/news/2021/02/developing-equitable-technology-for-food-security/.

98 Lee, Michael, Steve Daines, John Barrasso, Mitt Romney, John Thune, M. Michael Rounds, Chris Stewart, et al. "7.29.2020 Letter to DOJ - RE: Proposed Acquisition of Mountain States Rosen by JBS USA Holdings, Inc." 7.29.2020 letter to DOJ . Mike Lee, Senate, July 29, 2020. https://www.lee.senate.gov/_cache/files/e462cbb9-0546-4cea-b28b-2eb1a7ee926b/7.29.2020-msr-letter-to-doj.pdf.

98 Incorporate the business as a limited liability company, Sorvino, Chloe, and C. Robert Taylor. Interview on Pickett trial and monopsony issues with Auburn University's C. Robert Taylor. Personal, January 22, 2021.

98 Mobile slaughterhouses fashioned out of trailers, Grandin, Temple. "Temple Grandin: Alternative Business Models That Farmers Should Consider." Forbes, October 7, 2020. https://www.forbes.com/sites/templegrandin/2020/10/06/its-more-profitable-for-farmers-to-sell-direct-but-how-does-that-work/.

99 Missouri Prime Beef Packers, Sorvino, Chloe, Stacy Davies, and Derek Thompson. Interview with NextGen Cattle's Stacy Davies and Derek Thompson. Personal, March 4, 2021.

99 Humans' cavemen ancestors who likely ate organ meat, Draper, Isabel. "Should We Eat like Cavemen?" Think Twice. The University of Texas at Austin, July 23, 2019. http://sites.utexas.edu/think-twice/2019/07/23/should-we-eat-like-cavemen/.

CHAPTER 8

103 Stuck in one area, Nicole, Wendee. "Cafos and Environmental Justice: The Case of North Carolina." Environmental Health Perspectives 121, no. 6 (2013). https://doi.org/10.1289/ehp.121-a182.

103 Anaerobic bacteria work through the slurry, "Report Documents Waste Lagoons' Threats to Environment, Public Health." NRDC, July 24, 2001. https://www.nrdc.org/media/2001/010724.

103 Shed greenhouse gases, Leytem, A. B., D. L. Bjorneberg, A. C. Koehn, L. E. Moraes, E. Kebreab, and R. S. Dungan. "Methane Emissions from Dairy Lagoons in the Western United States." Journal of Dairy Science 100, no. 8 (August 2017): 6785–6803. https://doi.org/10.3168/jds.2017-12777.

103 Hog farm worker in Minnesota, "Hog Farm Co-Owner and Employee Die of Hydrogen Sulfide Poisoning in Manure Pit—Minnesota." FACE program: In-house Report 92-28. Centers for Disease Control and Prevention, November 18, 2015. https://www.cdc.gov/niosh/face/in-house/full9228.html.

103 Four family members and a farmworker died, Walker, Dionne. "5 Killed in Methane Gas Accident on Virginia Dairy Farm." Associated Press, July 4, 2007. http://archive.boston.com/news/nation/articles/2007/07/04/5_killed_in_methane_gas_accident_on_virginia_dairy_farm/.

104 Two different father-son pairs, Rodgers, Grant, and Donnelle Eller. "Iowa Father, Son Die from Manure PIT Fumes." USA Today, July 29, 2015. https://www.usatoday.com/story/news/nation/2015/07/28/iowa-father-son-die-manure-pit-fumes/30811157/.

104 Polluted mixture left over, "2020 Sustainability Impact Report." Smithfield Foods, 2020.

https://www.smithfieldfoods.com/getmedia/1fc9b578-4dff-4104-9706-ba0fbbc44f47/2020-Sustainability-Impact-Report.pdf.

104 Polluted mixture left over, Pornsukarom, Suchawan, and Siddhartha Thakur. "Assessing the Impact of Manure Application in Commercial Swine Farms on the Transmission of Antimicrobial Resistant Salmonella in the Environment." *PLOS One* 11, no. 10 (October 18, 2016). https://doi.org/10.1371/journal.pone.0164621.

104 Predominantly Black, Latinx, and Indigenous, Wing, Steve, and Jill Johnston. Rep. Industrial Hog Operations in North Carolina Disproportionately Impact African-Americans, Hispanics and American Indians, August 29, 2014. http://www.ncpolicywatch.com/wp-content/uploads/2014/09/UNC-Report.pdf.

104 Kravchenko, Julia, Sung Han Rhew, Igor Akushevich, Pankaj Agarwal, and H. Kim Lyerly. "Mortality and Health Outcomes in North Carolina Communities Located in Close Proximity to Hog Concentrated Animal Feeding Operations." North Carolina Medical Journal. North Carolina Medical Journal, September 1, 2018. https://www.ncmedicaljournal.com/content/79/5/278.

104 A clear example of environmental injustice, Wing, Steve, and Jill Johnston. "Industrial Hog Operations in North Carolina Disproportionately Impact African-Americans, Hispanics and American Indians." August 29, 2014. http://www.ncpolicywatch.com/wp-content/uploads/2014/09/UNC-Report.pdf.

104 A clear example of environmental injustice, Kravchenko, Julia, Sung Han Rhew, Igor Akushevich, Pankaj Agarwal, and H. Kim Lyerly. "Mortality and Health Outcomes in North Carolina Communities Located in Close Proximity to Hog Concentrated Animal Feeding Operations." *North Carolina Medical Journal* 79, no. 5 (2018): 278–88. https://doi.org/10.18043/ncm.79.5.278.

104 Death rates, Kravchenko, Julia, Sung Han Rhew, Igor Akushevich, Pankaj Agarwal, and H. Kim Lyerly. "Mortality and Health Outcomes in North Carolina Communities Located in Close Proximity to Hog Concentrated Animal Feeding Operations." *North Carolina Medical Journal* 79, no. 5 (2018): 278–88. https://doi.org/10.18043/ncm.79.5.278.

104 Some of the largest manure lagoons, "AgSTAR Project Profile: Ruckman Farm." EPA. Accessed January 31, 2022. https://beta.epa.gov/sites/default/files/2018-05/documents/agstar_profile_ruckman_2018.pdf.

104 Resident Elsie Herring testified, "House Committee on Energy and Commerce Building a 100 Percent Clean Economy: The Challenges Facing Frontline Communities: Testimony of Elsie Herring, November 20, 2019," 2019. https://www.congress.gov/116/meeting/house/110247/witnesses/HHRG-116-IF18-Wstate-HerringE-20191120.pdf.

105 Herring who died, Ikerd, John. "A Tribute to Elsie Herring." September 13, 2021. https://www.johnikerd.com/post/a-tribute-to-elsie-herring.

105 lagoons flood and the waste spreads, Heaney, Christopher D., Kevin Myers, Steve Wing, Devon Hall, Dothula Baron, and Jill R. Stewart. "Source Tracking Swine Fecal Waste in Surface Water Proximal to Swine Concentrated Animal Feeding Operations." *Science of the Total Environment* 511 (2015): 676–83. https://doi.org/10.1016/j.scitotenv.2014.12.062.

105 Hurricane Floyd, Pierre-Louis, Kendra. "Lagoons of Pig Waste Are Overflowing After Florence. Yes, That's as Nasty as It Sounds." *The New York Times*, September 19, 2018. https://www.nytimes.com/2018/09/19/climate/florence-hog-farms.html.

105 Hurricane Florence, Pierre-Louis, Kendra. "Lagoons of Pig Waste Are Overflowing after Florence. Yes, That's as Nasty as It Sounds." *The New York Times*, September 19, 2018. https://www.nytimes.com/2018/09/19/climate/florence-hog-farms.html.

105 Lagoons impacted, Kastrinsky, Josh. Letter to Chloe Sorvino. *Re: Request on Hog Manure Lagoons Overflow Figures*, May 10, 2022. With Josh Kastrinsky, Public Information Officer, Division of Energy, Mineral and Land Resources, North Carolina Department of Environmental Quality.

105 Antibiotics stew in those lagoons, "Sources of Eutrophication." World Resources Institute. Accessed September 7, 2021. https://www.wri.org/our-work/project/eutrophication-and-hypoxia/sources-eutrophication.

105 High concentrations of, Casanova, Lisa M., and Mark D. Sobsey. 2016. "Antibiotic-Resistant Enteric Bacteria in Environmental Waters." Water 8, no. 12: 561. https://doi.org/10.3390/w8120561.

105 High concentrations of, Li, X., Atwill, E.R., Antaki, E., Applegate, O., Bergamaschi, B.,

Bond, R.F., Chase, J., Ransom, K.M., Samuels, W., Watanabe, N. and Harter, T. (2015), Fecal Indicator and Pathogenic Bacteria and Their Antibiotic Resistance in Alluvial Groundwater of an Irrigated Agricultural Region with Dairies. J. Environ. Qual., 44: 1435-1447. https://doi.org/10.2134/jeq2015.03.0139.

105 Nearby rivers and streams, Helmer, Jodi. "Hurricane-Flooded Hog Farms Could Bring Superbugs to North Carolina Communities." NRDC, October 23, 2018. https://www.nrdc.org/stories/hurricane-flooded-hog-farms-could-bring-superbugs-north-carolina-communities.

106 A climate scenario analysis, "New Financial Modelling on Climate Shows Billions of Dollars at Risk in the Meat Sector." Farm Animal Investment Risk and Return, March 12, 2020. https://www.fairr.org/article/new-financial-modelling-on-climate-shows-billions-of-dollars-at-risk-in-the-meat-sector/.

106 The total footprint of beef production, Rotz, C. Alan, Senorpe Asem-Hiablie, Sara Place, and Greg Thoma. "Environmental Footprints of Beef Cattle Production in the United States." *Agricultural Systems.* Elsevier, November 27, 2018. https://www.sciencedirect.com/science/article/pii/S0308521X18305675.

106 Total US emissions, "Sources of Greenhouse Gas Emissions." Environmental Protection Agency. Accessed September 7, 2021. https://www.epa.gov/ghgemissions/sources-greenhouse-gas-emissions.

106 Emissions from agriculture account for, "Sources of Greenhouse Gas Emissions." Environmental Protection Agency. Accessed January 11, 2022. https://www.epa.gov/ghgemissions/sources-greenhouse-gas-emissions.

106 The bulk of the fertilizer used goes to row crops farmed for livestock feed, "Feedgrains Sector at a Glance." USDA, June 28, 2021. https://www.ers.usda.gov/topics/crops/corn-and-other-feedgrains/feedgrains-sector-at-a-glance/.

106 Roughly half of all US agricultural production emissions, Waite, Richard, and Alex Rudee. "6 Ways the US Can Curb Climate Change and Grow More Food." World Resources Institute, August 20, 2020. https://www.wri.org/blog/2020/08/us-agriculture-emissions-food.

107 Emitted as a potent greenhouse gas, Clark, Michael A., Nina G. Domingo, Kimberly Colgan, Sumil K. Thakrar, David Tilman, John Lynch, Inês L. Azevedo, and Jason D. Hill. "Global Food System Emissions Could Preclude Achieving the 1.5° And 2°c Climate Change Targets." *Science* 370, no. 6517 (2020): 705–8. https://doi.org/10.1126/science.aba7357.

107 The United Nations called curbing methane, Press Release. "Global Assessment: Urgent Steps Must Be Taken to Reduce Methane Emissions This Decade." United Nations Environment Programme, May 6, 2021. https://www.unep.org/news-and-stories/press-release/global-assessment-urgent-steps-must-be-taken-reduce-methane.

107 Enteric fermentation creates a lot of methane, Liu, Shule, Joe Proudman, and Frank M. Mitloehner. "Rethinking Methane from Animal Agriculture." *CABI Agriculture and Bioscience* 2, no. 1 (June 7, 2021). https://doi.org/10.1186/s43170-021-00041-y.

107 Methane from agricultural sources, Voiland, Adam. "Methane Emissions Continue to Rise." Earth Observatory. NASA, 2020. https://earthobservatory.nasa.gov/images/146978/methane-emissions-continue-to-rise.

107 Overall methane emissions, Fischer, Emily. "NASA at Your Table: Where Food Meets Methane." NASA, August 13, 2021. https://www.nasa.gov/feature/goddard/2021/esnt/nasa-at-your-table-where-food-meets-methane.

107 Failed to stymie the growth of methane, petitioned the federal government, Letter to U.S. Environmental Protection Agency. "Petition To List Industrial Dairy And Hog Operations As Source Categories Under Section 111(b)(1)(A) of the Clean Air Act." Center for Public Justice, June 6, 2021. https://food.publicjustice.net/wp-content/uploads/sites/3/2021/04/2021.04.06-Industrial-Dairy-and-Hog-CAA-111-Petition-FINAL.pdf.

107 Released an action plan, White House Briefing Room. "Fact Sheet: President Biden Tackles Methane Emissions, Spurs Innovations, and Supports Sustainable Agriculture to Build a Clean Energy Economy and Create Jobs." The White House, November 2, 2021. https://www.whitehouse.gov/briefing-room/statements-releases/2021/11/02/fact-sheet-president-biden-tackles-methane-emissions-spurs-innovations-and-supports-sustainable-agriculture-to-build-a-clean-energy-economy-and-create-jobs/.

107 A petition with California's Air Resources Board, "Before the California Air Resources

Board Petition for Rulemaking to Exclude All Fuels Derived from Biomethane from Dairy and Swine Manure from the Low Carbon Fuel Standard Program." n.d. https://food.publicjustice.net/wp-content/uploads/sites/3/2021/10/Factory-Farm-Gas-Petition-FINAL.pdf.

107 Producing biogas in North Carolina, Missouri, and Utah, "Renewable Natural Gas from Agricultural-Based AD/Biogas Systems." Environmental Protection Agency. Accessed January 31, 2022. https://www.epa.gov/agstar/renewable-natural-gas-agricultural-based-adbiogas-systems.

107 The civil rights concerns, "The Dirty Truth about Biogas Production and How to Take Action in NC." Southern Environmental Law Center, January 15, 2021. https://www.southernenvironment.org/news/the-dirty-truth-about-biogas-production-and-how-to-take-action-in-n.c/.

107 Nearly four times more nitrogen than if the lagoon was opened, Lupis, S. G., N. Embertson, and J. G. Davis. "Best Management Practices for Reducing Ammonia Emissions: Lagoon Covers - 1.631B." CSU Extension. Colorado State University Extension, March 29, 2016. https://extension.colostate.edu/topic-areas/agriculture/best-management-practices-for-reducing-ammonia-emissions-lagoon-covers-1-631b/.

107 Turning waste sludge from lagoons into biogas, "U.S. Methane Emissions Reduction Action Plan: CRITICAL AND COMMONSENSE STEPS TO CUT POLLUTION AND CONSUMER COSTS, WHILE BOOSTING GOOD-PAYING JOBS AND AMERICAN COMPETITIVENESS." The White House, November 2021. https://www.whitehouse.gov/wp-content/uploads/2021/11/US-Methane-Emissions-Reduction-Action-Plan-1.pdf.

108 Concentrations decline in a wide range of plant species, Provenza, Frederick D. *Nourishment: What Animals Can Teach Us about Rediscovering Our Nutritional Wisdom*. White River Junction, VT: Chelsea Green Publishing, 2018, p. 31.

108 Aquifers drying out in the Great Plains, Bessire, Lucas. *Running Out: In Search of Water on the High Plains*. Princeton, NJ, NJ: Princeton University Press, 2021.

109 Lost through surface runoff or leaching into groundwater, "Sources of Eutrophication." World Resources Institute. Accessed September 7, 2021. https://www.wri.org/our-work/project/eutrophication-and-hypoxia/sources-eutrophicatiion.

109 The Gulf of Mexico where the annual dead zone, more than the size of the state of Connecticut, "Northern Gulf of Mexico Hypoxic Zone." Environmental Protection Agency. Accessed January 31, 2022. https://www.epa.gov/ms-htf/northern-gulf-mexico-hypoxic-zone#:~:text=NOAA%2Dsupported%20scientists%20announced%20that,years%20is%205%2C380%20square%20miles.

109 Pollution stimulates algae growth and creates low-oxygen dead zones, "Low or Depleted Oxygen in a Water Body Often Leads to 'Dead Zone'—Regions Where Life Cannot Be Sustained." NOAA's National Ocean Service, March 14, 2019. https://oceanservice.noaa.gov/hazards/hypoxia/.

109 Nitrogen and phosphorus, "Estimated Animal Agriculture Nitrogen and Phosphorus from Manure." Environmental Protection Agency. Accessed January 31, 2022. https://www.epa.gov/nutrient-policy-data/estimated-animal-agriculture-nitrogen-and-phosphorus-manure.

109 High concentrations of these pollutants damage waterways, "The Sources and Solutions: Agriculture." Environmental Protection Agency. Accessed January 31, 2022. https://www.epa.gov/nutrientpollution/sources-and-solutions-agriculture.

109 Processed by municipal wastewater treatment plants or a slaughterhouse's own program, Aziz, Hamidi, Nur Puat, Motasem Alazaiza, and Yung-Tse Hung. "Poultry Slaughterhouse Wastewater Treatment Using Submerged Fibers in an Attached Growth Sequential Batch Reactor." *International Journal of Environmental Research and Public Health* 15, no. 8 (2018): 1734. https://doi.org/10.3390/ijerph15081734.

109 Processed by municipal wastewater treatment plants or a slaughterhouse's own program, Villarroel Hipp, María P., and David Silva Rodríguez. "Bioremediation of Piggery Slaughterhouse Wastewater Using the Marine Protist, Thraustochytrium Kinney Val-B1." *Journal of Advanced Research* 12 (2018): 21–26. https://doi.org/10.1016/j.jare.2018.01.010.

109 Pork plant in Beardstown, Wisniewski, Mary, and Christine Stebbins. "Midwest Farm Town, Transformed by Immigration, Thrives." Reuters, June 20, 2012. https://www.reuters

.com/article/us-usa-immigration-meatpacking/midwest-farm-town-transformed-by
-immigration-thrives-idUSBRE85J0FA20120620.

109 Among the country's worst in terms of water pollution, "Durbin Statement on JBS
Pork-Processing Plant Pollution in Beardstown: U.S. Senator Dick Durbin of Illinois."
Dick Durbin, United States Senator Illinois, October 15, 2018. https://www.durbin
.senate.gov/newsroom/press-releases/durbin-statement-on-jbs-pork-processing-plant
-pollution-in-beardstown-.

109 Among the country's worst in terms of water pollution, "Three Quarters of Large U.S.
Slaughterhouses Violate Water Pollution Permits." Environmental Integrity Project, October 11, 2018. https://environmentalintegrity.org/news/slaughterhouses-violate-water
-pollution-permits/.

109 Responsible for more than 1,800 pounds of nitrogen, Burkhart, Kira, Courtney Bernhardt,
Tom Pelton, Eric Schaeffer, and Ari Phillips. "Water Pollution from Slaughterhouses." Environmental Integrity Project, November 5, 2018. http://www.environmentalintegrity.org
/wp-content/uploads/2018/10/Slaughterhouse_Report_Final.pdf.

110 Tyson paid, Environmental Protection Agency. "Tyson Foods to Pay $7.5 Million for
Federal and State Clean Water Violations." EPA. Environmental Protection Agency, July
3, 2003. https://archive.epa.gov/epapages/newsroom_archive/newsreleases/51c2d19d5d
f66b4185257059006bbbff.html.

110 Sentenced in federal court, Press Release Number: 18-245. "Tyson Poultry Fined $2 Mil-
lion for Violating the Clean Water Act." Department of Justice Office of Public Affairs.
The United States Department of Justice, February 27, 2018. https://www.justice.gov
/opa/pr/tyson-poultry-fined-2-million-violating-clean-water-act.

110 JBS agreed to pay, to settle alleged violations of the federal Clean Water Act, Press
Release Number: 11-781. "Swift Beef Company to Pay $1.3 Million Penalty for Clean
Water Act and State Law Violations at Its Grand Island, Nebraska Beef Processing
Plant." Department of Justice Office of Public Affairs. US Department of Justice, June
16, 2011. https://www.justice.gov/opa/pr/swift-beef-company-pay-13-million-penalty
-clean-water-act-and-state-law-violations-its-grand.

110 Large operations have tightened their grip, Smit, Lidwien A., and Dick Heederik.
"Impacts of Intensive Livestock Production on Human Health in Densely Populated
Regions." GeoHealth 1, no. 7 (2017): 272–77. https://doi.org/10.1002/2017gh000103.

110 Passed off these problems to taxpayers, Sneeringer, Stacy. "Does Animal Feeding
Operation Pollution Hurt Public Health? A National Longitudinal Study of Health
Externalities Identified by Geographic Shifts in Livestock Production." American Journal of Agricultural Economics 91, no. 1 (2009): 124–37. https://doi.org/10.1111/j.1467
-8276.2008.01161.x.

110 Flooding streams and lakes with waste, "Combined Sewer Overflows (CSOs)." Environmental Protection Agency. Accessed January 31, 2022. https://www.epa.gov/npdes
/combined-sewer-overflows-csos.

110 Challenged the efficacy of the Clean Water Act in court, "Center for Biological Diversity v. Swift Beef." Public Justice Food Project. Public Justice, 2019. https://food.public
justice.net/case/center-for-biological-diversity-v-swift-beef/#:~:text=The%20Clean%20
Water%20Act%20prohibits,the%20Act's%20citizen%20suit%20provision.

110 Largely ignored disastrous levels of water pollution, Jones CS, Nielsen JK, Schilling
KE, Weber LJ. "Iowa Stream Nitrate and the Gulf of Mexico." PLoS ONE 13(4) (2018):
e0195930. https://doi.org/10.1371/journal.pone.0195930.

110 The impact of a CAFO in Iowa, "EWG Study and Mapping Show Big Cafos in Iowa
Up Fivehold since 1990." Environmental Working Group. Accessed September 7, 2021.
https://www.ewg.org/interactive-maps/2020-iowa-cafos/.

110 Predominantly Black, Indigenous, and Latinx, "EWG and Waterkeeper Alliance: Poultry
Factory Farms Disproportionately Threaten Black, Native American and Latino People
in North Carolina." Environmental Working Group, September 2, 2021. https://www
.ewg.org/news-insights/news-release/ewg-and-waterkeeper-alliance-poultry-factory
-farms-disproportionately.

111 Livestock requires a lot of resources to be turned into meat, "U.S. Could Feed 800
Million People with Grain That Livestock Eat, Cornell Ecologist ADVISES Animal
Scientists." Cornell Chronicle, August 7, 1997. https://news.cornell.edu/stories/1997/08

/us-could-feed-800-million-people-grain-livestock-eat#:~:text=Each%20year%20 an%20estimated%2041,million%20tons%20from%20forage%20crops.

111 Industrial meat is highly inefficient, Shepon, A., G. Eshel, E. Noor, and R. Milo. "Energy and Protein Feed-to-Food Conversion Efficiencies in the US and Potential Food Security Gains from Dietary Changes." *Environmental Research Letters* 11, no. 10 (2016): 105002. https://doi.org/10.1088/1748-9326/11/10/105002.

111 Propped up environmentally harmful farming practices, "A multi-billion-dollar opportunity—Repurposing agricultural support to transform food systems." Food and Agricultural Organization of the United Nations, 2021. https://doi.org/10.4060/cb6562en.

111 Crop insurance, price supports, and conservation, Schnepf, Randall Dean, and Megan Stubbs. "U.S. farm program eligibility and payment limits under the 2018 farm bill (P.L. 115-334)" (2019). https://sgp.fas.org/crs/misc/R45659.pdf.

111 Disaster payments, Dismukes, Robert, and Joseph Glauber. "Why Hasn't Crop Insurance Eliminated Disaster Assistance?" USDA, June 1, 2005. https://www.ers.usda.gov /amber-waves/2005/june/why-hasn-t-crop-insurance-eliminated-disaster-assistance/.

111 Mainly to commodity row crop farmers and dairy producers, "EWG's Farm Subsidy Database." EWG Farm Subsidy Database. The United States Conservation Database. Accessed October 29, 2021. https://farm.ewg.org/regionsummary.php.

111 More than $400 billion in subsidies, McFadden, J. R. and R. A. Hoppe. "Evolving Distribution of Payments From Commodity, Conservation, and Federal Crop Insurance Programs. EIB-184." USDA, 2017.

111 Subsidies supporting meat and dairy production, Joshi, Indira, Seetharam Param, Milind Gadre, and Irene. "Saving the Planet the Market for Sustainable Meat Alternatives." November 10, 2015. https://scet.berkeley.edu/wp-content/uploads/CopyofFINALSaving ThePlanetSustainableMeatAlternatives.pdf.

111 A third of America's corn crop annually, "Corn and Soybean Production up in 2020, USDA Reports." United States Department of Agriculture, January 12, 2021. https:// www.nass.usda.gov/Newsroom/2021/01-12-2021a.php.

111 "USDA Coexistence Fact Sheets Soybeans." USDA, February 2015. https://www.usda .gov/sites/default/files/documents/coexistence-soybeans-factsheet.pdf.

111 Antitrust concerns, Maxwell, Joe. Letter to The Honorable Jonathan Kanter Assistant Attorney General—Antitrust Division Department of Justice; The Honorable Lina Khan, Chair of the Federal Trade Commission The Honorable Tom Vilsack, Secretary of Agriculture. "Family Farm Action Alliance Letter to DOJ on Fertilizer Industry Antitrust." Family Farm Action Alliance, December 8, 2021. https://farmaction.us//wp -content/uploads/2021/12/FFAA_DOJ_Fertilizer_Investigation_Final.pdf.

111 Less than 1 percent of total US cropland, Bialik, Kristen, and Kristi Walker. "Organic Farming Is on the Rise in the U.S." Pew Research Center, January 10, 2019. https:// www.pewresearch.org/fact-tank/2019/01/10/organic-farming-is-on-the-rise-in-the-u -s/#:~:text=Still%2C%20organic%20farming%20makes%20up,acres%20of%20total%20 farmland%20nationwide.

111 Less than 1 percent of total US cropland, "Organic Production Documentation." USDA ERS. Accessed September 7, 2021. https://www.ers.usda.gov/data-products/organic -production/documentation.aspx.

112 A landmark study on soil erosion, Borrelli, Pasquale, David A. Robinson, Larissa R. Fleischer, Emanuele Lugato, Cristiano Ballabio, Christine Alewell, Katrin Meusburger, et al. "An Assessment of the Global Impact of 21st Century Land Use Change on Soil Erosion." *Nature Communications* 8, no. 1 (December 8, 2017). https://doi.org/10.1038 /s41467-017-02142-7.

112 Soils are getting worse, "Status of the World's Soil Resources." FAO, 2015. http://www.fao .org/3/i5199e/I5199E.pdf.

112 Already commands too much land, Bigellow, Daniel P., and Allison Borchers. "Major Uses of Land in the United States, 2012." USDA, August 2017. https://www.ers.usda.gov /webdocs/publications/84880/eib-178.pdf?v=2216.7.

112 Lost to other development, "Farms Under Threat: The State of the States." n.d. https:// farmlandinfo.org/publications/farms-under-threat-the-state-of-the-states/.

112 Erosion, Moyer, Jeff, Andrew Smith, Yichao Rui, and Jennifer Hayden. "Regenerative Agriculture and the Soil Carbon Solution." Rodale Institute, September 2020.

https://rodaleinstitute.org/wp-content/uploads/Rodale-Soil-Carbon-White-Paper_v11
-compressed.pdf.

112 Erosion, Pimentel, David, and Michael Burgess. "Soil Erosion Threatens Food Production." *Agriculture* 3, no. 3 (2013): 443–63. https://doi.org/10.3390/agriculture3030443.

112 Stressed soils, Jang, W. S., J. C. Neff, Y. Im, L. Doro, and J. E. Herrick. "The Hidden Costs
of Land Degradation in US Maize Agriculture." *Earth's Future* 9, no. 2 (February 2021).
https://doi.org/10.1029/2020ef001641.

112 A third of America's Corn Belt is degraded, Thaler, Evan A., Isaac J. Larsen, and Qian Yu.
"The Extent of Soil Loss across the US Corn Belt." *Proceedings of the National Academy
of Sciences* 118, no. 8 (February 23, 2021). https://doi.org/10.1073/pnas.1922375118.

112 Ten billion people could already be sustained, "How to Feed 10 Billion People." UN
Environment Programme, July 13, 2020. https://www.unep.org/news-and-stories/story
/how-feed-10-billion-people.

112 The amount of food wasted each year, "5 Facts about Food Waste and Hunger: World
Food Programme." UN World Food Programme, June 2, 2020. https://www.wfp.org
/stories/5-facts-about-food-waste-and-hunger.

113 Two billion people could be fed, "Monitoring Food Loss and Waste Essential to Hunger
Fight." United Nations Food And Agriculture Organization, October 21, 2013. https://
www.fao.org/news/story/en/item/203149/icode/.

113 Wasted per capita in America, Buzby, Jean C., Hodan F. Wells, and Jeffrey Hyman. "Economic Information Bulletin Number 121: The Estimated Amount, Value, and Calories
of Postharvest Food Losses at the Retail and Consumer Levels in the United States."
United States Department of Agriculture, February 2014. https://www.ers.usda.gov
/webdocs/publications/43833/43679_eib121_summary.pdf?v=0.

113 Chinese diets, Fan, Wenxin. "Feud at Smithfield Foods' Parent Company Shows Messy
Underside of Chinese Takeover." The Wall Street Journal. Dow Jones & Company,
November 11, 2021. https://www.wsj.com/articles/feud-at-smithfield-foods-parent
-company-shows-messy-underside-of-chinese-takeover-11636626600.

113 Acquired the iconic American ham maker, "Smithfield Foods, Inc. Schedule 14A." SEC,
August 19, 2013. https://www.sec.gov/Archives/edgar/data/91388/000119312513339679
/d554122ddefm14a.htm.

113 The largest acquisition of a US company by a Chinese business at the time, Chen, Ming-
Jer, Gerry Yemen, Ruo Jia, and Seb Murray. "The Smithfield Acquisition: Shuanghui
Buys the Whole Hog." Darden School of Business, August 13, 2019. https://ideas.darden.
virginia.edu/the-smithfield-acquisition.

113 The acquisition of California's largest pork processor, "Smithfield Foods Completes
Acquisition of Clougherty Packing LLC." Smithfield Foods, January 3, 2017. https://
investors.smithfieldfoods.com/2017-01-03-Smithfield-Foods-Completes-Acquisition
-of-Clougherty-Packing-LLC.

113 After rolling up the Smithfield deal with another, "Smithfield Foods to Acquire Farmer
John, Saag's Specialty Meats and Three Farm Operations." GlobeNewswire News Room,
November 21, 2016. https://www.globenewswire.com/news-release/2016/11/21/891867
/0/en/Smithfield-Foods-to-Acquire-Farmer-John-Saag-s-Specialty-Meats-and-Three
-Farm-Operations.html.

114 Business-as-usual climate scenario, "The future of food and agriculture—Alternative
pathways to 2050. Supplementary material." FAO, 2018. http://www.fao.org/3/CA1564EN
/CA1564EN.pdf.

114 Many views and ideas about Chinese and Western flavors, Fan, Wenxin. "Feud at Smithfield Foods' Parent Company Shows Messy Underside of Chinese Takeover." *The Wall
Street Journal*, November 11, 2021. https://www.wsj.com/articles/feud-at-smithfield
-foods-parent-company-shows-messy-underside-of-chinese-takeover-11636626600.

114 Cut deeper, Ping, Chong Koh. "Pork Giant's Shares Tumble after Father-Son Feud Intensifies." *The Wall Street Journal*, August 18, 2021. https://www.wsj.com/articles/pork
-giants-shares-tumble-after-father-son-feud-intensifies-11629282427.

114 Boiled over into a blowup, Fan, Wenxin. "Feud at Smithfield Foods' Parent Company
Shows Messy Underside of Chinese Takeover." *The Wall Street Journal*, November 11,
2021. https://www.wsj.com/articles/feud-at-smithfield-foods-parent-company-shows
-messy-underside-of-chinese-takeover-11636626600.

CHAPTER 9

117 A study Price worked on, Larsen J., A. Petersen, M. Sørum, M. Stegger, L. van Alphen, P. Vlentiner-Branth, L. K. Knudsen, L. S. Larsen, B. Feingold, L. B. Price, P. S. Andersen, A. R. Larsen, and R. L. Skov. "Meticillin-resistant Staphylococcus aureus CC398 is an increasing cause of disease in people with no livestock contact in Denmark, 1999 to 2011." Euro Surveill. 2015;20(37):10.2807/1560-7917.ES.2015.20.37.30021. doi: 10.2807 /1560-7917.ES.2015.20.37.30021. PMID: 26535590; PMCID: PMC4902279. https:// www.eurosurveillance.org/content/10.2807/1560-7917.ES.2015.20.37.30021.

117 Graduated with a doctorate, "Lance Price." Milken Institute School of Public Health. George Washington University. Accessed January 31, 2022. https://publichealth.gwu .edu/departments/environmental-and-occupational-health/lance-price.

117 Chicken workers near the Delmarva Peninsula, Price, Lance B et al. "Elevated risk of carrying gentamicin-resistant Escherichia coli among U.S. poultry workers." *Environmental Health Perspectives* vol. 115, 12 (2007): 1738–42. doi:10.1289/ehp.10191.

117 Employs about five hundred thousand people, "The Meatpacking Industry in Rural America during the COVID-19 Pandemic." USDA, October 28, 2021. https://www .ers.usda.gov/covid-19/rural-america/meatpacking-industry/#:~:text=Just%20over%20 500%2C000%20people%20work,industry%20in%20the%20United%20States.& text=While%20these%20counties%20make%20up,employment%20in%20the%20 United%20States.

117 CDC, "Antibiotic Resistance Threats in the U.S., 2013." Centers for Disease Control and Prevention, Department of Health and Human Services, 2013. https://www.cdc .gov/drugresistance/threat-report-2013/pdf/ar-threats-2013-508.pdf#page=6.

117 United Nations, "Stop using antibiotics in healthy animals to prevent the spread of antibiotic resistance." World Health Organization, November 2017. http://www.who.int /mediacentre/news/releases/2017/antibiotics-animals-effectiveness/en/.

117 United Nations, "Press Release—High Level Meeting on Antimicrobial Resistance," General Assembly of the United Nations, September 2016. https://www.un.org/pga/71 /2016/09/21/press-release-hl-meeting-on-antimicrobial-resistance/.

117 United Nations, "New Report Calls for Urgent Action to Avert Antimicrobial Resistance Crisis." World Health Organization. United Nations, April 29, 2019. https://www.who .int/news/item/29-04-2019-new-report-calls-for-urgent-action-to-avert-antimicrobial -resistance-crisis.

117 COVID-19's global death toll, Hannah Ritchie, Edouard Mathieu, Lucas Rodés-Guirao, Cameron Appel, Charlie Giattino, Esteban Ortiz-Ospina, Joe Hasell, Bobbie Macdonald, Diana Beltekian, and Max Roser. "Coronavirus Pandemic (COVID-19)." OurWorldInData.org, 2020. https://ourworldindata.org/coronavirus.

117 A study of deaths across 204 countries, Murray, Christopher JL, Kevin Shunji Ikuta, Fablina Sharara, Lucien Swetschinski, Gisela Robles Aguilar, Authia Gray, Chieh Han, et al. "Global Burden of Bacterial Antimicrobial Resistance in 2019: A Systematic Analysis." *The Lancet* (2022). https://doi.org/10.1016/s0140-6736(21)02724-0.

118 Contract an antibiotic-resistant disease, "2019 Antibiotic Resistance Threats Report." Centers for Disease Control and Prevention, November 23, 2019. https://www.cdc.gov /drugresistance/biggest-threats.html.

118 Suggests that's a low estimate, Burnham, Jason P., Margaret A. Olsen, and Marin H. Kollef. "Re-Estimating Annual Deaths Due to Multidrug-Resistant Organism Infections." *Infection Control & Hospital Epidemiology* 40, no. 1 (November 22, 2018): 112–13. https://doi.org/10.1017/ice.2018.304.

118 The nation's ninth- and tenth-leading causes of death, "FASTSTATS - Leading Causes of Death." Centers for Disease Control and Prevention, October 19, 2021. https://www.cdc .gov/nchs/fastats/leading-causes-of-death.htm.

118 An increase in temperature, MacFadden, D. R., S. F. McGough, D. Fisman, et al. "Antibiotic resistance increases with local temperature." *Nature Clim Change* 8 (2018): 510–514. https://doi.org/10.1038/s41558-018-0161-6.

118 The burden of antibiotic resistance is significantly underestimated, McGough, Sarah F., Derek R. MacFadden, Mohammad W. Hattab, Kåre Mølbak, and Mauricio Santillana. "Rates of Increase of Antibiotic Resistance and Ambient Temperature in Europe: A

Cross-National Analysis of 28 Countries between 2000 and 2016." *Eurosurveillance* 25, no. 45 (February 2, 2020). https://doi.org/10.2807/1560-7917.es.2020.25.45.1900414.

119 The hog may absorb more nutrients, Hughes, Peter, and John Heritage. "Antibiotic Growth-Promoters in Food Animals." United Nations FAO, 2004. https://www.fao.org /3/y5159e/y5159e08.htm.

119 The time it took to reach market weight declined, Graham, Jay P., John J. Boland, and Ellen Silbergeld. "Growth Promoting Antibiotics in Food Animal Production: An Economic Analysis." *Public Health Reports* 122, no. 1 (January 2007): 79–87. https://doi.org /10.1177/003335490712200111.

119 Nearly half of all hog producers that use the practice, Key, Nigel, and William D. McBride. "Antibiotics Used for Growth Promotion Have a Small Positive Effect on Hog Farm Productivity." USDA ERS, July 7, 2004. https://www.ers.usda.gov/amber-waves /2014/july/antibiotics-used-for-growth-promotion-have-a-small-positive-effect-on -hog-farm-productivity/.

119 Began requiring a veterinarian to sign off, "Timeline of FDA Action on Antimicrobial Resistance." US Food and Drug Administration, April 30, 2021. https://www.fda .gov/animal-veterinary/antimicrobial-resistance/timeline-fda-action-antimicrobial -resistance.

119 Cattle and hogs received the most antibiotics, "2020 Summary Report on Antimicrobials Sold or Distributed for Use in Food-Producing Animals." FDA Center for Veterinary Medicine. US Food and Drug Administration, December 2021. https://www.fda.gov /media/154820/download.

119 Lacing water and feed with antibiotics, "Fact Sheet: Veterinary Feed Directive Final Rule and Next Steps." Center for Veterinary Medicine. US Food and Drug Administration, February 11, 2021. https://www.fda.gov/animal-veterinary/development-approval -process/fact-sheet-veterinary-feed-directive-final-rule-and-next-steps.

119 Lacing water and feed with antibiotics, Zangaro, Casey. "Use of Antibiotics Administered in Water to Pigs in the Post-VFD Era." MSU Extension—Pork. Michigan State University, August 6, 2018. https://www.canr.msu.edu/news/use-of-antibiotics -administered-in-water-to-pigs-in-the-post-vfd-era.

119 Lacing water and feed with antibiotics, Muurinen, J., J. Richert, C. L. Wickware, et al. "Swine growth promotion with antibiotics or alternatives can increase antibiotic resistance gene mobility potential." *Sci Rep* 11, 5485 (2021). https://doi.org/10.1038/s41598 -021-84759-9.

119 Fair and humane reasons to administer, "Guidance for Industry the Judicious Use of Medically Important Antimicrobial Drugs in Food-Producing Animals." FDA Center for Veterinary Medicine, April 13, 2012. https://www.fda.gov/media/79140/download.

120 Random testing on a tiny fraction, "Food Safety and Inspection Service Annual Sampling Program Plan Fiscal Year 2021." Food Safety and Inspection Service, 2020. https://www.fsis.usda.gov/sites/default/files/media_file/2021-02/fsis-annual-sampling -plan-fy2021.pdf.

121 Antibiotics often persist, Kulkarni, Prachi, Nathan Olson, Greg Raspanti, Rachel Rosenberg Goldstein, Shawn Gibbs, Amir Sapkota, and Amy Sapkota. "Antibiotic Concentrations Decrease during Wastewater Treatment but Persist at Low Levels in Reclaimed Water." *International Journal of Environmental Research and Public Health* 14, no. 6 (June 21, 2017): 668. https://doi.org/10.3390/ijerph14060668.

121 Antibiotics often persist, Sabri, N. A., S. van Holst, H. Schmitt, B. M. van der Zaan, H. W. Gerritsen, H. H. M. Rijnaarts, and A. A. M. Langenhoff. "Fate of Antibiotics and Antibiotic Resistance Genes during Conventional and Additional Treatment Technologies in Wastewater Treatment Plants." *Science of the Total Environment* 741 (November 1, 2020): 140199. https://doi.org/10.1016/j.scitotenv.2020.140199.

121 Antibiotics often persist, Rodriguez-Mozaz, Sara, Ivone Vaz-Moreira, Saulo Varela Della Giustina, Marta Llorca, Damià Barceló, Sara Schubert, Thomas U. Berendonk, et al. "Antibiotic Residues in Final Effluents of European Wastewater Treatment Plants and Their Impact on the Aquatic Environment." *Environment International* 140 (July 2020): 105733. https://doi.org/10.1016/j.envint.2020.105733.

121 Antibiotics often persist, Hassan, Mahdi, Guangcan Zhu, Yong-ze LU, Ali Hamoud AL-Falahi, Yuan LU, Shan Huang, and Ziren Wan. "Removal of Antibiotics from Wastewater and Its Problematic Effects on Microbial Communities by Bioelectrochemical Technol-

ogy: Current Knowledge and Future Perspectives." *Environmental Engineering Research* 26, no. 1 (February 13, 2020). https://doi.org/10.4491/eer.2019.405.

121 Antibiotics often persist, Hsu, Charlotte. "Investigating Antibiotics in Wastewater." UB Now: News and views for UB faculty and staff. University at Buffalo, May 8, 2019. http://www.buffalo.edu/ubnow/campus.host.html/content/shared/university/news/ub -reporter-articles/stories/2019/05/aga-antibiotics-wastewater.detail.html.

121 The antibiotics stress soils, Lucas, Jane M., Bronte M. Sone, Dana Whitmore, and Michael S. Strickland. "Antibiotics and Temperature Interact to Disrupt Soil Communities and Nutrient Cycling." *Soil Biology and Biochemistry* 163 (December 2021): 108437. https://doi.org/10.1016/j.soilbio.2021.108437.

121 Domestic sales and distribution of antibiotics for livestock, "2020 Summary Report on Antimicrobials Sold or Distributed for Use in Food-Producing Animals." FDA Center for Veterinary Medicine. US Food and Drug Administration, December 2021. https:// www.fda.gov/media/154820/download.

121 Progress has stagnated, "FDA 2019 Report on Antimicrobial Sales For Food-Producing Animals." US Food and Drug Administration, 2019. https://www.fda.gov/animal -veterinary/cvm-updates/fda-releases-annual-summary-report-antimicrobials-sold-or -distributed-2019-use-food-producing.

121 Policy change created a moment of encouragement, Hyun, David. "Antibiotic Sales for Use in Food Animals Increased Again in 2019." The Pew Charitable Trusts, January 21, 2021. https://www.pewtrusts.org/en/research-and-analysis/articles/2021/01/21/antibiotic-sales -for-use-in-food-animals-increased-again-in-2019.

121 A 41 percent drop, "Animal Drug Companies Fulfill Commitment to Change Antibiotic Labels." The Pew Charitable Trusts, 2017. https://www.pewtrusts.org/en/research -and-analysis/articles/2017/01/03/animal-drug-companies-fulfill-commitment-to -change-antibiotic-labels.

121 Short-lived results, "Animal Antibiotic Sales Fall for 2nd Year." The Pew Charitable Trusts, 2018. https://www.pewtrusts.org/en/research-and-analysis/articles/2018/12/21 /animal-antibiotic-sales-fall-for-2nd-year.

121 Still down from peak sale years, "2020 Summary Report on Antimicrobials Sold or Distributed for Use in Food-Producing Animals." FDA Center for Veterinary Medicine. US Food and Drug Administration, December 2021. https://www.fda.gov/media /154820/download.

121 Dall, Chris. "FDA Reports Another Rise in Antibiotic Sales for Livestock." CIDRAP, December 16, 2020. https://www.cidrap.umn.edu/news-perspective/2020/12/fda-reports -another-rise-antibiotic-sales-livestock.

121 Paint a problematic picture, "FDA 2019 Report on Antimicrobial Sales For Food-Producing Animals." US Food and Drug Administration, 2019. https://www.fda.gov /animal-veterinary/cvm-updates/fda-releases-annual-summary-report-antimicrobials -sold-or-distributed-2019-use-food-producing.

121 Medically important antibiotics, Wallinga, David. "New Data: Animal vs. Human Antibiotic Use Remains Lopsided." NRDC, August 4, 2020. https://www.nrdc.org/experts /david-wallinga-md/most-human-antibiotics-still-going-us-meat-production.

122 Antibiotics used in livestock have not been developed specifically for them, Sneeringer, Stacy. "Developing Alternatives to Antibiotics Used in Food Animal Production." USDA, May 30, 2019. https://www.ers.usda.gov/amber-waves/2019/may/developing -alternatives-to-antibiotics-used-in-food-animal-production/.

122 Spending in the United States treating antibiotic-resistant infections alone is estimated at, "CDC Partners Estimate Healthcare Cost of Antibiotic-Resistant Infections." Centers for Disease Control and Prevention. US Department of Health & Human Services, April 1, 2021. https://www.cdc.gov/drugresistance/solutions-initiative/stories/partnership -estimates-healthcare-cost.html.

122 Will only get worse as, Burnham, Jason P. "Climate Change and Antibiotic Resistance: A Deadly Combination." Therapeutic Advances in Infectious Disease, (January 2021). https://doi.org/10.1177/2049936121991374.

122 Continue to come up with more evidence, Price, Lance B., Laura Rogers, and Kevin Lo. "Policy Reforms for Antibiotic Use Claims in Livestock." *Science* 376, no. 6589 (2022): 130–32. https://doi.org/10.1126/science.abj1823.

122 Peer-reviewed study published, Price, Lance B., Laura Rogers, and Kevin Lo. "Policy

Reforms for Antibiotic Use Claims in Livestock." *Science* 376, no. 6589 (2022): 130–32. https://doi.org/10.1126/science.abj1823.

124 Sold BN Ranch, "Blue Apron Acquires BN Ranch; Bill Niman to Join Blue Apron as President and Founder, BN Ranch." Extra Helpings. Blue Apron, October 2, 2019. https://blog.blueapron.com/blue-apron-acquires-bn-ranch/.

124 Inspector General Report, Rep, 2020. Controls Over Meat, Poultry, and Egg Product Labels - Office of the Inspector General: Audit Report 24601-0002-23 https://www.usda.gov/sites/default/files/audit-reports/24601-0002-23.pdf.

125 Survived cancer as a kid, credits to transitioning to an all-organic diet, "Lukas Walton." *Forbes*. Accessed January 31, 2022. https://www.forbes.com/profile/lukas-walton/.

125 Majored in environmentally sustainable business at Colorado College, de Jong, David, and Tom Metcalf. "A Wal-Mart Heir Is $27 Billion Poorer Than Everyone Thought." *Bloomberg*, November 6, 2015. https://www.bloomberg.com/news/articles/2015-11-06/a-wal-mart-heir-is-27-billion-poorer-than-everyone-calculated.

CHAPTER 10

127 José Andrés, Sorvino, Chloe, and José Andrés. Interview with José Andrés on future of restaurant business and humanitarian aid. June 2021.

128 Sought help from a food bank, 60 million, "Charitable Food Assistance Participation in 2020." Feeding America, September 2021. https://www.feedingamerica.org/sites/default/files/2021-09/Charitable%20Food%20Assistance%20Participation%20in%202020.pdf.

128 The hungry in America, Alisha Coleman-Jensen, Matthew P. Rabbitt, Christian A. Gregory, and Anita Singh. "Household Food Security in the United States in 2020, ERR-298." US Department of Agriculture. Economic Research Service, 2021. https://www.ers.usda.gov/webdocs/publications/102076/err-298.pdf?v=8810.9.

129 Lack consistent access to enough healthy food, 40 million, "Hunger in America Is Growing." Feeding America. Accessed September 8, 2021. https://www.feedingamerica.org/hunger-in-america.

129 Children live with pervasive hunger, 13 million, "Child Food Insecurity." Feeding America. Howard G. Bufett Foundation, 2018. https://www.feedingamerica.org/sites/default/files/research/map-the-meal-gap/2016/child/DC_AllCounties_CDs_CFI_2016.pdf.

129 Farmers whose sole income is raising chickens live below the poverty line, 71 percent, "The Business of Broilers: Hidden Costs of Putting a Chicken on Every Grill." The Pew Charitable Trusts, December 2013. https://www.pewtrusts.org/en/research-and-analysis/reports/2013/12/20/the-business-of-broilers-hidden-costs-of-putting-a-chicken-on-every-grill#:~:text=Few%20growers%20are%20able%20to,living%20below%20the%20poverty%20line.

129 Notoriously low paying, Sorvino, Chloe, and Mark Lauritsen. Interview with UFCW's Mark Lauritsen on meat-packer power. Personal, July 2020.

129 Barely enough to shell out for chicken himself, Sorvino, Chloe. "Fear and Closeness on Food's Front Line: A Poultry Worker Speaks out on the Cost of Being Essential." *Forbes*, April 12, 2020. https://www.forbes.com/sites/chloesorvino/2020/04/10/fear-and-closeness-on-foods-frontline-a-poultry-worker-speaks-out-on-the-cost-of-being-essential/.

129 The Supplemental Nutrition Assistance Program, "Policy Basics: The Supplemental Nutrition Assistance Program (SNAP)." Center on Budget and Policy Priorities, 2019. https://www.cbpp.org/research/food-assistance/the-supplemental-nutrition-assistance-program-snap.

129 Average benefit per person pre-pandemic, David Shepardson. "Biden Administration Confirms It Will Boost Food Stamps by Record Amount." Reuters, August 16, 2021. https://www.reuters.com/world/us/biden-administration-confirms-it-will-boost-food-stamps-by-record-amount-2021-08-16/.

129 Increased funding by $29 billion, "Fact Sheet: President Biden's New Executive Actions Deliver Economic Relief for American Families and Businesses amid the Covid-19 Crises." The White House, January 22, 2021. https://www.whitehouse.gov/briefing-room/statements-releases/2021/01/22/fact-sheet-president-bidens-new-executive-actions-deliver-economic-relief-for-american-families-and-businesses-amid-the-covid-19-crises/.

130 The first funding increase to SNAP since 2006, "USDA Modernizes the Thrifty Food

Plan, Updates SNAP Benefits: USDA-FNS." USDA, August 16, 2021. https://www.fns
.usda.gov/news-item/usda-0179.21.

130 The largest permanent spike in the program's six-decade history, DeParle, Jason. "Biden
Administration Prompts Largest Permanent Increase in Food Stamps." *The New York
Times*, August 15, 2021. https://www.nytimes.com/2021/08/15/us/politics/biden-food
-stamps.html.

130 Monthly allocations increased by an average of, DeParle, Jason. "Biden Administration
Prompts Largest Permanent Increase in Food Stamps." *The New York Times*, August 15,
2021. https://www.nytimes.com/2021/08/15/us/politics/biden-food-stamps.html.

130 The consumer opts for something processed, Moss, Michael. *Hooked: Food, Free Will,
and How the Food Giants Exploit Our Addictions*. Random House, 2021.

130 A diet full of processed foods can lead to serious disease and complicates the management of chronic illness, Seligman, Hilary K., Barbara A. Laraia, and Margot B. Kushel.
"Food Insecurity Is Associated with Chronic Disease among Low-Income NHANES
Participants." *Journal of Nutrition* 140, no. 2 (2009): 304–10. https://doi.org/10.3945
/jn.109.112573.

130 Households are more likely to have health problems from what they eat, "Importance of
Nutrition on Health in America." Feeding America. Accessed September 8, 2021. https://
www.feedingamerica.org/hunger-in-america/impact-of-hunger/hunger-and-nutrition.

130 Just enough aid, Nestle, Marion, and Kerry Trueman. *Let's Ask Marion: What You Need
to Know about the Politics of Food, Nutrition, and Health*. Oakland, CA: University of
California Press, 2020, pp. 66–68.

131 Poor Laws, Nestle, Marion, and Kerry Trueman. Let's Ask Marion: What You Need to
Know about the Politics of Food, Nutrition, and Health. Oakland, CA: University of
California Press, 2020.

131 Nearly half of SNAP recipients are children, "Snap Helps Millions of Children." Center
on Budget and Policy Priorities, April 26, 2017. https://www.cbpp.org/research/food
-assistance/snap-helps-millions-of-children.

131 Group 1 carcinogens, "IARC Monographs Evaluate Consumption of Red Meat and Processed Meat." International Agency for Research on Cancer. World Health Organization,
October 26, 2015. https://www.iarc.who.int/wp-content/uploads/2018/07/pr240_E.pdf.

131 Group 2A carcinogens, "Five Meats by the Slice: See How Little 50 Grams Actually Is."
CBCnews. CBC/Radio Canada, October 27, 2015. https://www.cbc.ca/news/canada
/saskatoon/five-meats-by-the-slice-see-how-little-50-grams-actually-is-1.3289822.

131 World Cancer Research Fund also suggests, "Limit Red and Processed Meat." World Cancer Research Fund International, August 11, 2021. https://www.wcrf.org/dietandcance
r/limit-red-and-processed-meat/#:~:text=Dietary%20goal,12%E2%80%9318oz)%20
cooked%20weight.

131 In some marginalized neighborhoods, Fryar, C. D., J. P. Hughes, K. A., Herrick, and
N. Ahluwalia. "Fast food consumption among adults in the United States, 2013–2016."
NCHS Data Brief 322 (2018): 1–8.

131 Phthalates, plasticizers, Edwards, L., N. L. McCray, B. N. VanNoy, et al. "Phthalate and
novel plasticizer concentrations in food items from U.S. fast food chains: a preliminary
analysis." *J Expo Sci Environ Epidemiol* (2021). https://doi.org/10.1038/s41370-021
-00392-8.

132 The top-purchased category for each, Garasky, Steven. "FOODS TYPICALLY PUR-
CHASED BY SUPPLEMENTAL NUTRITION ASSISTANCE PROGRAM (SNAP)
HOUSEHOLDS." USDA, November 2016. https://fns-prod.azureedge.net/sites/default
/files/ops/SNAPFoodsTypicallyPurchased.pdf.

132 Spent on industrially produced food, "Buyer Power and Economic Discrimination in
the Grocery Aisle: Kitchen Table Issues for American Consumers." National Grocers
Association, 2021.

132 Natural sources of nitrates, Provenza, Frederick D. *Nourishment: What Animals Can
Teach Us about Rediscovering Our Nutritional Wisdom*. White River Junction, VT: Chelsea Green Publishing, 2018.

133 Food production exported, 20 percent, "FAQs: How Important Are Exports to the U.S.
Agricultural Sector?" Economic Research Service U.S. DEPARTMENT OF AGRICUL-
TURE. Economic Research Service U.S. DEPARTMENT OF AGRICULTURE. Accessed

April 12, 2022. https://www.ers.usda.gov/faqs/#:~:text=Trade%20is%20essential%20to%20the,soybeans%2C%20corn%2C%20and%20wheat.

133 Only half a percent of US agricultural exports, Schechinger, Anne. "Think U.S. Agriculture Will End World Hunger? Think Again." Environmental Working Group, October 5, 2016. https://www.ewg.org/news-insights/news/think-us-agriculture-will-end-world-hunger-think-again.

133 "Sophia Roe Talks Happiness, Why Wellness Can Make Us Sick, & Being The 'Other' Bubble." Good American. Accessed January 2, 2022. https://www.goodamerican.com/blogs/good-times/sophia-roe-talks-happiness-why-wellness-can-make-us-sick-being-the-other-bubble.

CHAPTER 11

139 Bison killed each year, Sorvino, Chloe, and Bob Dineen. Interview with Bob Dineen. January 12, 2022.

139 Cattle annually, "The United States Meat Industry at a Glance." North American Meat Institute. Accessed January 31, 2022. https://www.meatinstitute.org/index.php?ht=d%2Fsp%2Fi%2F47465%2Fpid%2F47465.

140 Burning sage and a moment of silence, "Meet the Family." Wild Idea Buffalo. Accessed January 31, 2022. https://wildideabuffalo.com/pages/meet-our-founders#:~:text=Dan%20O'Brien%20started%20Wild,red%20meat%20on%20the%20planet.%E2%80%9D.

140 Producing bison meat this way for thirty years, O'Brien, Jill. "Meet Our Founding Father." Wild Idea Buffalo, June 6, 2018. https://wildideabuffalo.com/blogs/blog/meet-our-founding-father.

140 The long trailer, Amann, Denise, Trinia Greene, Ben Weaver, Kristopher Lewandowski, Kyra Harty, Larry Lyons, Adrian Lujan, et al. "An Introduction to Mobile Slaughter Units." USDA, February 21, 2017. https://www.usda.gov/media/blog/2010/08/30/introduction-mobile-slaughter-units.

141 Ensuring that the overall sustainability of the herd is maintained, "Humane Field Harvest." Wild Idea Buffalo. Accessed January 31, 2022. https://wildideabuffalo.com/pages/humane-field-harvest.

141 Fourth-largest individual landowner in the country, Land Report Editors. "Ted Turner Launches the Turner Institute of Ecoagriculture." The Land Report, September 10, 2021. https://landreport.com/2021/09/ted-turner-launches-the-turner-institute-of-ecoagriculture/.

143 A conservation trust, "Turner Ranches." Turner Enterprises. Accessed January 31, 2022. https://www.tedturner.com/turner-ranches/.

143 The wild bison population was as high as thirty-five million, Taylor, M. Scott. "Buffalo Hunt: International Trade and the Virtual Extinction of the North American Bison." 2007. https://doi.org/10.3386/w12969.

143 Loss of culture included the loss of a sustainable agricultural practice, "American Bison." NPS. Accessed January 31, 2022. https://www.nps.gov/common/uploads/teachers/lessonplans/American%20Bison20131.pdf.

143 Without bison hooves charging across, Isenberg, Andrew C. *The Destruction of the Bison.* Cambridge University Press, 2020. https://doi.org/10.1017/9781108848879.

143 Dust bowl that followed, Seager, Richard, and Celine Herweijer. "Causes and Consequences of Nineteenth Century Droughts in North America." Lamont-Doherty Earth Observatory. Columbia University. Accessed January 31, 2022. https://ocp.ldeo.columbia.edu/res/div/ocp/drought/nineteenth.shtml.

144 Practice of hunting only what was necessary and using every scrap kept the overall bison population strong, Wheat, Joe Ben. "A Paleo-Indian Bison Kill." *Scientific American* 216, no. 1 (1967): 44–52. https://doi.org/10.1038/scientificamerican0167-44.

144 Sustainability wasn't an afterthought, Bushnell, David I. "The Various Uses of Buffalo Hair by the North American Indians." *The William and Mary Quarterly* 23, no. 4 (1915): 299. https://doi.org/10.2307/1915280.

144 Did not till the land and repurposed wasted fish to fertilize soils, Mann, Charles C. *1491: New Revelations of the Americas before Columbus.* New York: Alfred A. Knopf, 2019.

145 Long bath in the smoker, Ferris, Shaldon. "Building a Business Rooted in Indigenous Values: Tanka Bar." *Cultural Survival Quarterly Magazine* (December 2020). https://

www.culturalsurvival.org/publications/cultural-survival-quarterly/building-business
-rooted-indigenous-values-tanka-bar.

145 Aimed to support the struggling Pine Ridge Reservation in South Dakota, "About Us."
Tanka Bar. Accessed January 31, 2022. https://tankabar.com/pages/about-us.

145 Goal was to eventually build a 100 percent Native-owned supply chain, Noble, Marilyn.
"Bison Bars Were Supposed to Restore Native Communities and Grass-Based Ranches.
Then Came Epic Provisions." *The Counter*, December 17, 2020. https://thecounter.org
/tanka-bar-general-mills-epic-provisions-bison-bars/.

145 Even more beholden to leverage, "Buyer Power and Economic Discrimination in the
Grocery Aisle: Kitchen Table Issues for American Consumers." The National Grocers
Association, 2021.

146 A market families relied on, Noble, Marilyn. "Bison Bars Were Supposed to Restore Native Communities and Grass-Based Ranches. Then Came Epic Provisions." *The Counter*,
December 17, 2020. https://thecounter.org/tanka-bar-general-mills-epic-provisions
-bison-bars/.

146 Distribution, revenue, Noble, Marilyn. "Bison Bars Were Supposed to Restore Native
Communities and Grass-Based Ranches. Then Came Epic Provisions." *The Counter*, January 24, 2020. https://thecounter.org/tanka-bar-general-mills-epic-provisions-bison-bars/.

146 Couldn't keep up with the hard-to-predict demand, Noble, Marilyn. "One Year after
Native-Owned Tanka Bar Had Lost Nearly Everything, the Buffalo Are on Their Way
Back." *The Counter*, February 21, 2020. https://thecounter.org/tanka-bar-niman-ranch
-bison-grassfed/.

147 Dr. George Washington Carver, Penniman, Leah, with foreword by Karen Washington.
Farming While Black. S.I.: Chelsea Green Publishing, 2018.

148 Percent of farmers were Black in 1910, "Farm Statistics by Race, Nativity, and Sex of
Farmer." US Census, 1920. https://www2.census.gov/library/publications/decennial/1920
/volume-5/06229676v5ch04.pdf.

148 Left out of federal help, Newkirk, Vann R. "The Great Land Robbery." *The Atlantic*,
June 16, 2020. https://www.theatlantic.com/magazine/archive/2019/09/this-land-was
-our-land/594742/.

148 Land was dispossessed, "2007 U.S. Census of Agriculture: Table 54. Selected Farm
Characteristics by Race of Principal Operator: 2007 and 2002." USDA, National Agricultural Statistics Service. Environmental Working Group, 2007. https://static.ewg
.org/reports/2021/BlackFarmerDiscriminationTimeline/2007_Ag-Census.pdf?_ga=
2.171760032.1834284671.1643399289-1257110918.1643089264.

148 Preferential lending terms to titles with sole holders, Reynolds, Bruce J., "Black Farmers
in America, 1865–2000: The pursuit of independent farming and the role of Cooperatives." 2002.

149 Other weaknesses in the legal framework, "Timeline: Black Farmers and the USDA,
1920–Present." Environmental Working Group. Accessed January 31, 2022. https://www
.ewg.org/research/black-farmer-usda-timeline/.

149 Didn't leave wills, Davy, Dãnia. "What Would a Pro-Black Farmer Policy Regime Look
like?" *Nonprofit Quarterly* (October 20, 2021). https://nonprofitquarterly.org/what
-would-a-pro-black-farmer-policy-regime-look-like/.

149 The USDA's last survey in 2017, "2012 Census of Agriculture—Table 62. Selected Principal Operator Characteristics by Race 2012 and 2017." USDA, 2012. https://www.nass.
usda.gov/Publications/AgCensus/2012/Full_Report/Volume_1,_Chapter_1_US/st99_1
_062_062.pdf.

149 Isn't as widespread as it should be, "Crop Acreage Data." USDA, 2021. https://www.fsa
.usda.gov/news-room/efoia/electronic-reading-room/frequently-requested-information
/crop-acreage-data/index.

149 Synthetics and monoculture dominate, Brown, Sarah E., Daniel C. Miller, Pablo J.
Ordonez, and Kathy Baylis. "Evidence for the Impacts of Agroforestry on Agricultural
Productivity, Ecosystem Services, and Human Well-Being in High-Income Countries:
A Systematic Map Protocol." *Environmental Evidence* 7, no. 1 (2018). https://doi.org
/10.1186/s13750-018-0136-0.

149 Patented seeds, "Recent Trends in GE Adoption." USDA, July 17, 2020. https://www.ers
.usda.gov/data-products/adoption-of-genetically-engineered-crops-in-the-us/recent
-trends-in-ge-adoption/.

149 Just six genotypes, Martin, Adam R., Marc W. Cadotte, Marney E. Isaac, Rubén Milla, Denis Vile, and Cyrille Violle. "Regional and Global Shifts in Crop Diversity through the Anthropocene." *PLOS One* 14, no. 2 (2019). https://doi.org/10.1371/journal.pone.0209788.

149 From planting cover crops to refusing to till soils, "Conservation Choices: Soil Health Practices." USDA. Accessed January 31, 2022. https://www.nrcs.usda.gov/Internet/FSE _DOCUMENTS/nrcseprd1318196.pdf.

149 A wide range of varied practices, "Soil Health Key Points." USDA. Accessed January 31, 2022. https://www.nrcs.usda.gov/Internet/FSE_DOCUMENTS/stelprdb1082147.pdf.

149 A wide range of varied practices, White, Charlie and, and Mary Barbercheck. "Managing Soil Health: Concepts and Practices." Penn State Extension. The Pennsylvania State University, July 31, 2017. https://extension.psu.edu/managing-soil-health-concepts-and -practices.

150 Contributes to soil erosion and the loss of biodiversity, Union of Concerned Scientists. "Tyson Foods Enrolled Less than Five Percent of Feed Acreage in Sustainability Program, Science Group Finds." Union of Concerned Scientists. Union of Concerned Scientists, 2022. https://www.ucsusa.org/about/news/tysons-feed-footprint.

150 Prairie strips, Asbjornsen, H., V. Hernandez-Santana, M. Liebman, J. Bayala, J. Chen, M. Helmers, C. K. Ong, and L. A. Schulte. "Targeting Perennial Vegetation in Agricultural Landscapes for Enhancing Ecosystem Services." *Renewable Agriculture and Food Systems* 29, no. 2 (June 2014): 101–25. https://doi.org/10.1017/s1742170512000385.

150 As much as 25 percent, "The Clean Lakes, Estuaries and Rivers Initiative Fact Sheet." Farm Service Agency. USDA, December 2019. https://www.fsa.usda.gov/Assets/USDA -FSA-Public/usdafiles/FactSheets/2019/crp_clear_initiative_prairie_strip_practice-fact _sheet.pdf.

150 Schulte, Lisa A., Jarad Niemi, Matthew J. Helmers, Matt Liebman, J. Gordon Arbuckle, David E. James, Randall K. Kolka, et al. "Prairie Strips Improve Biodiversity and the Delivery of Multiple Ecosystem Services from Corn–Soybean Croplands." *Proceedings of the National Academy of Sciences* 114, no. 42 (2017): 11247–52. https://doi.org/10.1073 /pnas.1620229114.

150 Improving water quality and biodiversity around croplands, Moore, Kenneth J., Robert P. Anex, Amani E. Elobeid, Shuizhang Fei, Cornelia B. Flora, A. Susana Goggi, Keri L. Jacobs, et al. "Regenerating Agricultural Landscapes with Perennial Groundcover for Intensive Crop Production." *Agronomy* 9, no. 8 (2019): 458. https://doi.org/10.3390 /agronomy9080458.

150 Organic carbon in those soils increases, Ontl, Todd A, and Lisa A Schulte. "Soil Carbon Storage." *Nature Education Knowledge* 3, no. 10 (2012). https://doi.org/10.1016/c2016 -0-03949-9.

151 Sold under its Grass Run label, "Frequently Asked Questions about Grass Fed Beef." Grass Run Farms, August 17, 2021. https://grassrunfarms.com/grass-fed-beef-frequently -asked-questions/.

151 Only one to have a large grass-fed division, "Grass Run Farms Producer Sustainability Pilot." JBS USA. Accessed January 31, 2022. https://sustainability.jbsfoodsgroup.com /stories/jbs-usa-beef-grass-run-farms-producer-sustainability-pilot/.

151 Among the top grass-fed producers, "Back to Grass: the Market Potential for U.S. Grassfed Beef." Stone Barns Center for Food and Agriculture, April 2017. https://www .stonebarnscenter.org/wp-content/uploads/2017/10/Grassfed_Full_v2.pdf.

151 Can be many different things, Lawler, Moira. "What Meat Labels like 'Organic' and 'Grass Fed' Actually Mean—and Whether You Should Care." Certified Humane, November 30, 2017. https://certifiedhumane.org/meat-labels-like-organic-grass-fed-actually -mean-whether-care/.

151 Grass feedlots where livestock eat grass pellets and are still kept in confinement, "Back to Grass: the Market Potential for U.S. Grassfed Beef." Stone Barns Center for Food and Agriculture, April 2017, p. 9. https://www.stonebarnscenter.org/wp-content/uploads /2017/10/Grassfed_Full_v2.pdf.

151 They pick a healthy mix of forage, Provenza, Frederick D. *Nourishment: What Animals Can Teach Us about Rediscovering Our Nutritional Wisdom*. White River Junction, VT: Chelsea Green Publishing, 2018.

152 The phytochemical richness of a landscape where animals were raised, Provenza, Fred-

erick D. *Nourishment: What Animals Can Teach Us about Rediscovering Our Nutritional Wisdom*. White River Junction, VT: Chelsea Green Publishing, 2018, p. 133.

152 Their meat tastes worse, Grandin, Temple. "The effect of stress on livestock and meat quality prior to and during slaughter." *International Journal for the Study of Animal Problems* 1(5) (2018): 313–37.

153 More data than any American producer, "Guidelines for the Safe Manufacture of Small-goods." Meat and Livestock Australia Ltd., 2003 Meat and Livestock Australia, 2011 Meat and Livestock Australia Meat Standards Australia beef information kit [2018-4-28]. https://www.mla.com.au/globalassets/mla-corporate/marketing-beef-and-lamb/documents/meat-standards-australia/tt_whole-set.pdf (2011).

153 Five hundred years or more to create an inch of fresh topsoil under natural conditions, "What on Earth Is Soil? Fact Sheet." USDA. Accessed January 31, 2022. https://www.nrcs.usda.gov/Internet/FSE_DOCUMENTS/nrcs144p2_002430.pdf.

154 "Study: White Oak Pastures Beef Reduces Atmospheric Carbon." PR Newswire. White Oak Pastures, May 1, 2019. https://www.prnewswire.com/news-releases/study-white-oak-pastures-beef-reduces-atmospheric-carbon-300841416.html.

154 Away from commodities peanuts and cotton, "Our Commitment." White Oak Pastures. Accessed January 31, 2022. https://whiteoakpastures.com/pages/our-commitment.

154 Soil organic matter, Rowntree, Jason E., Paige L. Stanley, Isabella C. F. Maciel, Mariko Thorbecke, Steven T. Rosenzweig, Dennis W. Hancock, Aidee Guzman, and Matt R. Raven. "Ecosystem Impacts and Productive Capacity of a Multi-Species Pastured Livestock System." Frontiers, December, 4, 2020. https://www.frontiersin.org/articles/10.3389/fsufs.2020.544984/full.

154 Aggregate stability increased ,"Carbon Footprint Evaluation of Regenerative Grazing at White Oak Pastures." Quantis, February 25, 2019.

154 A greenhouse gas footprint, "Study: White Oak Pastures Beef Reduces Atmospheric Carbon." Around the Farm Blog. White Oak Pastures, June 4, 2019. http://blog.whiteoakpastures.com/blog/carbon-negative-grassfed-beef.

154 Called into question the long-term potential of carbon sequestration, Yang, Judy Q., Xinning Zhang, Ian C. Bourg, and Howard A. Stone. "4D Imaging Reveals Mechanisms of Clay-Carbon Protection and Release." *Nature Communications* 12, no. 1 (January 27, 2021). https://doi.org/10.1038/s41467-020-20798-6.

155 Hotter temperatures made soils' carbon storage decline, Hartley, Iain P., Tim C. Hill, Sarah E. Chadburn, and Gustaf Hugelius. "Temperature Effects on Carbon Storage Are Controlled by Soil Stabilisation Capacities." *Nature Communications* 12, no. 1 (November 18, 2021). https://doi.org/10.1038/s41467-021-27101-1.

156 A map outlining America's top twenty nitrogen pollution hotspots, "The 20 Best Places to Tackle U.S. Farm Nitrogen Pollution." The University of Vermont Gund Institute for the Environment, February 16, 2021. https://www.uvm.edu/gund/news/20-best-places-tackle-us-farm-nitrogen-pollution.

156 Replace all the grain-finished cattle in the U.S. without using more land, "Back to Grass: The Market Potential for U.S. Grassfed Beef." Stone Barns Center for Food and Agriculture, April 2017. https://www.stonebarnscenter.org/wp-content/uploads/2017/10/Grassfed_Full_v2.pdf.

156 Rotational grazing could, Smith Thomas, Heather. "Ranchers Sing the Praises of Mob Grazing of Cattle." *Beef Magazine*, August 20, 2013. https://www.beefmagazine.com/pasture-range/ranchers-sing-praises-mob-grazing-cattle.

156 Currently pegged at, $4 billion, "Back to Grass: The Market Potential for U.S. Grassfed Beef." Stone Barns Center for Food and Agriculture, April 2017. https://www.stonebarnscenter.org/wp-content/uploads/2017/10/Grassfed_Full_v2.pdf.

156 Estimated total market size, "Sector at a Glance." USDA. Accessed January 31, 2022. https://www.ers.usda.gov/topics/animal-products/cattle-beef/sector-at-a-glance/.

157 Increasing stocking density, Gerrish, Jim. "Stocking Rate vs. Stock Density." *Beef Magazine*, December 16, 2011. https://www.beefmagazine.com/mag/beef_stocking_rate_vs.

157 Would increase America's methane emissions, Hayek, Matthew N, and Rachael D. Garrett. "Nationwide Shift to Grass-Fed Beef Requires Larger Cattle Population." *Environmental Research Letters* 13, no. 8 (July 25, 2018): 084005. https://doi.org/10.1088/1748-9326/aad401.

CHAPTER 12

159 Carbon to offset a relatively small, Rundquist, Soren, and Craig Cox. "In the Corn Belt, Planting of Cover Crops Plateaus, Even as Interest Grows in Their Potential to Address the Climate Crisis." Environmental Working Group, May 31, 2021. https://www.ewg.org /research/corn-belt-planting-cover-crops-plateaus-even-interest-grows-their-potential -address.

160 One in twenty acres of Midwestern cropland, "Cover Crops, Touted as a Climate Crisis Solution, Planted on Only 1 in 20 Acres of Corn Belt Cropland." Environmental Working Group, September 1, 2021. https://www.ewg.org/news-insights/news-release /cover-crops-touted-climate-crisis-solution-planted-only-1-20-acres-corn?auHash= ioiWVa36ve2wEibszrltj5FOLkAaUfO2wDdN8hb3dDo.

160 A natural preventive measure, "In the Corn Belt, Planting of Cover Crops Plateaus, Even as Interest Grows in Their Potential to Address the Climate Crisis." Environmental Working Group, May 31, 2021. https://www.ewg.org/research/corn-belt-planting-cover-crops -plateaus-even-interest-grows-their-potential-address?auHash=OgB5yPBpqsEnOpD8 caWxV8LR5yL6AIO6Bv1qiRBG0Kg.

162 You are what you eat, Gundry, Steven R., and Olivia Bell Buehl. *The Plant Paradox: The Hidden Dangers in "Healthy" Foods That Cause Disease and Weight Gain*. New York, NY: Harper Wave, an imprint of HarperCollins Publishers, 2018.

162 Fed soy and corn, Gundry, Steven R., and Olivia Bell Buehl. *The Plant Paradox: The Hidden Dangers in "Healthy" Foods That Cause Disease and Weight Gain*, p. 19.

162 Kelly Clarkson was promoting, London, Jaclyn. "The Doctor behind Kelly Clarkson's Weight Loss Speaks out about Her Using His Method." *Good Housekeeping*, June 3, 2019. https://www.goodhousekeeping.com/health/diet-nutrition/a21931116/plant-paradox -diet/.

162 Kelly Clarkson was promoting, Lowin, Rebekah. "Kelly Clarkson Swears by This Diet Cookbook—and It's on Sale Right Now." *Country Living*, January 6, 2020. https://www .countryliving.com/life/entertainment/a22229939/kelly-clarkson-plant-paradox-diet -cookbook/.

162 A fad that wouldn't work on everybody, "Weight Loss on the Plant Paradox." Cleveland Clinic, August 29, 2021. https://health.clevelandclinic.org/why-weight-loss-on-the- plant-paradox-diet-is-itself-a-paradox/#:~:text=What%20the%20Plant%20Paradox% 20does,re%20going%20to%20lose%20weight.%E2%80%9D.

162 Mayo Clinic cautioned against believing a lectin-free diet could, "Mayo Clinic Q and A: What Are Dietary Lectins and Should You Avoid Eating Them?" Mayo Foundation for Medical Education and Research. Accessed September 8, 2021. https://newsnetwork .mayoclinic.org/discussion/mayo-clinic-q-and-a-what-are-dietary-lectins-and-should -you-avoid-eating-them/.

163 Cornish Cross, Fanatico, Anne. "Meat Chicken Breeds for Pastured Production - Aviagen." National Sustainable Agriculture Information Service. National Center for Appropriate Technology. Accessed January 31, 2022. http://en.aviagen.com/assets/Public -Relations-Images/ATTRAMeatChickenBreeds.pdf.

164 Prized Angus cattle, "Breeds of Livestock." Department of Animal Science. Oklahoma State University. Accessed January 31, 2022. http://afs.okstate.edu/breeds/cattle/redangus /index-2.html/.

164 Bowlegged and can be sickly, "The Business of Broilers: Hidden Costs of Putting a Chicken on Every Grill." The Pew Charitable Trusts. Accessed January 31, 2022. https://www.pewtrusts.org/research-and-analysis/reports/2013/12/20/the-business-of -broilers-hidden-costs-of-putting-a-chicken-on-every-grill.

164 Days maturing before going to market, "Heritage Chickens." The Livestock Conservancy. Accessed January 31, 2022. https://livestockconservancy.org/heritage-chicken -definition/.

165 Aviagen is based in Huntsville, Alabama, *Walmart Inc. vs Pilgrim's Pride Corporation et al.* (US District Court for the Western Division of Arkansas Fayetteville Division, May 24, 2019).

165 BC Partners acquired Aviagen, Meikle, Brad. "BC Partners Sells Aviagen to Advent." Buyouts Insider, June 6, 2003. https://www.buyoutsinsider.com/bc-partners-sells -aviagen-to-advent/.

165 Changed hands to global private equity firm Advent International, "Advent International Closes $3.3B Buyout Fund." *Boston Business Journal*. Bizjournals.com, April 25, 2005. https://www.bizjournals.com/boston/stories/2005/04/25/daily10.html.

165 The last American breeder selling slow-growth chicken genetics, "Our Story." Groupe Grimaud. Accessed January 31, 2022. https://grimaud.com/en/our-story/.

166 Ffity percent of broiler genetics in the United States, *Walmart Inc. vs Pilgrim's Pride Corporation et al.* (US District Court for the Western Division of Arkansas Fayetteville Division, May 24, 2019).

166 Subsidiary Cobb-Vantress, *Walmart Inc. vs Pilgrim's Pride Corporation et al.* (US District Court for the Western Division of Arkansas Fayetteville Division, May 24, 2019).

CHAPTER 13

169 Humanity will not meet the goals that scientists have laid out, *Climate Change 2021: The Physical Science Basis. Contribution of Working Group I to the Sixth Assessment Report of the Intergovernmental Panel on Climate Change*. Masson-Delmotte, V., P. Zhai, A. Pirani, S., L. Connors, C. Péan, S. Berger, N. Caud, Y. Chen, L. Goldfarb, M. I. Gomis, M. Huang, K. Leitzell, E. Lonnoy, J. B., R. Matthews, T. K. Maycock, T. Waterfield, O. Yelekçi, R. Yu, and B. Zhou (eds.). Cambridge University Press. In Press.

170 Preparing for a potentially $10 billion public listing, Sorvino, Chloe. "Impossible Foods' CEO Says Going Public Is 'Inevitable.' So Why Have Most of 2021's Food Listings Spoiled?" *Forbes*, November 4, 2021. https://www.forbes.com/sites/chloesorvino/2021 /11/04/impossible-foods-ceo-says-going-public-is-inevitable-so-why-have-most-of -2021s-food-listings-spoiled/.

170 Impossible claims to use, Impossible Burger Environmental Life Cycle Assessment 2019. Quantis, 2019. https://impossiblefoods.com/sustainable-food/burger-life-cycle -assessment-2019.

170 Beyond touts, Heller, Martin C. "Beyond Meat's Beyond Burger Life Cycle Assessment." Center for Sustainable Systems. University of Michigan, September 14, 2018. https://css .umich.edu/sites/default/files/publication/CSS18-10.pdf.

170 Orlando, Brian. "Retail Sales Data." Plant Based Foods Association, April 7, 2021. https://www.plantbasedfoods.org/retail-sales-data/.

170 Barclays expects plant-based will rise to 10 percent of total meat consumption, "Carving up the Alternative Meat Market." Barclays Investment Bank, August 19, 2019. https:// www.investmentbank.barclays.com/our-insights/carving-up-the-alternative-meat -market.html.

171 One projection puts sales of alternative meat, eggs, dairy, and seafood products at, "Alternative-Protein Market to Reach at Least $290 Billion by 2035." BCG Global and Blue Horizon Corporation, March 23, 2021. https://www.bcg.com/press/23march2021 -alternative-protein-market-reach-290-billion-by-2035.

175 Not going to change, Santo, Raychel E., Brent F. Kim, Sarah E. Goldman, Jan Dutkiewicz, Erin M. Biehl, Martin W. Bloem, Roni A. Neff, and Keeve E. Nachman. "Considering Plant-Based Meat Substitutes and Cell-Based Meats: A Public Health and Food Systems Perspective." *Frontiers in Sustainable Food Systems* 4 (2020). https://doi.org/10.3389 /fsufs.2020.00134.

175 Genuinely blown away, Dai, Serena. "David Chang Adds Plant Based 'Impossible Burger' to Nishi Menu." Eater/VOX, July 26, 2016. https://ny.eater.com/2016/7/26 /12277310/david-chang-impossible-burger-nishi.

175 The most ever in the burgeoning industry's history, Keerie, Maia. "New GFI State of the Industry Reports Show Alternative Proteins Are Poised to Flourish Post-Covid-19." The Good Food Institute, January 22, 2021. https://gfi.org/blog/state-of-the-industry -2020/.

182 A stint in motivational speaking, "Joshua Tetrick: Speaker Agency, Speaking Fee." Speaking.com. Accessed January 31, 2022. https://speaking.com/speakers/joshua-tetrick/#:~ :text=Joshua%20Tetrick%20was%20named%20Rookie,linebacker%20with%20West% 20Virginia%20University.&text=Tetrick%20is%20the%20CEO%20and,social%20 entrepreneurs%20to%20micro%2Dinvestments.

183 Putting a hit on, Mohan, Geoffrey. "The Egg Industry Launched a Secret Two-Year War against a Vegan Mayonnaise Competitor." *Los Angeles Times*, October 7, 2016. https:// www.latimes.com/business/la-fi-egg-board-investigation-20161007-snap-story.html.

184 Buy back mayo from store shelves, Zaleski, Olivia, Peter Waldman, and Ellen Huet. "How Hampton Creek Sold Silicon Valley on a Fake-Mayo Miracle." *Bloomberg*, September 22, 2016. https://www.bloomberg.com/features/2016-hampton-creek-just-mayo/.

184 Just 1 percent of his 2014 sales, Zaleski, Olivia. "Inside the Board Resignations at Food Startup Hampton Creek." *Chicago Tribune*, June 3, 2018. https://www.chicagotribune.com/business/ct-hampton-creek-board-resignations-20170725-story.html.

184 Didn't want Tetrick making any decisions without, Zaleski, Olivia, Peter Waldman, and Ellen Huet. "How Hampton Creek Sold Silicon Valley on a Fake-Mayo Miracle." *Bloomberg*, September 22, 2016. https://www.bloomberg.com/features/2016-hampton-creek-just-mayo/.

CHAPTER 14

186 Acquire Netherlands-based Vivera, "Third Largest European Plant Based Producer Vivera Acquired by JBS S.A." PR Newswire, April 19, 2021. https://www.prnewswire.com/news-releases/third-largest-european-plant-based-producer-vivera-acquired-by-jbs-sa-301271538.html.

186 Tout its climate goals, Marion, Nestle. "Least Credible Food Industry Ad of the Week: JBS and Climate Change." Food Politics, April 25, 2021. https://www.foodpolitics.com/2021/04/least-credible-food-industry-ad-of-the-week-jbs-and-climate-change/.

187 No longer in good conscience avoid embracing, Brown, Pat. "How Our Commitment to Consumers and Our Planet Led Us to Use GM Soy." Medium, May 21, 2021. https://medium.com/impossible-foods/how-our-commitment-to-consumers-and-our-planet-led-us-to-use-gm-soy-23f880c93408.

191 Grown on about 840,000 US acres, "Crop Production 2009 Summary." USDA, January 2010. https://www.nass.usda.gov/Publications/Todays_Reports/reports/cropan10.pdf.

191 Just under one million acres planted, "Crop Production 2020 Summary." USDA, January 2021. https://downloads.usda.library.cornell.edu/usda-esmis/files/k3569432s/w3764081j/5712n018r/cropan21.pdf.

195 1897 guide, Falconer, William. *How to Grow Mushrooms*. Washington: US Department of Agriculture, Farmers' bulletin no. 53, 1897.

195 Composted urban waste, reuse manure, Meigs Beyer, David. "Impact of the Mushroom Industry on the Environment." Penn State Extension, September 6, 2021. https://extension.psu.edu/impact-of-the-mushroom-industry-on-the-environment.

196 Health concerns, Ficociello, Barbara & Casorri, Laura & Cichelli, Angelo & Pacioni, Giovanni & Masciarelli, Eva & Yan, Lijuan. (2019). The onset of occupational diseases in mushroom cultivation and handling operators: a review. Italian Journal of Mycology. 48. 10.6092/issn.2531-7342/9409.

196 Health concerns, "Controlling Exposure to Dust and Bioaerosols on Farms Growing Common Commercial Mushrooms (Agaricus Bisporus)." Factsheet Mushrooms. Horticulture Development Company, February 2011. https://www.hse.gov.uk/agriculture/resources/pdf/mushroom-factsheet-hdc.pdf.

196 Health concerns, Barney, Danny L. "CIS1077 Growing Mushrooms Commercially - Risks and Opportunities." UI Extension Publications and Multimedia, 2000. https://www.extension.uidaho.edu/publishing/html/CIS1077-Growing-Mushrooms-Commercially.aspx.

196 The worst environmental impact of all protein sources tested other than lab-grown meat, Smetana, S., Mathys, A., Knoch, A. et al. "Meat alternatives: life cycle assessment of most known meat substitutes." *Int J Life Cycle Assess* 20 (2015): 1254–1267 (2015). https://doi.org/10.1007/s11367-015-0931-6.

196 Energy it takes to run the industrial plants to farm fungi, Souza Filho, P. F., D. Andersson, J. A. Ferreira, et al. "Mycoprotein: environmental impact and health aspects." *World J Microbiol Biotechnol* 35, 147 (2019). https://doi.org/10.1007/s11274-019-2723-9.

196 Energy it takes to run the industrial plants to farm fungi, Souza Filho, Pedro F., Dan Andersson, Jorge A. Ferreira, and Mohammad J. Taherzadeh. "Mycoprotein: Environmental Impact and Health Aspects." *World Journal of Microbiology and Biotechnology* 35, no. 10 (2019). https://doi.org/10.1007/s11274-019-2723-9.

196 A sustainable, renewable energy source, "Sustainability." American Mushroom Institute. Accessed January 31, 2022. https://www.americanmushroom.org/main/sustainability/.

196 Transportation accounted, Dorr, Erica, Maximilien Koegler, Benoît Gabrielle, and Christine Aubry. "Life Cycle Assessment of a Circular, Urban Mushroom Farm." *Journal of Cleaner Production* 288 (2020): 125668. https://doi.org/10.1016/j.jclepro.2020.125668.

CHAPTER 15

199 Moved its listing, "Form 8-A MeaTech D Ltd." Sec.gov, March 5, 2021. https://www.sec .gov/Archives/edgar/data/0001828098/000117891321000926/zk2125706.htm.

199 A goal to raise $100 million investment in lab-grown meat, Stargardter, Gabriel. "Brazil's JBS Agrees to Buy Spanish Lab Meat Firm in $100 Million Push into Sector." Reuters, November 17, 2021. https://www.agriculture.com/markets/newswire/brazils -jbs-agrees-to-buy-spanish-lab-meat-firm-in-100-mln-push-into-sector.

200 Upside Foods, a $186 million series B round in 2020, "The Science of Cultivated Meat: GFI." The Good Food Institute, August 17, 2021. https://gfi.org/science/the-science-of -cultivated-meat/.

200 Peg the total investment figure, $2 billion, "Cellular Agriculture Investment Report." Cell Agri. Accessed September 8, 2021. https://www.cell.ag/reports.

201 Keerie, Maia. "New GFI State of the Industry Reports Show Alternative Proteins Are Poised to Flourish Post-Covid-19." The Good Food Institute, January 22, 2021. https:// gfi.org/blog/state-of-the-industry-2020/.

201 To feed its cell banks, "The Science of Cultivated Meat: GFI." The Good Food Institute, August 17, 2021. https://gfi.org/science/the-science-of-cultivated-meat/.

201 A race to get rid of animal-based serum, Paul-Gera, Kriti. "Cultivating Beef without FBS." Mosa Meat, January 13, 2022. https://mosameat.com/blog/cultivating-beef -without-fetal-bovine-serum.

201 A pricey challenge, "Where's the Beef? A First-Hand Assessment of Cultivated Meat Progress." Mosa Meat, November 11, 2021. https://mosameat.com/blog/cultivated -meat-progress.

203 Good Meat claims it doesn't use antibiotics, "Cultured Meat Faqs: Good Meat." Good Meat. Accessed September 8, 2021. https://goodmeat.co/faq.

203 Come under the microscope for its environmental impact, Lynch, John, and Raymond Pierrehumbert. "Climate Impacts of Cultured Meat and Beef Cattle." *Frontiers in Sustainable Food Systems* 3 (2019). https://doi.org/10.3389/fsufs.2019.00005.

203 A research study with data from five start-ups, "New Studies Show Cultivated Meat Can Benefit Climate and Be Cost-Competitive by 2030." The Good Food Institute, March 16, 2021. https://gfi.org/blog/cultivated-meat-lca-tea/.

203 Worse than industrial meat production, Smetana, Sergiy, Alexander Mathys, Achim Knoch, and Volker Heinz. "Meat Alternatives: Life Cycle Assessment of Most Known Meat Substitutes." *International Journal of Life Cycle Assessment* 20, no. 9 (2015): 1254–67. https://doi.org/10.1007/s11367-015-0931-6.

204 The fourth-highest net worth in the world, "Bill Gates." *Forbes*. Accessed September 8, 2021. https://www.forbes.com/profile/bill-gates/.

204 Rich nations should eat, Gates, Bill. *How to Avoid a Climate Disaster: The Solutions We Have and the Breakthroughs We Need.* London: Allen Lane, 2021.

204 The eighty poorest countries, Temple, James. "Bill Gates: Rich Nations Should Shift Entirely to Synthetic Beef." MIT Technology Review. MIT Technology Review, February 14, 2021. https://www.technologyreview.com/2021/02/14/1018296/bill-gates-climate -change-beef-trees-microsoft/.

205 Could value the start-up at $10 billion or more, Sen, Anirban, and Joshua Franklin. "Exclusive: Impossible Foods in Talks to List on the Stock Market." Reuters, April 8, 2021. https://www.reuters.com/article/us-impossible-foods-m-a-exclusive-idUSKBN2BV2SF.

205 Could value the start-up at $10 billion or more, Cavale, Siddarth, and Uday Sampath Kumar. "Analysis: Not Impossible, Just Unlikely: Wall Street's Plant-Based Love Wilts." Reuters, April 21, 2021. https://www.reuters.com/business/faux-meat-growth-doubts -give-market-food-thought-impossible-2021-04-21/.

205 Could value the start-up at $10 billion or more, Swarz, Jon. "Impossible Foods Prepping for $10 Billion IPO: Report." Morningstar, April 8, 2021. https://www.morningstar .com/news/marketwatch/20210408614/impossible-foods-prepping-for-10-billion-ipo -report.

205 Top farmland owner in the country, O'Keefe, Eric. "Bill Gates: America's Top Farmland

Owner: The Land Report." The Land Report | The Magazine of the American Land-owner, April 2, 2022. https://landreport.com/2021/01/bill-gates-americas-top-farm land-owner/.

205 Potatoes for McDonald's french fries, O'Keefe, Eric. "Bill Gates Is about to Change the Way America Farms." Successful Farming. Successful Farming, January 19, 2021. https:// www.agriculture.com/farm-management/farm-land/bill-gates-is-about-to-change-the -way-amer-ca-farms.

205 Potatoes for McDonald's french fries, "100 Circle Farms: A McDonald's Potato Supplier | McDonald's." McDonalds.com. McDonald's. Accessed April 12, 2022. https://www .mcdonalds.com/us/en-us/about-our-food/meet-our-suppliers/100-circle-farms.html.

205 Ask Me Anything interview over Reddit, Ellis, Jack. "Bill Gates Tells Reddit Why He's Bought so Much Farmland." AgFunder News. AFN, March 23, 2021. https://agfundernews .com/bill-gates-tells-reddit-why-hes-acquired-so-much-farmland.

205 Cause of concern, Packman, Hannah. "Why Farmers Are Worried about Bill Gates (and Other Non-Farming Land-Owners)." National Farmers Union, April 26, 2021. https://nfu.org/2021/03/29/why-farmers-are-worried-about-bill-gates-and-other-non -farming-land-owners/.

206 Genetically modified, Cohen, Larry. A Conversation with Bill Gates: GMOs. Other. *GatesNotes*, February 18, 2012. https://www.gatesnotes.com/About-Bill-Gates/A -Conversation-with-Bill-Gates-GMOs.

206 Reportedly cost $330,000, "World's First Lab-Grown Burger Is Eaten in London." BBC News, August 5, 2013. https://www.bbc.com/news/science-environment-23576143.

207 Produce a few burgers for the big reveal, "Launch of the World's First Cultured Meat Hamburger (August 5, 2013)." YouTube. Mosa Meat, 2018. https://www.youtube.com /watch?v=slslQLZL2EI.

CHAPTER 16

214 The four largest seed companies, "Vegetables." National Agricultural Statistics Service, US Department of Agriculture, September 6, 2002.

214 Dow Chemical and DuPont, Bartz, Diane, and Karl Plume. "Dow, Dupont Soar on Pros-pect of $130 Billion Merger 'Christmas Present'." Reuters. Thomson Reuters, Decem-ber 10, 2015. https://www.reuters.com/article/dow-m-a-du-pont/dow-dupont-soar-on -prospect-of-130-billion-merger-christmas-present-idINKBN0TS2F420151210.

214 Bayer and Monsanto, "Bayer closes Monsanto acquisition." Bayer, June 7, 2018. https:// media.bayer.com/baynews/baynews.nsf/id/Bayer-closes-Monsanto-acquisition#:~: text=Leverkusen%2C%20June%207%2C%202018%20%E2%80%93,sole%20owner%20 of%20Monsanto%20Company.

214 Monsanto's glyphosate lawsuits, "Bayer Reaches Settlement in Glyphosate Litigation." Bayer. Accessed April 12, 2022. https://www.bayer.com/en/roundup-litigation-five -point-plan.

214 Patented seeds, Bethany K. Sumpter, *The Growing Monopoly in the Corn Seed Industry: Is It Time for the Government to Interfere?*, 8 Tex. A&M L. Rev. 633 (2021). https://doi .org/10.37419/LR.V8.I3.6.

214 Bayer-Monsanto merger closed, "Bayer closes Monsanto acquisition." Bayer, June 7, 2018. https://media.bayer.com/baynews/baynews.nsf/id/Bayer-closes-Monsanto-acquisition #:~:text=Leverkusen%2C%20June%207%2C%202018%20%E2%80%93,sole%20owner %20of%20Monsanto%20Company.

214 Corteva, "History of Dow, Dupont and Pioneer." History of Dow DuPont & Pioneer Together | Corteva Agriscience. Accessed April 12, 2022. https://www.corteva.com/who -we-are/our-history.html.

216 Carrots, potatoes, Glaser, April. "Bill Gates Uses Farmland as an Investment Outlet Buying up Potato, Carrot and Onion Farms." NBCNews.com. NBCUniversal News Group, June 8, 2021. https://www.nbcnews.com/tech/tech-news/mcdonald-s-french -fries-carrots-onions-all-foods-come-bill-n1270033.

216 Can grow almost anywhere, "Here Is Background Information on How to Grow Grains Well-Suited to This Climate." Northern Grain Growers Association. Accessed Septem-ber 8, 2021. https://northerngraingrowers.org/growers/our-northern-grains.

216 Discourages weeds from growing and adds nitrogen to the soil, Jacobs, A. A. "Plant

guide for common barley (Hordeum vulgare L.)." USDA-Natural Resources Conservation Service. Jamie L. Whitten Plant Materials Center, 2016.

221 Grew mushrooms while escaping the devastating civil war, Barth, Dylan, Amelia Kosciulek, and Mark Abadi. "Mushrooms Used to Be Rare in Syria—but Thousands of Refugees Are Now Relying on Them to Survive." Insider, January 28, 2020. https://www.businessinsider.com/syria-refugees-mushrooms-civil-war-2020-1.

223 The first living thing to emerge after the atomic blast of Hiroshima, Tsing, Anna Lowenhaupt. *Mushroom at the End of the World: On the Possibility of Life in Capitalist Ruins.* Princeton University Press, 2021, p. 3.

223 Life without the promise of stability, Tsing, Anna Lowenhaupt. *Mushroom at the End of the World: On the Possibility of Life in Capitalist Ruins.* Princeton University Press, 2021, p. 2.

CHAPTER 17

229 A two-hundred-acre nonprofit farm, Wingert, Bridget. "Sharing the Bounty at Nonprofit Carversville Farm." Carversville Farm. Accessed January 31, 2022. http://www.carversvillefarm.com/news/cff-featured-bucks-county-herald/.

229 More than 90 percent goes to Philadelphia's soup kitchens, Briggs, Charlene. "An Interview with CFF's Tony D'Orazio." Carversville Farm. Accessed January 31, 2022. http://www.carversvillefarm.org/news/interview-cffs-tony-dorazio/.

229 An accidental entrepreneur, Levenson, Edward. "Successful Warminster CEO an 'Accidental Entrepreneur.'" *Bucks County Courier Times*, March 9, 2014. https://www.buckscountycouriertimes.com/article/20140309/NEWS/303099824.

231 Must send the cattle out, Rumley, Elizabeth R, and James Wilkerson. "Meat Processing Laws in the United States: A State Compilation." National Agricultural Law Center. University of Arkansas. Accessed January 31, 2022. https://nationalaglawcenter.org/state-compilations/meatprocessing/.

231 Per regulations, "Meat and Poultry Processing Regulations in Oregon: A Short Guide." OSU Extension Service. Oregon State University. Accessed January 31, 2022. https://extension.oregonstate.edu/animals-livestock/poultry-rabbits/meat-poultry-processing-regulations-oregon-short-guide.

CHAPTER 18

236 An even more severe future awaits, *Climate Change 2021: The Physical Science Basis. Contribution of Working Group I to the Sixth Assessment Report of the Intergovernmental Panel on Climate Change.* Masson-Delmotte, V., P. Zhai, A. Pirani, S. L. Connors, C. Péan, S. Berger, N. Caud, Y. Chen, L. Goldfarb, M. I. Gomis, M. Huang, K. Leitzell, E. Lonnoy, J. B. R. Matthews, T. K. Maycock, T. Waterfield, O. Yelekçi, R. Yu, and B. Zhou (eds.). Cambridge UniversityPress. https://www.ipcc.ch/report/ar6/wg1/downloads/report/IPCC_AR6_WGI_Full_Report.pdf.

237 Commodities-based systems often seek out vertical integration and overall concentrations of wealth and power over time, MacDonald, James M., "Contracts, markets, and prices: Organizing the production and use of agricultural commodities." 2004.

237 Commodities-based systems often seek out vertical integration and overall concentrations of wealth and power over time, Harwood, Joy L., "Managing risk in farming: Concepts, research, and analysis" (1999).

237 Commodities-based systems often seek out vertical integration and overall concentrations of wealth and power over time, Dongoski, Rob. "How Vertical Integration Is Impacting Food and Agribusiness." EY, August 4, 2021. https://www.ey.com/en_us/consumer-products-retail/how-vertical-integration-is-impacting-food-and-agribusiness.

237 Commodities-based systems often seek out vertical integration and overall concentrations of wealth and power over time, Flora, Cornelia B., and Luther G. Tweeten. *Vertical Coordination of Agriculture in Farming Dependent Areas.* Ames, IA: Council for Agricultural Science and Technology, 2001.

239 Annual third-party verification, "About B Corp Certification: Measuring a Company's Entire Social and Environmental Impact." Bcorporation.net. Accessed January 31, 2022. https://bcorporation.net/about-b-corps?gclid=Cj0KCQjwiqTNBRDVARIsAGsd9MpBPzqtL-LLnb55Pt-wsxwITH_KuUDfeimzBtsh4YewNSLicdYDcqMaAjUaEALw_wcB.

239 Balances profits with its impact on workers, environment, community, and customers, "General Questions." Benefit Corporation. Accessed January 31, 2022. https://benefitcorp.net/faq#:~:text=Does%20being%20a%20benefit%20corporation,tax%20law%20remains%20the%20same.

239 Over half the country, "State by State Status of Legislation." Benefit Corporation. Accessed January 31, 2022. https://benefitcorp.net/policymakers/state-by-state-status.

240 General Mills acquired Annie's in 2014, "Annie's to Be Acquired by General Mills for $46 Per Share in Cash." SEC. SEC, September 8, 2014. https://www.sec.gov/Archives/edgar/data/1431897/000119312514335723/d785894dex991.htm.

240 In a landmark 2016 deal, "Danone to Acquire WhiteWave, a USD 4 Bn Sales Global Leader in Organic Foods, Plant-Based Milks and Related Products." Danone, July 7, 2016. https://www.danone.com/content/dam/danone-corp/danone-com/investors/en-investor-conferences/2016/danone-to-acquire-whitewave/Presentation_Danone_WhiteWave.pdf.

243 Cut contracts with eighty-nine dairies, Rathke, Lisa. "Nearly 90 Northeast Organic Dairy Farms to Lose Their Market." Associated Press, August 27, 2021. https://apnews.com/article/lifestyle-business-234a7f83c0a19a782275799ffa9ce748.

243 Rathke, Lisa. "Horizon Organic to Extend Northeast Milk Contracts 6 Months." Associated Press, December 15, 2021. https://apnews.com/article/business-lifestyle-vermont-3b1f3458b548d3dc981e2e90cf9f677d.

245 Expected to start requiring climate and environmental impact disclosures in public filings, "Climate Disclosures and the SEC." Latham & Watkins Environment, Land & Resources. Accessed January 31, 2022. https://www.lw.com/thoughtLeadership/Climate-Disclosures-and-the-SEC.

245 A foundational part of the civil rights movement, Charles Black, "Annual Report 2020." Federation of Southern Cooperatives/Land Assistance Fund, 2020. https://federation.imagerelay.com/fl/637c70128a974f9a84ee3cfc0b5749b4.

246 The landmark class-action lawsuit *Pigford v. Glickman*, Cowan, Tadlock, and Jody Feder, "The pigford cases: USDA settlement of Discrimination Suits by Black Farmers" (2013).

247 The organic certification process, Greene, Catherine. "Support for the Organic Sector Expands in the 2014 Farm Act." USDA, July 7, 2014. https://www.ers.usda.gov/amber-waves/2014/july/support-for-the-organic-sector-expands-in-the-2014-farm-act/.

247 A formal raise with the Securities and Exchange Commission, "Facilitating Capital Formation and Expanding Investment Opportunities by Improving Access to Capital in Private Markets." SEC, November 2, 2020. https://www.sec.gov/corpfin/facilitating-capital-formation-secg.

248 Regulation crowdfunding, "Facilitating Capital Formation and Expanding Investment Opportunities by Improving Access to Capital in Private Markets." U.S. Securities And Exchange Commission, March 10, 2021. https://www.sec.gov/corpfin/facilitating-capital-formation-secg.

248 Regulation crowdfunding, "Regulation Crowdfunding." U.S. Securities And Exchange Commission, May 4, 2017. https://www.sec.gov/education/smallbusiness/exemptofferings/regcrowdfunding#:~:text=permit%20a%20company%20to%20raise,a%2012%2Dmonth%20period%20and.

248 Accredited investors, "Accredited Investors—Updated Investor Bulletin." SEC, April 14, 2021. https://www.investor.gov/introduction-investing/general-resources/news-alerts/alerts-bulletins/investor-bulletins/updated-3.

248 The rate is 7.5 percent, "What Do You Charge?" Wefunder. Accessed January 31, 2022. https://help.wefunder.com/getting-started-for-founders/303756-how-does-wefunder-make-money#:~:text=It's%20free%20to%20create%20a,There%20are%20no%20other%20fees.

249 Doesn't charge a fee, "Borrow." Kiva. Accessed January 31, 2022. https://www.kiva.org/borrow.

250 US senators unveiled a bill that would make school lunch free for all, "Sanders, Omar, Gillibrand, and Moore Seek to Expand and Make Permanent Universal School Meals." Bernie Sanders US Senator for Vermont, May 7, 2021. https://www.sanders.senate.gov/press-releases/news-sanders-omar-gillibrand-and-moore-seek-to-expand-and-make-permanent-universal-school-meals/.

250 The United Nations was promoting the idea of universal access to food in its "resilience"

track, "United Nations Food Systems Summit Action Track 4." United Nations. Accessed January 31, 2022. https://www.un.org/sites/un2.un.org/files/fss_action_track_4_-_wave _2_ideas_paper_final.pdf.

250 West Virginia policymakers recently proposed adding a right to food to the state's constitution, "ARTICLE III. Bill of Rights. §23. Right to Food, Food Sovereignty and Freedom from Hunger." Introduced House Joint Resolution 30. West Virginia Legislature 2021 Regular Session, March 5, 2021. http://www.wvlegislature.gov/Bill_Status/bills _text.cfm?billdoc=hjr30+intr.htm&yr=2021&sesstype=RS&i=30&amp ;houseorig=h&billtype=jr.

250 Maine's House of Representatives overwhelmingly voted, "RESOLUTION, Proposing an Amendment to the Constitution of Maine To Establish a Right to Food." 130th Maine State Legislature, January 13, 2021. https://legislature.maine.gov/legis/bills/getPDF.asp ?paper=HP0061&item=1&snum=130.

251 The future is structuring food companies and retailers as public utilities, Ikerd, John. "The Corporatization of America." University of Missouri, July 2001. http://web.missouri .edu/~ikerdj/papers/OhioCorporatization1.html.

251 A Community Food Utility, Ikerd, John. "Enough Good Food for All: A Proposal." *Journal of Agriculture, Food Systems, and Community Development* (2016): 1–4. https://doi .org/10.5304/jafscd.2016.071.001.

251 A vertical cooperative with a board of directors, Ikerd, John. "Enough Good Food for All: A Proposal." *Journal of Agriculture, Food Systems, and Community Development* (2016): 1–4. https://doi.org/10.5304/jafscd.2016.071.001.

252 Slotting fees or free product that supplier brands must pay to stay on store shelves, "In-Store Promotions Explained." Rodeo CPG. Accessed March 1, 2022. https://www .rodeocpg.com/knowledge-share/in-store-promotions-explained.

252 Supplier brands shell out roughly $225 billion or the equivalent in free product annually, "2020 Marketing Spending Industry Study: What's Your P/E?" Cadent Consulting Group, n.d.

252 Drumming up support for a program within Austin's city government, Schweizer, Errol. "Why We Need a Public Food Sector." The Checkout Radio, April 7, 2021. https://www .thecheckoutradio.com/writing/why-we-need-a-public-food-sector.

252 A concept that first emerged in the 1990s in Latin America and Europe, Laville, Jean-Louis. "The Solidarity Economy: An International Movement." *RCCS Annual Review*, no. 2 (2010). https://doi.org/10.4000/rccsar.202.

253 More than two hundred food hubs nationwide, Neal, Arthur. "Food Hubs—Building Businesses and Sustaining Communities." USDA, February 21, 2017. https://www .usda.gov/media/blog/2013/11/20/food-hubs-building-businesses-and-sustaining -communities.

254 As much local produce as it could fit, "Case Study: World Central Kitchen and the Common Market Texas." The Common Market. Accessed January 31, 2022. https:// www.thecommonmarket.org/about/reports/case-study-world-central-kitchen-and-the -common-market-texas.

254 Adopt shares to save more profits for their farms, Vittek, Shelby. "You Can Thank Black Horticulturist Booker T. Whatley for Your CSA." *Smithsonian Magazine*, May 20, 2021. https://www.smithsonianmag.com/innovation/you-can-thank-black-horticulturist -booker-t-whatley-your-csa-180977771/.

254 Adopt shares to save more profits for their farms, Anstreicher, Kate. "The Untold History of CSA." Glynwood. Center for Regional Food and Farming, July 14, 2020. https:// www.glynwood.org/connect/news.html/article/2020/07/14/the-untold-history-of-csa.

254 Whatley pushed farmers, Zawora, Weronika. "Dr. Booker T. Whatley: Pioneer of Community Supported Agriculture." Stearns Farm CSA, July 28, 2021. https://stearnsfarmcsa.org /2021/06/28/dr-booker-t-whatley-godfather-of-community-supported-agriculture/.

254 About 40 percent of all US farmland is rented, "Visualizing U.S. Farmland Ownership, Tenure, and Transition." USDA, November 13, 2020. https://www.ers.usda.gov/data -products/data-visualizations/other-visualizations/visualizing-us-farmland-ownership -tenure-and-transition/.

258 More meat is being sold online than ever before, "Trends in U.S. Local and Regional Food Systems: Report To Congress." USDA, January 2015. https://www.ers.usda.gov /webdocs/publications/42805/51173_ap068.pdf.

259 Industrial flavors often made as a by-product of petroleum production, Sorvino, Chloe and International Flavors and Fragrances, Interview and Tour of IFF in New Jersey. Personal, May, 2021.

260 Said to be exploring in 2021 to the tune of $2 billion, Tse, Crystal, and Gillian Tan. "Thrive Market Is Considering an IPO at $2 Billion-Plus Value." *Bloomberg*. Accessed July 8, 2021. https://www.bloomberg.com/news/articles/2021-07-08/thrive-market-is -said-to-plan-ipo-at-2-billion-plus-value.

260 About eight thousand exist in America, "National Farmers Market Managers Survey." USDA, 2019. https://www.ams.usda.gov/services/local-regional/research-publications /fmms#:~:text=NASS%20conducted%20the%20survey%20in,in%20the%20lower%20 48%20states.&text=NASS%20mailed%20the%20survey%20to,the%20survey%20 was%2058.8%20percent.

261 Roughly $1 billion worth of food sells annually at farmers' markets nationwide, Johnson, Renée, "The role of local and regional food systems in U.S. farm policy" (2018). https:// sgp.fas.org/crs/misc/R44390.pdf.

261 Compared to more than $1 trillion spent on food in America annually, "Food Prices and Spending." USDA ERS, December 27, 2021. https://www.ers.usda.gov/data-products /ag-and-food-statistics-charting-the-essentials/food-prices-and-spending/.

261 Federal assistance payments cover just 2 percent of total farmers' market purchases, "Food Prices and Spending." USDA ERS. USDA, December 27, 2021. https://www .ers.usda.gov/data-products/ag-and-food-statistics-charting-the-essentials/food-prices -and-spending/.

262 Pacific Foods acquired by Campbell Soup Co. for $700 million, "Campbell Completes Acquisition of Pacific Foods." Pacific Foods of Oregon, December 12, 2017. https://www .pacificfoods.com/news/campbell-completes-acquisition-of-pacific-foods/.

AFTERWORD

265 Curves for ten miles, Felix, Carla. Letter to Chloe Sorvino. RE: JBS Grand Island—Factchecking Help, June 14, 2024. Felix is a Public Information Officer Section Supervisor at Nebraska's Department of Environment and Energy.

265 Wastewater lagoon snapped, Windhorst, Jason, ed. Rep. JBS Swift January 2024 ENVIRONMENTAL CONCERN (NOEC) INVESTIGATION REPORT. Lincoln, Nebraska: Department of Environment and Energy, n.d. Windhorst is an inspector at Nebraska's Department of Environment and Energy.

265 Two million gallons of sludge, Windhorst, Jason, ed. Rep. JBS Swift January 2024 ENVIRONMENTAL CONCERN (NOEC) INVESTIGATION REPORT. Lincoln, Nebraska: Department of Environment and Energy, n.d. Windhorst is an inspector at Nebraska's Department of Environment and Energy.

265 Flowed downstream into the Wood River, Windhorst, Jason, ed. Rep. JBS Swift January 2024 ENVIRONMENTAL CONCERN (NOEC) INVESTIGATION REPORT. Lincoln, Nebraska: Department of Environment and Energy, n.d. Windhorst is an inspector at Nebraska's Department of Environment and Energy.

265 Dripped from burst pipes, Windhorst, Jason, ed. Rep. JBS Swift January 2024 ENVIRONMENTAL CONCERN (NOEC) INVESTIGATION REPORT. Lincoln, Nebraska: Department of Environment and Energy, n.d. Windhorst is an inspector at Nebraska's Department of Environment and Energy.

265 Dead and dying fish, Windhorst, Jason, ed. Rep. JBS Swift January 2024 ENVIRONMENTAL CONCERN (NOEC) INVESTIGATION REPORT. Lincoln, Nebraska: Department of Environment and Energy, n.d. Windhorst is an inspector at Nebraska's Department of Environment and Energy.

265 Tested positive, Michl, Greg. Rep. MEMORANDUM: Swift Beef Company (FID 24352) – Instream Water Sampling Summary Report NOTIFICATION NUMBER (NOEC): 010624-JB-0800. Lincoln, Nebraska: Department of Environment and Energy, n.d.

266 Letter, Peterson, Board Chair Hall County Board of Commissioners, Ron. Letter to JBS 555 S Stuhr Road Grand Island, NE 68801. To Whom It May Concern. "Hall County Board of Commissioners Letter to JBS." Grand Island, Nebraska: 121 South Pine Street, February 13, 2024. Emailed to Chloe Sorvino, March 6, 2024.

266 Twenty properties' wells, Felix, Carla. Letter to Chloe Sorvino. RE: JBS Grand Island—

Factchecking Help, June 18, 2024. Felix is a Public Information Officer Section Supervisor at Nebraska's Department of Environment and Energy.

266 Response letter, Lang, Plant Manager at JBS Grand Island, Tony. Letter to Ron Peterson, Board Chair Hall County Board of Commissioners. "JBS Response Letter to Hall County Board of Commissioners Letter." Grand Island, Nebraska: 121 South Pine Street, February 26, 2024.

266 Extensive erosion, Windhorst, Jason, ed. Rep. JBS Swift January 2024 ENVIRONMENTAL CONCERN (NOEC) INVESTIGATION REPORT. Lincoln, Nebraska: Department of Environment and Energy, n.d. Windhorst is an inspector at Nebraska's Department of Environment and Energy.

266 Other leaks, Windhorst, Jason, ed. Rep. JBS Swift January 2024 ENVIRONMENTAL CONCERN (NOEC) INVESTIGATION REPORT. Lincoln, Nebraska: Department of Environment and Energy, n.d. Windhorst is an inspector at Nebraska's Department of Environment and Energy.

266 Meat production is growing. As is consumption, USDA. "Excel on Meat Supply and Disappearance Tables, Historical." USDA Economic Research Service. Accessed May 22, 2024. https://www.ers.usda.gov/webdocs/DataFiles/104360/MeatSDFull.xlsx?v=5312.

266 Hottest year ever recorded, National Oceanic and Atmospheric Administration U.S. Department of Commerce Press Department. "2023 Was the World's Warmest Year on Record, by Far." National Oceanic and Atmospheric Administration, January 12, 2024. https://www.noaa.gov/news/2023-was-worlds-warmest-year-on-record-by-far#:~:text=Earth's%20average%20land%20and%20ocean,0.15%20of%20a%20degree%20C).

266 Died from extreme heat and lack of water, Polansek, Tom. "Heat, Humidity Kill Hundreds of US Cattle during World's Hottest Month." Reuters, August 7, 2023. https://www.reuters.com/world/us/heat-humidity-kill-hundreds-us-cattle-during-worlds-hottest-month-2023-08-07/.

266 Died from extreme heat, Gilbert, Mary, and Holly Yan. "Extreme Heat Kills Nearly 2 Dozen Cattle, Forces Evacuations from a Nursing Home and Shuts down an Ice Cream Parlor." CNN, August 24, 2023. https://www.cnn.com/2023/08/23/weather/heat-dome-record-temperatures-climate/index.html.

268 Indigenous land, Mendonça, Ricardo. "Indigenous People from Pará Challenges JBS in the U.S." Valor International, October 20, 2023. https://valorinternational.globo.com/agribusiness/news/2023/10/20/indigenous-people-from-para-challenges-jbs-in-the-us.ghtml.

268 Buying cattle raised on cleared acres, Environmental Investigation Agency. "Who Bought Apyterewa's Illegal Cattle?" EIA.org, May 29, 2024. https://us.eia.org/report/who-bought-apyterewas-illegal-cattle/.

268 New York attorney general also filed, James, New York State Attorney General, Letitia. "Attorney General James Sues World's Largest Beef Producer for Misrepresenting Environmental Impact of Their Products." New York State Attorney General, February 28, 2024. https://ag.ny.gov/press-release/2024/attorney-general-james-sues-worlds-largest-beef-producer-misrepresenting.

268 Review boards, National Advertising Review Board Newsroom. "NARB Recommends JBS Discontinue 'Net Zero' Emissions by 2040 Claims." National Advertising Division of BBB National Programs, June 20, 2023. https://bbbprograms.org/media-center/dd/narb-jbs-net-zero-emissions.

268 JBS appealed, National Advertising Review Board Newsroom. "JBS Appeals NAD Recommendation to Discontinue 'Net Zero' Claims." National Advertising Division (NAD) of BBB National Programs, February 15, 2023. https://bbbprograms.org/media-center/dd/jbs-net-zero-emissions.

269 Letter from Vilsack, VILSACK, THOMAS J. Letter to THE HONORABLE CAROLYN B. MALONEY Chair Committee on Oversight and Reform U.S. House of Representatives. "JBS USA and Their Affiliates." Washington, DC: Washington, DC, November 2, 2022. Published on Politico.com. https://www.politico.com/f/?id=00000185-8812-de44-a7bf-e817657f0000.

269 POLITICO report, Brown, Marcia. "Federal Government Won't Stop Buying Food from Meatpacker Tied to Bribery Case." Politico, January 10, 2023. https://www.politico.com/news/2023/01/10/usda-meatpacker-bribery-case-00077093.

269 $176 million, Weir, USDA, Shilo. Letter to Chloe Sorvino. Media Request: Factchecking Deadline 7/1, June 26, 2024.

269 Documents filed, JBS S.A. "NOTICE TO THE MARKET: ANNOUNCES FILING OF REGISTRATION STATEMENT FOR PROPOSED EXCHANGE OFFERS." Sec. gov Exhibit 99.1, March 27, 2024. https://www.sec.gov/Archives/edgar/data/1450123 /000121390024026281/ea020268001ex99-1_jbssa.htm.

269 Convert their common shares to preferred, JBS S.A. "PROSPECTUS JBS S.A. Offers to Exchange All Outstanding Unregistered Notes of the Series Specified Below for New Notes Which Have Been Registered under the Securities Act of 1933." Sec.gov, July 24, 2023. https://www.sec.gov/Archives/edgar/data/1450123/000121390023059236/ f424b30723_jbssa.htm#T10. Filed Pursuant to Rule 424(b)(3). Registration No. 333-272099. Page 93.

269 Thirty-one years old, Freitas, Tatiana, and Daniel Cancel. "Wesley Batista Filho Is on Deck to Run Brazilian Meat Company JBS." Bloomberg.com, May 18, 2023. https:// www.bloomberg.com/news/articles/2023-05-18/wesley-batista-filho-is-on-deck-to -run-brazilian-meat-company-jbs.

270 JBS USA CEO, JBS S.A. Press Office. "JBS USA Announces New CEO - JBS Foods." JBS USA, April 27, 2023. https://jbsfoodsgroup.com/articles/jbs-usa-announces-new-ceo.

270 Traveling with Lula to China, Paraguassu, Lisandra, and Ana Mano. "With Stakes High, Brazil Meat Industry Dominates Lula Delegation to China." Reuters, March 22, 2023. https://www.reuters.com/markets/commodities/with-stakes-high-brazil-meat-indus try-dominates-lula-delegation-china-2023-03-22/.

270 Lula visited a JBS plant, Iglesias, Simone, and Gerson Freitas. "Lula Reunites with Billionaire JBS Brothers as Brazil's China Ties Deepen." Bloomberg.com, April 12, 2024. https://www.bloomberg.com/news/articles/2024-04-12/lula-reunites-with-billionaire -jbs-brothers-as-brazil-s-china-ties-deepen.

270 $3.2 billion fine, case sealed, Boadle, Anthony. "Brazil Meatpacker JBS Owner Fights to Cut $3.2 Bln Corruption Fine-Sources." Nasdaq, August 9, 2023. https://www.nas daq.com/articles/brazil-meatpacker-jbs-owner-fights-to-cut-$3.2-bln-corruption-fine -sources. Originally published on Reuters.

270 End J&F's fines, Mendes, Lucas. "Toffoli Suspende Multa de Mais de R$ 10 Bilhões Do Acordo de Leniência Da J&F." CNN Brasil, December 20, 2023. https://www.cnnbrasil. com.br/politica/toffoli-suspende-multa-de-mais-de-r-10-bilhoes-do-acordo-de-lenien cia-da-jf/#.

270 J&F confirmed, Workman, J&F Spokesman, Daniel. Letter to Chloe Sorvino. RAW DEAL Afterword Factchecking for J&F and the Batistas, July 3, 2024.

270 Profits dropped, Tyson Newsroom. "Tyson Foods Reports Fourth Quarter and Fiscal 2023 Results." Tyson Foods, November 13, 2023. https://www.tysonfoods.com/news /news-releases/2023/8/tyson-foods-reports-fourth-quarter-2023-results.

271 Closed eight plants, Tyson Newsroom. "Tyson Foods Reports Fourth Quarter and Fiscal 2023 Results." Tyson Foods, November 13, 2023. https://www.tysonfoods.com/news /news-releases/2023/8/tyson-foods-reports-fourth-quarter-2023-results.

271 Perry, Iowa, Polansek, Tom. "Tyson Foods to Close Iowa Pork Plant with 1,200 Workers." Reuters, March 11, 2024. https://www.reuters.com/markets/commodities/tyson -foods-close-iowa-pork-plant-with-1200-workers-2024-03-11/.

271 Tyson also laid off, Lee, Ron. "Tyson Foods Plant to Lay off Hundreds of Workers in Wilkesboro." https://www.wbtv.com, September 29, 2023. https://www.wbtv.com /2023/09/29/processing-plant-lay-off-hundreds-workers-wilkesboro/.

271 Corporate workforce, Polansek, Tom. "Tyson Foods to Eliminate 10% of Corporate Jobs, 15% of Senior Leaders." Reuters, April 26, 2023. https://www.reuters.com/business/ tyson-foods-eliminate-10-corporate-jobs-memo-2023-04-26/.

271 USDA decided, USDA Newsroom. "USDA Launches Effort to Strengthen Substantiation of Animal-Raising Claims." USDA, June 14, 2023. https://www.usda.gov/media/ press-releases/2023/06/14/usda-launches-effort-strengthen-substantiation-animal -raising.

271 Affidavits, USDA Newsroom. "USDA Launches Effort to Strengthen Substantiation of Animal-Raising Claims." USDA, June 14, 2023. https://www.usda.gov/media/ press-releases/2023/06/14/usda-launches-effort-strengthen-substantiation-animal -raising.

271 Tyson announced reversing its policy, Thomas, Patrick. "WSJ News Exclusive | Tyson Foods to Drop 'No Antibiotics Ever' Label on Some Chicken Products." *Wall Street Journal*, July 2, 2023. https://www.wsj.com/articles/tyson-foods-to-drop-no-antibiotics-ever-label-on-some-chicken-products-13f417cf.

271 Coresistance, Sorvino, Chloe, and Lance Price. Interview with Dr. Lance Price. Personal, March 18, 2024.

271 Remain in waterways and soil, Hansen, Martin, Erland Björklund, Kristine A. Krogh, and Bent Halling-Sørensen. "Analytical Strategies for Assessing Ionophores in the Environment." *TrAC Trends in Analytical Chemistry* 28, no. 5 (May 2009): 521–33. https://doi.org/10.1016/j.trac.2009.01.008.

271 Remain in waterways and soil, Sun, Peizhe, Delphine Barmaz, Miguel L. Cabrera, Spyros G. Pavlostathis, and Ching-Hua Huang. "Detection and Quantification of Ionophore Antibiotics in Runoff, Soil and Poultry Litter." *Journal of Chromatography* A 1312 (October 2013): 10–17. https://doi.org/10.1016/j.chroma.2013.08.044.

271 Can make farmland less productive, Sassman, Stephen A., and Linda S. Lee. "Sorption and Degradation in Soils of Veterinary Ionophore Antibiotics: Monensin and Lasalocid." *Environmental Toxicology and Chemistry* 26, no. 8 (August 2007): 1614–21. https://doi.org/10.1897/07-073r.1.

272 Sales of antibiotics, FDA, Center for Veterinary Medicine. "2022 Summary Report on Antimicrobials Sold for Food-Producing Animals." U.S. Food and Drug Administration, December 7, 2023. https://www.fda.gov/animal-veterinary/antimicrobial-resistance/2022-summary-report-antimicrobials-sold-or-distributed-use-food-producing-animals.

272 Sales increased, Center for Veterinary Medicine. "FDA 2022 Report on Antimicrobial Sales for Food-Producing Animals." U.S. Food and Drug Administration, December 7, 2023. https://www.fda.gov/animal-veterinary/cvm-updates/fda-releases-annual-summary-report-antimicrobials-sold-or-distributed-2022-use-food-producing.

272 Killing a record, Animal and Plant Health Inspection Service U.S. DEPARTMENT OF AGRICULTURE. "Confirmations of Highly Pathogenic Avian Influenza in Commercial and Backyard Flocks." HPAI Confirmations in Commercial and Backyard Flocks, 2022. https://www.aphis.usda.gov/livestock-poultry-disease/avian/avian-influenza/hpai-detections/commercial-backyard-flocks.

272 Dairy cows, Stobbe, Mike, and Jonel Aleccia. "Dairy Cattle in Texas and Kansas Test Positive for Bird Flu." AP News, March 26, 2024. https://apnews.com/article/bird-flu-dairy-cattle-usda-kansas-texas-c3040bb31a9a8293717d47362f006902.

272 Texan dairy worker, "Highly Pathogenic Avian Influenza A(H5N1) Virus Infection in a Dairy Farm Worker." *New England Journal of Medicine*, May 3, 2024. https://doi.org/10.1056/NEJMc2405371.

272 Fatal in humans, Centers for Disease Control and Prevention. "Highly Pathogenic Avian Influenza A(H5N1) Virus in Animals: Interim Recommendations for Prevention, Monitoring, and Public Health Investigations." Centers for Disease Control and Prevention, May 14, 2024. https://www.cdc.gov/flu/avianflu/hpai/hpai-interim-recommendations.html.

272 New norm, Sorvino, Chloe, and Lance Price. Interview with Dr. Lance Price. Personal, March 18, 2024.

272 Panera, Cunningham, Waylon. "Exclusive: Panera Loosens Ingredients Standards Ahead of IPO, Internal Documents Show | Reuters." Reuters, March 6, 2024. https://www.reuters.com/business/panera-loosens-animal-welfare-ingredients-standards-ahead-ipo-internal-documents-2024-03-06/.

272 Chick-fil-A, Chick-fil-A. "Our Chicken Commitment." Chick-fil-A. Accessed May 21, 2024. https://www.chick-fil-a.com/our-chicken-commitment.

272 More than one million chickens were killed, Lyman Director of Marketing & Communications, Arkansas Department of Agriculture, Ann. Letter to Chloe Sorvino. *Press Request—Factchecking on Cooks Venture Farm Euthanasia in 2023*, March 29, 2024.

273 $150 million raised, PitchBook. "Cooks Venture Overview–PitchBook." PitchBook. Accessed May 22, 2024. https://pitchbook.com/profiles/company/277243-48#overview.

275 The state government of Arkansas had to kill, Lyman, Director of Marketing & Communications, Arkansas Department of Agriculture, Ann. Letter to Chloe Sorvino. *Press Request — Factchecking on Cooks Venture Farm Euthanasia in 2023*, March 29, 2024.

275 Farms at risk, Mobley, Andrew. "Arkansas Poultry Company Closure Leaves Farmers High and Dry, 1.3 Million Birds Euthanized." KATV, February 14, 2024. https://katv.com/news/local/arkansas-poultry-company-closure-leaves-farmers-high-and-dry-13-million-birds-euthanized-cooks-venture-senator-bryan-king-madison-county-car roll-dustin-maybee-chicken-department-of-agriculture-secretary-wes-ward-avian-influenza-bird-flu-patrick-fisk.

275 Farms at risk, "Arkansas State Legislature Handout on Cooks Venture." PDF. Accessed May 21, 2024. https://www.arkleg.state.ar.us/Home/FTPDocument?path=/Assembly/Meeting+Attachments/685/I10254/Handout+-+1++Connect-AR.pdf.

275 Group of fifty, Marsh, Dan. "Former Growers Seek Answers at Tense Meeting." *Madison County Record*, December 13, 2023. https://mcrecordonline.com/stories/former-growers-seek-answers-at-tense-meeting,35961.

275 Left holding the bag, Hoffman, Michael. "Company Moves Ahead with Plans to Euthanize Hundreds of Thousands of Chickens across Northern Arkansas." https://www.ky3.com, December 14, 2023. https://www.ky3.com/2023/12/14/company-moves-ahead-with-plans-euthanize-hundreds-thousands-chickens-across-northern-arkansas/.

275 Left holding the bag, Hoffman, Michael. "Arkansas Farmers Still Skeptical after Cooks Venture Shares Update on Chicken Euthanizations." https://www.ky3.com, December 9, 2023. https://www.ky3.com/2023/12/09/arkansas-farmers-still-skeptical-after-cooks-venture-shares-update-chicken-euthanizations/.

275 Chapter 7 bankruptcy, "Cooks Venture, Inc. Bankruptcy (1:24-BK-10828), Delaware Bankruptcy Court." PacerMonitor Federal Court Case Tools, April 19, 2024. https://www.pacermonitor.com/public/case/53187439/Cooks_Venture,_Inc.

275 Mary's Free-Range Chicken, Mary's Free-Range Chicken. "Mary And Her Family." Mary's Free-Range Chicken. Accessed May 23, 2024. https://www.maryschickens.com/maryandherfamily.htm.

276 Start-ups raised, Good Food Institute. "A Deeper Dive into Alternative Protein Investments in 2022: The Case for Optimism." Good Food Institute, February 16, 2023. https://gfi.org/blog/alternative-protein-investments-update-and-outlook/.

276 Secured nearly $16 billion in all, GFI Media, Good Food Institute. Letter to Chloe Sorvino. Re: Press Inquiry // Alt Protein Funding Report, March 14, 2024.

276 Fifty-two companies, PitchBook Emerging Tech Research. "Q4 2023 Foodtech Report." PitchBook, March 15, 2024. https://pitchbook.com/news/reports/q4-2023-foodtech-report.

276 70 percent less money flowed, PitchBook Emerging Tech Research. "Q4 2023 Foodtech Report." PitchBook, March 15, 2024. https://pitchbook.com/news/reports/q4-2023-foodtech-report.

276 2023, plant-based deals dropped, PitchBook Emerging Tech Research. "Q4 2023 Foodtech Report." PitchBook, March 15, 2024. https://pitchbook.com/news/reports/q4-2023-foodtech-report.

277 Cut back on research spending, Sorvino, Chloe, and Peter McGuinness. Interview with Impossible Foods CEO Peter McGuinness. Personal, March 14, 2024.

277 Debt swelled, YCharts: Beyond Meat Total Long Term Debt (annual). Accessed May 21, 2024. https://ycharts.com/companies/BYND/total_long_term_debt_annual.

277 Loans are coming due in 2027, Beyond Meat. "SEC Filing: Beyond Meat, Inc." SEC Filing | Beyond Meat, Inc., December 31, 2023. https://investors.beyondmeat.com/node/11676/html.

277 Cash dropped, Ycharts: Beyond meat cash and equivalents (annual). Accessed May 21, 2024. https://ycharts.com/companies/BYND/cash_and_equivalents_annual.

277 The most shorted stock across the entire stock market, Scheid, Brian. "Short Sellers Boost Bets against Energy Stocks as Prices Fall." S&P Global, December 18, 2023. https://www.spglobal.com/marketintelligence/en/news-insights/latest-news-headlines/short-sellers-boost-bets-against-energy-stocks-as-prices-fall-79806698.

277 39 percent of Beyond shares were shorted, "YCharts: Beyond Meat–Short Interest." YCharts. Accessed May 21, 2024. https://ycharts.com/companies/BYND/short_interest.

277 The most among any food stock, Scheid, Brian, and Annie Sabater. "Short Sellers Cut Bets against Most Sectors, Raise Positions against Materials." S&P Global, June 21, 2024. https://www.spglobal.com/marketintelligence/en/news-insights/latest-news-headlines/short-sellers-cut-bets-against-most-sectors-raise-positions-against-materials-82147504.

278 All-time-high of $234, "Ycharts: BYND Stock Price & Charts: Beyond Meat." BYND Stock Price & Charts, Beyond Meat. Accessed May 21, 2024. https://ycharts.com/companies/BYND.

278 $6 per share, "Ycharts: BYND Stock Price & Charts: Beyond Meat." BYND Stock Price & Charts | Beyond Meat. Accessed May 21, 2024. https://ycharts.com/companies/BYND.

278 meatballs that shuttered by January 2023, Atkinson, Ray. Letter to Chloe Sorvino. *Smithfield — Plant-Based?*, March 6, 2024.

278 Kroger and Albertsons, Sorvino, Chloe. "The World's Largest Meat Seller Embraces Plant-Based Proteins as Pandemic Demand Surges." Forbes, June 18, 2020. https://www.forbes.com/sites/chloesorvino/2020/06/18/the-worlds-largest-meat-seller-embraces-plant-based-proteins-as-pandemic-demand-surges/.

279 $95 million valuation; $30 million raised, PitchBook. "Smallhold Overview–PitchBook." PitchBook. Accessed May 22, 2024. https://pitchbook.com/profiles/company/178113-97#overview.

279 Minority shareholder Monomyth, Chapter 11 Case No. 24-10267 (CTG) Smallhold Inc, CAMBER ROAD PARTNERS, INC.'S OBJECTION TO DEBTOR'S FIRST AMENDED PLAN OF REORGANIZATION (UNITED STATES BANKRUPTCY COURT FOR THE DISTRICT OF DELAWARE 2024).

279 Chapter 11 bankruptcy, "Smallhold, Inc. Case # 24-10267." Epiq 11, February 18, 2024. https://dm.epiq11.com/case/smallhold/documents.

279 Allegedly at a loss, Chapter 11 Case No. 24-10267 (CTG) Smallhold Inc, CAMBER ROAD PARTNERS, INC.'S OBJECTION TO DEBTOR'S FIRST AMENDED PLAN OF REORGANIZATION (UNITED STATES BANKRUPTCY COURT FOR THE DISTRICT OF DELAWARE 2024).

280 Lab-grown chicken from start-up, Carmen, Tim. "Lab-Grown Chicken Promises Guilt-Free Meat, but the Hurdles Are Steep." *Washington Post*, September 15, 2023. https://www.washingtonpost.com/food/2023/09/15/cell-cultured-chicken-lab-grown-good-meat-upside-foods/.

280 112 sold in all, Whitney, Upside Foods, Brooke. Letter to Chloe Sorvino. *Upside Questions & Factchecking*, March 20, 2024.

280 Lab-grown chicken from Good Meat, Good Meat. "The Future of Meat." GOOD Meat. Accessed May 21, 2024. https://www.goodmeat.co/eat/cultivated-chicken.

280 China Chilcano, "Experience Good Meat Cultivated Chicken at China Chilcano: Washington, DC." China Chilcano. Accessed May 21, 2024. https://www.chinachilcano.com/event/good-meat/.

281 Good Meat claims it didn't track, Kabat, Good Meat, Carrie. Letter to Chloe Sorvino. *Good Meat / Eat Just Questions & Factchecking*, April 3, 2024.

281 Not in Florida, Staff, News Releases. "Governor Desantis Signs Legislation to Keep Lab-Grown Meat out of Florida." Florida Governor Ron DeSantis, May 1, 2024. https://www.flgov.com/2024/05/01/governor-desantis-signs-legislation-to-keep-lab-grown-meat-out-of-florida/.

281 $3 billion in the past five years, Good Food Institute. "State of the Industry Report: Cultivated Meat and Seafood: GFI." Good Food Institute, May 15, 2024. https://gfi.org/resource/cultivated-meat-eggs-and-dairy-state-of-the-industry-report/.

281 BioTech Foods, JBS Newsroom. "JBS Defines the next Step for the Cultivated Protein Research Center." JBS Foods, May 12, 2022. https://mediaroom.jbs.com.br/noticia/jbs-defines-the-next-step-for-the-cultivated-protein-research-center.

281 World's largest cultivated meat plant, JBS Newsroom. "JBS Company Initiates Construction of the World's Largest Cultivated Beef Protein Plant." JBS Foods, June 14, 2023. https://mediaroom.jbs.com.br/noticia/jbs-company-initiates-construction-of-the-worlds-largest-cultivated-beef-protein-plant.

282 Raw materials, "The B Corp Standard Is at Risk." Fair World Project, December 6, 2022. https://fairworldproject.org/the-b-corp-standard-is-at-risk/.

282 Regenerative Organic certification, Rodale Institute. "Regenerative Organic Certified." Rodale Institute, September 27, 2023. https://rodaleinstitute.org/regenerative-organic-certification/.

Index

About the Author

Chloe Sorvino leads coverage of food, drink, and agriculture at *Forbes*. Her work has been featured by NPR, *Women's Wear Daily*, and the *Financial Times*.

She grew up gardening in New Jersey. While studying journalism and international economics at George Washington University, she spent most of her time learning as a news editor at the independent student newspaper, the *GW Hatchet*. She resides in New York City with her husband, Nick, and their composting worms.

Find out more at ChloeSorvino.com and follow her on X @ChloeSorvino.